THE RED THREAD

THE RED THREAD

BUDDHIST APPROACHES TO SEXUALITY

BERNARD FAURE

PRINCETON UNIVERSITY PRESS

PRINCETON, NEW JERSEY

Copyright © 1998 by Princeton University Press

Published by Princeton University Press, 41 William Street, Princeton, New Jersey 08540

In the United Kingdom: Princeton University Press, Chichester, West Sussex

Library of Congress Cataloging-in-Publication Data

Faure, Bernard.

[Sexualités bouddhiques. English]

The red thread : Buddhist approaches to sexuality / Bernard Faure.

p. cm.

Includes bibliographical references and index.

ISBN 0-691-05998-5 (cloth : alk. paper). — ISBN 0-691-05997-7

(pbk. : alk. paper)

1. Sex—Religious aspects—Buddhism.   2. Buddhism—Social aspects.

I. Title.

BQ4570.S48F3813   1998   294.3′37857—dc21   98-16645   CIP

This work is an expanded and revised edition of *Sexualités bouddhiques: Entre désirs et réalités,* originally published by Le Mail, in 1994

This book has been composed in Sabon

Princeton University Press books are printed on acid-free paper and meet the guidelines for permanence and durability of the Committee on Production Guidelines for Book Longevity of the Council on Library Resources

http://pup.princeton.edu

Printed in the United States of America

10 9 8 7 6 5 4 3 2 1

10 9 8 7 6 5 4 3 2 1

(Pbk.)

CONTENTS

THE RED THREAD

INTRODUCTION

OVER THE PAST two decades, a number of scandals have shattered Buddhist communities in North America and Europe. The San Francisco Zen Center, the oldest Zen center in the United States, repudiated its *rōshi*, Richard Baker, when the latter was accused of having an affair with one of his female students. In the Vajradhatu community, one of the largest American communities practicing Tibetan Buddhism, a scandal broke out in 1988 when members learned that one of their masters, Osel Tendzin, well known for his active sexuality, had contracted AIDS three years earlier. Other scandals, having to do with alcoholism, embezzlement, or generically eccentric behavior, involved American, Japanese, Korean, and Tibetan Buddhist teachers. In 1983, for instance, the Japanese master of the Los Angeles Zen Center had to be treated for alcoholism. More remarkably, Trungpa Rimpoche, the great Tibetan master of the Vajradhatu community, allegedly the eleventh reincarnation of Trungpa Tulku, invoked his "crazy wisdom" to justify his alcoholism, womanizing, and financial eccentricities. More recently, the American branch of the Shinshū sect of Japanese Buddhism has come under heavy criticism. In a 1985 article in the *Yoga Journal*, entitled "Sex and Lives of the Gurus," Jack Kornfield, a psychologist and co-founder of the Insight Meditation Society, reveals that among fifty-four cases he had studied of Buddhist, Hindu, and Jain teachers in North America, thirty-four had sexual relationships with their disciples.[1]

Such scandals only reinforced the negative impression that a part of the public had of Buddhist religious sects. They cannot always be interpreted, however, as the consequences of the cynicism or ambition of a few charismatic individuals. On the one hand, the interest of the media for such scandals points toward the possibility, in some cases, of a scapegoat mechanism. But far from being mere accidents due to individual personalities, they may also be seen as structural problems, having deeper social, psychological, and cultural roots. These behaviors found some doctrinal justification in the teachings of Mahāyāna or Great Vehicle—particularly in its most radical versions, Vajrayāna and Chan/Zen. The problem is by no means limited to Western interpretations of Mahāyāna: it is also found in Asian forms of Mahāyāna and Theravāda, as recent

---

[1] See Kornfield 1985; see also on that question Butler 1990.

scandals in the Japanese sect of Jōdo Shinshū and in Thai Buddhism show.[2]

To give a full account of the various social, psychological, and cultural factors of Buddhist antinomianism is beyond the scope of this book. I want to emphasize, however, doctrinal elements that may have caused or justified antinomian behavior, as well as attempt to give an historical background to help us make more sense of some of these bewildering developments.

THE TWO ROADS

The question of sexual ethics has been a thorny one for the Buddhist tradition. Buddhists have always claimed the moral high ground and attempted, with more or less success, to maintain an exigent ideal of purity. Any spiritual practice is fated to confront the obstinate realities of human existence, however. The desire for purity is in itself unable to rule out the defilement of lust. Buddhism was no exception to this rule. Nevertheless, it distinguishes itself by the ambivalent fashion in which it problematized the issue of desire. From the outset the Buddhist tradition has been divided between the most uncompromising moral rigorism and a subversion of all ideals in the name of a higher truth, transcending good and evil. Mahāyāna Buddhism, in particular, argued that the ultimate truth can be discovered only by those who awaken to the reality of desire and are able to transmute it.

In this tradition, a paradigmatic story is that of the two monks Prasannendriya and Agramati, as told in the *Dazhidulun* (Treatise of the Great Perfection of Wisdom), a work attributed to Nāgārjuna. Despite his ideal of purity, Agramati eventually falls into hell because of his false views, whereas Prasannendriya, for all his infringements of morality, obtains salvation. The story seems to assert the superiority of transgression, its status as proof of awakening.[3] As Rolf Stein remarks, the concept of "pivoting" or "overturning" (Skt. *paravṛtti*) seems to lie behind the view that rather than negating passion, desire, and sexuality, one can transmute them. This "revulsion" is indeed what allows the bodhisattva, in various Buddhist scriptures, to indulge in sex without being defiled by it. In the *Śūraṃgama-sūtra*, for instance, a bodhisattva makes love to the daughters of the demon Māra in order to save them.[4] The story of Prasannendriya and Agramati illustrates a cardinal tenet of Mahāyāna Bud-

---

[2] See Gordon Fairclough, "Sacred and Profane: Monks Embroiled in Sex and Plagiarism Scandal," *Far Eastern Economic Review*, March 3, 1944: 22–23.

[3] Lamotte 1944–1980, 1: 399; see also Stein 1974: 505.

[4] Stein 1974: 504–6.

dhism, the theory of the Two Truths, ultimate and conventional. Ultimate truth is the truth that transcends all limited viewpoints, sublating conventional truth, that is, the truth perceived from a limited, all-too-human perspective. Traditional morality, as it is found in canonical scriptures, must therefore be transcended—or rather, *transgressed*, that is to say, both violated and preserved as law.

Other variants of this paradigm are known. In another revealing story, the Vinaya master Daoxuan encounters the Tantric master Śubhakarasiṃha. This encounter is anachronistic, since Daoxuan, founder of the Chinese Vinaya school, died in 667, several decades before Śubhakarasiṃha's arrival in China in 713. But this anachronism is unimportant, since here we are dealing with two ideal types: the ideal of the rigorist monk, and the ideal of the (apparently) laxist monk, representing two diametrally opposed (and complementary) conceptions of monastic discipline, or Vinaya. Śubhakarasiṃha is described as someone who drank wine, ate meat, and generally behaved rudely. Although it is not said explicitly that he engaged in sex, the fact that he was also the transmitter of Tantric practices makes it likely that sexual transgression is implied. Unsurprisingly, the orthodox Daoxuan intensely disliked the Indian master. According to tradition, Śubhakarasiṃha once shared a cell with Daoxuan at the Ximing Monastery. In the middle of the night, Daoxuan caught a flea. At that very moment, Śubhakarasiṃha shouted: "The Vinaya master has killed a child of the Buddha!" Then Daoxuan realized that Śubhakarasiṃha was a bodhisattva, whose behavior cannot be fathomed by ordinary men. The next day he paid obeisance to him.[5]

In Korea as well, we find the well-known hagiographical contrast illustrated by the "lives" of the two monks and friends, Ŭisang (625–702) and Wŏnhyo (617–686). Ŭisang was a strict observer of Buddhist precepts: when a young Chinese girl attempted to seduce him, "his heart was like a rock and could not be moved."[6] Wŏnhyo, on the other hand, was a regular customer of whorehouses, famous for his eccentric behavior. Along the same lines, the *Samguk yusa* tells us how, during the Unified Silla period, two monks withdrew to the mountains in order to practice meditation. They lived in cells next to one another. One evening a beautiful young woman, having lost her way, came to ask hospitality for one night. The first monk told her that he could not let her enter his cell. The woman was given shelter by the second monk, who took pity on her. After taking a bath, the woman asked him to step into the tub. When he did so, he found that his mind was in a state of concentrated bliss, his skin took a golden color, like that of the bath water, and the tub turned

---

[5] See Chou 1944–1945: 269, and *Song gaoseng zhuan*, T. 50, 2061: 791b.
[6] *Song gaoseng zhuan*, ibid., 729a.

into a lotus pedestal. The woman revealed herself as the Bodhisattva Avalokiteśvara. At that moment, the other monk, full of righteous indignation, burst into the room, only to find his friend seated on a pedestal with a golden body like that of the future Buddha Maitreya. He was in turn invited to step into the golden water and was also transformed into a buddha. Upon hearing of the miracle, the villagers flocked to see the two saints and to hear them preach the Dharma. After they had finished speaking, the two friends ascended to heaven.[7] This story shows that the monk who is ready to transgress the precepts out of compassion reaches enlightenment faster than other monks, and is also able to save the others who strive toward holiness through the slower path of meditation.

The paradigm of the two paths to holiness is still alive and well in Korea. A recent Korean film, *Mandala* (1981), takes up this theme and modernizes it.[8] The film describes the friendship between Pobun, a young monk striving for purity, and Jisan, an eccentric (and alcoholic) older monk. The personality of Jisan fascinates Pobun, and the two monks set out on a journey together. One night they end up in a brothel, where Jisan is well known. While Jisan drinks with the prostitutes, Pobun retires to his room. Fast asleep, he has a delicious dream, in which he runs in paradisiac fields to the accelerating beat of of a drum (his heart). At the moment of experiencing the climax of enlightenment, Pobun wakes up, and realizes with a shock that the source of these oneiric delights was a young woman who had crept into his room. Running away from this den of iniquity, Pobun vows never again to follow his pernicious companion. Later on, however, Pobun revises his judgment when he hears villagers praising Jisan for helping them, at the risk of his life, during a severe epidemic. Pobun then understands that Jisan is truly a bodhisattva. The two monks resume traveling together. However, the film ends on a dark note. On a winter night, Jisan, refusing the shelter offered by a villager, leaves in search of a tavern. In the early morning Pobun discovers his body, covered with snow, and incinerates it.

[7] See Ilyŏn 1972: 239–42; see also ibid., 305–11.

[8] This film by the Korean filmmaker Im Kwont'aek is based on a novel by Kim Sundung entitled *Mantra*. There is also a feminine version of this theme by the same filmmaker, entitled "Higher, Still Higher." It tells the story of two nuns, whose spiritual quest takes two apparently opposed roads. The order of Korean nuns has attempted to prevent the release of this film, judged contrary to Buddhist morality. Korean nuns also protested against the shooting of a film called *Piguni* (The Nun), the story of a beautiful woman who became a nun and had to struggle to keep her worldly passions under control. The film, which depicted explicit scenes of a nun masturbating and the heroine's sexual trysts after she had taken the monastic vows, was never completed, as the filmmaker voluntarily acceded to the sensibilities of the protesters. Again in 1986, the Chogye Order raised strong objections to the filming of the life of Jung-kwang the Mad Monk (with Jung-kwang himself starring), and to its being shown at movie theaters.

Korea is familiar with these eccentric monks, who seem to pay no attention to moral values and enjoy provoking scandals. A contemporary case in point is that of the painter-monk Jung-kwang, a living Buddha according to some, a demon according to others. When accused of the worst transgressions, Jung-kwang merely replies that he is a "Buddhist mop," which "cleans everything while getting itself dirty."[9] Jung-kwang's case is admittedly an extreme one, but it calls attention to the radical consequences of Buddhist antinomianism, particularly in sexual matters.

The first part of this book examines the essential ambiguity or tension between what we could call the two centers of the Buddhist ellipse, or the "two sources" of Buddhist religion, philosophy, and ethics. The main problem confronted by the monastic community as well as by the individual, one which has until now found no satisfying solution—indeed, how could it?—is desire. Before examining in the second part various implications of this question for East Asian Buddhism, we will investigate two kinds of normative texts: first, doctrinal texts, in particular the sermons attributed to the Buddha and their scholastic commentaries dealing with the nature of ultimate reality and the path leading to it; second, disciplinary rules constituting the Vinaya, rules allegedly promulgated by the Buddha for his monastic community.

To understand how the traditions stemming from these two sources articulate with each other, one must consider briefly the evolution of Buddhism after the death of its founder. As is well known, several councils attempted to lay down the teaching of the Buddha, first orally, then in writing. In other words, these councils attempted to prevent the proliferation of Buddhist discourse by closing the canon. They did not entirely succeed, however. During one of them a schism divided Buddhism between two factions, the conservative faction of the "Elders," the predecessor of modern Theravāda (lit. "Way of the Elders"), a form of Buddhism now practiced in Sri Lanka and Southeast Asia, and the "majority" faction (Mahāsaṅghika, lit. "Great Assembly"), the predecessor of the Mahāyāna ("Great Vehicle"), which spread to and developed in East Asia.

Whereas Theravāda doctors remained attached to the letter of the ser-

---

[9] Jung-kwang 1979: 36; see also ibid., 6. In the Western tradition, the idea that monks purify the world by taking its dirt on them is expressed by Rabelais's Gargantua, who explains as follows why monks are shunned by the world: "The conclusive reason is that they eat the world's excrement, that is to say, sins; and as eaters of excrement they are cast into their privies—their convents and abbeys that is—which are cut off from all civil intercourse, as are the privies of a house." See Rabelais 1955: 125–26. This passage calls to mind Chan figures like Mingzan, nicknamed Lancan, "Refuse-eater."

mons of the Buddha and to the strict observance of Vinaya, Mahāyāna Buddhism saw an eclosion of doctrinal texts, in which free rein was given to theoretical experimentation and mythological imagination—texts which their authors had no qualms in attributing to the Buddha himself. In scriptures like the *Lotus Sūtra,* the Buddha assumes a superhuman stature and becomes, like the great gods of Hinduism, the beginning and the end of the great cosmic game. He is no longer—if he ever was, except in the imagination of some practitioners and scholars—merely a man who has achieved perfection after long struggles against desire and the thirst for existence. One can then understand why these two types of normative texts should have very different positions regarding the question of desire. One must not, however, exaggerate the difference and draw a too sharp distinction between Vinaya and doctrinal rigorism on the one hand, Mahāyāna thought and antinomianism on the other. Just as the doctrinal position of Theravāda evolved greatly and went beyond (or at least, relativized) the early Buddhist emphasis on renunciation, Mahāyāna periodically experienced "purist" reforms that seemed to contradict or contain its doctrinal open-endedness. As for the Vinaya, we could—at the risk of oversimplifying—distinguish two main versions: the rigorist, which spread through South, Southeastern, and East Asia; and the "liberal" version, found in Tibet, China, and Japan, influenced by the doctrinal developments of Mahāyāna. Although he is in many ways a typically Mahāyāna Buddhist, the Vinaya master Daoxuan represents the rigorist approach, whereas the Tantric master Śubhakarasiṃha represents the more open approach. It is no mere coincidence that Chan masters were particularly interested in the Tantric precepts brought to China by Śubhakarasiṃha at the beginning of the eighth century. Tantric (or Vajrayāna) Buddhism contained a number of sexual elements that were not always expurgated from the Chinese translations.

Buddhist Sexualities

Desire lies at the heart of Western sexuality. Does its presence at the heart of Buddhist discourse, then, imply that we are dealing with Buddhist sexuality? Is there a Buddhist "sexuality," in the sense meant by Michel Foucault in his *History of Sexuality,* as "the correlative of that slowly developed discursive practice which constituted the *scientia sexualis*"?[10]

---

[10] For Foucault, "sexuality was defined as being 'by nature': a domain susceptible to pathological processes, and hence one calling for therapeutic or normalizing interventions; a field of meanings to decipher; the site of processes concealed by specific mechanisms; a focus of indefinite causal relations; and an obscure speech (*parole*) that had to be ferreted out and listened to." See Foucault 1980: 68.

Sex never was the object of a specific discourse, of a *scientia sexualis* in Buddhism. Foucault at one point contrasted an *ars erotica*, characteristic of civilizations such as India, China, or Japan, with a "science of sex," which would be the monopoly of the modern West.[11] According to him, this science is characterized by the importance of the penitential technique of the "confession"—a compulsory revelation of the subject's sexual secrets that is the exact opposite of the initiatory "secret" concerning sexual union. Quite obviously this opposition needs to be nuanced, and Foucault himself, incidentally, already noted that the *ars erotica* was not entirely unknown in the West.[12] On the Buddhist side too, the existence—in concert with Tantric sexual initiations—of a penitence system based on confession makes this opposition less appropriate. With confession, we are a long way from the "learned initiation into pleasure [of the *ars erotica*], with its technique and its mystery."[13] In Buddhism, however, confession did not lead to the elaboration of a "scientific" discourse, as in the Christian West. Even in Tantrism, sex may have become the object of a discourse, but not of a science: it is a sexual soteriology, not a "sexology."

At any rate, there is indeed a modern Chinese or Japanese discourse in sexuality. The fact that such a discourse may be heavily indebted to Western "sexology" must not hide the fact that it also grows from deep roots in cultures impregnated by Buddhism and other Asian religions. As long as we do not read the modern system back into the past, we are therefore entitled to look for the Buddhist origins of this sexuality, just as Foucault looked for the Greco-Roman and Christian origins of Western sexuality.

Not only do Asian cultures differ in their relation to sex, but Buddhism itself, and within it major trends like Theravāda, Tantrism, or Chan/Zen, offer such a degree of inner complexity that any generalization in this domain would be improper. My goal in Chapter One is therefore not to describe or discuss *the* orthodox Buddhist tradition regarding sexuality—an enterprise that would be, at best, anachronistic—but to circumscribe a few problems, and to follow not only in the texts of mainstream Buddhism but also on its margins the emergence of discursive formations, or at least of fragments of a *discours amoureux* (or *anti-amoureux*). Indeed, as in Western culture, we are dealing not with one discourse, a monolithic ideology, but with polymorphous (and sometimes perverse) discourses, with Buddhist sexualities. These are "fragments" because, as one Westerner remarked concerning Zen, "sex and love are neglected, . . . although one is treated to a host of details regarding la-

---

[11] Foucault 1980: 57–58.
[12] Ibid., 70.
[13] Ibid., 62.

trines and 'shit sticks.'" The main difficulty is that there exists in Buddhism no systematic discourse on sex; as such, the object of our study is an elusive, perhaps nonexistent one. But is such a (to us) conspicuous silence merely the sign of a lack of concern, or is it the symptom of a ritual avoidance? And is the tradition really silent about sex (and love)? It remains true that in Buddhism sex never became a legitimate object of inquiry; it always appears as an element of other domains (moral, technical, disciplinary, soteriological). If *sex* seems simultaneously repressed and celebrated in Buddhism (unlike most religions, which either repress or celebrate, but not both), Buddhism never treats sex in isolation, but always as an element of general discourses on desire or power. We cannot infer, from certain discursive "patterns" in which we, modern interpreters, recognize the contours of something we call "sex," the existence of an underlying reality that would be the Buddhist sexuality."[14] Sometimes the "erotic" element is present only in a sublimated form, as a discursive figure of transgression. Often it is entirely diverted, distorted, sublimated in discussions of more fundamental forms of desire, such as hunger or the search for immortality. Sexuality was perhaps not, as it is in our society, the central, organizing principle around which the notion of self crystallized. Ironically, the only full-fledged *discours amoureux* in Japanese Buddhism is concerned with male youths, not with women.

Should Buddhist discussions of sexuality be interpreted in socio-economic terms (for instance, against the backdrop of feudalism and the rise of a patriarchal system), or do they constitute a type of discourse that has a relative autonomy? At first glance, Buddhist sexuality is only one of the by-products of ideology, and the Buddhist institution seems to play a relatively passive role, ratifying (sometimes reluctantly) the official ideology. However, does this mean that what Foucault called the "repressive hypothesis" is entirely verified? This hypothesis itself may indeed have repressive effects on our reflection. Should we consider that the discourse merely reflects the practice? What role does Buddhism play in practice with its taboo/transgression paradigm? What are the statuses (not merely the status) of women? Are we dealing with the articulation of complex networks of practices (in particular, discursive practices), or with a

[14] The same point is made by Charlotte Furth in her criticism of van Gulik's famous history of "sexual life" in China: "Although Van Gulik recognizes medical, religious, and literary genres among his sources, he imposes on all types and every period the unquestioned assumption that discussions of sexual practices, wherever they may be found, are evidence for the historical presence of a discrete erotic domain: a self-consciously understood cultural sphere for the experience and understanding of sexual pleasure, in and of itself. The presence of such a domain is assumed to be the natural by-product of human instinct, and this universal category of experience leaves its historical traces as *ars erotica*." (Furth 1994: 129)

simple confrontation of two monolithic realities (such as "Buddhism" and "woman")?

Much of what we know about Buddhist sexual "normality" and "deviance" comes from the norms edicted in the Vinaya. These norms, when they are clearly stated, should be understood as they were allegedly promulgated, that is, in an ad hoc manner. Unfortunately, we no longer have the "stage directions" for these ritual performances of monastic repentence and, like the Buddhists themselves, we tend to confuse highly localized statements with universal laws.[15] Another obvious difficulty is the predominantly male nature of this discourse. Women have an important function in it but they are almost totally passive (except perhaps in Tantrism, if we are to believe Miranda Shaw).[16] We have very few documents written by Buddhist women, and even those, like those of many female Christian mystics, use a predominantly male language and imagery. From a certain feminist standpoint, one could even consider that their discourse reinforces dominant male norms instead of rejecting or subverting them.

This work is primarily a study in collective representations, focusing on their inherent dynamics and their social inscription. In order to reveal enduring common (sometimes even cross-cultural) structures, I have wandered freely across geographical borders and historical periods— much to the dismay of some of my historian friends. I have at times exaggerated the picture, for the sake of argument, and I am acutely aware that some contrasts have to be nuanced, contextualized, qualified.

Finally, I should make it clear that, for heuristic and didactic purposes, I have assumed here the existence of a generic Buddhism, a singular norm, which many will question. But this norm will, of course, turn out to be irreductibly plural, multivocal, to the point that we may have to speak of Buddhisms in the plural, or rather, of Buddhist norms and sexualities, of Buddhist approaches to sexuality (without reifying Buddhism any longer, just as one may speak of religiosity without necessarily being able to define or willing to objectify religion). It might not be enough to define from the outside a norm that is fundamentally ambivalent (the two ways represented by Prasannendriya and Agramati), but let me say that they are meant to symbolize (and may be unable to subsume) this diversity. The references to Indian and Tibetan Buddhism should be seen as mere heuristic counterpoints or introductions to a work that has, due to specific circumstances, come to focus mainly on Chinese and Japanese Buddhism. The *Dazhidulun,* despite its clear polemical intent, has been used as a compendium representative of this admittedly problematic

[15] On the constraints of interpretation, see Winkler 1990.
[16] See Shaw 1994.

"common Buddhism" (what modern Japanese Buddhists like to call *tsū bukkyō*), and no systematic attempt has been made to contextualize historically the materials presented in the first part. It is impossible to do justice in a single book to the wealth of materials on the topic, but I wanted at least to address briefly other traditions for which I claim no expertise. Indulgence is required from the reader, as this work is meant to be a heuristic device to attract specialist from other areas to Asian materials that may seem at first glance irrelevant.

In Chapter One, I draw from normative doctrine to examine a number of Buddhist hermeneutics of desire. In Chapter Two, I take a closer look at the Vinaya rules concerning "illicit" sex. In Chapter Three, I discuss various forms of Buddhist transgression and their subversive claims. Textual transgression does not always translate into social transgression, and in this context as in many others, the gender line remains the great divide. Chapter Four, opening the second part of the book, is a discussion of the discrepancy between monastic norms and ideals and what seems to be (at first glance) the social reality. Chapters Five and Six examine one specific Buddhist discourse on sexuality, in this case Japanese male homosexuality, or more precisely, "male love" (*nanshoku*). The first chapter—and this is true for the rest of the book as well—is not an attempt at a "cartography of desire," or even a Buddhist *carte du tendre*. It is not a map of Buddhist sexuality—not even one of those premodern maps that leave many blanks, "virgin" lands for future intrepid explorers to fill—but rather a Buddhism (and sexuality) *à la carte*. It is rather, to use the distinction between the map and the itinerary, an attempt at following a few paths in the diverse intellectual and cultural landscapes of my "own private" Buddhism—a place that, like Barthe's Japan, is neither quite the same as nor different from the "real thing." It is only a cultural *promenade,* an intellectual peregrination, one which I hope will be stimulating to the reader's appetite (or digestion). This work is to be read as a divertissement—in other words, a very serious (and hygienic) activity.

Another caveat has to do with my references to Western sources. These references should not be misconstrued as a simplistic attempt at comparativism: they mean rather that, unlike some historians, I believe that my research has a subjective, transferential relation with its subject matter (object). In this subjective discourse about a constructed object, which also becomes a pretext (Buddhist sexualities), my own Western standpoint, as well as Western references or counterpoints, are constantly at work behind the scenes. If so, better to acknowledge it than deny it.

A shorter version of this text was published in French in 1994 under the title *Sexualités bouddhiques: Entre désirs et réalités*. At that time, I followed the traditional (yet problematic) "three countries" model and tried to use examples from Indian, Chinese, and Japanese Buddhism. In the process of rewriting this book, however, in the second half, in particular, I have privileged medieval Japanese Buddhism. This emphasis is in part due to personal circumstances (a recent stay in Japan), but also to the abundance of documents and the quality of recent historiography, as well as for reasons having to do with the historical specificity of Japanese Buddhism (at least in the context of sexuality and gender). It is indeed in Japan that one can most easily study the assimilation of Mahāyāna Buddhism to local culture. In that country, as in Tibet—although to a lesser degree—but more than in China or Korea, Buddhism became part of mainstream culture. Furthermore, the abundance of documents and the quality of recent historiography allow a much richer and complex study. This specificity, far from being the manifestation of some perennial Japanese "essence"—as partisans of *nihonjinron* ideology claim—was the result of a variety of historical "accidents" such as:

The systematic combination of Buddhism with local cults (through the so-called *honji suijaku*, or "essence-trace" theory) and culture (for instance, in the arts of entertainment, *geinō*).

The extreme development of the notion of feminine impurity and the resulting exclusion of women from sacred places and events (temples, mountins, rituals, festivals).

The wide tolerance for monastic sex (*nyobon*) and the existence of married monks.

The development of the *hongaku* (innate enlightenment) theory, which paved the way to certain forms of antinomianism.

The elaboration of a state ideology based on Buddhist notions such as the identity of royal law and Buddhist Law (*ōbō soku buppō*), and the medieval exegesis leading to the creation of a "sexual theology."

The tradition of male homosexuality (*nanshoku*), seen as specific of Buddhist monastic culture.

This book owes much to many people. At the end of this long search for sources, I feel like one of the protagonists in Allison Lurie's novel, *Foreign Affairs,* an American scholar whose work, "like all scholarship emptied of will and inspiration, has . . . degenerated into a kind of petty highway robbery: a patching together of ideas and facts stolen from other people's books."[17] I can only hope that my debt to other people has been duly acknowledged, and that the synthesis I have attempted to achieve amounts to slightly more than a "patching together of ideas and facts," even if it is definitely not a "seamless stūpa."

[17] See Lurie 1984: 390.

At the risk of discouraging the weary implied reader, I should add that this volume is the first instalment of a two-volume book, itself the first part of a two-part project. I have therefore left out the gender issues for another forthcoming book, *Purity and Gender*. As Honoré de Balzac wrote in the epigraph of one of his novels "Homo duplex, said our great Buffon: why not add: Rex duplex? Everything is double, even virtue. Thus Molière always presents the two sides of any human problem. . . . My two novels are therefore forming a pair, like two twins of different sex."[18] My books may not quite qualify as novels, but they are deeply concerned with the question of polarity (the yin-yang that will constitute medieval "sexual theology")—not to mention a certain inherent duplicity. Thus it is only fitting that they would come in pairs. In the first part, woman is often conspicuously absent, or she appears inasmuch as she is an element of the Buddhist discourse on sexuality: not for herself, as individual, but as one pole of attraction or repulsion in a gendered male discourse about sex. Denied the role of a subject in this discourse, she is primarily the emblem of larger generative, karmic, or social processes, with positive or negative soteriological value. At best a partner in a Tantric yab-yum, male-female pair, she rarely stands (or lies) alone, or with other women. In a second part she will return to haunt Buddhism not only as the prime object of a discourse, which, even when it is about woman's salvation, is still uttered by men and is hardly more than an exorcism, but also as the subject of a narrative in (and through) which she becomes able to poach freely in male preserves, to reassert her voice, and to steal the show. A final word: like most historical works, this book is largely fictitious. Any resemblance with persons living or dead is to a large extent a coincidence.

[18] Honoré de Balzac, "Dédicace à Don Michel Angelo Cajetani, prince de Tréano," in (1846) 1993.

Chapter 1

THE HERMENEUTICS OF DESIRE

> By whatever thing the world is bound, by that
> the bond is unfastened.
> (*Hevajra-tantra*)

> One who, possessing desire, represses desire, is living a lie.
> (*Caṇḍamahāroṣana-tantra*)

AFTER SIX YEARS of ascesis, Śākyamuni realized the ultimate truth under the bodhi tree and became the Buddha, the Awakened. What is this truth according to the first Buddhist orthodoxy (for as we will see, there have been several)? It is expressed in the form of a tetralemma known as the "four noble truths": suffering, the cause of suffering, the possibility of ending suffering, and the method of achieving that end. The first two rubrics describe the world of saṃsāra, the cycle of transmigration through birth-and-death. The driving force of this cycle is desire. Actually, desire is itself produced by ignorance, which makes one believe in the existence of an enduring self where the sage sees only fleeting states of consciousness. The third rubric deals with nirvāṇa, the ultimate quiescence and extinction of all defilements or passions; the fourth describes the path to nirvāṇa—the so-called eightfold path.

Some of these ideas were common in the Indian culture of the time. They were not radically new to Śākyamuni himself. Despite the attempts of his own father, King Śuddhodana, to shield him from the harsh realities of the outside world, Śākyamuni had encountered these realities—in the form of a sick man, an old man, a corpse and an ascetic—during four excursions outside the palace.

It is another event that led him to leave the palace, however. One night, he awoke and looked at the women of his gynaeceum, asleep around him in unflattering postures—frozen in a corpselike slumber. Sleep had stripped them of their charms, and revealed their ugliness. This scene revealed to Śākyamuni the vanity of his hedonistic life. He thus came to understand that everything, including pleasure, is ephemeral and painful in the end, and that suffering takes root in desire and the illusion of a self. More precisely, he came to understand the nature of sexual desire, which ties humans to their earthly body, to the circle of rebirths, and inscribes them in a long line of ancestors and descendants. This first insight, which led Śākyamuni to abandon his wife and his newborn son, would eventually mature into full awakening under the bodhi tree. By renouncing the world, Śākyamuni "left the family." The expression "leaving the family" soon came to designate monastic ordination, and this is why, in Theravāda, the postulant ritually reenacts the founder's "flight from the palace." By an ironic turn of events, this ordination, in East Asian Buddhism, came to be seen as an adoption into another (spiritual) family, an affiliation to the "lineage of the Buddha": Chinese and Japanese monks bear the patronym Shi (Śākya). More generally, Buddhist monks and nuns are called "children of the Buddha."

Whereas Śākyamuni left his wife Yaśodhara and the other women of his gynaeceum without regrets, such renunciation was not always as easy for his disciples, as shown by the case of his half-brother Nanda. After entering the Buddhist order at the request of the Buddha, on the day he was to get married, Nanda was unable to forget his love, the beautiful Sundarī. To help him take his mind off her, the Buddha showed him successively the most extreme ugliness—a dead and disfigured she-monkey—and of beauty—the celestial nymphs in Trāyastriṃśa Heaven. Nanda came thus to realize that, from an aesthetic standpoint, the distance between the nymphs and Sundarī was greater than that between Sundarī and the monkey. The stratagem turned out, however, to be a double-edged sword, as Nanda now became infatuated with the nymphs. Therefore, the Buddha promised him one of them as a wife if he would only persevere in his practice. Fortunately, the mockery from his codisciples brought Nanda to his senses (or rather, away from them, back to reason), and thereafter he devoted himself to the practice of meditation. The story affirms that he was eventually able to realize the vanity of all desires and the emptiness of beauty. He consequently untied the Buddha from his promise and renounced the nymph he had so coveted.[1]

PROTEAN DESIRE

Śākyamuni succeeded in cutting off desire, but his disciples were not always as successful. In the later Buddhist tradition, desire was usually displaced, intensified, modified in manifold ways. Even when repressed in its sexual form, desire was often merely displaced to thirst for power. Political ambition, in turn, seems to have legitimated sex. Political success multiplies temptations and opportunities and, as we all know, "opportunities make the thief." A truly vicious circle.

---

[1] The story was well known in Japan. See, for instance, the *Konjaku monogatari shū*, "How the Buddha Converted Nanda and Caused him to Renounce Secular Life," in Ury 1979: 35–37.

Sexual desire belongs to the realm of the senses, and these senses are deluding us. We might recall Laozi's saying that the five senses make a person blind and deaf. Only the mind, a sixth sense according to Buddhists, can reveal things as they really are—provided that it can detach itself from sense perceptions. Buddhist soteriology teaches that there are three obstacles to deliverance: passions, acts, and their retribution. According to the the *Dazhidulun,* a commentary on the *Prajñāpāramitā-sūtra* (Great Perfection of Wisdom) attributed to Nāgārjuna: "Among these three obstacles, the act is the greatest." Indeed, it is the act that brings retribution, but only because it is itself caused by passion. The *Dazhidulun* insists on the inescapable nature of karmic retribution:

> The wheel of transmigration pulls man
> With his passions and hindrances.
> It is very strong and revolves freely,
> No one can stop it. . . .
> The waters of the ocean may dry up,
> The earth of Mount Sumeru may become exhausted,
> But the acts of former existences
> Will never be consummated or exhausted.[2]

Desire is almost as defiling as the act itself, however: "He who enjoys looking at women, even in painting, is not detached from the act."[3] In the traditional Buddhist classification, there are three passions: hatred, love, and ignorance. Desire, in the form of love (*rāga,* a word meaning color, but also lewdness, concupiscence, lust, attraction), is therefore one of the "three poisons" that pollute and maintain human existence. According to this conception, all existence (human or nonhuman, because this is true even for the gods) is fundamentally defiled.

The Buddhist notion of desire is not limited to sexual desire; it encompasses all sensual desires. Desire is usually described with ten similes: it is said to be like a dry meat bone, a piece of meat for which many birds are fighting, a torch made of straw carried against the wind, a pit full of burning coal, a dream of a beautiful landscape, borrowed things, a tree laden with fruit on which it is dangerous to climb, a slaughterhouse, the point of a sword, a snake's head.[4] Carnal desires are commonly associated with hunger and thirst, more precisely eating meat and drinking alcohol, and therefore nondesire implies not only chastity but vegetarianism and sobriety as well.[5] Buddhist desire—this "creeper of existence"

[2] Lamotte 1944–1980, 1: 347.
[3] La Vallée Poussin 1927: 79.
[4] *Majjhima-nikāya* 1: 133–34.
[5] Likewise, for the Encratites (from the Greek *enkrateia,* "continence"), the abstention from meat and alcohol was intimately tied to sexual renunciation, for the eating of meat,

according to the *Dhammapada*—is reminiscent of what the Romans called *cupiditas,* greed in all its forms. As Peter Brown remarks, the true struggle of the ascetic is as much against his belly as against his under-belly.[6] Significantly perhaps, the Buddha is said to have died from indi-gestion after eating meat, not from venereal disease. In modern Thera-vāda monasteries, the major obstacle to monastic life is not chastity but the—apparently minor—rule of fasting in the afternoon. In Japan, monks have got round this rule by calling their evening meal a "medication."

Buddhists distinguish between sensual desire and a subtler desire, the "thirst for existence"—including the desire to be reborn in paradise. To these two forms of desire they add a third one, the desire for annihilation, the thirst for nonexistence. However, the Buddhist position on this point is somewhat ambivalent. Whereas in early Buddhism this desire for nir-vāna was judged to be good, later Buddhists came to deny its nature as desire (for its paradoxical object, nirvāna, is neither being nor nonbeing). In Mahāyāna Buddhism, however, this longing for deliverance is often perceived as the most dangerous form of the desire to exist, because it is the most subtle: as the simile goes, a sandalwood fire burns one just as well as as an ordinary fire.[7]

Some modern commentators have noted the apparent paradox of a "desire" for enlightenment.[8] Of course, the term *desire* is misleading in this context, since we are not talking here of lust in the strict sense. How-ever, even if one cannot speak of a "lust for enlightenment" (Stevens) or of a "passionate enlightenment" (Shaw), the question of a will that would condition enlightenment, relativize the absolute, remains a vexing one. We can distinguish on that point two main types of practitioners: those for whom any desire, even that of awakening, is harmful or at least superfluous; and those for whom, due to an ultimate ruse of ultimate

---

like the sexual act, was supposed to identify humans with animals, and alcohol is well known for its aphrodisiac effects. See Brown 1988: 93.

[6] Ibid.

[7] The two sources of desire, physical and visual, sometimes merge for the best. Here is, for instance what Mujū writes in his *Shasekishū:* "I have heard that after Eshin [Genshin, 942–1017] aroused the Aspiration for Enlightenment, he venerated the two characters *myō-ri* ["fame"]. He considered that it was from a desire for prestige that he had studied; and it was by virtue of his learning that his Aspiration for Enlightenment arose. Without his desire for fame, there would have been no learning, and without learning, no wisdom. Without wisdom it would have been difficult for the Desire for Enlightenment to have arisen. The *Vimalakīrti Sūtra* speaks of entering the Way after being caught on the fish-hook of desire. It says that when there is attachment to the sensuous, the Bodhisattva becomes a beautiful woman as a device for leading people into the Way of the Buddha." (Morrell 1985: 130)

[8] See, for instance, in Plutarch's *Life of Alexander,* the discussion between Alexander and the Indian sages, as it is analyzed by Dumézil 1983: 69–70.

reality, desire is still needed to put an end to desire. Thus, in Tantrism, desire, once refined, may serve as fuel to awakening. In his study on rationality (and the subversion thereof), Jon Elster points to the paradox of states that are "by-products" and cannot be the direct effect of a cause.[9] Likewise, desire cannot lead directly to awakening, yet the latter derives from it—but it is only a paradoxical by-product, not a direct effect. The Chan master Shenhui, for instance, distinguished two kinds of illusion, the gross and the subtle. Gross delusion is to be attached to passions, subtle delusion is to attempt to get rid of passions in order to reach awakening.

Desire for beauty belongs to the second category of delusion. Infatuation with beauty can remain long after physical craving has disappeared. We recall the story of Nanda, who was infatuated with the beauty first of a mortal woman and later of a celestial nymph, but who was eventually able to overcome fire with fire. Alienation not only in someone else's beauty but also in one's own beauty may become a stumbling block, as Narcissus learned at his own expense (or expanse). Likewise, the handsome Ānanda confronts dangers and difficulties unknown to the austere-looking Mahākāśyapa. Women fall in love with him, and he is lured into temptation by them. Sometimes, this love at first sight has disastrous consequences. The *Jurin shūyō shō,* for instance, explain that monks no longer have their shoulder bare because a woman who was drawing water was troubled by the sight of Ānanda and his skin "white as snow," and as a result let the child she carried fall into the well. Sometimes, however, Ānanda is able to use his beauty as an instrument of conversion. In the *Jikidan shō,* the well-known episode of the seduction of Ānanda by the courtesan Mātaṅga becomes a moral victory for Ānanda, who declares: "If you want to become my wife, become a nun." In the *Sanbō ekotoba,* we find that Ānanda was, toward the end of the Heian period, the object (*honzon*) of a penance ritual for women.[10]

The "historical" Buddha himself is said to have been very handsome and he became at times the object of sublimated desire, in spite of the hagiographical or iconographical topos of the thirty-two corporeal marks that depicts him with hands reaching his knees, webbed fingers, and many other features that hardly meet our classical canon of beauty. Nevertheless, transfigured by spirituality, his beauty can be beneficial, making him an object of devotion, an instrument of conversion.[11] Even after his death, the fragmented body of the Buddha in the form of

---

[9] See Elster 1983: 57.

[10] See Kamens 1988: 272–73.

[11] See, for instance, the story of the brahman Vākkhalithera who, after seeing the Buddha once, longed to see him constantly, and became a monk just for that reason, although the Buddha scolded him for preferring the view of his foul body to that of the Dharma. Malalasekera 1961–, s.v. "Beauty," fasc. 6: 599.

"relics" (śarīra), remained an object of desire and fetishism, and almost caused a "war of the relics." In this case, people wanted to appropriate some of the spiritual power of the Buddha, an efficacy or charisma that was reflected (or embodied) in his corporeal beauty.

For ordinary monks, beauty can be a mixed blessing. For nuns (and women in general), it is simply a curse. In a man, beauty is often perceived as the effect of a good karma, whereas in a woman it is usually seen as the result of a past sin—paradoxically enough, because it produces attachment in men. For this reason, the beautiful Eshun, sister of the Zen priest Emyō, had to disfigure herself to be accepted as a nun.[12] Such drastic measures are not always necessary, since attachment can also be thwarted by means of contemplation. In order to understand the ephemeral nature of the body, monks are exhorted to contemplate impurity and ugliness, for instance to meditate on a corpse. The *Dazhidulun* explains the necessity to "reject colors"—that is, all forms of beauty.[13] While emphasizing that "love or hatred depend on the person, and color in itself is indetermined," it argues that practitioners must reject both the feeling and its external cause, because "when melted gold burns your body and you want to get rid of it, you cannot simply avoid the fire while keeping the gold; you must reject both the gold and the fire."[14]

Desire and Rebirth

What makes desire so nefarious according to Buddhism? It is the force that gets us bogged down in being, making us fall into what Augustine called the "slide of temporality" (*in lubrico temporalis*). According to the idealist version of Buddhist thought, desire produces the act; the craving thought produces the three worlds. Every person is thus the product of his or her own karma, and this karma manifests itself both subjectively and objectively, as the individual consciousness and its environment, the world in which the individual is immersed at birth. Therefore, desire plays a properly ontological, or even ontogenic, role: it is what drives beings, after death to be reincarnated in a certain maternal womb. According to the scholastic conceptions of the *Abhidharmakośa-śāstra*, a kind of Buddhist *Summa Theologia*, after death, the human being exists in the form of an "intermediary being" (Skt. *antarābhava*) until the time when, seeing a man and a woman making love, he or she feels, due to his

---

[12] See *Rentōroku* in *Sōtōshū zensho* 16, Shiden 1: 301–2.

[13] The Chinese word meaning "color" (Ch. *se*, J. *shiki*), and by extension the forms of the empirical world, also connotes feminine beauty, feminine charm, and carnal desire. Hence the various possible interpretations of the famous Buddhist stanza: "Form (color) is emptiness, emptiness is form."

[14] Lamotte 1944–1980, 2: 990.

or her karma, irresistibly attracted toward one of the partners and repelled by the other. According to this Buddhist version of the Oedipus complex, he or she will be reincarnated as a child of this couple—as a girl (if the attraction comes from the male partner) or as a boy (if it comes from the woman).

Rebirth is by no means always human, however, and the intermediary being, depending on past deeds, may well be reborn in one of the five other destinies (gati)—among heavenly beings (devas), hungry ghosts (pretas), titans (asuras), animals, or the damned in hell. All these destinies belong to the world of desire: even the devas, who live in constant bliss, are motivated by desire. According to Dirghāgama, in the Trāyastriṃśa Heaven male and female gods are able to achieve orgasm simply by thinking about each other.[15] The Dazhidulun also says: "Heavenly women (apsaras) have no eunuch to keep them, / They are free from the troubles of pregnancy. / [With them] pleasure and debauchery [have only joys]. / After a meal, no need to go to pass a motion."[16] Sensual pleasure is in this case admitted because it does not create new acts, since it is much more subtle than that of humans. However, these celestial beings are themselves still chained to the wheel of saṃsāra, condemned to fall back into a lower rebirth sooner or later, when their good karma is exhausted. This realm of desire is the lowest of the three worlds that constitute the Buddhist universe. The two others are the world of subtle matter and the immaterial world, which can be reached only by those who, having "entered the stream" of the Buddhist Path, are on their way to becoming arhats.

Māra

In Buddhist mythology, one particular figure incarnates the vital—yet deadly—drive that animates and binds all beings. This mythical figure is Māra, the Evil One, also conceived of as Kāma, Desire. We are told that when Śākyamuni was about to reach Awakening, Māra, afraid of losing dominion over the human world, sent his daughters to seduce him. This is one of the "three attempts" made in vain by Māra to weaken Śākyamuni's resolve and prevent him from becoming a Buddha. Georges Dumézil has argued that the episode should be read in the context of the Indo-European ideology of the three functions (justice/sovereignty, war, and sensuality/fecundity). In this schema, desire belongs essentially to the third function. Māra's goal was to make Śākyamuni fall "in the trap of one of the highest values admitted in pre-Buddhist societies: the riposte to

[15] Dirghāgama, 133c.
[16] Lamotte 1944–1980, 2: 823.

aggression, spiritual perfection, and the procreation of heirs."[17] One could argue that Śākyamuni had almost fallen into Māra's trap by marrying the beautiful Yaśodhara and begetting a son. However, it is nowhere implied that Māra used Yaśodhara to lure the Buddha, although she is presented in an ambivalent light as both chaste and seducive, forlorn and dangerous. In the *Buddhacarita,* a life of the Buddha compiled by Aśvaghoṣa, Māra, after his three vain attempts, realizes that he has lost control over Śākyamuni. He tries, however, to limit the damage by painting the perspective of a spiritual lineage in glowing colors: "Let the Perfect One return home and procreate with his legitimate wife many sons, who will in turn become Perfect Ones."[18] According to the most widespread version, Māra subsequently makes one last attempt to convince the Buddha to enter into nirvāṇa without further delay, so that he would not share with men his realization of the Dharma. Although he ultimately fails, the Buddhist tradition has been at times troubled by the apparent hesitation of the Buddha.

Desire is therefore the "law of the genre" in the French sense (of gender, but also of *genus*—human and nonhuman). Sexuality is dangerous, above all because it binds men, as if with a "red thread," to human existence and to lineage. A Greek euphemism for penis is "necessity."[19] In Japanese, too, the popular etymology connected *mara* (penis) with the homonymous Sanskrit terms *māra* (obstacle, killing) and Māra (the lord of obstacles or of Death). Śākyamuni's son was also called Rāhula, another word meaning "obstacle." According to some brahmanical texts, a son's performance of appropriate rituals assures his father of one kind of immortality ("below the navel"), physical immortality. However, a higher kind of immortality ("above the navel," that is, spiritual immortality), advocated in the *Upaniṣad,* is lost through the birth of a son and the resultant ties to saṃsāra.[20] The Buddhist notion of continence ran against Indian and Chinese notions of lineage. It was ironically turned against the Buddhists themselves in the *Huahu jing* (Scripture on the Conversion of the Barbarians), a Daoist polemical tract. In this work, Laozi plays the part of the Buddha. In one variant, he even enters the womb of Queen Māya. However, the main episode is that in which a barbarian king who has refused allegiance to him is subdued by his divine power. Although the king repents, Laozi/Buddha punishes him and his subjects by ordering them to practise asceticism—that is, to wear red-

---

[17] Dumézil 1983: 37–45.
[18] Ibid., 42.
[19] Brown 1988: 84.
[20] See Wendy Doniger O'Flaherty, "Karma and Rebirth in the Vedas and Purāṇas," in O'Flaherty, ed., *Karma and Rebirth in Classical Indian Traditions* (Berkeley and Los Angeles: University of California Press, 1980), 3–5.

brown garments like criminals, mutilate their bodies, and abstain from sexual intercourse in order to put an end to their rebellious seed. If, the authors of the tract argue, Laozi taught the barbarians in order not to save them but to humiliate and weaken them, and eventually to destroy them, would it not be insane to introduce this teaching to China?

THE BUDDHIST ECONOMY OF DESIRE

The newborn infant is bound with the threads of marital alliance.
How many springs have the scarlet blossoms opened and fallen?

(Ikkyū, *Kyōunshū*)

The desire to exist, analyzed in Indian Buddhism as one of the twelve *nidānas* (causes of existence), tended to merge in Chinese Buddhism with the popular Chinese conception of a "fundamental destiny" (*benming*). According to this conception, every person receives at birth a certain destiny, and if he/she dies before fulfilling this destiny, he/she wanders about, like a lost soul, unable to renounce his/her memory and to fuse into the great cosmic woof of the Dao, or into the social woof of lineage. Victims of violent death, who still have a portion of life remaining, cannot be inscribed into familial memory: they are out of place, outlawed, out of the "economy" (*oikos nomos*, the "law of the house"). To prevent them from harming the living, an attempt is made to reintegrate them into that socio-cosmic economy: they are turned into gods or ancestors through elaborate rituals. By taking charge of the cult of the dead, Buddhism was able to take root in China.

We recall that Māra's last attempt to divert the Buddha from preaching the Law was an argument for the continuation of Śākyamuni's physical (and spiritual) lineage: "Beget many sons who will reach awakening." Śākyamuni rejected this temptation, thereby forsaking his duties (and his name) as an heir and leader of the Śākya clan. The rise of the Buddhist saṅgha coincides with the destruction (for karmic reasons, we are told) of this lineage and of his father's kingdom.

Like the Christian message according to Peter Brown, the early Buddhist message was *un*familiar in both senses of the word: "It was a message of which those caught in the narrow confines of the family could have no inkling."[21] The Buddha himself had apparently cut off what Paul Eluard called "the dreadful snake coils of the blood ties." This anti-familial and antisocial aspect of early Buddhism drew sharps criticisms for the new doctrine: "At that time, sons of well-known and distinguished families from the country of Magadha were practicing the reli-

[21] Brown, 1988: 89.

gious life under the guidance of the Blessed One. This upset and angered people: 'He is on a path which takes away [people's] children, the monk Gotama. He is on a path which makes widows, the monk Gotama. He is on a path which destroys families, the monk Gotama.'"[22]

From a Chinese perspective in particular, the apparent lack of filial piety of the Buddha raised serious issues. In response to this criticism, Chinese Buddhists worked hard to assert a typically Buddhist form of filial piety: the Buddha even went to heaven, we are told, to preach the Dharma to his mother. He also took good care of his father: tradition has it that when King Śuddhodana died, the Buddha and his half-brother Nanda were at his pillow, and Ānanda and Rāhula at his feet. At the time of the funerals, the Buddha is said to have shouldered his father's coffin, "in order to admonish sentient beings in our latter age against ingratitude for our fathers' and mothers' loving care."[23] According to the apocryphal *Fanwang jing*: "When Śākyamuni Buddha sat under the bodhi tree and attained supreme awakening, that was when he first enjoined the bodhisattva precepts and filial submission toward parents, teachers, clergy, and the Three Jewels. Filial submission is the Dharma of the ultimate path. Filial piety is called *śīla*, it is also called restraint."[24]

The fact remains that the Śākyas' seed became extinct with the Buddha, or rather because of him, with his son, who became a monk under him. Incidentally, tradition has it that Śākyamuni's begetting of a son was merely intended to prove to the world that he was a real man: "And it occurred to him: 'Lest others say that the Prince Śākyamuni was not a man, and that he wandered forth without 'paying attention' to Yaśodharā, Gopikā, Mṛgajā, and his other sixty thousand wives, let me now make love to Yaśodharā.' He did so, and Yaśodharā became pregnant."[25] As noted earlier, the child's name, Rāhula (lit. "Obstacle"), tells a lot about the fatherly feelings of the Buddha. In a Sanskrit variant of the tale, the Buddha's relationship with his wife and son is radically different. To quote John Strong's synopsis: "Rāhula is not born on the eve of the Great Departure but only engendered then, when the future Buddha makes love to his wife to prove his manhood and to fulfil his duties to his family. . . . There ensues an interesting parallelism between his career as a quester and [Yaśodharā's] own pregnancy, which develops at home. . . . Finally, when he attains enlightenment at Bodh-gaya, she gives birth at home, having, according to this legend, borne her son in her womb six

22 Vinaya 1: 43, quoted in Wijayaratna 1990: 90.

23 Tominaga 1990: 40.

24 *Fanwang jing*, 1004a. The 35th light precept of the *Fanwang jing* also begins with a vow of filial obedience (ibid., 1007b). However, the 40th precept says that monks should not pay obeisance to rulers or parents, nor honor kin and spirits (ibid., 1008c).

25 See Strong 1995: 10.

years! Here her son's name, Rāhula, is not associated with the word for fetter but with the divinity Rāhu, who eclipses the moon at the moment of his birth, just as his father, upon attaining enlightenment, is thought to outshine the sun."[26]

The image of the Buddha as an ascetic rejecting marital life and blood ties was sometimes questioned by family-oriented Buddhists. In many Japanese stories, the marital sequence in the life of the Buddha was on the contrary emphasized, and sometimes served as an excuse for monks who wanted to break their vows: thus, in an otogizōshi (narrative book) entitled *Sasayakitake monogatari,* a priest of Kurama-dera (on the northern outskirts of Kyoto), Saikōbō, argues that if Śākyamuni, before achieving enlightenment, plighted his troth to Yaśodharā and fathered the child Rāhula, there is no reason why he could not himself have at least an affair with the girl he is infatuated with.[27] We learn also that the Buddha had other wives, with whom he fathered a child.[28] One, in particular, Gopā, now takes the front seat (or the main bed). Tantric Buddhists argued that the Buddha, before leaving the palace, learnt from her all the secrets of sex, although in this case sex was not aimed at procreation.[29]

Paradoxically, the message of some of these stories is that whereas the ascetic denial of sexuality can lead to evil results, apparent transgressions may end well. In the famous Dōjōji legend, a monk died as a result of refusing to respond to a young girl's love. She turned into a monstrous snake, and followed the monk to his hiding place, the bell of Dōjōji. Coiling around the bell, the snake reduced the monk to ashes through the intense heat of her anger. Although some people hearing this story may have concluded that women are intrinsically evil, others may have thought that it would have been better for both the monk and the girl to have followed the human course of events.

In the Mahāyāna tradition, Vimalakīrti is said to represent the ideal of the householder, but we hear nothing of his family, his wife and children. This family man does not indulge in family pleasures any more than he indulges in sex while visiting brothels. Another famous "family man," at least in the Chan/Zen tradition, is a disciple of Mazu Daoyi named "Lay-

---

[26] Ibid.

[27] See Kavanagh 1996: 232–33. We find distant echoes of this theory in Japan. For instance, Yoshitsune, trying to seduce a young woman, cynically resorts to this argument. In a parodic text of the Edo period criticizing Confucian and Buddhist sexual morality, the *Onna tairaku hōkai,* we find a list of similar arguments. See Minamoto 1993: 105–6.

[28] According to the Vinaya of the Mūlasarvāstivādin, for instance, the Buddha had three wives, named Yaśodharā, Gopā, and Mṛgajā—not to mention the sixty-thousand women of his gynaeceum. See T. 24, 1450: 111–12.

[29] Shaw 1994: 143.

man" Pang. In his case, we do hear about his family—a strangely nuclear family in Tang times, consisting of his wife and daughter. They all live like pure Chan adepts, and their lineage comes to an end with them, since there is no male heir. To make matters worse (from a Chinese viewpoint), Pang destroys his family's wealth by throwing it in the river. Furthermore, his daughter, who apparently never considers marriage as an option, turns out to be quite unfilial (at least by Confucian standards) by chosing to die before her parents.

The Buddhist ascetic, in a sense, wanted to be irresponsible. Responsibility means to respond to the call of the other, to trade solitude for solidarity, the silence of nature for the bustle of society; it is to reintegrate the economy.[30] Yet Buddhism was eventually reintegrated into the "economic circle" and diverted from its early ideal of renunciation in the name of the collectivity. An example of such relapse is found in the following tale, which shows how an eminent monk could fall into the trap of lineage. Shi Hao, the prime minister of the Song Emperor Xiaozong, despaired of having a male heir. Having heard that one way to get one was to lure an old hermit and hope for his death, so that the latter would be reborn as a male child in one's lineage, Shi Hao invited an eminent priest named Jue. Despite his many years of ascesis, Jue was dazzled by the wealth of his host, and the thoughts of envy that arose at the moment of his death caused him to be reborn in the house of the minister. Later, he became a cruel and corrupted statesman. Beyond the karmic morality of this tale, which shows us the fall of an insufficiently virtuous monk in the whirlpools of evil, its interest is to illustrate the belief in the possibility of the transformation of spiritual power into vital power, of divesting moral virtue to the profit of procreative *virtus*.

A similar motif is found in the biography of Kumārajīva. The Indian translator was the son of a monk who had been forced to marry a Kuchean princess against his will.[31] After the boy had come of age, another Kuchean king attempted to force the young Kumārajīva to marry yet another princess, a proposition the young monk steadfastly refused. Undaunted, the king then forced Kumārajīva to become drunk one night and locked him in a "secret chamber" with the girl, after which time, we are told, Kumārajīva "surrendered his integrity." After Kumārajīva ar-

---

[30] In Japan, the Buddhist refusal of the economy finds its ultimate expression (not without compromises with reality) in the principle of *muen* (unrelatedness, autonomy) analyzed by Amino Yoshihiko. Monastic institutions were one expression of this utopian realm, in which the normal economic "relations" (*en*) of credit and debt, and the derived social relations (lord and vassal, etc.) were no longer acknowledged. See Amino 1978.

[31] See *Gaoseng zhuan*, T. 50: 330a. According to one version, he agreed to marry the princess so that the son born from this union might transmit to China the original icon of the Buddha stolen by his father. See Frank 1968: 78–79.

rived in China, the northern ruler Yao Xing, impressed by the monk's intelligence, forced him to cohabit with no fewer than ten courtesans, arguing that otherwise the "seeds of the Dharma would bear no offspring!" "From this point on," the biography continues, "Kumārajīva no longer lived in the monks' quarters."[32] However, as Antonino Forte points out, "What is usually presented as the imposition of a barbarian king (constraining him to have relations with many women in order to procreate many geniuses like himself) could well be the result of an idea of the clergy which is not strictly monastic but more secular."[33]

The popular transformation of spirituality into vital force is also illustrated in an episode of the Chinese novel *Xiyou ji* (Journey to the West). In this episode, an ogress passes herself off as a bodhisattva and fools the priest Xuanzang. However, when the supernatural monkey Sun Wukong perceives her true identity and ties her to a tree, she confesses that she wanted to become an immortal by copulating with the Chinese monk, a man who has practiced since childhood and has never lost a drop of his primordial yang.[34] In another episode, Xuanzang is captured by four demons, who explain to their master: "We had heard for long that this Chinese monk had a dharma body formed through the practice of purity during ten successive incarnations: to eat a bit of it would indefinitely prolong our life."[35]

In the *Nihon ryōiki* we find a story about an eminent monk, Zenshū, who was reborn as a prince. This monk had a large birthmark on the right side of his chin. When he was about to pass away, a diviner was called to give an oracle about his life after death, Then Zenshū's spirit, having possessed the diviner, said, "I will enter the womb of Tajihi no Omina, a wife of the emperor of Japan, to be reborn as a prince. You shall know his identity owing to the same birthmark as mine on the prince's face." After Zenshū's death, the imperial consort gave birth to a boy who had the same birthmark as the late priest, but the boy died after three years. In this case, we seem to be dealing with the rebirth of a

[32] See *Xu gaoseng zhuan*, 330–33; and André Lévy 1978, 4: 86. In Korea, we find the case of Wŏnhyo, already mentioned: the Silla king, wanting to obtain "seeds of sainthood," invites him to the palace and has him sleep with a princess. The child begotten from this union will become one of Silla's Ten Sages, and his son will be sent as an emissary to Japan. See Ilyŏn 1972: 306–7.

[33] Forte 1995: 77. In the *Jin shu* 95: 2501, we read that Kumārajīva was overtaken by an uncontrollable sexual desire in the middle of a lecture. He came down from the podium and said to the emperor: "Because of the hindrance of desire I need a woman." The emperor sent him a courtesan immediately and the union was blessed with two children (ibid.). The Iranian translator An Shigao, also initially an hostage, was another monk with very prosperous offspring.

[34] *Xiyou ji* 16: 80; Lévy 1978, 2: 580–81.

[35] *Xiyou ji* 15: 73; Lévy 1978, 2: 437.

bodhisattva, a last rebirth whose function is to exhaust some karmic residue. The story is ambivalent, however, because of the widespread belief that children who died before their third year were actually demons, incarnated in a human family to expunge some karmic debt. The *Nihon ryōiki* mentions another case, that of a famous hermit known as Bodhisattva Jakusen. When he was about to die, Jakusen told his disciples that he would be reborn twenty years later as a prince named Kamino. He is, says Kyōkai, the present emperor, a truly a sage ruler, although some have unduly criticized him due to the occurrence of droughts and plagues under his reign.[36] The point of this story for us is that the rebirth of the priest is clearly seen as the reincarnation of a bodhisattva, an expedient motivated by compassion to help people.

More often, it is attachment to life (or to a living being) that causes the desire to be reborn in this world, despite all its suffering. In the worst case, such desire can create ghosts with "unfinished business," unable to move on along the path, trapped forever in a liminal realm. In Japanese literature, for instance, we have several instances of a monk's rebirth as a "malevolent spirit" (*onryō*) because of a burning love. Thus, when Lady Nijō tells Emperor Go-Fukakusa that she has had an affair with the Ninnaji priest Ariake, he says, "None of this bodes well for the future, for events from the past teach us that passion respects neither rank nor station. For example, the spirit of the high priest Kakinomoto pursued Empress Somedono relentlessly, and it was beyond the power of the buddhas and bodhisattvas to prevent her from yielding to his malevolent spirit. The holy man of the Shiga Temple was also smitten by passion, but he was luckily returned to the true way by the sympathy and skill of the lady he loved."[37]

When Ariake comes to take leave of Nijō, after she has given birth to a child who is taken from her, and he has contracted a fatal disease, he tells her:

> Sometime after our sorrowful parting on that far-away dawn I learned that you had gone into hiding, and having no one else to turn to, I began copying out five of the Mahāyāna sūtras. In each chapter I inserted a phrase from one of your letters with the plea that we might be united in this world, so deep are my feelings. The sūtras are copied now but not dedicated. I shall dedicate them after we have been reborn together. If I store the more than two hundred chapters in the treasure hall of the dragon king, I will certainly be reborn to this life, and then I shall dedicate them to Buddha. To accomplish this I plan to take the sūtras with me after death by having them added to the fuel of my funeral pyre.

---

[36] See Nakamura 1973: 284–86.

[37] According to one version of the legend, the lady in question was empress Kyōgoku, consort of Emperor Uda (r. 887–897). See Brazell 1973: 123. On Empress Somedono and the Shiga priest, see below, chapter 3.

Lady Nijō comments, "His futile attachment to this world distressed me. 'Just pray that we may be reborn together in paradise.' 'I cannot, for I am unable to relinquish my love for you. That is why I wish to be reborn as a human. When I die, as all creatures must, my smoke rising to the vast and empty sky will surely drift toward you.' He spoke with a grave sincerity which touched me deeply."[38]

We should not interpret the apparent contradictions of Buddhism only as concessions to popular piety. Admittedly, Buddhism first defined itself as an ascesis—moderate but efficacious—that is, as a more or less violent attempt to weaken the physical vitality in oneself so as to allow the growth of a spiritual principle. By renouncing the world, the Buddhist ascetic joins the "living dead." Paradoxically, some of these saints became in popular devotion "deities of life." In China, the most well-known cases are the two friends Hanshan and Shide, worshiped as "gods of union." In Japan, certain self-mummified saints were worshiped in order to enhance fertility. In one particular case, the object of devotion was the dried genitals of the saint. This unexpected return of vitality is inscribed in the inner dynamics of Buddhism, in particular in the ritual renunciation. According to Maurice Bloch, such rituals of renunciation aim, above all, at letting the violence of the ascetic act rebound in the form of vitality.[39] At any rate, the otherworldly teaching of Buddhism, like that of Christianity, eventually confronted the two major aspects of sexuality underscored by Michel Foucault: discipline and demography. Inasmuch as it became part of an ideology that was promoting fecundity, it came to promote "deities of life." The Buddhist emphasis on funerary rituals was another way to promote fertility, the regeneration of life, but this time without the mediation of sexuality. As Bloch points out, sexuality is opposed to fertility: "It is associated with flesh, decomposition and women, while true ancestral fertility is a mystical process symbolized by the tomb and the (male) bones."[40] Thus, "the fertility of 'life' which is affirmed in funerary practices is above all legitimate fertility often contrasted . . . with illegitimate individual polluting sexuality."[41]

ASCETIC LUST

For early Buddhists, continence was imperative in order to break the vicious circle of human existence. Buddhism was also influenced in this respect by Hindu conceptions. In Hinduism, desire was also seen as perturbating the self-control of the ascetic. In yoga, for instance, chastity

[38] Brazell 1973: 147–48.
[39] See Bloch 1992.
[40] Bloch and Parry 1982: 21.
[41] See ibid., 226.

was essentially a way to accumulate spiritual energy. The consummation of the sexual act is usually perceived by the male as a vital depredation: the loss of semen—the vital essence par excellence—entails a loss of energy. Similar conceptions were also formulated in Daoism, and they may have reinforced the ascetic and misogynistic tendencies in Chinese Buddhism. From this viewpoint, sex is not only a hindrance but it can also make one lose the benefits of a long ascetic practice. This is what happens to many ascetics who lose all their powers at the mere sight of feminine beauty.

The paradigmatic example is that of the hermit Unicorn, an ascetic so powerful that, in a moment of anger, he imprisoned the dragon kings, deities of rain, and provoked a terrible drought. To bring the rain back, the king sent five hundred beautiful maidens into the mountain where the hermit dwelt. One of them seduced him, and the dragons were able to escape, bringing on a sudden deluge. The courtesan took refuge in a cave with the hermit, who fell in love with her. After a few days, when the rain stopped, she decided to return to the city, and the hermit showed her the way. At one point, he offered to carry her on his back to cross a stream. When they entered the city, he was still carrying her on his back, and thus became an object of ridicule. When he attempted to fly off back to his mountain, he realized to his great dismay that he had lost all his powers.[42] In one Japanese variant, the hermit, under the name Kume Sennin, returns for good to the profane world: "One day, whilst he was flying over a river, his eye was so violently caught by the unusual whiteness of the legs of a young, lovely washerwoman that instantly he lost all his miraculous gift, and fell down before her quite topsy-turvy. Subsequently, he married her, but persisted in adding the title 'Ex-Saint' to his sign-manual."[43]

[42] According to some sources, the ascetic Unicorn is none other than a former incarnation of the Buddha. As we will see, ascetic power can be destroyed not only by the vision of maiden but also by that of boys, as in the Japanese case of the old hermit of Shishigatani: "From the moment he chanced to see these two splendid boys, his concentration failed him and the good deeds he had accumulated in previous incarnations went to naught." See Saikaku 1990: 61. Men are not the only fallible ones, however, as is shown in the story of the ascetic nun who lost her concentration and assumed again her human form (she had become a stone) because of a thought of desire provoked by the sight of a monk. See Frank 1968: 116–17.

[43] See Minakata 1973, 10: 193. The legend often appears in Japanese literature. See, for instance the *Konjaku monogatari shū*, in Frank 1968: 70–74; "Ikkaku Sennin," in Waley (1921), 1976: 245–46; and Urabe Kenkō's *Tsurezuregusa*: "Did not the fairy Kume lose his supernatural powers when he saw the white legs of a girl washing clothes? And well he might, at the sight of the bare unpainted skin of those arms and legs beautifully glossy and plump!" in *The Miscellany of a Japanese Priest,* translated by William N. Porter (Putney, VT: Charles Tuttle, 1974 : 14). The *Shichi daiji junrei shiki* by Ōe no Chikafusa and the *Konjaku monogatari shū* contain an interesting follow-up about Kume and the pillars of

A similar topos is found in Chinese novels. In the *Jinpingmei,* for instance, a group of monks who have come for the funeral of the husband of the beautiful Golden Lotus become victims of her charms: "At the sight of the deceased's wife, all these monks felt their Buddha nature becoming clouded, and their mind of meditation getting lost; none of them was able to control the monkey-like agitation of his thoughts and the running wild of his desires. . . . Their strenuous ascesis was in one instant annihilated, and thousand thunders could not have reestablished it."[44]

Another entertaining example is that of the test inflicted by the third patriarch Upagupta on one of his disciples who bragged that he had overcome the temptations of the flesh. One day, when he was crossing a ford, this disciple felt compelled to rescue a young woman who was about to drown. Aroused by the contact of her soft skin, he suddenly forgot his years of ascetic practice and decided that her debt toward him should be repaid right away in nature:

> Forcing her to the ground, he lay between her legs, intent on violating her—and at that moment he looked at her and found that instead of a woman he had hold of the holy sage who was his master. Aghast, he tried to pull away, but Upagupta held him fast between his legs, and cried out, "Why do you torment an aged priest in that manner? Are you the saintly man who has gained enlightenment and is untainted by sexual desire?" The disciple was overwhelmed with shame and struggled to get free from Upagupta's legs, but they held him in a vice-like grip and would not let go. As the master went on upbraiding him, a crowd of passers-by gathered to watch, and the disciple was overcome with shame and mortification.[45]

Owing to Upagupta's skillful means, however, the disciple was able to recover himself and to preserve some of the benefits of his earlier practice. Often, as we will see, reform was achieved by much less humorous means.

The Demonization of Desire

Desire seems to stem from inside oneself, yet most desires are external to the self and come from the outside world. In spite of the dogma of no-

---

Tōdaiji. After marrying and living a profane life under the name of Kume no Sukune, he was one day drafted with others to build Tōdaiji. He then used his remaining powers to make the trees fly, and these trees became the pillars of Tōdaiji. According to Tanaka Takako, Kume's true ascetic nature was fully manifested only after he came into contact with women and returned to profane life. See Tanaka 1992: 67.

[44] See Lévy 1985, 1: 163.

[45] *Uji shūi monogatari,* translated by Mills 1970: 396.

self, Buddhist ascetics, like Indian yogis and Greek Stoics, seem to have conceived the self as a citadel besieged by the external world.[46] Their renunciation to the world was above all an attempt to regain self-possession, and it therefore implies a rejection of desire. Because of its association with desire, the world was perceived as evil, and vice-versa. In order to eradicate desire, extirpate its root, they also had to negate the phenomenal world. Such a conception, resonating with that the Gnostics, seems far from the Middle Way between asceticism and hedonism advocated by the Buddha. Once the world is perceived as impure, salvation lies at the end of a long and painful process of purification. By the same token, sexuality, until then merely a technical obstacle, a potential stumbling block for ascetics, is now identified with defilement, and is loaded with moral affect. In other words, it becomes a form of vice. Buddhist depreciations of the body, a fortiori the female body, aim at provoking a holy horror of sensual desire.[47]

Although sexual desire may not be the most fundamental form of desire, sex is usually the essential object of continence. Because they meet the vital needs of the individual, other forms of avidity (hunger and thirst) may be controlled, but they cannot be entirely suppressed. They reach their limits more easily, however, whereas sexual desire, based in great part on imagination, can lead an individual to his or her doom.

The goal of desire, fulfillment, or pleasure, is itself ontologically deficient. The emptiness of pleasure is a leitmotif of the *Dazhidulun:*

He who enjoys pleasures is never satiated;
He who is deprived of them suffers greatly;
When he does not possess them, he wants to possess them;
When he possesses them, he is tormented.

The joys of pleasure are rare.
The grief and pain that it exudes are plenty.
Because of it, men lose their life,
Like moths dashing into a lamp.[48]

The fire of desire is often described in similar terms in later Buddhist literature. In the *Chōnōki,* for instance, it is said that the body devoured

[46] According to the Sāṃkhyā doctrine, desire is produced at the stage following the union of *puruṣa* (mind) and *prakṛti* (matter). Nondesire is therefore in itself insufficient for emancipation; it must be accompanied by correct knowledge. There must be a direct (nonrational) knowledge of puruṣa.

[47] These descriptions remind us of the words of Odilon of Cluny: "This feminine grace is only . . . blood, humors, gall. Consider what is hidden in the nostrils, in the throat, in the belly: everywhere filth. And we, who are reluctant to touch with our fingertips vomit or dung, how can we desire to clasp in our arms the bag of excrement itself?"

[48] Lamotte 1944–1980, 2: 989.

by love is like a moth being drawn to the flame of a lamp.[49] We also find in the *Dazhidulun* the story of a fisherman who burns to death in the flames of his own passion when unable to sleep with a beautiful princess.[50]

Buddhist continence, like its Christian counterpart, has been the object of various judgments.[51] It is traditionally exalted as an effort toward a state of perfection in which the individual develops all his or her potentialities, reaching a plenitude incomparably superior to the illusory pleasures of the senses. Some modern commentators, on the contrary, think that it reflects a fear of sexuality, and more generally an anxiety toward life, a withdrawal into oneself through fear of losing one's physical and above all spiritual energy. The loss of energy caused by the sexual act—the so-called "small death"—was obviously a major concern for ascetic virtuosos.[52] For the ordinary monk, however, the karmic consequences of desire seem to have been more important. The sexual act is the karmic act par excellence, because it inserts the person into two different processes, individual retribution and collective perpetuation of the lineage. Desire creates "impregnations" of consciousness, germs that sooner or later will develop, bringing about the constitution of new physical and mental series geared toward perpetuating or reproducing a false sense of self. It also contributes to the perpetuation of the human species, and more specifically, of the clan or lineage. The "red thread" that runs through the lives of individuals and connects them to the collectivity is also that of the blood in their veins. To consummate the conjugal act amounts to sacrificing the autonomous self on the domestic altar.[53] However, if reproduction is essential for the survival of the species as well as that of the individual in his descendants, it also anticipates, or even precipitates, the individual's death. To this fatal sequence, the ascetic opposes a blunt refusal. When the warrior Koremori longs for his wife, a holy man tells him:

> The heretic demon king in the sixth heaven [Māra], who rules as he pleases over all six heavens in the world of desire, resents the efforts of that world's inhabitants to escape the cycle of life and death, and thus he hinders them by

[49] See Strong 1994: 410. The story is quoted by Kūkai in his *Sangō shiki,* in *Kōbō Daishi Kūkai zenshū,* 1984, 6: 22, cited in Strong 1994: 411.

[50] See *Dazhidulun,* 166.

[51] On Christian views regarding continence, see Brown 1988.

[52] This interpretation is found among various Western commentators on Buddhism, such as the anthropologist Melford Spiro apropos Burmese monks. Georges Bataille wonders if it is not precisely fear that provides a basis for the sexual sphere and its attraction. See Bataille 1957.

[53] In this sense, Bataille is right to argue that the sexual act in some ways resembles a sacrifice. See ibid., 200.

assuming the guise of a wife or a husband. The Buddhas of the Three Worlds, who regard all mankind as their children, and who seek to lead us to the Pure Land from which there is no return, have issued strict injunctions against loving the wives and children who have chained us to the wheel of transmigration from remote antiquity to the present.[54]

The individual karmic perspective seems at first glance to contradict the perspective of the lineage, but in practice their effects reinforce each other: to reach awakening, one must not only "leave the family," putting an end to the lineage from which one stemmed (we know that it is precisely on this point that Chinese Buddhists were criticized by Confucianists), but in Buddhist orthodoxy one must also "leave the cosmos"—a structure created and maintained by one's deluded consciousness. According to the Yogācāra teaching, from which an important part of Mahāyāna Buddhism derives, the three worlds—of desire, form, and formlessness—are indeed nothing but the product of our mind, they are conditioned by our thought. In order to transcend them, therefore, it is essential first to purify one's mind, to put an end to thought by depriving it of its fuel—deep-rooted desire stemming from ontological ignorance.

Cutting Off Desire at the Root

One could also say that the source of all evil is the penis (appropriately called the "root"). The sting of carnal desire can be felt by the most hardened ones, as the Chinese erotic novel the *Rou putuan* (The Carnal Prayer Mat) makes clear apropos its hero Weiyangsheng who, after a youth spent in debauchery, has decided to become a monk:

> But any young man joining the order has certain problems he must face. However strongly he tries to rein in his lusts, however firmly he tries to extinguish his desires, prayer and scripture reading will get him through the day well enough, but in the wee hours of the morning that erect member of his will start bothering him of its own accord, making a nuisance of itself under the bedclothes, uncontrollable, irrepressible. His only solution is to find some form of appeasement, either by using his fingers for emergency relief or by discovering some young novice with whom to mediate a solution. (Both methods are regular standbys for the clergy.) Had Weiyangsheng done so, no one who caught him at it would have been disposed to criticize. Even Guanyin herself would have forgiven him, if she had come to hear of it; she would hardly have had him consumed in the fires of his own lust! Weiyangsheng felt differently, however. He maintained that those who joined the order ought to accept its commandment against sexual desire as a cardinal rule, whether or not their

---

[54] See *Heike monogatari,* in McCullough 1988: 349.

standbys took the form of actual adultery. Even if the standbys broke no rules and brought no dishonor to those practicing them, they represented a failure to suppress desire just as surely as adultery itself. Moreover, the handgun led to intercourse, and homosexual relation to heterosexual. Sight of the make-believe causes us to yearn for the reality, and one act leads to another by an inexorable process that we must not allow to get started.[55]

In a belated upsurge of virtue, Weiyangsheng choses to emasculate himself, despite the fact that castration was clearly denounced by the Buddha. We are told that when the Buddha was in Śrāvastī, there was a monk who castrated himself by severing his penis in order to cut off desire. The Buddha scolded him, saying: "This foolish man, monks, cut off one thing when another should have been cut off. Monks, one should not cut off one's own organ. If anyone should cut it off, there is a grave offence."[56]

Despite this clear-cut indictment, Weiyangsheng's case was not exceptional, and there were occasionally cases of self-inflicted mutilation. Let us just give one other example, that of the scion of a great family, Guangyi, who at the time of Wu Zetian's usurpation became a monk to escape the empress's fury. With the restoration of the Tang he was invited to court, and on his way to the capital he happened to lodge in the house of a distant relative named Li Shijun. When Li Shijun's daughter fell in love with him, rather than to respond to her advances he preferred to castrate himself. His "relics" were enshrined by Emperor Zhongzong in a monastery of the capital, and became the object of a flourishing cult.[57]

In Japan, too, there are cases of an individual castrating himself by cutting his "jade shaft." This form of castration differed from the traditional cutting of the testicles performed for eunuchs. Called *rasetsu* (literally, "cutting [*setsu*] the [*ma*]*ra* [penis]"), it was sometimes a penal punishment. Like their distant contemporary Abelard, and for similar reasons, some of Hōnen's disciples were subjected to this ordeal. Minakata Kumagusu, commenting on the term *rasetsu*, writes: "The virile energy is vulgarly called *mara*. This is why, cutting the beginning, one says *ra*. In my view, nowadays there are people who are castrated to punish them for adultery. This does not harm their life, but their sexual energy is naturally not very strong any more." However, Minakata is skeptical on that point, and he mentions the case of a monk who, toward the end of the Edo period, castrated himself out of remorse for having sinned. Later, during the early Meiji period, when the interdiction against

[55] Li Yu 1990a: 304.
[56] See Vinaya 2: 110; quoted in Fiser 1993: 58.
[57] See *Song gaoseng zhuan*, T. 50, 2061: 873b.

monks having sex was lifted, this monk took a mistress and, despite his diminished sex, succeeded in giving her a child.[58]

Sometimes the mutilation was displaced toward lesser anatomical parts. A case in point is that of the monk Jōshō (alias Saga Sōzu, abbot of Kongōbuji on Kōyasan, d. 983), who applied a Buddhist version of the biblical principle, "If your right hand makes you sin, cut your right hand": "Jōshō never violated the precepts on women, but he just once happened to touch a woman with his index finger. He said, 'By touching a woman with my finger, I have committed the sin of attachment. This, my finger, is the cause of sin.' He repented by burning his index finger, and paid homage to the Three Treasures. He feared such a minor sin so greatly, how could he commit any major sin?"[59]

The importance of a "wholesome" body is well illustrated in the *Shōbōgenzō,* where Dōgen, to illustrate the mysterious ways of karmic retribution, tells the story of the eunuch who, seeing a herd of five hundred bulls taken to be castrated, thinks: "Although I have a human body, because of my evil past karma, I am unable to function as a man. I should truly use my wealth to save these animals from a similar destiny." Therefore he buys the animals and frees them. "As a result of his good karma the eunuch's male functions were restored."[60] Dōgen seems unaware of the ironic element of the story, since the good karma, in this case, restores the procreative power that will tie the redeemed eunuch to existence. The notion of the integrity of the body, the corporeal compensation that results from this indemnification, is more important to Dōgen than an asceticism at all costs (although in other passages he advocates "crushing one's body" in order to reach the spiritual goal). Furthermore, the number five hundred is, by an uncanny coincidence, that of the arhats, spiritual castrati.

The root of desire, in the case of a woman, could be cut just as "radically" in other ways. A particularly implacable exemplum is the following story, relating the conversion of a lustful woman named Miaoyi. To achieve this conversion, the Buddha conjures a handsome youth who seduces her. At first, Miaoyi experiences sheer bliss, but after a full day of lovemaking she grows tired and wants to get some rest and food. The youth will not relent, however, telling her that he practices a sexual method of long life according to which one cannot rest before twelve

---

[58] Minakata 1991: 200. Minakata also tells the story of the "castrated priest" (*rasetsu oshō*), who was perceived as a symbol of cutting the passions. He also mentions the existence of reliquaries containing the organs of vassals who castrated themselves instead of following their lord in death (ibid., 201–2).

[59] See *Dainihonkoku hokekyō kenki,* in Dykstra 1983: 66.

[60] See *Shōbōgenzō,* "Sanji gō" (Karmic Retribution in the Three Stages of Time"), in Yokoi 1976: 143.

days. Her continuous orgasms soon turn into a nightmare. After four days of this plethoric diet, she feels as if she had been run over by a cart; after five days, as if she had swallowed iron balls; after six days, as if her heart had been pierced by arrows. Now utterly disgusted, she vows never to have sex again. The youth gets angry, accusing her of spoiling his practice. When, ashamed by his failure, he says that he wants to kill himself, she does nothing to stop him. Without getting off her, he cuts his throat, splashing blood over her. Panicked, she realizes that she cannot disengage herself from his corpse, which soon begins to putrefy, decomposing so quickly that after seven days only stinking bones remain, adhering to her as if glued to her body. From the depth of her despair, Miaoyi implores the gods, but it is the Buddha who appears, accompanied by Ānanda, and he frees her, readily obtaining her conversion.[61]

Passions and Impregnations

Desire is only one of the three fundamental defilements or "poisons" that vitiate all existence, along with anger and ignorance. Buddhist deliverance results from metaphorically cutting off these passions. It is much more difficult, however, to destroy their tenacious impregnations. The concern about impregnations, perceived as distinct from the passions themselves, moved to the front stage with the development of Mahāyāna. The problem seems to have arisen from the need to explain why the arhats, who were supposedly free of all defilements, still behaved sometimes as ordinary men. As the *Dazhidulun* puts it: "If certain corporeal or vocal acts do not conform to knowledge, they seem to stem from passions, and those who do not know the thought of others see them as such and have for them a feeling of horror. Actually this has nothing to do with passion, but those who have long obeyed passions perform acts of this kind. Likewise a prisoner long laden with chains, when freed, still walks hesitantly, although he has no more chains."[62]

The *Dazhidulun* gives several specific examples from among the direct disciples of the Buddha, ascetics who were still affected by the stench of the "three poisons." Thus, due to the impregnation of lust, Nanda could not help staring at women in the assembly; due to the impregnation of anger, Śāriputra overreacted when the Buddha accused him of eating impure food; due to the impregnation of hatred, Mahākāśyapa, after the Buddha's death, expelled Ānanda from the group of the arhats with harsh words.[63]

---

[61] See *Guanfo sanmeihai jing*, T. 15, 643: 685b.
[62] Lamotte 1944–1980, 3: 1760.
[63] Ibid., 1760–61. See also *Shasekishū*: "Among the Buddha's disciples, Śāriputra gave

Ānanda had not at that point extinguished the passions in himself, but after his public humiliation he rapidly succeeded, so we are told, and was thus able to join the arhat community. What should we think, however, of Piṇḍola, whose gluttony led him to show off his supernatural powers? This so angered the Buddha that he condemned him to remain in the world and to wait for the coming of the future buddha Maitreya.[64] Are we dealing here with passions or merely with impregnations? Piṇḍola became the first of the Sixteen (or Eighteen) Arhats, assuming the function of guarantor of ritual orthodoxy. The motif of gluttony, however, did not disappear: due to an offence committed in a past life (according to a Japanese source, he had broken his vow of chastity) he is said always to be hungry.

The question of residual impregnations should perhaps be raised in the case of the Buddha himself. Sometimes the words of the Enlightened One sound like those of a Victorian clergyman. When one reads the episodes during which he set the rules of what would become monastic discipline or Vinaya, one cannot but be struck by statements that reflect gross sexist prejudice. Certain episodes in the life of the Buddha are also puzzling. Is it not said, for instance, that he died from diarrhea caused by pork meat?[65] Later commentators have tried to downplay that shocking detail by arguing that the word for meat was used metaphorically, referring actually to a kind of mushroom. The Buddha was eventually exonerated when Buddhist doctors decreed that, although the impregnations of desire remain in the case of saints, they were in his case entirely destroyed.[66] To the same end, the *Dazhidulun* resorts to a comparison between ordinary and cosmic fires: if arhats still have impregnations of passion, it is because the fire that destroyed their passions is like an ordinary fire; when this ordinary fire has burnt its fuel, there still remain ashes and coals, because its strength is not sufficient to consume them; whereas the fire of omniscience, which destroys the passions of the Buddha, is like the fire that destroys the universe at the end of a cosmic period.[67]

In the third century B.C.E., the question of the purity of the Buddhist saint became the pretext of a famous controversy in which scholars see

---

the appearance of anger because during five hundred lifetimes he had been a serpent. Nanda had been deeply immersed in sensuality, and even after he attained the fruit of arhatship, he still had an eye for women. When wise men are so, who among ordinary men will not have this flaw?" Quoted in Morrell 1985: 217.

[64] See Strong 1979.

[65] In this respect, the Buddha differs from the Christ who, according to the Gnostics, "ate, drank, but did not defecate." In later Buddhist hagiography, however, the Buddha stops excreting.

[66] Bapat 1957 and Lamotte 1974.

[67] Lamotte 1944–1980, 3: 1761.

the distant origin of the split between Mahāyāna and Hīnāyāna (or, more correctly, Theravāda). A monk named Mahādeva argued that the arhats may still show signs of defilement. The emergence of this notion may reflect a criticism of the arhats, stemming from lay Buddhists. It could also be a justification on the part of the monks, trying to explain why, in practice, they seemed less perfect than the arhats described in the scriptures. They could argue that, in their cases, appearances were misleading, since residual impregnations, which are merely the effects of a karma about to become exhausted, did not by any means call into question their purity. At any rate, this theory, together with a number of ideological and social factors, caused a breach in the uncompromising stance of early Buddhism toward desire. It allowed a reasonable doubt, a margin of tolerance toward behaviors that seemed characteristic of an impassioned mind to a noninformed observer. This paved the way to a more positive conception of desire in Mahāyāna.

THE TREND REVERSAL

With the emergence of Mahāyāna Buddhism, a trend reversal takes place—or perhaps one should speak rather of a progressive shift toward more positive conceptions of desire and passions. Mahāyāna is generally said to have advocated a less ascetic, more tolerant (or laxist, depending on the viewpoint) conception of Buddhist practice. As noted above, the rise of Mahāyāna is attributed to the schism of the Sarvāstivādins at the time of King Aśoka. Paradoxically, the Theravāda interpretation of the schism remained the official version, even in Mahāyāna countries. According to this version, the schism resulted from the "five false views" of Mahādeva, a character charged with the worst sins: committing incest with his mother, killing his parents, and killing a monk. King Aśoka himself, by mistakenly taking his side, is implicitly blamed for the Sarvāstivādins' exile to Kashmir. Even in death, Mahādeva was smeared by his enemies—literally, since we are told that, when the sandalwood of his cremation pyre would not burn, someone advised smearing his corpse with dog excrement, after which the fire finally erupted. It is ironic that this story, clearly originating within the Theravāda faction, would still be propagated centuries later in Japan, in popular Buddhist collections of tales such as the *Konjaku monogatari shū* and the *Sangoku denki*.[68]

With the development of Mahāyāna, radically new doctrines like the Two Truths theory came to the forefront. The pervading logic of nonduality that led to the identity of the Two Truths implied a revalorization of everyday life, of the phenomenal world, according to the principle that

[68] See Mair 1986. On Mahādeva's "false views," see La Vallée Poussin 1910.

saṃsāra is none other than nirvāṇa, that passions are no different from awakening. This evolution was most radical in Vajrayāna and Chan/Zen.

Many factors have contributed to this revalorization of the world, of the body, and of desire. On the social level, the emergence of a lay Buddhism was more down to earth, more preoccupied with tangible benefits —happiness in this world, a better rebirth in the next—than with a distant ideal of perfection reserved to monks. Among the doctrinal elements, let us simply mention, at the risk of oversimplifying, Mahāyāna expressions of nonduality such as the identity of wisdom and compassion; speculations regarding the immanence of the Buddha nature; and finally, the inner dialectic of the *prajñā* (wisdom), according to which the mind should abide nowhere. This dialectic is found in particular in texts of the Perfection of Wisdom (*prajñāpāramitā*) tradition. Thus, according to the *Dazhidulun,* "one must fulfil the virtue of morality by relying on the non-existence of sin and its contrary."[69] Nevertheless, the person who transgresses the eight kinds of precepts of traditional discipline is still said to fall into the three evil destinies after death.

The emphasis on values specific to Mahāyāna, in particular compassion, allows one in some cases to break the rule. According to the apocryphal *Fanwang jing* (Brahma Net Sūtra), for instance, although transgression ordinarily reveals a lack of compassion, it can, conversely, be used as a vehicle of compassion. In Mahāyāna scriptures, the formal criteria regarding what constitutes transgression tend to disappear. According to Asaṅga, the risk that compassion may lead to desire or attachment is relatively minimal compared to the fault that would consist in taking a dislike to others: "By doing the good for others, / There is neither offense nor attachment; / But our dislike is always in contradiction / With [the interest of] all living beings."[70] In other words, nothing is formally condemnable for a bodhisattva. If a (male) lay practitioner acts out of love and compassion, everything he does is a bodhisattva action, and none of his acts can be considered to be an offense. Normal ethical rules can therefore be transgressed when needed. Nevertheless, the rule against illicit sex for monks and nuns is not lifted, and even in the case of a lay practitioner it is allowed only if the other person who benefits from the act does not become attached to it. As Asaṅga puts it in his *Bodhisattvabhūmi* (Treatise on the Stages of the Bodhisattva [Career]):

> When a woman is alone and her thought is prey to the agony of the desire to put an end to her celibacy, the lay Bodhisattva approaches her with the dharma of sexual union. He then thinks: "May she not develop a thought of unfriendliness, which would lead to demerits. May she on the contrary, under my influ-

[69] Lamotte 1944–1980, 2: 770.
[70] See *Mahāyānasūtrālaṃkāra,* quoted in Tatz 1986: 247.

ence, abandon her unwholesome thoughts, so that the object of her desire becomes a root for good."

Adopting this thought of pure compassion, he resorts to the dharma of copulation, and there is no error; but this produces on the contrary many merits.[71]

Nevertheless, Asaṅga takes care to specify that for a bodhisattva-monk to transgress the rule of celibacy remains out of question. If Asaṅga and other commentators refuse to extend to monks the authorization they give to lay practitioners, its is because, more than any other serious crime, sexual transgression remains particularly attractive.

Although still inscribed in the negative tradition regarding the body, a text like the Vimalakīrtinirdeśa contributed largely to modify attitudes regarding desire and sexuality. This trend did not develop without hesitations, even in the apparently most radical texts, like the apocryphal Śūraṃgama-sūtra. This text warns among other things against the dangers of desire. It opens with the famous episode in which Ānanda, about to succumb to the charms of a courtesan, is rescued in extremis by the Bodhisattva Mañjuśrī. The Śūraṃgama attempts to refute "heretical" teachings that equate desire with awakening. We find in some esoteric texts an affirmation of heterosexual love and the thesis that "desire in itself is pure," since all things, including the "exquisite rapture" of sex, belong to the pure realm of the bodhisattva. The Tantric master Yixing, in his commentary on the Mahāvairocana-sūtra, glosses the term bhagavat ("Blessed One") as bhaga, which means "woman" and "designates the origin."[72] It is precisely in this kind of esoteric text that one finds the identity between desire and awakening, dharma body and human body, sense organs and "true abodes," or bodhi and nirvāṇa. This theory was the object of the fierce criticism of the apocryphal Śūraṃgama—a work which is itself strongly impregnated with Tantrism.

The sūtra also tells the stories of a monk and a nun who, convinced of the emptiness of everything, fell into hell—the nun, for having had sexual relations with a man, the monk, for having committed a murder. The latter story contrasts with that of the two monks mentioned by Jizang in his commentary on the Vimalakīrtinirdeśa. To hide the fact that one monk had sex with a village girl, his friend caused the girl's death. When the two monks confessed their offenses to Upāli, "the first keeper of Vinaya" told them that they could not be forgiven. Fortunately, the layman Vimalakīrti happened to pass by, and he told the monks that their crime, having been produced by thought, was illusory.[73] Realizing this, the monks were freed from remorse and produced the thought of awakening.

[71] See Asaṅga's text and Tsong-kha-pa's commentary ibid., 215–16.
[72] Yixing's commentary, T. 39, 1796: 579c; Stein 1975: 483.
[73] See Weimojing yi shu, T. 38, 1781: 944c.

Variants of this story are found in Chan texts such as the *Damo lun* (Treatise of Bodhidharma), but the description of the offenses is generally omitted. As the *Zhengdao ge* (Song on Realizing the Way) by Yongjia Xuanjue (fl. 8th c.) puts it: "There were two monks. One transgressed the vow of chastity, the other the precept against murder. / But the ephemeral wisdom of Upāli could only tighten the knot of the fault. / The Mahā-sattva Vimalakīrti was able to put an end to their doubts, / as the warm sun melts frost and snow."

In Mahāyāna, the pleasures of human existence seem derisory in light of the pure bliss of nirvāṇa. Buddhist nirvāṇa was initially defined as a pure extinction, about which nothing can be said except that it has none of the characteristics of this world. But the Mahāyāna teaching went one step (or several) further, causing by the same token a mental revolution. Nirvāṇa is now described with four terms: permanence, bliss, subjec-tivity, and purity. Compared to this supreme bliss the pleasures of this world grow pale, however attractive they may at first appear. Pleasure is thus twice vitiated because it is ontologically twice deficient: on the one hand it is impermanent; on the other, even in its positive character it is only a pale reflection of the plenitude of nirvāṇa. The notion of nirvāṇa becomes identified with that of awakening, that is, a pure experience that, instead of putting an end to the world of the senses, sanctifies it and takes place within that world. Far from being a rejection of the world, awakening becomes a sovereign affirmation of it, an ultimate enjoyment of this world purified of all its negative aspects. As Vimalakīrti tells Śāri-putra, who complained of living in a too imperfect world: "When your mind is pure, the world becomes a pure land." In the same way, he scolds Subhūti when the latter hesitates to accept a bowl of fragrant rice: "Rev-erend Subhūti, take this food if, falling in all false views, you reach nei-ther the middle nor the extremes; . . . if, identifying with defilement, you do not reach purification; if you associate with all the Māras and with all the passions."[74] Let us note in passing that Śāriputra and Subhūti sym-bolize the two opposite ideals of solitary ascesis and life in a monastic community. Having dismissed these two paragons of traditional Buddhist practice, Vimalakīrti concludes: "Sons of good family, without entering the great sea it is impossible to get the precious pearls; likewise, without entering the sea of passions it is impossible to produce the all-knowing thought."[75]

The paradoxical character of the Mahāyāna teaching appears clearly in the following dialogue between a goddess (*devī*) and Śāriputra. When the devī tells the arhat that "the identity of all dharmas is the holy deliver-

[74] See ibid., 158.
[75] Ibid., 291.

ance," he is puzzled: "But is not the destruction of love, hatred, and ignorance what constitutes deliverance?" The devī then reveals to him that the Buddha defined deliverance as "destruction of love, hatred, and ignorance" only for deluded people. For the others, he said that love, hatred, and ignorance are in themselves deliverance.[76] The poor Śāriputra feels utterly lost. He eventually accepts the new Law, but his arhat mind, infatuated with purity, needs to be reassured. It will be when he understands that the love mentioned by the devī is that of the bodhisattva, a feeling that shows no trace of desire. We have here a kind of contradiction in terms, which preserves the old Buddhist morality while pretending to overthrow it. True, bodhisattvas voluntarily "manifest themselves as courtesans to attract men, but, having seduced them with the hook of desire, they establish them in the knowledge of the buddhas."[77] The bodhisattva "follows the way of love, but he is detached from the pleasures of love. . . . He follows the way of all passions, but he is absolutely undefiled and naturally pure."[78] Vimalakīrti himself, although he frequents brothels, does so only with pure intentions, to teach prostitutes the disadvantages of debauchery.[79] As many edifying stories suggest, the monk may through ascesis extinguish in himself the fire of passions, but there would only remain then dead ashes. He is consequently condemned to "play with fire," to draw from it the essential spiritual energy, that of compassion, hoping to become "well cooked" rather than burnt at this dangerous fire.

The primacy of compassion is highlighted in a famous Zen anecdote, in which an old woman supported a hermit for twenty years, until one day she decided to test him. She sent a young girl to serve him food, and told her to make overtures to him. The man rejected the girl's advances, saying: "I am like a withered tree propped up against a cold boulder after three winters without warmth." When the old woman heard the girl's report, she said angrily: "Twenty years wasted feeding a phony layman!" Then she burned his hut. Commenting on this case, Ikkyū wrote the folloving poem:

The old woman's kindness was like lending a ladder to a thief;
Thus, to the pure monk she gave a girl as wife.
Tonight, if a beautiful woman were to entwine with me,
A withered willow would put forth fresh spring growth.[80]

---

[76] Ibid., 274.
[77] Ibid., 298.
[78] Ibid., 286–87.
[79] Ibid., 128.
[80] Kyōunshū 94: untitled poem; translation based on Arntzen 1986: 102, and Sanford 1981.

In another passage of the *Vimalakīrtinirdeśa,* two monks come to confess a fault to Upāli, who admonishes them severely. Thereupon Vimalakīrti appears, and says: "Reverend Upāli, without further aggravating the fault of these two monks or harming them, destroy the remorse that they have from their sin. Reverend Upāli, sin exists neither inside, nor outside, nor in between. . . . All dharmas arise from imagination, like the moon in the water and the reflection in the mirror. Those who know that are called the true keepers of discipline; those who know that are well disciplined."[81] In another passage, Vimalakīrti explains to Śāriputra how truly to meditate: "Not to destroy passions that belong to the realm of transmigration, but to enter nirvāṇa, that is how to meditate." The same idea is expressed as follows: "The bodhisattva must exert patience toward his own passions and must not cut off his ties. Why? Because if he cut off these ties, the disadvantage would be too great: he would fall to the rank of arhat and would not differ from a man deprived of his senses. This is why he stops his passions, but does not cut them off."[82]

We have seen how the two Buddhist paths constituted by impassive ascesis and deliverance through passions were opposed through the exemples of the two monks Prasannendriya and Agramati.[83] According to Agramati, "love is characterized by passion"—in other words, it is nefarious. According to Prasannendriya, however: "Love is the Path, / Hatred and ignorance are also the Path. / In these three things are enclosed / Innumerable states of Buddha." Prasannendriya nevertheless is careful to point out: "Love is not born, nor does it perish, / It cannot give cause for worry. / But if a man believes in the self, / Love will lead him to evil destinies."[84] The *Perfection of Wisdom* in 150 verses, translated by Amoghavajra, states: "The Bodhisattva takes his posture in the purity of touch, he takes his posture in the purity of concupiscence, he takes his posture in the purity of pleasure, he takes his posture in the purity of passion."[85]

Desire in Chan/Zen

The ambivalence of Chan/Zen regarding desire and passions finds its paradigmatic expression in the verses composed by Shenxiu (606–706) and Huineng (d. 713) in their contest for the rank of sixth Chan patriarch. Shenxiu is (dis)credited with the gradualist viewpoint, according to

[81] Lamotte 1962: 174–76.
[82] Ibid., 144.
[83] See Lamotte 1944–1980, 1: 398–402.
[84] Ibid., 401.
[85] Quoted in Strickmann 1996: 279–80.

which the practitioner must strive on all occasions to "polish the mirror of the mind" and prevent it from tarnishing, that is, to purify the mind from all defilements. Huineng's verse, on the other hand, denies the very reality of defilements, which, to use a Buddhist metaphor, are mere "flowers in the sky"—hallucinations of a feverish mind. Does the fever, and the mind itself, have some kind of reality? For Huineng, or at least for his "biographer," none of these things, insofar as they depend on false notions, retain any ontological status.

The Chan repudiation of desire is suggested by the story of the bath offered by Empress Wu Zetian to Shenxiu. The old master (he was then in his nineties but, we are told, had an imposing allure) was entrusted to the expert care of ladies-in-waiting. Seeing that he kept a perfect composure, the empress, duly impressed, sighed: "Only in the bath can one see the great man." This comment could be interpreted allegorically, the hot water of the bath meaning the passions that cannot move the sage. Perhaps the canonical age of the Chan patriarch played a role, although the empress herself, hardly younger, had lost none of her flame. The story also appears in a chronicle of Japanese Buddhism, the *Genkō shakusho,* next to that of a monk—actually an avatar of the bodhisattva Kannon—who had sexual relations with an empress in order to convert her. From that viewpoint, Shenxiu was not yet a true bodhisattva—or perhaps the Japanese empress was more attractive.

This hagiographical topos of the temptation of the Buddha by the daughters of Māra is often imitated in the "lives" of Chan/Zen masters. In the autobiography of Dhyānabhadra (Zhikong), an Indian master who traveled all the way to Korea, we hear about an experience he had while staying in a Central Asian kingdom: "In this country, the king is an infidel and, knowing that my vows forbid any violence or lasciviousness, he ordered a dancer-girl to take a bath with me. I showed the most complete indifference, being no more disturbed than if I had been a corpse. The king sighed, saying: 'Here is truly someone extraordinary!'" The same anecdote is found in a more recent "autobiography," that of the Chan Master Xuyun (d. 1952): "During the night, I felt that someone touched my body. I woke up and saw a girl near me undressing and offering her body to me. I did not dare say anything and got up promptly, sitting with legs crossed, and recited a mantra. She dared not move after that."[86]

A similar anecdote is told by the Zen master Shidō Bunan (1603–1676): "Once, when my master was taking a bath, a woman washed his back and front, all the parts of his body. I believe that this is a rare event

---

[86] See Waley 1932a: 363; and Xu Yun, *Empty Cloud: The Autobiography of the Chinese Zen Master Xu Yun,* translated by Charles Luk (Longmead: Element Books, 1988), 10.

among us."[87] The bath seems to have played an important role in Buddhist imagination. The Chan master Hanshan Deqing (1546–1623), for instance, once dreamt that he ascended to Tuṣita Heaven and was invited to take a bath in Maitreya's palace. The apparent presence of a woman in the bath horrified him at first, but he regained his serenity when it turned out to be a man, and Hanshan let the man scrub him without feeling the least troubled.[88]

Desire is clearly affirmed in another Chan story, in which Empress Wu questions Shenxiu as well as several other Chan masters (Xuanyue, Laoan, Xuanze, and Zhishen). When the empress asks them whether they still have desires, Shenxiu and the others answer negatively, whereas Zhishen—whom the story is intended to lionize—declares that he has desires. When pressed by the empress, he explains: "That which is born has desire, that which is not born has no desire."[89] Zhishen's answer could be read in several ways, but obviously it does not simply reflect conventional wisdom, which in this case is represented by the other monks and their quasi-Hīnayāna belief that desire is wrong. Zhishen directly expresses the Mahāyāna identity of passions and awakening.[90] Instead of searching to please the empress, Zhishen reacts in a perfectly spontaneous way (or at least this is what the authors of the chronicle attempt to suggest).

Passions Are Awakening

Starting from the identity of awakening and passions, Chan did not reach the same practical or ritual conclusions as did the Vajrayāna, at least in its Indo-Tibetan form. As a matter of fact, the Chan teaching, which recapitulates on that point the various positions of Mahāyāna, is more ambivalent—or less consistent—than Tantric Buddhism, characterized by its extremism, its rejection of any morality, and its taste for despised aspects of physical or social reality. True, these elements are also present in Chan, for instance with Linji Yixuan, but on the whole the emphasis is on more sublime (or sublimated) realities.

Linji comments as follows on Mazu's dictum, "the ordinary mind is the Way":[91] "What are you looking for, worthies? These unsupported monks now in front of me, clear and distinct, listening to the Law, have

---

[87] See Kobori and Waddell, trans., 1970–1971: 4(2): 122.

[88] See Luk 1971: 90.

[89] See *Lidai fabaoji*, T. 51, 2075: 184a.

[90] This dialogue also resonates with a passage of the Analects, in which Confucius asks his disciples to express their dearest wish. Whereas the other disciples try to show their wisdom, and compete with pious wishes, Xeng Xi admits that he would simply like to take a bath, which brings him Confucius's approval. See *Lun'yu* 11.26.

[91] Let us note in passing that the Chinese term *dao*, "Way," has been used to translate the Sanskrit *bodhi*, "awakening."

never lacked anything." Linji seems to consider the individual as a spiritual monad, intrinsically identical to the Buddha in its natural perfection: "From my standpoint, adepts, you are no different from Śākya. Today, amidst so many activities of all kinds, what are you lacking? The spiritual radiation from your six senses never stops! Whoever can see things thus will be during his entire life a man without affairs." What Linji means by being "without affairs" is to know how to remain ordinary—"to shit and piss, to put on clothes and eat." No need, therefore, to waste time in vain practices such as reciting scriptures—or even sitting in meditation, the eponymous practice of Chan. All this amounts to producing karma, to bringing about karmic retribution: "It is said everywhere, adepts, that there is a Way to cultivate, a Law to experience. Tell me which Law, which Way? What are you lacking in your present activity? What do you need to complete through cultivation?"[92]

This kind of quietism already appears in the work of early Chan masters. We find, for instance, in the *Liaoyuan ge* (Song of the Realization of the Origin), attributed to Tengteng, the following passage: "You cultivate the Way, but the Way cannot be cultivated. . . . In awakening, there is fundamentally neither observance nor transgression. . . . No need to study much, nor to show discrimination and intelligence. Forget the phases of the moon and the intercalary months. Passions are awakening, the blue lotus grows in the mud and on manure."[93]

In the apocryphal *Śūraṃgama,* a text widely used in Chan, we find several warnings against the excesses to which the teaching on non-duality may lead. The text rejects in particular the eccentric behavior of Chan "madmen" or of Tantric siddhas. The ambivalence of Chan appears well in this text which, despite its Tantric ideas, is deeply moralizing in its condemnation of desire. We recall that it opened with the episode of the almost successful attempt at seduction of Ānanda by a courtesan. Nevertheless, if it emphasizes the importance of morality and Vinaya, it seems at times to advocate an easier path and even provides an incantation to get "at once"—a reference to the sudden teaching dear to Chan—the deliverance from passions. Another formula allows one to avoid all the heretical views of those who believe that "passions are awakening," and more precisely, that the sex organs are the "true abodes" of awakening and nirvāṇa.[94]

The Tantric Turning of the Wheel

Whereas in early Buddhism continence was an absolute necessity because of the fear of a sexuality that binds us to existence(s), and in classi-

---

[92] See Fuller Sasaki 1975: 10–12.
[93] See *Jingde chuandeng lu,* T. 51, 2076: 461b.
[94] Stein 1974: 504.

cal Yoga continence was prescribed to discard perturbations of self-mastery and to find an increase of energy through renunciation, in Tantrism sexuality, once dominated, may be used as a source of spiritual energy, owing to the theoretical symbolism of sublimation inherited from the *Upaniṣad*.

Tantric Buddhism drew that ultimate consequence from the cardinal tenet of the Mahāyāna teaching, nondualism, in other words the identity of passions and awakening at the level of ultimate truth. But it even goes further when it asserts that the energy of the passions is the necessary catalyst of awakening. Desires must be used according to the principle that "one nail drives another," "poison expels poison." As long as the aim is to drive away evil through evil, passions are recognized to have a soteriological virtue. Such is, for instance, the standpoint of Yixing (d. 727) in his commentary on the *Mahāvairocana-sūtra*, one of the basic texts of Sino-Japanese Tantrism: "Ordinarily, Buddhism teaches [you] to treat animosity through kindness, attraction through nonattraction, false views through correct views. But now I teach [you] to expel animosity through greater animosity, to treat any attraction through a greater attraction. . . . These are things difficult to believe. Thus will one say: 'How strange!' "[95]

Sexual Allegories

By emphasizing the identity of passions and awakening, Vajrayāna Buddhism developed the notion of Wisdom (*prajñā*) as Bliss, and asserted the possibility of becoming a buddha in this very body. The pairing of meditation (*samādhi*) and wisdom (*prajñā*) was interpreted (and perhaps enacted) symbolically as a ritual union between two partners, one representing the male principle (*vajra*, diamond, the male organ), the other the female principle (lotus, the female organ).

Indo-Tibetan Tantric rituals also achieve the transmutation of two fundamental passions, hatred and desire. Hatred is transmuted by ritual murder, love by ritual coitus. In both forms of ritual, we are told, the aim is to "free" human beings, women through love, men through death. Many tantric texts contain fairly explicit references to sexual practices. Recall, for instance, Yixing's commentary according to which the Buddha, the "Blessed One" (*bhagavat*), dwelt originally in the *bhaga*, that is, the sex organ, of the goddess.[96] As Louis de La Vallée Poussin puts it: "In

[95] T. 39, 1796: 685b–c.

[96] See Malalasekera 1961–, s.v. "Bhaga." See also the *Hevajra-tantra*, T. 18, 892: 587c; and Yixing's commentary on the *Mahāvairocana-sūtra* (T. 39, 1796: 579). For a discussion, see Stein 1975: 481–83.

the same way as Śiva organically united with his consort, the Buddha [Vajrasattva] rests in the mysterious *bhaga* of the Bhagavatīs; this sublime embrace . . . , essential to the diamond body, realizes the *mahāsukha* [Great Bliss] and in the *mahāsukha* the perfect *sambodhi* [Illumination]. Buddha is inseparable from Tārā. . . . It is through love and for love that the world becomes double, and in love that it finds again its original unity and its eternal non-differentiation."[97] The sexual elements play a central role in Tibetan Vajrayāna, whereas they have been marginalized in Chinese and Japanese Vajrayāna. They did not disappear, however, and were even canonized, becoming an integral part, although often in symbolic guise, of Sino-Japanese Buddhism.[98] Some tantras such as the *Hevajra* and the *Guhyasamāja* were translated into Chinese only during the Song, and then in a fairly euphemized form, since the transcription of Sanskrit terms often made the sexual meaning less obvious. However, the sexual metaphor was at work in the very notion of their lineage of transmission. The lineage of the *Hevajra* was that of the Mother (emphasizing *prajñā*, wisdom), that of the *Guhyasamāja* that of the Father (emphasizing *upāya*, means).[99] In Japan, the sexual features resurface in the "heretical" teaching of the Tachikawa-ryū, a branch of Shingon that became quite popular during the Kamakura period.

If sexual union is often expressed metaphorically in Chinese translations of Tantric texts, in some cases it becomes itself the "metaphor" for the samādhi of the Buddha Vajrasattva. Instead of interpreting certain terms with erotic connotations as metaphors of the sexual act, commentators came to interpret certain explicit sexual expressions as metaphors for a mystical state, metaphors too often misunderstood by partisans of a literal interpretation. We know that a similar kind of spiritual hermeneutics was also common in the effusions of the Christian mystics, which, rather than interpreting erotic representations of mystical union as expressions of a sublimated sexuality, saw on the contrary in human sexuality a pale reflection of a mystical *coincidentia oppositorum*.

The Buddhist doctrine is expressed through a network of symbolic oppositions that lend themselves to sexual metaphors. One may wonder what led people to use the sexual act as a metaphor for samādhi and to give a symbolic and classificatory value to sexual representation. At any rate, these metaphors and symbols may have contributed to revalorizing the sexual act, and leading in some cases to quite literal interpretations of certain injunctions that were essentially ritual—or even serving to justify laxist behavior.

[97] Quoted in Chou Yi-liang 1944–1945: 327.
[98] See Stein 1975: 481.
[99] See ibid., 486.

The pairing of wisdom (*prajñā*) and skillfulness in means (*upāya*), or wisdom and compassion (*karuna*)—as representing the female and male principles—is also expressed on the mythological plane by the representation of the Buddha with a feminine companion (*śakti*), symbolizing his energy. This perfect union, *prajñōpāya,* can be concretized by the union of a male practitioner with a female partner (the Tibetan *yab-yum*). The Great Bliss (*mahāsukha*) that ensues coincides with the realization of Emptiness (called *vajra,* diamond or thunderbolt). During the sexual union, the male practitioner is supposed to meditate "in the forehead or in the sex organ."[100] This meditation is also called *samapatti,* a term that in Mahāyāna means the achievement of a state of equanimity in which all mental constructs are gradually eliminated, but that in Vajrayāna refers more specifically to the union of Hevajra and his female companion Nairātmya. During the preliminary ritual "invocation" of the deity, it is a meditation through which the practitioner sees himself as male (Tib. *yab*) united to a goddess (Tib. *yum*), or as a female (*yum*) united to a god (*yab*). In the course of the ritual, this mental copulation can be translated into a real coitus with a "wisdom woman" (*vidyā*), or "seal" (*mudrā*). During the act, the practitioner must concentrate on his *bodhicitta,* a term that in Mahāyāna refers to a psychic and mental state, the "thought of awakening," but that is used here in a more specific sense, to designate the semen. The thought of awakening (*bodhicitta*) is identified with the *bindu,* the "drop," that is, the product of the fusion of the seed (*sukla,* the "white," semen = *upāya*) with the ovum (*rakta,* the "red," the menses = *prajñā*).[101] The *bindu* is the egg, the germ, just as the thought of awakening is the germ of a new being. This practice is related to the "coitus reservatus" with a female partner (*mudrā*). The trick is to stir this seminal essence without losing it through ejaculation, so that it may ascend through the central artery into the seat of Great Bliss located in the brain. The process, which is said to lead ultimately to the union of Bliss and Emptiness, can be practiced either alone during meditation, or with a female partner. Likewise, the term "Great Bliss" (*mahāsukha*) means not only a spiritual state but also "sexual fluid."[102]

This basic schema receives an interesting development in some Tantric texts describing the initiation of the disciple through the *sahaja* rite. The *sahaja,* "simultaneously arisen," is usually connected with the Tantric ritual of consecration (*abhiṣeka*), where it refers to the relation between the ultimate and the preliminary joys. The master first unites with the

---

[100] See ibid., 91.

[101] See van Gulik: "The female energy acquired from the woman stimulates the *bodhicitta* of the man, it blends with his activated but unshed semen into a new, powerful essence now called *bindu,* the drop [semen]" (van Gulik 1961: 342).

[102] On this term, see Astley 1994: 931–46.

female partner, ejaculates, and deposits his *bodhicitta* in her lotus receptacle. Then, after consecrating the disciple in his union with the female partner, he confers on him the five sacraments.

As Per Kvaerne points out, the term *abhiṣeka* is commonly used for the act of impregnation, and perhaps retains this connotation in those cases where the *abhiṣeka* involves a "sacred union" (*hieros gamos*). The term referred initially to an "aspersion," consecration by sprinkling with holy water, and this idea was never lost.[103] Indeed, "while there were only two actors in the minor consecrations, the neophyte and the preceptor, there now enters a third, the heroine, one might say, of the sacred drama, namely a young woman variously known . . . as *mudrā* ('Seal'), *vidyā* or *prajñā* ('Wisdom'), or simply *devī* ('Goddess')."[104] Summing up the ritual according to the *Hevajra-tantra* and the *Sekoddeśaṭīka* by Nāḍapāda, the first three major consecrations can be characterized as follows: in the first, the disciple is permitted to touch the breast of the woman (*mudrā*), "thus experiencing the subsequent bliss by anticipation, as it were"; in the second, this bliss is actually experienced by the preceptor, and its essence, in the form of the Thought-of-Enlightenment [*bodhicitta*, that is, the preceptor's semen], is transferred [actually, swallowed] by the disciple, who is thereupon permitted to regard the Lotus [the sex] of the Seal, that is, the source of bliss; and in the third, the disciple is himself united with the Seal, thus fully experiencing the bliss of union for himself."[105] Here is how the *Hevajra-tantra*, for instance, describes the Consecration of the Secret: "The Prajñā [girl] of sixteen years [no longer twelve] he clasps within his arms, and from the union of the vajra and bell the Master's consecration comes about. . . . Then with thumb and fourth finger he drops the *bindu* [that is, the *bodhicitta*, or semen] in the pupil's mouth."[106] Likewise, in a fifteenth-century text entitled "Fundamentals of Buddhist Tantras": "The procedure of conferring the initiation is as follows: the red-and-white element of the 'Father-Mother' union are taken from the 'lotus' of the mother with the thumb and ring-finger of the 'Father-Mother' and placed on the tip of their own tongue."[107] The *Sekoddeśaṭīka* further elaborates this point: "Having by means of his own Vajra-Jewel . . . had intercourse with a beautiful maiden, twelve years of age, adorned with all ornaments and like molten gold [in hue] [so that she becomes] impassioned, having [moreover] realized the purity

---

[103] Kvaerne 1975: 89–91.

[104] Ibid., 95. In one source she is supposed to be "trembling, . . . twelve years old and in all respects perfect" (ibid., 96). We seem to be far from the equalitarian relationship described in Shaw 1994.

[105] Kvaerne 1975: 101.

[106] *Hevajra-tantra* II, 3, 13–14, quoted ibid.

[107] Lessing and Wayman (1968) 1983, p. 319, quoted ibid., 99.

of the disciple, and having thrust the Vajra with its seed into the mouth [of the disciple], only then is his own Seal to be given [to the disciple]."[108] However, it is made clear that the rite "is not taught for the sake of enjoyment," but for the purpose of attaining buddhahood. It is sacred. According to Snellgrove, "one might even claim that these new elements, far from issuing in a degeneration brought about a rejuvenation, nourished in the hidden well-springs of Indian religious life."[109]

As Kvaerne points out: "Dealing with the tantras, it is, in fact, difficult to say where a ritual, whether external or interior, is described in sexual terms, and where a sexual act is expressed in ritual terms."[110] The tendency to interiorize practice, which led to a denial of the flesh-and-blood woman, was also found in Hinduism. Whereas the *Brāhmaṇas* interpret the ritual in sexual terms, the *Bṛhadāraṇyaka-upaniṣad* identifies the sexual act with the fire ritual: "Woman, in truth, is Agni. Her bosom is the combustible, her [pubic] hair the smoke, her vulva the flame, what one introduces in it the charcoal, bliss the sparks. In this fire, the gods offer the sperm; from this offering man is born."[111]

Thus, the Tantric consecration implied the ejaculation of the master (in the second consecration), although not of the disciple (in the third consecration). The disciple, actually, must not emit his bodhicitta. (He will be authorized to ejaculate only when he has become a master initiating his own disciple.) The union of the red and white (of the semen of the master and menstrual blood of the woman, that is, of wisdom and skillful means) produces an embryo that is transferred to the disciple, who is, as it were, impregnated. Although the woman cannot be entirely dispensed with as an intermediary, we seem to have here an attempt to create a male lineage.

Profane orgasm is merely a reflection of the *sahaja*, the joy "arisen simultaneously" through an orgasm without emission. The state of sahaja is said to be ineffable, blissful, timeless, omniscient, nondual, cosmic, transcendental, sacred, the luminosity of one's own mind.[112] The *Tibetan Book of the Dead,* however, connects the sahaja with the act of conception.[113]

As noted earlier, Tantric ritual is a sacred union (*hieros gamos*), yet one

---

[108] M. E. Corelli, quoted ibid.

[109] Snellgrove 1959a: 40.

[110] Kvaerne 1975: 107.

[111] See *Bṛhadāraṇaka-upaniṣad* VI. 2. 13; and Silvain Lévi, *La doctrine du sacrifice dans les Brāhmanas* (Paris: Presses Universitaires de France, 1898): 107.

[112] Kvaerne 1975: 126–28.

[113] W. Y. Evans-Wentz, *The Tibetan Book of the Dead,* 3rd ed. (London: Oxford University Press, 1957), 179.

"utterly void of connection with 'fertility' of any kind; its sole legitima-
tion resides in the restoration of wholeness—or, which is the same, the
'holiness'—of the Buddha-nature, the unity of Wisdom and Means."[114]
In some cases, Tantric sexual practice, not unlike the Chinese "art of the
bedchamber," evokes a kind of sexual battle in which the woman, just
like the man, can reach the ultimate stage if she is able to draw up,
"through a skillful contraction," the male *bindu* and to keep it, thus
increasing her power.[115] Paradoxically, this sterile *unio mystica* lends itself to the symbolism of gestation and fertility.

The motif of the couple in sexual embrace can have at least two different, yet related meanings: it can indeed symbolize the conjunction of opposites, or hierogamy; it can also represent the submission of evil forces.
Tantrism constitutes from this standpoint an attempt to save (by conversion, or taming) all beings, even the most evil. This explains in part the
Tantric taste for terrible deities, the only ones able to impress impenitent
people. Above all, this motif derives from the notion that buddhas and
bodhisattvas adapt themselves to beings to convert them by the most
appropriate method. They therefore manifest the fundamental passions,
hatred and love, in order to transmute them into their opposites. In other
words, the buddhas take the same appearance and act in the same way as
the beings they must tame.[116] Thus, the bodhisattva Avalokiteśvara
(Guanyin/Kannon) assumes the appearance of, and copulates with, the
demons that he/she wants to "tame." A well-known example is her taming of the elephant-headed demon Vināyaka (J. Shōten or Kangiten).

According to some sources, one of the eight supranormal powers of the
Buddha is the transmutation of desire or of the sexual act, a transmutation that allows him to remain in Great Bliss and to avoid any defilement
in the midst of the passions. The Tantric notion of transmutation of desires seems to originate in the Buddhist notion of "revulsion," which was
one of the main features of the "epistemological" Yogācāra school. The
goal is "not to reject or run away from phenomena, the body, the passions, but to transmute them through such revulsion or metamorphosis, a
kind of simple inversion from a negative sign into a positive one."[117] Let
us note in passing that the term translated by "transmutation" (or "revulsion," *paravṛtti*) is also applied, on the mythological level, to the
change of gender of the figures of the pantheon. This notion, which appears as early as the third century C.E. with Asaṅga, will be taken up

[114] Kvaerne 1975: 133–34.
[115] See *Hathayogapradīpikā*, verse 99, translated by Tara Michael (Paris: Fayard, 1974).
[116] See Stein 1974: 502.
[117] Ibid., 504.

in China, in particular in the "apocryphal" *Śūraṃgama-sūtra,* which describes the "inversion" or "reversal" of the impure into the pure. Likewise, the idea of conversion through sex appears in canonical texts such as the *Gaṇḍavyūha,* in which the young Sudhāna is "initiated" by the courtesan Vasumitra.

The Tantric reinterpretation in physiological terms of spiritual categories like bodhicitta shows that the Tantras give a great importance to the human body, and in particular to the sexual act. We are dealing here with an eroticized mystique that attributes an active role to the male principle, and a passive one to the female principle. Since the phenomenal world results from a primordial differentiation of reality through these two principles, deliverance is conversely conceived as a return to this reality: it is the awareness of their essential unity. Paradoxically, the enjoyment of sex is supposed to lead to detachment; whereas ordinary desire leads to attachment to self and the defilement of passions, the "great desire" makes the practitioner lose his/her self into pure bliss: "the functioning of desire, quickly and violently, in the way that an arrow flies; as an arrow points to its target, sexual desire turns to the opposite sex and begins to move. Desire develops and one loses sight of one's ego-self." [118]

THE AMBIVALENT BODY

The changes regarding desire result from (and in turn cause) changes in the conception of the body, to which we now turn. In early Buddhism, the body was perceived as an impure thing. Many Buddhist descriptions resonate with Augustine's famous statement: "We are born between excrement and urine" (*Inter faeces and urinam nascimur*). One Buddhist locus classicus can be found in *Vimalakīrtinirdeśa,* a scripture that had a great influence on Chinese Buddhism:

> This body is like a ball of foam, unable to bear any pressure. It is like a water bubble, not remaining very long. It is like a mirage, born from the appetites of the passions. It is like the trunk of the plantain tree, having no core. Alas! This body is like a machine, a nexus of bones and tendons.[119] It is like a magical illusion, consisting of falsifications. It is like a dream, being an unreal vision. It is like a reflection, being the image of former actions. It is like an echo, being dependent on conditioning. It is like a cloud, being characterized by turbulence and dissolution. It is like a flash of lightning, being unstable, and decaying

[118] Nakamura 1981: 1398b, s.v. "yoku-sen," "arrow of desire," referring to T. 8, 243: 784b2.

[119] This passage brings to mind the "machines désirantes" in Deleuze and Guattari 1997.

every moment. The body is ownerless, being the product of a variety of conditions.[120]

The ideal layman Vimalakīrti emphasizes that the body is impermanent, fragile, unworthy of confidence, and feeble. It is insubstantial, perishable, short-lived, painful, filled with diseases, and subject to changes. As if that were not enough, the body is also unreal, void, inanimate, insensate; filthy, being an agglomeration of pus and excrement. It is false, afflicted by the four hundred and four diseases. Constantly overwhelmed by old age, it ends in death. Its five aggregates and four elements are compared to murdererers and poisonous snakes.[121] As Etienne Lamotte points out, this long litany reflects the typically Buddhist conception according to which illness is the normal state of the body.[122] Even when one grants to it a minimum of existence, the body is usually the object of negative judgments: it is ephemeral, condemned to dissolve into its constitutive aggregates; it is what makes us fall into illusion, succumb to the temptation of the senses, and what chains us to saṃsāra, the continual whirl of karmic retribution.

The Female Body

If the body is generally deficient in every respect, the female body is even worse. Even the bodies of the goddesses are no exception. Here is how the Buddha, always gallant, describes the body of Māra's three daughters, Lust, Discontent, and Craving, when they try to trap him "with the snare of lust": "This body [of yours] is a swamp of dirt, / a filthy heap of impurities. / In these wandering latrines, / How could one revel?"[123] In another famous episode, when the brahman Māgandiya wants to marry his beautiful daughter to the Buddha, the latter tells him about the unsuccessful attempt of Māra's daughters to tempt him and adds that, compared to them, Māgandiya's daughter is like a corpse with the thirty-two impurities, "an impure vessel painted without," and he would not touch her even with his feet. As if to add insult to injury, this contempt for the female body had be internalized by women. Here is, for instance, how the monastic rule deals with novice nuns: "Let the novice hate her impure

[120] See Thurman 1976: 22.

[121] Ibid.

[122] Lamotte 1944–1980, 1: 584

[123] Ibid., 2: 883. Women are "wholly snares of Māra," and their bodies are metaphors for all sensual desires; see *Aṅguttara* 3, edited by R. Morris and E. Hardy, 67. See also Lamotte 1944–1980, 2: 880–81. The refrain of the *Theragāthā's* verses ("Like a snare of Lord Death laid out") presents man as the prey, Māra as the hunter, and woman as the baited snare. See Lang 1986: 70–71. Some of the verses in the *Therīgāthā* are by ex-courtesans reflecting on the transiency of beauty. See *Therīgāthā*, 253, 265, 269.

body as a prison where one is locked up, as a cesspool into which one has fallen. Let her fear passion as fire, as the encounter with bandits."[124]

This conception of the female body is illustrated by many stories. We recall the episode in which the future Buddha, seeing the women of his gynaeceum plunged into an ugly slumber—exclaimed in disgust: "I live in truth in the midst of a cemetary!" At that very moment, life appeared to him in its true light (or darkness), as a mask of death. This abrupt realization, which precipitated Śākyamuni's conversion, prepared him for his encounter with Māra's daughters.[125]

Early Buddhist texts have often resorted to the rhetorical strategy that consists in deforming the female body, turning it into a memento mori. This imaginary transformation of the feminine body actually corresponds to a common visualization technique.[126] One of the best examples is the story of Upagupta and Vasavadattā, a famous courtesan of Mathurā. Vasavadattā hears about a young perfume salesman named Upagupta, and sends her servant to propose a love meeting to him. Upagupta refuses. Thinking that he may have misunderstood her offer, she sends her servant again to explain that it is a free service. Upagupta refuses again. Later on, Vasavadattā kills her lover in order to find a more powerful patron. Her crime is discovered, and she has her hands and feet, nose and ears cut off—the usual punishment for the crimes of murder and adultery—and is exposed on the cremation ground. Upagupta now visits her, but she tries to hide from him. When she asks him why he has finally come, he answers: "Sister, I did not come to you driven by desire, I came to see the intrinsic nature of desires and impurities. When you were covered with splendid clothes and various other external ornaments arousing passion, those who looked at you could not see you as you really are, even when they tried. But now, free from these ornaments, your form is visible in its intrinsic nature."[127] The righteous Upagupta, who can turn everything into spiritual grist in his mill, reaches deliverance thanks to this vision of the maimed courtesan. The story does not tell how Vasavadattā reacted, nor what happened to her afterward.

A further edifying apologue is the story of the beautiful Sirimā, a courtesan of Rājagṛha, with whom a monk had fallen in love. When she died prematurely, the Buddha asked the king to expose her corpse, and proceeded to auction it. But, as no one made an offer, he gradually lowered the price, and eventually offered to give the corpse away—again without success. He concluded his demonstration with a sermon on impermanence. The monk in love, who had been witness to all this, was radically

124 Wieger 1910: 189.
125 See Malalasekera 1961–, s.v. "Beauty," 598.
126 See Wilson 1995.
127 Aśokāvadāna, quoted in Strong 1983: 181.

cured from his infatuation with physical beauty. The motif of the contemplation of the corpse—or more generally the contemplation of impurity (aśubhābhāvanā), a psychological method to understand the true nature of things—was developed by Buddhist preachers into the "nine phases" of the decay of the female body, a body whose owner was, in Japan, seen to be the famous courtesan Ono no Komachi.[128]

The horrible transformation of the female body serves both to thwart its power of seduction and to reveal its true nature. These stories betray a fundamental ambivalence toward the female body: feared and despised, fascinating and grotesque, it constitutes a stumbling block for the male practitioner. Death is not the only event that reveals the horrible reality of the female body; another such "moment of truth" is menstruation. Because its outflow threatens the self-enclosure of the body, menstruation became a convenient emblem of defilement, and its cyclical nature served as a reminder of change and decline.[129] Corporeality renders women particularly vulnerable: they can be—and are often—penetrated, and cannot help overflowing their bodily limits, spilling an impure blood. Their body is therefore open, passive, and expansive. Thus, despite the Buddhist advocacy of nonduality, it seems practically impossible for them to transcend sexual difference.

These descriptions of the female body remind us of Bakhtin's evocation of the grotesque body of Western popular culture in his work on Rabelais. According to Bakhtin, the Rabelaisian character (Gargantua, Pantagruel) is characterized by his/her open body—in stark contrast with the closed body of "classical" culture. The grotesque body is essentially orifices and excreta. It is "emphasized as a mobile, split, multiple self, a subject of pleasure in processes of exchange; and it is never closed off from either its social or ecosystemic context. The classical body on the other hand keeps its distance." Yet the morality of Buddhist exempla is hardly Rabelaisian: they aim precisely at denying procreation and regeneration. Even the "immaculate" birth of Gargantua reads like a parody of the birth of the Buddha (and of course of that of Christ). Gargamelle, Gargantua's mother, is no Queen Māya, either.[130]

---

[128] On this motif, see Sanford 1988 and Lachaud 1997.

[129] On the sociological meaning of bodily fluids, see Douglas 1967.

[130] For Bakhtin, see Stallybrass and White 1986: 22. Here is how Rabelais describes Gargamelle's delivery: "A little while later she began to groan and wail and shout. Then suddenly swarms of midwives came up from every side, and feeling her underneath found some rather ill-smelling excrescences, which they thought were the child; but it was her fundament slipping out, because of the softening of her right intestine—which you could call the bum-gut—owing to her having eaten too much tripe. . . . At this point a dirty old hag of the company . . . made her an astringent, so horrible that her sphincter muscles were stopped and constricted. . . . By this misfortune the cotyledons of the matrix were loosened at the top, and the child lept through them to enter the hollow vein. Then, climbing through

However, there is another side to these stories, another message that should not be ignored. The writers of texts such as the *Lalitavistara* have dwelt on the physical beauty of Māra's daughters more than necessary—even if only as a narrative device—to show the Buddha's superhuman detachment. The contrast between the details of this beauty and the gruesome description of the underlying reality by the Buddha is all the more striking. However, we find precisely a similar description in the case of the devīs and heavenly nymphs, but also in that of Buddha's mother, Māya.[131] For instance, Māya is said to have given birth to the Buddha in a position identical with that commonly given to yakṣīs and devatās (female demigods). This suggests that, as in the rest of rest of Indian culture (think of the sculptures of Khajurao), feminine beauty was still felt in Buddhism to be a positive element. Like the Virgin Mary (and unlike Gargamelle), Māya is what Max Weber calls a *theotokos,* and her semi-divine nature is expressed by her physical beauty.

The Opened and Closed Body

Buddhist practice seems to be aimed at bringing about the physical and mental closure of the practitioner, by reinforcing first his corporeal barriers. One is reminded here of Mary Douglas's point about the importance of boundaries for the individual body as metaphor for the social body. We will see later the importance of the rules of corporeal behavior in the Vinaya. The goal is to reach physical, but also and above all mental, chastity. In contrast with the porous mind of the profane, which is like a sieve or like a leaking roof, the mind of the Buddhist saint is hermetically sealed, like a waterproof roof.

Several conceptions seem to have coexisted (or alternated). We have noted above the negative judgment passed on the body because of its transitory nature. This conception paved the way to the Mahāyānist dogma that the human body is illusory, and, more fundamentally, empty. According to the *Heart Sūtra* (Skt. *Hṛdaya-sūtra,* J. *Hannya shingyō*), for instance, it is not only the empirical, corporeal self that is empty but also the "series" or psychosomatic "aggregates" that constitute it. The unstable, fluid, execrable body of early Buddhism was concurrent with (and often superseded by) an immutable, immortal, admirable body, one that was emptied, precisely, of its organic impurity.

According to Vimalakīrti, the practitioner, revulsed by and in despair over his perishable body, should cultivate admiration for the body of the

---

the diaphragm to a point above the shoulders where this vein divides in two, he took the left fork and came out by the left ear." See Rabelais 1995: 52.

[131] See Falk 1974: 109.

Tathāgata. This may sound somewhat paradoxical for an advocate of nonduality! And how should one answer the objection of those who argue, on the basis of the scriptures, that the Buddha's body itself was foul, subject to illnesses such as diarrhea? The question of the Buddha's corporeal frailty and decay has worried his disciples. According to a widespread belief, after Buddha cut off his hair and beard on the day of renunciation, these polluting exuviae never grew back. Finally, the physical weaknesses of the Buddha, just like those of Vimalakīrti, are explained away as skillful means. According to the *Mahāvastu*:

> The conduct of the Exalted One is transcendental, his root of virtue is transcendental. The Seer's walking, standing, sitting, and lying down are transcendental. . . . The Buddhas conform to the world's conditions, but in such a way that they also conform to the traits of transcendentalism. . . . It is true that they wash their feet, but no dust ever adheres to them; their feet remain clean as lotus leaves. This washing is mere conformity with the world. It is true that the buddhas bathe, but no dirt is found on them. . . . This washing is mere conformity with the world. . . . They keep their dark and glossy hair cropped, although no razor ever cuts it. This is mere conformity with the world.[132]

Certain followers went one step further. The *Kathāvattu* mentions, for instance, "heretical" sects like those of the Andhakas and the Uttarāputtakas, which held that the excreta of the Buddha excelled all fragrant things.[133] At any rate, it is on the imperishable body of the Buddha, the body of the Dharma "born of innumerable good works," and not on his transient body, that the adepts must focus their desire. The essential practice in Tantric Buddhism, as in Chan, consists in identifying oneself, in this very body, with the Buddha—as his successor Mahākāśyapa did. Beginning with him, all the patriarchs became one with the Buddha, and this identity was expressed in the physical mode. Keizan Jōkin (d. 1325) describes it in typical Zen fashion: "When you realize your inner self, you see that Kāśyapa can wriggle his toes in your shoes. . . . Therefore, no need to go back two thousand years in the past. If only you practice with zeal today, Kāśyapa will be able to appear today in the world, without any need for you to go to Mount Kukkuṭpāda. Thus, the flesh of Śākyamuni's body will still be warm, and Kāśyapa's smile will bloom again."[134]

Since the first Mahāyāna sūtras, the body that must be reproduced (not only in the formal sense of imitation of a meditative posture but indeed be engendered within oneself) has been the object of a very precise description. It would be revealing to study the underlying symbolism of the

---

[132] *Mahāvastu* 1: 132–34.
[133] *Kathāvattu* 18: 4.
[134] See Keizan, *Denkōroku*, T. 82, 2585: 346a.

forty main marks and the eighty-two secondary marks of the imaginary body of the Buddha. Endowed with all its marks, this body is properly speaking a semiotic body, a kind of living symbol that embodies the Buddhist teaching. It constitutes a "religious program," an illustration and a memento of the Buddhist doctrine. This physical "body of Law," counterpart of the metaphysical Dharma body, is a kind of "Table of the Law" on which the Buddhist (and Hindu) *imaginaire* is inscribed.[135]

Some of these corporeal characteristics have aroused the Buddhist imagination, for instance the "cryptorchidy" of the Buddha—the belief that "the secret part of [his] abdomen is contained in a sheath, as in the case of an elephant or a horse."[136] The Buddha is said to have shown his penis to suppress doubts in his listeners on several occasions. This shocked some commentators, who attempted to "encrypt" the story and the sacred pudenda under prudish glosses. It is for showing this superlative sexual organ to women during the funerary wake of the Buddha—in order to convert them!—that Ānanda was scolded by Kāśyapa and excluded from the assembly.[137] According to Nancy Barnes, "The sheathed penis symbolizes that [the Buddha's] genital virility is controlled and contained and is replaced by his oral 'virility.'" Noting that another of these

---

[135] In a sūtra it is said, "If all those who slander the Mahāyāna sūtras, or steal the property of monks, or commit any of the Five Transgressions, or violate any of the Four Great Prohibitions will contemplate one of these marks or signs of the Buddha for one day and one night with great concentration, all their sins will be erased, and eventually they shall not fail to see the Buddha." See *Sanbō ekotoba* in Kamens 1988: 101–2.

[136] This is the origin of the "horse-penis samādhi," or, more precisely, the "samādhi of the sheath of the horse-penis" [J. *Meonzō sanmaji*], on which see *Mikkyō daijiten*, edited by Mikkyō daijiten saikan iinkai (revised ed., 6 vols., Kyoto: Hōzōkan, 1970), 5: 2151c. According to the Japanese commentator Raiyū, it is another name of the "samādhi to get rid of all obstacles," and it means that the production of the bodhicitta is like the fact that, when the horse feels desire, its penis comes out, and when desire is appeased, its penis is hidden. The locus classicus for the horse-penis samādhi is the "Chapter on King Rāgarāja," in the *Yuqi jing* (T. 18, 867), translated by Vajrabodhi. See also *Jakushōdō kokkei shū*, in *DNBZ* 149: 35a.

[137] Buddhist monks act as though, like the Buddha, they had no sexual organs. Sex remains hidden in their discourse. But Japanese Buddhist sculptors came to represent the Buddha and Buddhist divinities as being like all men in this: a first attempt was made with the representation of viscera inside the famous statue of Śākyamuni at the Seiryōji (Shakadō) in Saga, on the Western outskirts of Kyoto. However, it stopped short of revealing the secret mark of the Buddha. Unlike the Mahāvira in Jainism, the Buddha is never represented naked. The same is not true of other lesser Buddhist figures. For instance, when the clothes are removed from certain statues of Jizō and Benten they reveal a fairly realistic anatomy. But Buddhism, on the whole, remains rather anatomically shy. In the Vinaya, nakedness is rejected by the Buddha: "Nakedness would not be suitable for monks, but unworthy of them. This is not the right thing to do. How could you, ignorant man, adopt nakedness as it is practiced by other ascetics?" See *Mahāvagga*, in Vinaya 1: 305, quoted in Wijayaratna 1990: 43. Here, however, the point seems to be to distinguish Buddhist monks from other ascetics, such as the Jains.

marks, the "long, broad tongue," is closely connected in the earliest textual references with that of the sheathed penis, Barnes argues that the Buddha is the father of sons and daughters "who are born of his mouth, that is, of the truth he teaches." His procreative energy, in other words, has been "displaced upward" to his tongue.[138]

Another conception of the human body, apparently more optimistic, was found in the traditional cosmologies of India and China, in which the body is perceived as a microcosm. Through this microcosm one may reach into the macrocosm and eventually realize its underlying principle, or the other way around. Through Tantrism in particular, Buddhism came to be influenced by these cosmological conceptions. The point here is that the body becomes the indispensable organ for contact with the absolute. The *Śrīkālacakra,* for instance, argues that supreme bliss cannot be realized in this life without the body.[139]

From a different standpoint, the development of funerary rituals leads to the notion of a twofold body—mortal and immortal, individual and social. The aim is to transmute the mortal body into the immortal, or at least to transfer a vital principle from the former into the latter. Cremation, which was seen at first like a mere destruction, becomes a recreation, a reincorporation. What matters in relics is the creation of an immortal ritual body. By contrast with the self-contained body of the meditator, closed on itself, the "fragmented body" (*śarīra*) is a disseminated body. However, the opposition must not hide the fact that in both cases the goal is to obtain, or to rediscover under the gangue of gross sensations, an incorruptible "adamantine body."

Like the body of the Tathāgata, which "does not flow through the nine orifices, because he does not have the nine orifices," the ideal body of the Buddhist practitioner was a closed body, without "outflows" (a metaphorical designation for defilements).[140] The latent symbolism of the meditative posture—of control and recollection—seems to contradict some of the aims of meditation, a dissolution of the self that recalls the "oceanic feeling" described by Romain Rolland, and analyzed by Freud as primary narcissism.[141] As Peter Brown points out in the case of Christian ascetics, "Virginity involved the heroic defence of the integrity of a specifically male or female body. . . . Bodies defended with such care were not destined to melt away in some distant transformation. Far from being a superficial and transitory layer of the person, sexual differences,

---

[138] Nancy Schuster Barnes, "Buddhism," in Arvind Sharma, ed., *Women in World Religions* (Albany: State University of New York Press, 1987), 7–8, and 259 n. 11.

[139] T. 18, 892: 595c.

[140] See T. 375, quoted in *Hōbōgirin* 1: 2a

[141] See Freud (1930) 1944.

and the behavior appropriate to them, were validated for all eternity."[142]
A revealing case, in which continence truly becomes the contrary of incontinence, is that of Wulou, a Korean monk living during the Tang,
whose name, meaning "Without Outflows," was interpreted literally by
hagiographers who attributed to him the gift of never excreting.[143]

This conception made perfection much more difficult, if not impossible, for women, whose body is open to inflows and outflows, penetration
and menstruation. However, Buddhist texts also describe an open body,
in which sexual differences, as in the West according to Thomas Laqueur,
were a matter of degree rather than nature.[144] It is in the social construction of gender, based on clear-cut juridical, social, and cultural distinctions, that the difference became radical. In early Buddhism at least, a
bad karma could lead to a change of sex in this very life.[145]

The metaphor of defilements/outflows, as it is used by "spiritual" Buddhism, draws our attention to "properly" physical outflows, in particular
to excreta.[146] One has a feeling that the "unthought" of the tradition—
not only what one may call its "soft underbelly" but also its most radical
undermining of dualistic thinking—might find its expression in excretal
imagery. In its desire for purity and neat boundaries, mainstream Buddhism refused the refuse. Excreta, evacuated from its official discourse,
return in its twilight language. In a nondualistic teaching, impurity is not
as easy to eliminate or contain as in a dualistic (or trinitarian) religion
like Christianity.[147] We are reminded of the feigned perplexity of the
Chan monk who has just been told that the entire world is the pure
Dharma realm, the sphere of ultimate reality: "If this is so, where can I
shit?" To the traditional Buddhist practitioner, still relying on dualities
like pure and impure, mind and body, the Chan master Linji Yixuan
opposes the ideal of the "man without affairs," a fellow who is content to

[142] Brown 1988: 383.
[143] See *Song gaoseng zhuan*, T. 50, 2061: 845c.
[144] See Laqueur 1990.
[145] Similar examples are found in the Western tradition. See ibid., 144.
[146] We recall that the "historical" Buddha died from diarrhea, a death which Christians
reserved to heretics. Thus, St. Hilaire attributes to a mortal diarrhea the death of the heretic
Arius—whose impure soul had to leave through his lower body. See Gaignebet and Périer
1990, 1: 838.
[147] The Christian dualism is pleasantly expressed by Martin Luther, who in his *Table
Talks* tells the story of a monk who is visited by the Devil while being in the latrine: "Mon-
achus super latrinam / Non debet orare primam?" / —"Deo quod supra / Tibi quod cadit
infra" ([The Devil:] "The monk in the latrine, should he not recite his prayer?" / —[The
monk:] "To God what is above / to you what falls below"); ibid., 1: 833. There is actually
in esoteric Buddhism a "god of the latrine" who destroys defilement, Ucchuṣma (J. Usu-
sama Myōō). His cult became particularly important in Zen monasteries, in which the
latrine was one of the three "silent places" (*sanmokudō*), together with the bath and the
meditation hall (or the refectory). See Frank 1991: 158–59.

"shit and piss when he feels like it." Buddhist hagiography goes one step further, for instance with the "mad monk" Jigong who, in a Rabelaisian move, turns "excrement into sacrament." When drunk, Jigong vomits on Buddhist statues, and his vomit becomes a splendid gilding.[148] His Japanese counterpart, Ikkyū, urinates on a Buddha statue, thereby covering it with gold. Whereas anti-Buddhist iconoclasts were usually punished by some supernatural illness when they desecrated Buddhist images in this manner, the apparent desecration committed by these monks turned into a consecration and revealed their saintly nature. Their excreta were thus sanctified (and sanctifying), and they were even at times bought by people for their alleged medicinal virtues.[149] The ambivalence (execrable/precious) perhaps explains their "uncanniness," their properly *unheimlich* capacity to serve in Chan/Zen or Tantric discourse as a metaphor for the transcendent unity of contraries. This ambivalence may also have something to do with the economic importance of human excreta as fertilizers in the horticultural economy of Zen monasteries.

· · · · ·

All the examples examined above suggest that salvation or awakening has to do, in one way or another, with sex—whether sexuality is denied (abstinence), affirmed, or displaced (usually in a ritual context). As Georges Bataille pointed out, the experiences of sex and of mysticism, although they cannot be reduced to each other, nevertheless communicate and express a similar sense of "plethora" or fullness. Confronted with such a plethora of materials, the most striking fact is the diversity of the Buddhist hermeneutics of desire. The standpoint usually presented as orthodox—the initial rejection of desire—is after all only one among others. We may wonder whether if, rather than the rule of the game itself, it is not only the opening move on an ideological chessboard, or better a go board, all the positions of which will be gradually occupied, all the virtualities explored. In the end, we should perhaps downplay the "moral" or "soteriological" interpretations of sexual desire, of its denial or affirmation. In most cases, what is at stake is neither purely consensual sex or individual awakening, but rather collective strategies aimed at the preservation of the lineage.

[148] Robert 1989: 202.

[149] According to the *Sanbō ekotoba*, the bath water of the monks has healing virtues. See Kamens 1990: 261: "If you prepare a bath for monks and take the water used for the bath and wash your pockmarks with it, they will heal immediately." The custom of drinking the urine of saints as a panacea (as in the case of the Pure Land ascetic Tokuhon) was quite widespread in Japan. In this case, excrement truly becomes sacrament. See also Bourke 1891.

Chapter 2

DISCIPLINING SEX, SEXUALIZING DISCIPLINE

I F DESIRE was a much-discussed topic among Buddhist philosophers, the regulation of sex was, more pragmatically, one of the main
concerns of the early Buddhist order. Thus, the dogmatic discourse of
Buddhist doctrine (the Dharma) was eventually linked to another normative discourse, that of monastic discipline (the Vinaya). As one text puts
it, "The speech of the Buddha is twofold due to the doctrine and the
discipline" (*dharmavinayaśena dvividham*).[1] This twofold speech would
be doubled by the twofold truth of Mahāyāna exegesis. As a corpus of
disciplinary rules, the Vinaya (and its extracanonical epitome, the *Prātimokṣa*) presents itself as a long list of prohibitions proclaimed by the
Buddha from time to time, in response to various problems faced by the
new community. It is therefore marked by a pragmatic concern that distinguishes it from the philosophical teaching of certain sūtras. Compared
with theoretical or metaphysical conceptions on the nature of desire or
passions, these disciplinary rules strike us at first glance by their circumstantial origin. They were dictated by concerns for propriety and collective harmony and, in many cases, for public perception of the saṅgha.
Nevertheless, once established, these rules became a moral imperative
and their application was in principle independent of any particular so-
ciocultural context.

These two types of discourses were never completely heterogeneous, of
course, and the distinction between the Dharma and the Vinaya (two of
the "Three Baskets," Skt. *Tripiṭaka*) was never clear-cut.[2] In practice, as
we will see, the repercussions of the theoretical reform that took place
within the Great Vehicle did affect the Vinaya. The elaboration in China
and Japan of a Mahāyānist Vinaya, in response to cultural changes and
to doctrinal developments, strongly linked these two normative views
and greatly changed the doctrinal basis and soteriological import of the
Vinaya. The biweekly recitation of the *Prātimokṣa*, or list of rules, at the
time of the *poṣadha* (Pāli *uposatha*, penance ritual), came to be seen retrospectively as a form of practice that was not only complementary to the
doctrine but identical to it. Although prohibitions may originally have

[1] Lamotte 1958: 156.

[2] The *Vinayapiṭaka* is composed of three sections: the *Sūtra-vibhaṅga*, the *Skandhaka*,
and the *Appendices*. Strictly speaking, the *Prātimokṣa*, or inventory of offences, is not part
of it, but we will include it in our discussion of the Vinaya.

been a pragmatic matter and not a soteriological issue, one also observes in the Vinaya a tendency to shift from the utilitarian to the ethical and spiritual levels, for instance by qualifying sexual intercourse as inherently wrong. According to Mohan Wijayaratna:

> The strictness shown here can be explained in two ways: with respect to the rules of the Community, and with respect to doctrine. First, the Community's rules, accepted by all who joined it, did not allow members to have sexual intercourse, because this would change the nature of the organization. . . . There would be no more communal and free life: monks and nuns would be ordinary fathers and mothers in monastic dress. Secondly, at the doctrinal level, the aim was to remove everything which impeded inner progress. Monks and nuns trying to achieve selflessness must be detached from all sources of sensual pleasure. . . . It was in order to avoid this danger that Buddhist monasticism decided to prohibit sexual intercourse completely.[3]

LAW, ORDER, AND LIBIDO

This "pragmatic" explanation of the origins and function of Vinaya may itself raise a few questions. There is something naive in the view that the Vinaya was there simply to further the practice of monks and nuns. The truly worthy goal of Buddhist practice, deliverance, does not completely account for the strikingly detailed and legalistic nature of the monastic code. As the *Samantapāsādika,* a Vinaya commentary that constitutes a kind of "Hite Report" on Buddhist sexuality, puts it: "When the Tathāgata prescribes the rule of a *pārājika* offense [offense entailing a "defeat," that is, exclusion from the community], he prescribes it in such a way that it covers all the possible cases, leaving no loophole which is not covered by it."[4] Apparently, the point was to guard against all eventualities, even the most unlikely—assuming that the infractions discussed have occurred at least once, giving rise to the specific scolding by the Buddha out of which the rule arose. However, nothing confirms that hypothesis; on the contrary, certain clues suggest that the individual rules came fully formed from the minds of the legislators and that the etiological anecdotes that accompany them have served only as a posteriori justifications.

Although the Vinaya may not be simply a random collection of rules made up by monks, it seems hard to follow the traditional view that it reflects the truly liberating Dharma. If the concern for leaving no loophole in the theoretically monolithic edifice of Vinaya explains the quasi-

---

[3] Wijayaratna 1990: 95.
[4] T. 24, 1462: 723a21; translated by Bapat and Hirakawa 1970: 201.

obsessive plethora of details, it does not bridge the gap between the Vinaya and other elements of the Dharma—for instance the Two Truths theory, whose structural ambivalence significantly weakened the theoretical scaffolding of Vinaya. This gap may reflect in part the division of Buddhism between conservative and progressive factions, followers of the letter or the spirit of the Law—a division symbolized by the tension between Kāśyapa and Ānanda. The hesitation between strict observance and accommodation appears, for instance, in the case of the nun Thullanandā, who sides with Ānanda when the latter is criticized by Kāśyapa for his shortcomings. The author of the *Mahāvastu,* one of the main commentaries on the Vinaya, is divided between his admiration for this nun and her loyalty to Ānanda, on the one hand, and the need to condemn her for insubordination on the other.[5]

The Vinaya deserves to be analyzed as a "literary" document and not as a legal document, a mere recording of admonitions. It should also be examined in its performative function, and not simply as a series of behavioral prescriptions. One may in particular wonder what effect was produced on the monks and nuns by the regular recitation of this list of 250 or more rules or "precepts"—a ritual enumeration of properly "insane" or unhealthy acts, topics that were not allowed for discussion in any other circumstances. Did this lengthy litany of prohibitions—many of them of a sexual nature—simply reinforce the cleric's conscience of his or her duty, or did it produce, apart from a feeling of guilt, a kind of cathartic fascination? In other words, do we not have here a phenomenon of displacement in the Freudian sense, that is, a displacing of energy that, under the cover of denial, produces intense pleasure?[6] One could argue that early Buddhist monks, in their attempt to understand reality "as it is," did not avert their gaze from sexuality but rather confronted head on the "facts of life," in the same way as they dwelt on the "contemplation of impurity" during their meditation. But it may also be argued that Vinaya commentators show a rather unhealthy fascination for the

---

[5] See Strong 1990.

[6] In "Obsessive Actions and Religious Practices," Freud points out that a characteristic of obsessional neurosis (but also of religious ritual and, namely, of penance) is that "its manifestations . . . fulfill the conditions of being a compromise between the warring forces of the mind. Thus they always reproduce something of the pleasure which they are designed to prevent; they serve the repressed instinct no less than the agencies which are repressing it." (Grimes 1995: 215) Freud also argues that the mechanism of psychical displacement "from the actual, important thing on to the small one which takes its place" succeed in "turning the most trivial matter into something of the utmost importance and urgency." Thus, the "petty ceremonies of religious practice gradually become the essential thing and push aside the underlying thoughts." (ibid., 216) In the Buddhist case, the displacement is from the sexual instinct to a ritualized recitation of the rule against sexuality. It simultaneously denies the thought which it affirms by bringing it to mind.

trivial and defiling aspects of human existence. Even before being threatened by external accommodations, the rule is already shaped from within by narrativity. The Vinaya is not only a juridical corpus, it is a mine of spicy anecdotes. As Charlotte Furth writes regarding another kind of literature: "The gravity of intention [of these texts] may be subverted by the proliferation of detail ready to entangle the reader in the very appetites which the adept is being warned he must control. Such texts always say more than they mean."[7] This also brings to mind Thomas Laqueur's comment, referring to texts such as *Onania, or the Heinous Sin of Self-Pollution,* or Samuel-Auguste Tissot's *L'Onanisme:* "Here is a literature that generates erotic desire in order to control it."[8] Even if Vinaya texts were not among these "books that one reads with only one hand," Buddhist monastic discipline seems traversed through and through by desire. Is it merely a coincidence that the title of an important Tantric scripture, the "Book on Vinaya," refers not to Vinaya but Vināyaka? Perhaps Vināyaka, the personification of the dark side of Gaṇeśa, the elephant-headed god of obstacles, who would become one of the "sexual deities" of Japanese Tantrism, was also the lord of Vinaya practice.

We cannot dwell here on the rules regarding lay morality, a morality that promises a better rebirth to those who observe the five precepts concerning murder, theft, illicit love, lying, and the use of intoxicants. According to Louis de La Vallée Poussin, this "morality of the paradises" does not have very high ethical standards. It nevertheless attempted to regulate sex between lay men and women. According to the *Abidharmakośa-śāstra,* "illicit love" for laymen comes in four forms: sexual intercourse with a "forbidden" woman (adultery), sexual intercourse with one's wife through a "forbidden way" (fellatio, cunnilingus, sodomy), having sex in the wrong place (hermitage, etc.), or at a wrong time (when a woman is pregnant, when she is feeding, or when she has—with her husband's authorization!—made a vow of chastity).[9]

As noted above, the core of monastic discipline is contained in the *Prātimokṣa,* the list of rules that monks and nuns must observe and recite twice a month, at the new moon and full moon, during the *poṣadha* (Pāli *uposatha*) ceremony. According to I. B. Horner, "This recitation served

---

[7] Furth 1994: 136.

[8] Laqueur 1990: 263.

[9] La Vallée Poussin 1927: 47. This list is strangely reminiscent of another, drawn by the German medieval canonist Burchard of Worms, about the "abuse of wedding." According to the latter, he must do penance who, with his spouse or another, "has mated from behind, 'in the fashion of dogs'; or has mated with a wife made impure by her menses or because she is pregnant; he who has defiled himself with his wife on Sunday or during holidays [Christmas, Lent], or else while he was drunk, or finally in a public place." Quoted in Le Goff 1991: 185–86.

the double purpose of keeping the rules fresh in the minds of the monks and nuns, and of giving each member of the monastic community the opportunity, while the rules were being repeated or recited, to avow an offense that he or she had committed."[10] Raffaele Pettazzoni points out that this *Prātimokṣa* "is less a list of sins properly speaking than a list of monastic offenses, which for the most part are such only in the eyes of a community of monks. Likewise, the sanctions provided for are concerned less with the sin in itself or the sinner than with the relations of the sinner and the community (explusion, suspension, etc.). There is no talk of either absolution or pardon: these concepts are incompatible with the pure doctrine of Buddhism."[11] Although Pettazzoni's notion of a "pure" Buddhist doctrine is questionable, his remark has nevertheless the merit of emphasizing the functional (or rather dysfunctional) nature of the offense. If the sexual act, in particular, is severely condemned by Buddhist penitentials, it is not so much in the name of morality, nor because, as in ascetic discourse, it would entail desire and loss of energy; but rather because it can provoke troubles within the saṅgha and within the community at large, on whom the monks rely for support. The viewpoint of the legislators, who borrow the authority of the Buddha, is quite different from that of the Buddhist philosophers or moralists. The often-invoked argument, according to which monastic rules aim above all at preserving the monks' morality, leading to mind purification and thus allowing progress in meditation, does not seem to apply to Vinaya very well. Indeed, unlike canonical texts that define morality as part and parcel of an "ascesis" in Foucault's sense—oriented toward an ethics and constituting a form of individuation—Vinaya texts are merely codes of behavior that define what is allowed and what is forbidden.[12] However, as John Winkler puts it: "To know when any such male law-givers—medical, moral, or marital, whether smart or stupid—are (to put it bluntly) bluffing or spinning fantasies or justifying their 'druthers' is so hard that most historians of ideas—Foucault, for all that he is exceptional, is no exception here—never try."[13] Sex is, of course, always blacklisted in the Vinaya, but for various reasons that, if they usually tend to be mutually reinforcing, can also sometimes weaken each other.

However, there soon appeared a tendency, which became extensive in Mahāyāna, to consider the offense as defilement that requires purification. Henceforth, the elimination of the offense took the form of a ceremony aiming at exorcising defilement, rather than the form of an autocritique aimed at restoring the collective harmony through psychological

---

[10] Horner 1949–1966, 1: xii.
[11] Pettazzoni 1932: 187.
[12] See Foucault 1985: 30–31.
[13] Winkler 1990: 6.

devices. Pettazzoni sees there a return to the magico-religious conceptions of Brahmanism—perhaps also, in the cases of China and Japan, of local cults. This return to pre-Buddhist sources helps to explain, according to him, what looks like an inconsistency in the case of the bimonthly ceremony of poṣadha, during which offenses are ritually confessed: indeed, "the three questions which conclude each section of the *Prātimokṣa* have meaning only in relation with the answer which anyone who felt guilty of one of the offenses listed in the section read should give. Probably that answer originally constituted the confession: a public confession . . . in relation to which the [prior] confession of the monks between themselves constituted in all likelihood a secondary and posterior development."[14] Pettazzoni points out that in Brahmanism the uposatha was the seclusion observed by the priest before the sacrifice.

> In Buddhism, because one suppressed the sacrifice to retain only the vigil, *i.e.*, the *uposatha*, the devotional practices of the vigil took the place of the ancient cultual ceremony. . . . In due time . . . , the character of liturgical ceremony of the *uposatha* was emphasized. Because the sacrificial solemnity had disappeared, what had been the "vigil" took the place of the "feast": the "day of fasting" became the day of the solemn meeting. In the same way, the confession, already practiced as a spiritual preparation to the celebration of the feast, retained that preparatory character vis-à-vis the *uposatha* when the latter replaced the former. What was probably connected originally—*uposatha* and confession—became separated: whereas the recitation of the Rule [*Prātimokṣa*] became the essential matter of the *uposatha* celebration, the confession, which had been an integral part of it, took precedence over it, as a preliminary and preventive practice, becoming the *sine qua non* condition for a monk to take part in the *uposatha*.[15]

This tendency to redefine confession as a collective rite of purification reactivated the latent meaning and function of the *Prātimokṣa*. Charles Prebish, following Sukumar Dutt, suggests that the word itself, when it was first introduced in the Buddhist vocabulary, had little to do with confession, and meant rather an "external bond of union"[16] The ritualization of the *Prātimokṣa* reflected this evolution toward collective puri-

---

[14] Pettazzoni 1932: 172.

[15] Ibid., 174–77. On the exclusion of those who are not monks, see *Sanbō ekotoba*, in Kamens 1990: 265–66: "While the recitation proceeds, those who are not monks may not watch or listen. When the Buddha was in this world, there was a certain boy who hid himself and overheard the monks in convocation. The Buddha was not present, but he knew about this, and he sent Vajrapāṇi to drive him away. Vajrapāṇi struck the boy on the head and killed him; it was then seen that he was not, in fact, a real boy. The convocation is certainly an important element of monastic life and an ancient artifact of the Buddha's teachings."

[16] Dutt 1960: 70; quoted in Prebish 1975: 18.

fication and affirmation of group identity. It can also be seen as part of a scapegoat mechanism through which offenders (like Ānanda at the first council) are mercilessly excluded in order to purify the group and reaffirm its boundaries. Finally, we should keep in mind that these texts are normative, and we rarely hear the voices of the monks and nuns who were affected by them.

Let us examine more closely the list of rules, or rather the lists, because the *Prātimokṣa* of the nuns, although it repeats that of the monks, is considerably more developed: 348 rules instead of 250. The list of offenses is divided into eight sections in both penance manuals, in order of decreasing gravity. The first section concerns offenses leading to exclusion (*pārājika*). It contains four clauses for monks and eight for nuns. The next five sections deal with offenses that are the object of variable penances. First come thirteen offenses (seventeen for women) called *saṅghādiśeṣa*, for which the sanction imposed by the community consists in temporary exclusion; then two indeterminate offenses, carrying variable sanction according to case (expulsion, suspension, penance); thirty lighter offenses, which are mere failures to observe the rule of poverty, but still liable to confession and penance; ninety offenses (178 for women) merely requiring confession, and four special offenses (eight for women). Finally, the seventh and eighth sections list a hundred minor rules of etiquette or purity, and seven rules of procedure to settle conflicts. As we can see, these rules deal not only with the five "offenses of nature" (murder, etc.), but also with many "offenses of disobedience," whose character is sometimes very arbitrary or circumstantial.

Such a fault-provoking system, as Foucault suggests in the case of Christian penance manuals, may have contributed to the individualization of monks and nuns and facilitated their control by the community.[17] These texts are prescriptive, and we have to read between the lines to guess how these men and women could experience these rules. The apparently heterogeneous litany of possible or simply imaginable offenses, recited every fortnight, could not fail to produce certain perverse effects, even in the most clever minds. It constitutes as it were a system of "double bind"—because, on the pretext of defining the offenses, it evokes their possibility in the minds of the audience at the same time that it underscores the guilt of the intention. As Minakata Kumagusu points out, regarding the Japanese context: "The profusion of laws is a logic that increases the number of culprits. Monks, who had leisure, when they read such things, came to acts of singular perversity through mere curiosity, and lay people too, studying this, eventually established such things

---

[17] See also Legendre 1974.

as the *wakashu jorō* [lit. the 'ephebe-courtesan']."[18] The poṣadha list provides very precise suggestions indeed, and Buddhist compilers or commentators seem to have developed a strange fascination in evoking the most unlikely turpitudes and perversions. At the same time, the purely ritual nature of the question addressed by the officiating monk to the monks assembled for the poṣadha turned this list into a kind of incantatory or exorcistic discourse, which gratified both individual and collective imaginations.

Before continuing, a remark on method is in order. Sukumar Dutt, among others, has pointed out that the classification of the offenses in the *Prātimokṣa* "does not appear to have been made on any initially recognized principle, but is more or less haphazard and promiscuous."[19] Despite textual variants, and the rather haphazard organization of the text, we should consider the *Prātimokṣa* as a whole and regard it as a coherent value system.[20] According to this perspective, one might object that it is fallacious to dwell on some rules dealing with sexuality, after extracting them from their context. However, a global analysis of the *Prātimokṣa* (let alone of the various forms of Vinaya) would take us too far afield, and I will have to limit myself to a brief survey. When reading these manuals, one cannot but be struck by the sometimes unexpected, but nevertheless significant, sequence of various prohibitions. Obviously, their original meaning is not the one that imposes itself upon the modern interpreter, who judges them according to his/her own cultural prejudices. We must therefore try to contextualize these examples, and remember in particular that the notions of "natural" or "unnatural" acts are neither everywhere nor always the same. Often, offenses judged at first glance to be against nature turn out to be reversals of social hierarchy, that is, offenses "against culture."[21] As we shall see later, transgression obeys a variety of motivations. Following John Strong, we may distinguish at least three types of Vinaya violators: the "latitudinarians"; those who, finding loopholes in the Dharma, allow the Dharma to evolve; and finally, potential schismatics who have a different vision of what Bud-

---

[18] Nakazawa 1991: 124.

[19] Dutt 1960: 78–79.

[20] I am aware, of course, that there are many discrepancies between the monastic codes of various schools (Dharmaguptaka, Mahāsaṅghika, etc.). These divergences often led to divisions and schisms. Thus, we greatly oversimplify the matter when we speak of Vinaya as a whole, just as we speak of "the Buddhist teaching" in the singular. However, a case can still be made for a certain underlying unity, textual and conceptual, of these codes. Whereas the rules may differ, the "rule" of their production seems fairly stable. For a discussion of the differences between *Prātimokṣa* texts of various Hīnayāna schools, see Prebish 1974; and Lamotte 1958: 181–97.

[21] See Winkler 1990: 21.

dhism should be.[22] Some of these transgressive attitudes reflect the blurring of the borders between monks and laymen, the fact that monks are too engaged in active life and too close to their parishioners. As the case of the six "heretic" monks of Kitāgiri suggests, the Vinaya served first of all as a demarcation line: in this instance, the Buddha himself chose to prevent a schism by excluding these monks from his community. As Pierre Bourdieu points out, rites of passage (such as ordination) are above all rites of demarcation.[23] In practice, it was divergences on points of discipline—not of doctrine, as in Christianity—that gave rise to Buddhist schisms. Conversely, "philosophical" transgression constitutes a rejection of social values, in their mundane as well as in their monastic form.

Ordination

The recitation of the rules takes place at two moments of peculiar intensity: the initial ordination and the periodical repentance.[24] In the ordination ritual, after the postulant has answered to all the questions concerning his aptitudes, the officiating priest asks the chapter of monks three times to admit him if no one sees any objection. Then he explains to the postulant the four cases leading to *pārājika,* "defeat," that is, expulsion from the community: heterosexual relations, theft, murder, and boasting of psychic powers. If the postulant agrees never to transgress these fundamental rules, he is finally accepted.

The procedure is the same for female postulants, with a few major differences. After having been declared acceptable, the novice must vow not to commit the four pārājika offenses, to which are added another four: to touch the body of another person or of an animal "between the armpits and the knees"; to touch the hand or the clothes of a man, or withdraw with him to a solitary place, stay there, talk with him in private; or to take a walk with him, get close to him, or arrange a meeting with him; to hide anyone's serious offenses; and to take side with a monk or novice who has been censored. Whereas these four kinds of offenses are punishable by penitence for monks, they lead to immediate exclusion for nuns.

During the ordination ceremony, the female postulant must answer an apparently heterogeneous list of questions. The criteria that govern that list are of several orders: moral—not to have committed the five major offenses (murder of father or mother, of a saint, wounding a Buddha, dividing the saṅgha); juridical and social—to be juridically emancipated and free of any debt toward society (the king, the administration, the

[22] Strong 1990.
[23] Bourdieu 1990: 118.
[24] See Wieger 1910: 197.

family, the Buddhist community); medical—to be in good health (the list of illnesses is significant: skin diseases, lung diseases, epilepsy, flatulence, dropsy, illnesses of the spleen, diabetes); and finally sexual—not to be sexually deviant (androgynous, asexual, having an aversion to men). However, the main difference between monks and nuns regarding ordination is that the female postulant, after having convinced her superiors of her physical and moral integrity, must still appear in front of the assembly of monks, which will in the last instance decide her admission.

Confession

The formal, collective confession is preceded by an individual confession to another monk. For each section of the monks' formulary, the enunciation of the precepts is followed by a threefold question, by which the officiating priest asks the monks whether they are free of the offenses recited. He concludes rather hastily from their silence that such is the case. Here, for instance, is the preamble of the *Sūtra of the Mūlasarvāstivādin*: "O Venerable Ones, the introduction of the *Prātimokṣa Sūtra* recitation has been recited by me. Therefore, I ask the Venerable Ones— Are you completely pure in this matter? A second and also a third time I ask—Are you completely pure in this matter? Since there is silence, the Venerable Ones are [completely pure] in this matter. Thus do I understand."[25]

Among the thirteen cases requiring penance, the first five have to do with the sexual act: if a monk, moved by desire, touches the body of a woman; if he says exciting words; if he boasts in front of her and asks her to serve him; finally if he serves as a go-between. The ninety miscellaneous offenses are relatively minor, and a number of them have to do with cases in which a monk can be temporarily isolated with a person of the opposite sex—even with the laudable intention of explaining a scriptural passage to this person. The important point is always to remain visible, if not transparent. Some rules are without any apparent relation with sexuality, such as the rules against destroying the dwelling place of a spirit (for instance by cutting a tree) or bathing more than twice a month when one is not sick.

Most striking, however, is the properly ritual nature of confession, to which, paradoxically, only pure monks are admitted. The *Prātimokṣa* even explicitly excludes the *paṇḍaka* (a term often improperly translated as "eunuchs"), considered to be passive homosexuals. We know that it is on that point that Foucault distinguishes homosexuality—as a cultural construct specific to some cultures—from sodomy, a term referring to a spe-

[25] See Prebish 1975: 49.

cific type of prohibited act. The Vinaya interdiction seems to aim at a type of "man," not only at a type of act.[26] Furthermore, if confession may have played, as Foucault thinks, an individualizing role in the Christian case, in Buddhism it seems to have served above all to assert the ritual purity and the unity of the group. From that standpoint, the prohibition of sexuality in the Vinaya is based not so much on a puritanical morality or on the fear of losing painfully acquired psychic powers as on the monks' will to distinguish themselves ritually from laymen and other religious groups, and to prevent or exorcise centrifugal forces within the saṅgha. Renunciation is what "distinguishes" the monk, and the rules aim above all at avoiding all promiscuity, not only with outsiders but also, within the community, with those who threaten its cohesion and its borders.

SEXUAL OFFENSES

Let us turn to the major offense, the sexual act itself. The Indian Vinaya is not sparing of details on this topic and sex is not only forbidden in principle but also seriously constrained in practice by an assortment of rules. As Wijayaratna admits, "Despite the well-known tenet of the 'Middle Way', Buddhist monasticism seems to have held an extreme position on this issue."[27] Apart from the precept on chastity, whose transgression leads to exclusion from the community, various cases of penitence belong to this rubric, including onanism, fondling, saucy talk, "platonic" love. The first pārājika offense for monks is defined as follows: "When a monk . . . has carnal relations with a being of the female sex, of whatever species, he is expelled from the community." The heterosexual act is therefore strictly prohibited, "even so much as with an animal."[28] Bestiality seems actually less reprehensible than heterosexual relations with a consenting human partner.[29] This clause is traced back to the case of a monk

---

[26] Ibid., 467, 471.

[27] See Wijayaratna 1990: 94.

[28] "If a monk who has accepted the Discipline, who has not rejected the Discipline and has not pronounced himself unable to continue [with the religious life], has sexual intercourse, even with an animal, he commits an offense entailing defeat. That monk is one who is defeated; he is not in communion." (*Vinayapiṭaka* 3: 23). This is more detailed in *Mahāvagga* (ibid. 1: 96): "It is prohibited for a monk to have sexual intercourse, even with a female animal. A monk who has sexual intercourse is not a monk any more, nor a son of the Śākyans. As a man who has been beheaded cannot live with only a body, so a monk who has had sexual intercourse is not a monk any more, nor a son of the Śākyans." See also Prebish 1975: 50–51.

[29] Compare with the Western hierarchy of sin, as found in Thomas of Chobham (fl. 1200–1233), *Summa Confessorum*, edited by F. Broomfield (Louvain: Editions Nauwelaerts, 1968), 400: "It is shameful when a man takes pleasure with a woman in an

who had tamed a female monkey, and his vice was discovered when the monkey candidly offered herself to other monks.[30] Although the pārājika offense covers what Japanese Buddhists call *nyosan nanni* (the three female [orifices], the two male [orifices]), homosexual relations between men, not to mention between women, are on the other hand conspicuously downplayed.[31]

The structure of the Vinaya creates a kind of gradation of acts, from the few major offenses to the multitude of minor breaches. By putting the sexual act at the summit or at the center, it is as if the fundamental sexual taboo was diffracted, reverberating at other lower levels. But above all, this structure implies that any act falls under the domination of the Law, any action is caught in the web of a guilty desire. Even apparently insignificant acts are liable to minor infractions. We recall that it is precisely on the point of minor infractions that Ānanda was accused of not having asked enough instructions from the Buddha. In due time, and with the stiffening of the casuistic apparatus and the increase of ritualism, the properly amusing aspects of the commentary become invisible, at least within the magical and hallucinated circle of the community, and if they invite laughter it is only among "heretics." The importance of the system is to lead to an absolute certitude that all particular cases will necessarily find a place in the classificatory whole. As Pierre Legendre points out in the Western context, we observe the "constancy of the sexual theme in underscoring the indisputable nature of the Law."[32]

The rule against carnal relations with the other sex is said to originate with the case of Sudinna, a young man who had left his parents and his wife to become a monk.[33] After the death of his father, his mother came to beg him to go back home or at least to procreate the child who could continue the family lineage. After some hesitation, Sudinna eventually yielded to her request and fulfilled his filial and marital duties. Having heard the story, the Buddha scolded him as follows:

> It were better for you, foolish man, that your male organ should enter the mouth of a terrible and poisonous snake, than that it should enter a

---

unnatural way; it is more shameful to take pleasure in one's own organs; it is most shameful when women take pleasure among themselves or men among themselves; it is diabolic when a man or a woman excite themselves with an animal (Turpe autem est innaturaliter virum in muliere, turpius in membris propriis, turpissimum mulieres inter se et viros inter se, diabolicum si vir vel mulier exerceant cum bruto animali).

[30] See *Sifen lü*, T. 22, 1428: 571a; and *Samantapāsādikā*, T. 24, 1462: 715c; Bapat and Hirakawa, trans. 1970: 169.

[31] For a Sōtō Zen analysis of the sex pārājikā, see *Zenkai shō*, 649–50.

[32] See Legendre 1974 :125.

[33] On Sudinna, see *Sifen lü*, 570b; and *Samantapāsādikā*, 713b; Bapat and Hirakawa, trans. 1970: 159.

woman. . . . It were better for you, foolish man, that your male organ should enter a charcoal pit, burning, ablaze, afire. . . . What is the cause of this? For *that* reason, foolish man, you would go to death, or to suffering like unto death, but not on that account would you pass at the breaking up of the body after death to the waste, the bad bourn, the abyss, hell. But for *this* reason, you would pass to the waste, the bad bourn, the abyss, hell.[34]

Sudinna was eventually expelled from the community, and the Buddha pronounced the above rule to prevent the occurrence of a similar case. This, however, was to remain wishful thinking. The *Samantapāsādikā*, a commentary attributed to Buddhaghosa (5th c.), defines the sexual act as a "grave offense, at the end of which one must use water [to wash oneself]," one which "is practiced by two people in a secret place"; more precisely, "when the external part of the male organ is inserted, even as much as a sesame seed, into the female organ—the humid region where the wind itself does not reach." The act comprises four phases: "the initial entrance, the time of staying in, the time of taking out, and the subsequent period. If the monk feels pleasure during any of these four phases, he is guilty; otherwise he is innocent."[35]

But clarifications do not stop here, and they betray one of the hidden functions of Vinaya: to exclude certain categories of beings from the elected flock. The commentary, concerned about the identity of potential partners, lists "three kinds of females," two types of "neuters" (paṇḍaka, each type being further divided into three subtypes), and three kinds of males—thus a total of twelve kinds of people with whom sexual intercourse results in a pārājika offense. Significantly, male partners have been added in the commentary, whereas they were omitted in the rule itself—which, however, considered all the possible categories of females. At any rate, through a complicated calculation based on the principle that some of these categories of beings (human females and hermaphrodites, nonhumans, and animals) have "three ways," whereas others ("neuters" and human, nonhuman, and animal males) have only two, the commentator reaches a total of thirty "ways" into which the insertion of a monk's penis—"even to the extent equal to the length of a sesame seed"—constitutes an act involving "defeat" and requires exclusion from the community.[36] The Vinaya regulation against "eunuchs" has also to do

[34] I. B. Horner 1949–1966, vol. 1 (*Suttavibhanga*) 36

[35] *Samantapāsādikā*, 722b, Bapat and Hirakawa, trans. 1970: 199. See also *Sifen lü*, 572a.

[36] *Samantapāsādikā*, 722b; Bapat and Hirakawa, trans. 1970: 197–98. There were also rules against fellation: see *Mahāsānghika Vinaya*, T. 1425: 234c; and Raniero Gnoli, ed., *The Gilgit Manuscript of the Sanghabhedavastu: Being the 17th and Last Section of the Vinaya of the Mūlasarvāstivādin* (Rome: Istituto per il Medio ed Estremo Oriente, 1977, 2: 158. One canonical reference is traced back to King Ajātaśatru. We are told that this king

with the fact that monks must be capable of performing sexually while controlling their desire to do so. Given these regulations, we find very few instances of monks making themselves eunuchs for the sake of nirvāṇa.[37] This selection of potential partners was done on the basis of various criteria, most prominently sexual ones. It becomes clear that, as much as with the sexual act itself, sexual offenses have to do with the fact of mixing with the wrong people. It serves to elaborate a taxonomy that recalls those analyzed by Mary Douglas.[38]

Despite the Buddhist claim of nondualism, male homosexuality itself helped to reinforce gender boundaries and social boundaries defined by gender. Paradoxically, both hermaphroditism—a kind of hypersexuality —and impotence—a "hyposexuality"—were seen as characteristic of the paṇḍaka, and as such, were threatening and/or despised. The same is true for castration, although the condemnation of the latter was in some cases attenuated by its ascetic motivations. Japanese Buddhists were also aware that the feminization of the novices (*chigo*), while temporary, could lead to significant psychological or physical changes that would transform the object of their love into a strange being, close to the paṇḍaka of canonical literature. But even the hermaphrodite, neither fish nor fowl, was not forever "exiled from either gender." Far from being fixed in his/her nature, he/she was already in movement toward one or the other sex. Transsexuality, although not encouraged, was not condemned, either. It was judged weird and slightly pitiful, as shown by Japanese stories in which a monk turns into a woman and is later recognized by his former fellows.[39]

---

took in his mouth the penis of his son Udayabhadra, bitten by an insect, to extract the venom from it. See Durt 1997.

[37] See supra, Chapter One, on castration. The *Mahāsāṅghika Vinaya*, 417c, describes "six types of unmanliness"; it also reports how one night after the lights go out in the monastery, some of the monks feel someone fondling them. By the time they light the lamp, the culprit has vanished. The next night, the scoundrel tries it again, but this time one of the monks is ready for him and catches him—as it turns out, he too is a monk. They then take the rascal to the Buddha who asks him who he is. The monk responds, "I am a princess." Then the Buddha asks him/her what kind of woman he/she is. The monks says, "I go both ways. I am neither man nor woman," and then explains that he/she became a monk because he/she heard that monks needed wives and he/she wanted to help out. This is followed by a long passage about how unmanly men should not be allowed into the saṅgha. Minakata Kamagusu, quoting the *Mahāprajñāpāramitā-sūtra*, refers to the five kinds of "Yellow Gates" (J. *kōmon*, that is, *paṇḍaka*, impotent males, or "nonmales"). See Minakata 1971– 1975, bekkan, 585. He also mentions the case, reported in the *Wu zazu*, of an individual who is male at the hour of the rat and of the horse, female at the hour of the ram and the pig. On the "Yellow Gates" see also ibid., 589, 603, 607.

[38] See Douglas 1967.

[39] Ibid., 301. The *Kii zōdan* reports, for instance, the story of a young monk who once came to spend the night in a village of Kōshū. He was handsome and looked like a nun. The

Another border that could be blurred by deviant sexuality was that between humans and animals. As if not sufficiently obvious, the animal category is detailed in the Vinaya commentaries in a way that borders on taxonomic delirium. This description is reminiscent of Jorge Luis Borges's famous account of an imaginary Chinese encyclopedia.[40] Thus, among inferior animals, with or without legs (snakes, chickens, cats, and dogs), the "snake" class comprises everything that crawls, including centipedes; the "fish" class also includes tortoises, iguanas, and frogs. Like the bodies of cats, dogs, and other animals, the body of these beings has three parts, the smallest penetration of which would consitute a pārājika offense. Regarding cavities, however, there are some caveats: the commentator observes that although the mouth of a frog may be very large, to introduce one's penis in it would hardly produce any pleasure and would therefore constitute an offense liable only to penitence.[41] The same is true when the sexual act takes place in the trunk of an elephant, or in other—nongenital—parts of domestic animals like the horse, the cow, the donkey, the camel, or the buffalo.[42]

A too readily sociohistorical reading of passages of this kind, suggesting that bestiality and other similar vices were rampant in India at the time of the Buddha, would reinforce the worst colonial clichés about

---

next day, due to bad weather, he could not leave. In the morning, he seemed completely like a woman—even his voice. When the innkeeper questioned the monk, the latter said that he was from Echigo and that after two or three years in Tanba he was returning home. When asked whether he was a monk or a nun, he replied that he was a nun. The patron fell in love with him and eventually married him. The young bride let her hair grow. She soon became pregnant and gave birth. When the child was twelve or thirteen, a group of monks passed by. Among them was an old monk, whom the woman recognized as her former master. After some hesitation, the former monk decided to explain everything. He said that, after coming to this village, he had dreamt that he was transformed into a woman, and when he/she woke up his male organ had been replaced by a female one. His/her voice had changed too. She had finally married the innkeeper and for fifteen years lived in this house. She had hidden from her husband the fact that she was originally a monk. She had heard of a "woman becoming a man," but not of the opposite. Was this due to her bad karma? The master reassured her, composed a verse, and told her to continue studying her kōan, without fearing her karma. In a similar story, two monks return home after studying several years in the capital. Some ten years later, while traveling again to the capital, they find that the hostess of the inn looks like one of their former fellow monks. The woman eventually admits that she was this monk, and explains how, once when returning from the capital and spending the night in an inn, his/her genitals began to hurt and eventually fell off, leaving a scar looking like a female organ. He/she subsequently married the innkeeper and had children. Having heard her story, the two monks leave, perplexed. The *Wakan sansai zue*, after mentioning these two cases, also gives Chinese precedents. See Terashima Yoshiyasu, ed., *Wakan sansai zue* (Tokyo: Tōkyō bijutsu, 1970).

[40] See Borges, quoted in Foucault 1973.
[41] See Bapat and Hirakawa 1970: 196.
[42] Ibid., 202.

Asians.[43] Apart from its questionable ethnocentric or racist nature, this type of conclusion would also rest in the present case on a fundamental misunderstanding of the textual nature of the Vinaya. After all, one could draw from reading the Pantagruelic "descriptions" of François Rabelais similar, or even worse, conclusions regarding the sexual life of Renaissance Frenchmen. Humor is more obvious in Rabelais than in Vinaya texts, but it is also at work in the latter—even if not in their authors' minds (this quality is rather rare among lawmakers), at least in that of their audience. Pushed to its extreme, Vinaya legalism produces comic effects that must not have been lost on its readers.

The mania for details can have other "perverse"—even macabre— effects, as can be seen from passages like the following: "If in a corpse, everything is rotten except the three ducts, and one practices the sexual act in those ducts, one is guilty of a *pārājika* offense. If, however, only one part is left intact, one commits only a *thullacaya* (minor) offense."[44] The commentary persists, sparing no detail in the description of the corpse. Whatever one may think of this kind of literature, such a detailed description, although it may have been intended to have a deterrent effect, also suggests that one can get used to anything, even the obscenity of death. Even the contemplation of corpses, recommended by the Buddha as an antidote to sensual desire, was perhaps no longer judged sufficient by the compilers of Vinaya.

Rules for the Nuns

Often the rules and warnings against the other sex are parallel for monks and nuns.[45] This is in principle the case for the pārājika rule regarding sex: "If a nun voluntarily has carnal relations, even with an animal, she is excluded, and no longer shares the religious life." But the difference lies in interpretation of this rule, which is much more detailed, due to the assumption of the imperfection of female nature that renders women more subject to desire. Monastic glosses zero in on the problem, and their proliferation results in a rich casuistry. To give just a sample: "If a nun has carnal relations with a human male, with a human eunuch; if, the

[43] Even Arnold van Gennep, in his classic study on the rites of passage, mentions among examples of "rites of incorporation," and of the belief in the "magical efficacy" of coitus, "the custom of intercourse with hens, ducks, etc., which is so widespread in Annam that a European must never eat one of these fowl if it has not been killed in his presence." See van Gennep 1960: 173–74.

[44] *Samantapāsādikā,* T. 24, 1462: 723a; Bapat and Hirakawa, trans. 1970: 201.

[45] See, for instance, the *Aṅguttara-nikāya* I: 1 and 2: "Monks, I know of no physical appearance . . . which reduces a man's mind to slavery as does that of women." But the reverse is equally true: "I know of no physical appearance . . . which reduce a woman's mind to slavery as [that] of a man do[es]."

male organ being introduced in the female organ—among the impure orifices: the mouth, the anus, the vagina—she suffers from it and, having suffered, finds pleasure in it; if she finds pleasure at the beginning, finds pleasure during it, finds pleasure at the end; if she is delighted with it, if she finds pleasure in it, she is excluded. If she does not get pleasure at the beginning, but gets pleasure in the middle, gets pleasure at the end; . . . or if she does not find pleasure in the beginning, nor in the middle, but finds pleasure in the end. . . . [in all these cases] she is excluded. If she does not find pleasure in the beginning, in the middle, or in the end, there is no offense." She is also excluded "if the male organ of a sleeping or dead [human], being introduced in the female organ, she suffers from it, etc.; likewise if the male organ of a nonhuman [male or] eunuch, of an animal male or eunuch [is introduced] in any of the three impure orifices, etc."[46]

The commentary also defines three variables of the act, namely, the nature of the partner, his mental state, and the place of penetration: "A nun is excluded in three cases: with a human, with a nonhuman, and with an animal; and in three others: in the mouth, in the anus, in the vagina; and in three others: when [the partner] is sleeping, when he is dead, when he is awake. A nun is excluded in two [cases]: with a male and with a eunuch." The condition of the nun—and above all her reaction—are also taken into account: "If the nun is asleep, or drunk, or mad; if a man comes near her and sits on her, or lies on her, or penetrates her; and if, taking part in it then, she finds pleasure at the beginning, in the middle, at the end, she is excluded." However, certain extenuating circumstances are considered, and we can see that, despite the formalism of Vinaya, it is the intention, together with the pleasure taken or not taken (*mens rea* and *actus rea*), that determine in last analysis whether the act is guilty or not: "How must she be taken as nonconsenting? If it is due to ignorance, or to confusion; when believing that it is licit; with a shameless individual; under the grip of passion, hatred, delusion—there is no offense. For she whose mind is absent, who remains passive, who does not commit [the sexual act], there is no offense."[47]

The fifth parājika rule, regarding touching, establishes that "if a nun in prey to desire allows a man who is prey to desire to touch her, to grab her 'below her shoulders or above her knees,' this nun is excluded, she no longer takes part in religious life." Following the basic definition, we find a variation on each of its terms. Thus, "if a nun in prey to desire accepts from a woman in prey to desire, etc.—she commits an infraction of discipline liable to restraint." The sixth parājika rule defines as follows the "eight things" entailing exclusion: "If a nun in prey to desire remains

[46] Nolot 1991: 62.
[47] Ibid., 64–65.

close at hand to a man in prey to desire, or talks with him, or accepts that he holds her hand, or that he holds her cloth, or if she rejoices from his coming, or if she invites him to sit down, or if she stretches her body toward him, or if she goes to a rendezvous, this nun too is excluded, she no longer has a share in religious life." However, until the seventh "thing" or stage there is merely an accumulation of serious offenses, and the exclusion properly speaking takes place only at the eighth stage: "If she commits gradually, one after the other, these eight things, when she has committed them all, her act constitutes a pārājika offense."[48]

Homosexuality

Although there exists in Indian Buddhism no such inclusive term as "homosexuality" or "lesbianism," Vinaya authors were obviously aware of the reality of some of the practices designated by these terms and they were bent on preventing them—within the limits of reason or custom. In most sexual offenses considered by the Vinaya, we are dealing with acts requiring only penance, not exclusion. Significantly, homosexual acts are passed over practically in silence in the case of monks. One of the rare explicit references to sodomy appears incidentally in an anatomic gloss of the *Samantapāsādikā* about the "passage of cereals" or "passage of faeces": "If a bhikkhu practises the sexual act in the passage of faeces by effecting an entrance to the extent of a sesamum, then he becomes guilty of a pārājikā offense."[49] Unless, of course, he finds no pleasure in it. At any rate, this (textual) passage is the only one in which a case of homosexuality is judged liable of exclusion. In another instance, the Buddha judges a case of homosexuality implicating two novices but, significantly, it is their preceptor, Banantuo, whom he reproaches for his laxity.

On the whole, however, the Vinaya pays little attention to these deeds and does not punish offenders severely—particularly when one compares its relative tolerance in that matter with the rigor with which heterosexual acts are condemned and the wealth of details with which they are described. Although (as we will see in Chapter Five) male homosexuality became a prominent feature of the Japanese Buddhist landscape and was raised to the level of a discursive object, such was never the case with female homosexuality. What we would call lesbianism, but for which the Buddhists have no name, was at best perceived as a poor imitation of heterosexual relations—or a preparation for them—and as such condemned. As John Winkler points out in the Greek context, only men count as significant, whereas women do not signify: they are, properly speaking, insignificant. Sexual relations between women are equally in-

[48] Hirakawa 1982: 121.
[49] *Samantapāsādikā*, T. 24, 1462: 722b; Bapat and Hirakawa, trans. 1970: 198.

significant and can be formulated only through male language.[50] The same situation prevailed in the Western context, and we see (pseudo) Inquisitors like Sinistrari d'Ameno, bent on finding everyone guilty, taking great pains to define a "female sodomy" that would be the equivalent of male sodomy.[51] Sinistrari d'Ameno's solution—the discovery of a lesser, female, penis, that allowed some penetration, that is, the clitoris— shows the extent of his predicament. For Buddhist abbots too, as we can infer from the wealth of details regarding *olisboi,* the main problem seems to have been penetration, an act that, implying a breach of the body's integrity, metaphorically signified a breach of the identity of the group.[52]

All forms of promiscuity with other women, in the bath or in the latrine, or of autoeroticism, were forbidden. It is, for instance, prohibited for a nun to undress in the presence of another woman (or even to use the water of her bath!), to be massaged by her, for two women to examine each other while joking, to discuss sexual matters, to sit on the bed of a woman or a young girl, or to examine her wardrobe. Nuns must never sleep two in the same bed, unless one of them is sick. An etiological anecdote traces back the latter interdiction to an episode during which six nuns, having shared the same bed, broke it. The story does not tell how, but the commentary states that if two nuns are obliged in some circumstances to share the same bed, they must at least keep between them an appropriate distance.[53] It is also said that "no woman of bad conduct must be admitted; those whose sexual organs are not normal or who have some secret illness must not either be accepted." Once more we detect the obsessive fear of anything that might threaten the Buddhist

[50] Winkler 1990: 8.

[51] See Chapter 5, note 35 below. The possibility that the work attributed to Sinistrari d'Ameno may be a hoax does not diminish its value; on the contrary: its parodic intent merely accentuates a tendency that might otherwise remain less visible.

[52] Discussing the most revealing item on Artemidoros's oneirological list, a dream in which "a woman penetrates a woman," Winkler argues that the phrase "must not be domesticated by a soft-focus translation, such as 'lesbianism,' for that would be to gloss over the very point where ancient Mediterranean sexual significations diverge from our own, hence the point where they are most revealing. . . . Sexual relations between women can only be articulated here in the significant terms of the system, penetrator vs. penetrated, not as what we would call lesbianism. Sexual relations between women are here classed as 'unnatural' because 'nature' assumes that what are significant in sexual activity are (i) men, (ii) penises that penetrate, and (iii) the articulation thereby of relative statuses through relations of dominance. . . . To penetrate is not all of sex, but it is that aspect of sexual activity which was apt for expressing social relations of honor and shame, aggrandizement and loss, command and obedience, and so it is that aspect which figured most prominently in ancient schemes of sexual classification and moral judgment." See Winkler 1990, 39–40. See also Sinistrari d'Ameno.

[53] Hirakawa 1982: 329–30.

community from outside. But, to quote Sinistrari d'Ameno, "Et haec satis de hoc turpissima iniquitate" (Enough with this shameful iniquity!). Let us move to the next item on our list.

Autoeroticism

We recall how the hero of the *Rou putuan* could find no other escape than castration to end his solitary vice. Not all monks resorted to such drastic methods. Masturbation seems to be a fairly serious offense for members of the monastic community, since it leads to temporary exclusion, and the texts formally prohibit the emission of semen, "except during sleep." Various minor rules aim at divesting the monk's mind from any autoerotic temptation: "When a novice relieves himself, let him do so without looking down"; likewise, the interdiction against taking a bath more than twice a month if one is not sick. The main rule is traced back to the case of the monk Seyyasaka, who, tormented by desire, resorted to masturbation on the advice of an elder monk. Interestingly enough, the story, while denouncing masturbation, emphasizes its beneficial effects on the health of the monk, who soon became "nice looking with round features, of a bright complexion, and a clear skin."[54] Having aroused the suspicion of his fellow monks, he eventually confessed to them, and was chastised in these terms: "Your peace is an illusion. Should we not repel evil thoughts? You, on the contrary, find peace by satisfying your passions!" The Buddha, when told about this, scolded the culprit in much more severe terms: "Imbecile, you publicly hold out your hand to receive alms, and with the same hand you commit horrors." Then he pronounced a new rule, and concluded: "Afraid that this imbecile may later have imitators, I prescribe that the following text be inscribed in the formulary: If a monk, touching his genitals, causes the semen to flow, this monk must confess his offense in front of the chapter and be submitted to canonical penance. . . . However, the fact of having experienced a pollution during sleep does not fall under this prohibition."[55]

Despite this strong condemnation, masturbation was not always taken with as much seriousness as one may expect from a reading of the normative texts, at least in Japan, as we can see from the following anecdote in the *Uji shūi monogatari*:

> Again, long ago there was a man known as Masatoshi the Minamoto Major Counsellor from Kyōgoku. Once when he had sponsored a Buddhist service,

[54] *Vinayapiṭaka* 3: 110, quoted by Fiser 1993: 61.

[55] Wieger 1910: 351. The main rule against masturbation for monks is the *Saṅghādiseṣa* rule 1, *Vinayapiṭaka* 2: 109; for nuns, the *Pācittiya* rules 3 and 4, *Vinayapiṭaka* 4: 259–61, and *Pācittiya* rule 93, *Vinayapiṭaka* 4: 342.

engaging priests to ring bells before the Buddha and choosing men of lifelong chastity to preach on the Sūtra, a priest went up on to the rostrum and with a strange expression on his face seized the bell-stick and brandished it, but failed to strike the bell. After a while the Major Counsellor began to wonder what was wrong. For some time the priest remained silent and everybody began to feel uneasy, then suddenly he quavered, "Does masturbation count?"[56] The whole congregation exploded with laughter, and a retainer called out, "How many times have you done it?" Inclining his head doubtfully, the priest replied, "I did it only last night." At this, the place rang with laughter, and the priest took advantage of the confusion to make a hurried exit.[57]

Autoeroticism could sometimes take strange forms, which the Vinaya duly prohibits. The Dharmaguptaka Vinaya mentions the case of a monk whose body was so supple that he could put his sex into his mouth. He had a doubt, however, and asked the Buddha whether he had committed a pārājika offense. The Buddha said that he had. Another monk, we are told, had a penis so long that he could stick it into his anus. When he inquired whether he had committed a pārājika offense, the Buddha, not surprisingly, answered that he had.[58]

More generally, for the offense to be complete, a monk has to "imagine, masturbate, ejaculate." If he imagines and masturbates but does not ejaculate, there is an offense. However, if he imagines, but does not masturbate and does not ejaculate, no offense.[59] In the end, it seems that the "solitary vice" is vicious precisely because it is solitary: it is not only that masturbation drains the precious juice of life of the individual, or that it represents a moral defeat of the individual addicted to his desire, but it threatens the community by undermining the social behavior of individuals.

The important restriction made by the Buddha, according the Vinaya, about offenses committed in a dream was to give rise to copious commentaries.[60] The *Samantapāsādikā*, for instance, glosses the passage as follows: "The Buddha has laid down precepts to govern bodily activity and not to govern mental activity. Therefore, if the emission is in a dream, then there is no offense."[61] Another commentary describes various possible scenarios: "A bhikkhu dreams that he is carrying on a sex-

---

[56] Mills points out that the word used here, *kawatsurumi*, could mean "sodomy." See Mills 1970: 148 n. 2.

[57] See Mills 1970: 148.

[58] *Dharmaguptaka Vinaya (Sifen lü)* 55. Quoted in a letter from Minakata, to Iwata Jun'ichi, dated 1932/12/11, in Nakazawa 1991–1992, 3: 485. The story of the monk who commits fellatio on himself is also found in the *Mahāsaṅghika Vinaya*.

[59] See Fiser 1993: 60.

[60] See for instance *Sifen lü*, T. 22, 1428: 579b.

[61] *Samantapāsādikā*, T. 24, 1462: 759c; Bapat and Hirakawa, trans. 1970: 356.

act with a woman, or that he embraces her, or that he sleeps with her and if there are, in series, acts of passion like this, which you should yourself know, then even when semen is emitted there is no offense. While the semen is just coming out, if he awakes and, because of his relish in the act of emission, if he holds his organ with his hand, or if he presses it down between his two thighs, then he becomes guilty of an offense. Therefore, if a wise bhikkhu dreams in his sleep, he should be alert and if he should make no movement, then so far so good. If the semen comes out, then lest his clothes and beddings be spoilt, if he holds his organ with his hand and goes to a place where he can wash, then there is no offense."[62]

In the *Zhi chanbing biyao fa* (Secret Essentials to Cure Dhyāna illness, 5th c.), practitioners are warned about the existence of an evil yakṣiṇī named Buti (Skt. Bhūtī?), also called the demon(ess) of dreams, who, among other obstacles to the practice of monks, causes wet dreams.[63] When a monk sees her in a dream and emits semen, he must repent.[64] When semen is emitted voluntarily, "even to the extent sufficient to satiate a fly"—an interesting variant of the sesame seed metaphor—this is an offense liable to temporary exclusion. Before discussing the four main kinds of dreams, the Vinaya commentary distinguishes, in a quasi-Aristotelian style, between seven (sometimes ten) kinds of semen—blue, yellow, red, white, wood-colored, butter-colored, the color of ghee (clarified butter).[65] Ivo Fiser argues that "while these practices were strictly hidden from the eyes of the outside world in most . . . other monastic orders, in the Buddhist Order they were lucidly described, seriously investigated and duly penalized. . . . The calm tone of these passages dealing with sexual problems, the pedantic classification of all the details of facts, possibilities and/or probabilities, and the importance given to these passages in the *Sutta-Vibhanga* are signs of the moral strength of the Order."[66]

Thus, two elements seem to determine the importance of the offense:

[62] Ibid., 761a, p. 362. We find similar statements in the Christian context. See for instance Gratian, Distinction 6, canon 3: "Is it a sin to let oneself be abused by nocturnal images?—There is no sin, when they abuse us despite ourselves; but there is a sin, if by certain movements of our thought we have provoked them." Quoted in Legendre 1974: 158.

[63] Dhyāna illness is a pathological mental or physical state caused by misguided meditation.

[64] T. 15, 620: 341a–b, quoted in Strickmann 1996: 316–17.

[65] *Samantapāsādikā,* 760a; see *Vinayapiṭaka* 3: 114–15. Again: "In the Vinaya, there are seven kinds of semen, but in the *Vibhāṣya* [commentary] are explained in detail ten kinds. Which are those ten? Blue, yellow, red, white, of the colour of wood, of the colour of skin, of the colour of oil, of the colour of milk, of the colour of butter or curds and of the colour of ghee." See Bapat and Hirakawa, trans. 1970: 356–57.

[66] Fiser 1993: 57.

penetration and loss of semen. Ivo Fiser argues that "in all cases of sexual misconduct, at issue is not just control of genital organs but, more importantly, control over a higher organ, the mind. . . . The source of the passion that Buddhists combat is not the penis per se but rather the mind." Thus, there is no offense when semen is emitted unintentionally (for instance in a dream, while defecating, urinating, cherishing lustful thoughts, or bathing in hot water).[67] However, as the above commentary shows, there seems to have been some disagreement on that point. At any rate, the loss of semen is not condemned primarily for its delibitating effects, and early Buddhism on this point differs from Brahmanism or Daoism (and from later Tantrism), for which the retention of semen is of "quintessential" importance for the accumulation of spiritual energy. As Fiser points out: "In what seems almost a parody of the brahmanical notion that a man's physical health is dependent upon retention of his semen, the Vinaya records the case of a young monk who regains his vitality after he begins to masturbate daily."[68]

Generally speaking, a dream is consired blameworthy when it includes commission of a murder, a theft, or an illicit sexual act. To the objection that arises then, namely, that the actions of the dream should, like any other act, lead to retribution, the commentary answers that this is not the case, because the mental actions in the dream are too weak to produce effects.[69] Thus wet dreams, a major bone of contention in early Buddhism, do not constitute an offense according to the Vinaya, which invokes the "exception of the dream" mentioned earlier.[70] However, there may be an offense if the monk goes to sleep with the intention of having a wet dream, or even if he tries without success.[71]

For nuns, too, masturbation is the object of severe and particularly

---

[67] *Vinayapiṭaka* 3: 112. See also the *Samantapāsādikā* gloss: "'The semen is released from its original source': The original source is in the waist. There are others who say: it is not so; the whole of the body has semen, excepting only the hair, nails, dried skin which have no semen. If the semen is released from its original source, whether it enters the [discharging] duct or does not enter the [discharging] duct, and when it comes out even to the extent of what a fly can be satisfied with, then the person becomes guilty of a *saṅghādisēṣa* offense. However, while a man is working hard, or while he is taking an athletic exercise, or when he is sick, if the semen comes out by itself, then there is no offense." See *Samantapāsādikā*, 759c; Bapat and Hirakawa, trans. 1970: 356.

[68] Fiser 1993.

[69] Bapat and Hirakawa, trans. 1970: 62.

[70] Lamotte 1958: 300–1. According to Lamotte, the five propositions advanced by Mahādeva, according to which arhats could have wet dreams, were an attempt to question the privileged status of the arhats in the early Buddhist community, and reflected the viewpoint of lay followers. See also La Vallée Poussin 1927.

[71] Bapat and Hirakawa, trans. 1970: 62.

detailed warnings.[72] In order to prevent it, nuns must above all watch their corporeal attitudes: "Before the night rest, nuns must invoke the Buddha, and fall asleep lying on the side, the body bent, without stretching their legs, their head inclined over their chest, and entirely covered; their hands must stay away from their private parts." All the possibilities—or almost all—are envisaged; for instance, "if a nun masturbates with the palm of her hand, or with a bowl, . . . a small brass cup . . . , or with anything else, and thereby satisfies her sensual desire, she commits an infraction to discipline." The interdiction is the same for all kinds of penetration: thus, a rule concerning the lacquer olisboi states that "if a nun fabricates the replica of a phallus, introduces it in her vagina, and thereby satisfies her sensual desire, she commits a grave offense." The rule concerning personal hygiene is motivated by a question of the nun Prajāpati Gautamī, aunt and adoptive mother of the Buddha: "Blessed One, the sex of women stinks; is it permitted, Blessed One, to wash it?" "It is permitted," answers the Buddha. Then the nuns washed superficially; they still smelled as bad. Gautamī questioned the Buddha about this matter: "Blessed One, is it permitted to wash inside?" "It is permitted." The Buddha then proclaimed the following rule: "The nun who washes herself must do it by introducing a finger wrapped [with cloth]; it is not proper to introduce it too far and thus to satisfy sensual desire; if a nun introduces her finger too far and thus satisfies sensual desire, she commits a serious offense."[73] However, the Pāli Vinaya is less detailed than its Sanskrit counterpart with respect to female masturbation. It gives only one example of self-gratification, called "a slap with the palm of the hand" (on the cunnus), *tala-ghātakam*: "Now at that time two nuns, tormented by sexual urge, having entered an inner room, slapped with the palms of the hand." The *Mahāsaṅghika-bhikṣunī-vinaya* speaks of a nun who "was overcome with passion and patted her pubic region with the hand."[74] Other examples include a nun who, while washing her organ, inserts her finger further than the first knuckle so as to satisfy her sexual desire; or who, for the same purpose, pushes a cloth

[72] Here is how Lamotte, in a footnote to the *Traité*, describes this offense, in veiled (Latin) terms (which must remain veiled): "Si qua religiosa voluntarie semen emiserit, aliter ac in somno, erit pātayantikā" (quoting *Shi song liu,* T. 1435: 344b27). Cf. T. 212: 664b6, " 'emisit semen super terram.' Etenim prohibitio emissionis seminalis (lingua sanscrita, śuk-ravisṛṣṭi; lingua sinica che tsing) a primo saṃghāvaśeṣadharma, quae continetur in regula religiosorum (*bhikṣuprātimokṣa*), reassumitur in regula relogiosarum (*bhikṣunīprātimok-ṣa*)." See Lamotte 1944–1980, 2: 807 n. 4.

[73] Nolot 1991; Hirakawa 1982: 392–94.

[74] See *Vinayapiṭaka* 4: 260 (*Pācittiya* 3), quoted in Fiser 1993: 61; and see translation by Hirakawa 1982: 392.

into her organ during her menstrual period, or flushes her organ with falling water; or, taking a bath in a rapid stream, stands with her organ against the stream; or, finally, pushes up her organ various kinds of roots (turnip roots, small onions).[75]

Precautions against the autoerotic temptations of the woman, who is by (Buddhist) definition a creature controlled by her sexual desires, do not stop here. Thus, the rule concerning menstrual cloth gives the following details: "The woman who has her menses and loses blood must wear a cloth. It is not proper to wear it too tight; it is not proper to introduce it too far, in order to thus satisfy sensual desire; on the contrary it must be introduced in a very loose fashion into the vagina. If a nun introduces it too far or too tight, so that she satisfies her sensual desire, she commits a serious offense." Likewise, the rule concerning the bath: "If a nun keeps her sex under a water nozzle, under the jet of a jug, . . . or under the water of a duct, and thus satisfies sensual desire, she commits a serious offense. If she bathes in a lake, in a stream, or under the water of a duct, she must not bathe facing the water flow." Finally, to leave nothing to chance as far as olisboi are concerned, there exists a rule regarding the vegetal substitutes for the penis: "If a nun satisfies herself with a radish, an onion, a cabbage, a root of horseradish, a creeper, a cucumber, a colocynth, a gourd, a pumpkin, or any other object, and thus satisfies sensual desire, she commits a serious offense."[76] The nuns must also on all occasions avoid arousing desire in others. Among the various rules, there is even one regarding the way of sitting: "It is not proper for a nun to sit with her legs crossed [in lotus or half-lotus position]; on the contrary, she must sit in crossed position with a single foot and cover her vagina with the heel of the other."[77] Furthermore, "when she puts on a band to cover her breasts, she must do it so that her breasts are compressed."[78] All these rules suggest that the woman—nun or laywoman—remains an object of desire for the monk. Possessed by an inclination to lust that is difficult to control, she becomes even more dangerous. The entire Vinaya seems to derive from this fundamental asymmetry between genders, an asymmetry to which we will have occasion to return.

[75] This latter form of self-gratification became, we are told, the cause of the death of Empress Shōtoku. See Chapter 3 at n. 103.

[76] Nolot 1991 par. 274.

[77] In the *Mahāsaṅghika Vinaya*, this posture is said to prevent snakes from entering the woman's vagina. See *Minakata Kumagusu zenshū*, vol. 2: 475–77. Stories of lustful snakes attracted by women's genitalia are frequent in Japanese Buddhist collections of tales like the *Nihon ryōiki* or the *Konjaku monogatari shū*. See Nakamura 1973 and Frank 1968.

[78] See Nolot 1991 par. 263; Hirakawa 1982: 394–98.

THE RISE OF MAHĀYĀNA PRECEPTS

Compared to the "orgy" of details in the Indian Vinaya, the Chinese and Japanese commentaries, as well as the "Pure Rules" (Ch. *qinggui*, J. *shingi*) of Chan/Zen (which should be distinguished from the Vinaya properly speaking), are rather discreet with regards to sexual prohibitions. Perhaps the interiorization of Buddhist ethics made the formalism of the earlier period look at first glance superfluous.

One of the rare Chinese monastic regulations to elaborate on the question of sexuality seem to be that of the Ming Chan master Zhuhong. In his *Ten Things for the Cultivation of the Self*, Zhuhong describes the "seventh thing" as follows: "Do not go near women: If one enters into friendship with young nuns, adopts a woman from the outside world as a godmother, goes frequently to relatives' homes to visit relatives or dependants, or even if one lives with his mother who is not yet seventy, oblivious of ridicule and suspicion; all these are regarded as being near women."[79] Zhuhong is also famous for his double-entry moral bookkeeping. In his *Record of Self-Knowledge* (*Zizhi lu*), he puts a price on every good and bad deed.[80] On the whole, however, perhaps due to Confucian influence, Chinese and Japanese monastic rules remain extremely abstract and euphemized; or perhaps there was not much to add to the overwhelming detail of Indian Vinaya. Mahāyāna precepts were influenced by the notion that "defilements are awakening, saṃsāra is no different from nirvāṇa." The development of a new type of Mahāyāna precepts, called "bodhisattva precepts" (Ch. *pusajie*, J. *bosatsukai*), results in part from the awareness of the excessive rigor of Indian Vinaya, judged ill-adapted to Chinese realities and to the compassionate ideal of Mahāyāna. In order to transform the ritualism of Indian Vinaya, Chinese Buddhists have tended to interiorize its observance and to emphasize the

[79] See Yü 1981: 205.

[80] This is how Zhuhong evaluates the following "miscellaneous bad deeds": To have sexual intercourse with extremely close kin counts as fifty demerits. To have sexual intercourse with a prostitute counts as two demerits. To have sexual intercourse with a nun or a chaste widow counts as fifty demerits. If upon seeing a beautiful woman of a good family, one desires to make love to her, count two demerits. (This is for lay people. In the case of a monk, no matter whether the woman is related to oneself or not, of good family, or of lowly origin, to commit such an offence will be counted uniformly as fifty demerits, and to have the desire to make love to her will be counted uniformly as two demerits." (Yü 1981: 252) This kind of moral bookkeeping had a long history in Daoism, and it is found in Buddhist apocrypha such as the *Tiwei jing* (Sūtra of Trapuṣa [and Ballika], 5th century). See Ms. 2051 in the Stein Chinese Collection of Dunhuang Manuscripts, British Museum, London; and Ms. 3732 in the Pelliot Chinese Collection of Dunhuang Manuscripts, Bibliothèque Nationale, Paris.

state of mind of the practitioner rather than the detail of the prohibitions. However, the contrast between these two types of discipline must be nuanced. There are all kinds of intermediary Vinayas, and counterexamples abound. Thus, whereas intention plays a significant role in the "Hīnayānist" Vinaya, the *Fanwang jing* is in some respects extremely ritualistic.

In China, monastic discipline had already aroused a renewed interest during the Tang with the constitution of a "Vinaya school" (*Lü zong*) by Daoxuan (597–667) and the appearance of many ordination platforms. Meanwhile, the new Chan school, in its theoretical extremism, had come to challenge the very notion of a Buddhist "morality"—or at least to empty its content by reinterpreting it in a purely spiritual fashion. The fourth Chan patriarch Daoxin (580–651), for instance, on the basis of an often-quoted passage from the *Puxian guan jing* (Sūtra on the Contemplation of Samantabhadra), defines the "primordial repentance" as follows: "Those who want to repent, let them sit correctly and concern themselves with ultimate reality!" The point is to realize, through sitting meditation, that all acts, whether good or bad, are fundamentally empty. A similar notion is found in the *Platform Sūtra,* that of an "informal repentance" or of "formless precepts"—said to correspond to ultimate reality, or the realization of the fundamental principle of all things, rather than to the literal observance of Vinaya, which still belongs to the realm of phenomenal multiplicity and conventional truth. Another example is provided by a passage of the *Damo lun* (Treatise of Bodhidharma), in which the second patriarch Huike answers as follows to a disciple who asked to be confessed:

HUIKE: "Bring me your offenses, and I'll confess you."

DISCIPLE: "My offenses have neither form nor graspable character, how could I bring them to you?"

HUIKE: "You are therefore confessed by me. Go back to your cell. If you had committed an offense, you would indeed have to confess it; but since you don't find any, you don't need confession."

DISCIPLE: "Tell me how to cut off my passions."

HUIKE: "Where are they, that you want to cut them off?"

DISCIPLE: "I don't know."

HUIKE: "If you don't know, it is because they are like space. What idea of space do you have, to speak of cutting it off?"

DISCIPLE: "Is it not said in a sūtra: cut all evil, cultivate all good, and you will become a buddha?"

HUIKE: "Those are false notions objectified by your mind."[81]

---

[81] See Faure 1986: 131.

According to the *Wusheng fangbian men* (Gate of the Non-Born Upā-ya) attributed to the Northern Chan master Shenxiu (d. 706), "The bodhisattva precepts consist in observing the 'mind precepts,' whose essence is no other than the buddha nature [in everyone]. As soon as the mind is aroused, one goes astray from this buddha nature, which amounts to transgressing the bodhisattva precepts. Conversely, he who prevents the mind from being aroused conforms to the buddha nature, and by the same token, he observes the bodhisattva precepts."[82] Likewise, in the *Platform Sūtra* attributed to Shenxiu's rival, the "sixth patriarch" Huineng, the adept is invited to take refuge in its fundamental nature: any attempt to control the mind vitiated by the three poisons is judged superfluous. From this standpoint, as the *Dunwu zhenzong lun* puts it, "to consider that there are precepts is to lose the [true] precepts."[83] The emphasis was laid on a "formless repentance" that aimed at realizing the emptiness of passions, rather than on actual transgressions. Already present in early Chan, for example in texts such as the *Wusheng fangbian men* or the *Platform Sūtra*, this tendency seemed to lend itself to laxity. This is, at least, what is suggested by criticisms like that of Zongmi (780–841) against the Bao Tang school of Chan, or that of the Tokugawa Zen master Dokuan Genkō (1630–1698) against monks who neglected the Vinaya and the Buddhist teachings on the authority of Huineng and the *Platform Sūtra*.[84]

Various canonical writings, including several "apocryphal" scriptures, played an important role in the development of the bodhisattva precepts. *The Sūtra of Brahma's Net* (*Fanwang jing*), by far the most popular, reduces the number of precepts to fifty-eight (from 250)—consisting of ten major interdictions and forty-eight minor ones. This new kind of precepts are characterized above all by their altruistic nature, and they are supposed to express the three aspects of Buddhist morality: to stop committing evil, to cultivate goodness, and to act for the benefit of others. The ordination ritual defined by this text is also considerably simplified. We witness an interiorization of the precepts as a function of contemplative practice, since the goal is to transmute the "three poisons" (hatred, love, and ignorance) through spiritual contemplation.

The ten major precepts of the *Fanwang jing* deal with not killing, not stealing, not indulging in sexual misconduct, not lying, not drinking alcohol, not speaking about the faults of others, not praising oneself while denigrating others, not reviling others, not bearing a grudge, and not speaking ill of the Three Jewels (Buddha, Dharma, Saṅgha). Offense

[82] See Suzuki 1968: 168.
[83] T. 85, 2835: 1279b.
[84] Cf. *Dokuan dokugo*, T. 82, 2597: 565a.

against these ten precepts make a man *pārājika,* that is, unworthy; but they do not lead, as in early Buddhism, to the expulsion of the culprit, since the "essence of the precepts," once acquired, can never be lost: once a bodhisattva, always a bodhisattva. Thus, the culprit can now rehabilitate himself through his own repentence and through the merits of others.[85] This attractive feature may, incidentally, have contributed to the moral decline of the clergy.

The third precept emphasizes the importance of chastity:

> A son of the Buddha must refrain from sexual misconduct, by committing an improper act himself, by causing someone else to engage in such acts, or by indulging in sexual relations with women. There are causes and conditions, methods and acts that lead to illicit sex. He must never intentionally engage in sexual relations with animals, celestial beings, or spirits of the opposite sex. He must never use the unnatural ways.[86] A bodhisattva whose state of mind conforms to filial piety must lead others to liberation and teach the pure Dharma to people. If, on the contrary, he were to produce lustful thoughts with regard to beings, such that without distinguishing between animals, on the one hand, and his mother, daughters, sisters, and the six types of relatives, on the other, he were to engage in illicit sex, lacking the spirit of compassion, this would constitute a pārājika offense for this bodhisattva.[87]

The thirty-sixth rule returns to that point: "When a son of the Buddha has produced the ten great vows, upholding the precepts of the Buddha, he must also make the following vow: I would rather throw myself into a roaring fire, or onto a mountain of swords, than break the precepts of the buddhas of the three periods by commiting impure acts with women."[88] As de Groot points out, whereas sexual incontinence is prohibited, it seems that carnal relations are not absolutely forbidden. Nevertheless, they are checked by every means: monks must in particular abstain from alcohol or aliments such as the five strong flavors (garlic, onions, ginger, Chinese chives, leeks), which are held to be aphrodisiac.

The *Fanwang jing* manifests its ecumenism by clearly taking the opposite course from classical Vinaya with regard to criteria for inclusion into or exclusion from the monastic community. The fortieth rule, in particular, establishes that one must not discriminate between those who come to receive the bodhisattva precepts—kings and princes, great ministers and public officials, monks and nuns, laymen and laywomen, heavenly beings, people of no sex or hermaprodites, eunuchs or slaves, demons or

---

[85] See Pettazzoni 1932: 197–98.

[86] Ishida Mizumaro glosses *feidao,* "unnatural ways," as the nongenital orifices (anus, mouth) in the case of a woman. See Ishida 1971: 88–89.

[87] See de Groot 1893: 34.

[88] See Ishida 1971: 216; de Groot 1893: 67.

spirits. Bodhisattva precepts are open to all, even "eunuchs, lascivious women, demons, and beasts."[89] However, as Paul Groner points out, "it is not clear that the universal assembly of people of all classes envisioned in the *Fan-wang ching* ever existed."[90]

This apocryphal—that is to say, Chinese—"sūtra," and the trend of the bodhisattva precepts as a whole, are generally perceived as representative of a Mahāyāna tendency to interiorize religious experience. They would represent a kind of Buddhist Protestantism, marking the passage from a purely external and formalist morality to an interiorized ethic. Even if there is some truth to this, it would be wrong to push the comparison too far. It is important to note the way in which this text has also contributed to revalorizing, and at the same time denying, the human body, which it turns into an object of sacrifice. The forty-eighth rule, concerning offerings to the scriptures, stipulates indeed that a "son of the Buddha" must worship and copy the scriptures, and in order to achieve this must not shrink from any sacrifice. He must be ready to use his skin as parchment, his blood as ink, his marrow as liquid to dilute the ink (a typically Chinese detail), and his bones as brushes. Although this aspect has gone unnoticed by most commentators, the *Fanwang jing* also incites one to real mutilations—and perhaps contributed significantly to the vogue of immolation in China after the sixth century: "If one does not burn one's body, one's arm, one's finger as an offering to the Buddhas, . . . one is not a bodhisattva."[91]

Admittedly, Mahāyāna morality is no longer simply the first of the traditional "three studies": morality (*śīla*), concentration (*samādhi*), and wisdom (*prajñā*). As the privileged expression of Buddhist compassion, it acquires an ethical dimension that allows it to subsume all other practices. The *Fanwang jing* defines transgression as an offense inasmuch as it implies a lack of compassion, but it adds that a transgression can sometimes result from compassion, in which case there is no offense. As we can see, the formal criteria that allowed automatic judgment of the nature of the act tend to vanish. It is perhaps in reaction to this tendency that Zhuhong will try to determine in such a precise—and quasi-automatic—fashion the value of every act.

In a curious manner, this interiorization of morality, which tends to

[89] See the comment in *Sanbō ekotoba*, in Kamens 1988: 321–22: "On this basis, in both China and Japan generations of emperors and empresses and gentlemen and ladies of good family, inspired with faith, have asked monks to administer these precepts to them. Eunuchs may be thought of as degenerates; lascivious women are sensual sinners. Spirits and demons have fierce hearts; dumb animals dwell in ignorance. But all have access to this blessing."

[90] Groner 1990: 256.

[91] De Groot 1893: 207.

give priority to the intention over the act, is found in the same texts that reflect an increasing ritualization of penance and of the act. Pettazzoni saw in this ritualization, perhaps mistakenly, a return to ideas and forms of material and magical elimination of sins that "original" Buddhism was supposed to have left behind.[92] By the same token, according to him, contrition was eventually relegated to the background, particularly in Japan, where "an act of inner religiosity as deep as Buddhist penance was in the beginning becomes therefore a collective rite of elimination of sins for the good of the community."[93] Thus, during the six days of monthly fasting of the poṣadha, one recites the fifty-eight rules of the *Fanwang jing* in front of the images of buddhas and bodhisattvas. Ritual confession and repentence for offenses have also become prolegomena to ordination. According to the twenty-third minor rule of the above sūtra: "When a son of Buddha, after the nirvāṇa of the Buddha, with the right frame of mind wants to receive the bodhisattva precepts, he must personally vow in front of the images of buddhas and bodhisattvas to receive the precepts. Then he must during seven days repent in front of the buddhas. If auspicious signs appear, he has received the precepts; otherwise, he must continue during twice seven days, during thrice seven days, even during one year until these signs appear."[94] We have here, obviously, a form of ritual that implies the active and absolving presence of Buddhist deities in their icons. This pietistic atmosphere, at first glance, does not seem to predispose to laxity or antinomianism, as some have accused the bodhisattva precepts of doing. The majority of Buddhists were no longer concerned with awakening, but rather with the accomplishment of ritualized, routinized existence, dominated by the monastic rule.

In Japan, orthodox Vinaya was first transmitted in 736 by the Northern Chan monk Daoxuan (J. Dōsen, not to be confused with the homonymous Vinaya master). However, it is only with the arrival of Jianzhen (J. Ganjin, 688–763) and his disciples in 753 that orthodox ordination became possible. After founding Tōshōdaiji, Ganjin conferred the *shami* (novice) precepts to the retired emperor Shōmu and his consort Kōmyō, and to their daughter, Empress Kōken, under the impassive gaze of the Great Buddha of Tōdaiji. After him, the Japanese Ritsu school became an active school. However, this reform rejected as irregular a large number of clerics who had been ordained previously under the authority of the state. Before that, Buddhist clerics were regulated by the state through the *Sōniryō*, "Rules for Monks and Nuns," based on both the Indian Vinaya and the *Fanwang jing*. The two types of Vinaya coexisted in the

[92] Pettazzoni 1932: 206.
[93] Ibid., 208.
[94] Ishida 1971: 186; de Groot 1893: 56.

so-called Vinaya of the Southern capital (Nara), according to the belief that "Hīnayāna penances have the effect of erasing minor transgressions; Mahāyāna penances effectively save us from heavy sins."[95] With the development of Tendai during the Heian period, however, the bodhisattva precepts became autonomous. Whereas in China these precepts were eventually added to traditional precepts without supplanting the latter, only in Japan, within the Tendai school—and owing to the efforts of its founder Saichō (762–822)—did the Mahāyāna precepts succeed in superseding the precepts of the so-called Lesser Vehicle. By the same token, the Tendai obtained its independence from the traditional Buddhist schools of the ancient capital Nara: its adepts, in order to become monks, no longer needed to ascend the official ordination platforms of the great Nara monasteries. The Tendai school emphasized the importance of the so-called perfect and sudden precepts (endonkai), in other words, of a spontaneous action deriving from fundamental awakening. These precepts were those of the Fanwang jing, which until then had played a subsidiary role.[96] The structure of ordination remained the same, however. The three preceptors of traditional ordination were merely replaced by invisible preceptors—Śākyamuni, Mañjuśrī, and Maitreya—whereas the seven witnesses became all the buddhas of the ten directions. With this new type of ordination, the observance of the precepts (and therefore their transgression) became purely interiorized.

The trend of the "mind precepts," initiated in early Chan, found one expression during the Kamakura period in the so-called Bodhidharma school (Damo zong) or in the Shinshū school. For other masters like Yōsai, however, the Zen school "takes Vinaya as its fundamental principle."[97] The "One-Mind precepts," as they are transmitted in Zen, are for some the same as the "perfect and sudden" precepts of Tendai, and are consequently incompatible with Indian Vinaya. But in the end, one emphasizes the necessity of practicing the two disciplinary systems jointly. In some cases, it seems that the will to interiorize discipline led to a challenging of all norms; in other cases (with Yōsai, Dōgen, and other masters of the Kamakura period), it led to a renewal of Vinaya and to a return to the notion of "joint practice" of the Hīnayāna and Mahāyāna precepts. However, the impact was felt even in traditional Buddhism. As Mujū Ichien (1226–1312), a Zen master who became paradoxically a spokesman for Nara Buddhism, puts it: "Although something may be forbidden by the regulations, do not neglect to form a favorable karmic affinity with it if you believe that such an affinity will bear fruit; and even though

[95] Sanbō ekotoba, in Kamens 1988: 255.
[96] On this question, see Groner 1990.
[97] See Kōzen gokokuron, T. 80, 2543: 79.

something may be advocated in the sūtras, if you suspect that it may contain an impediment to salvation, eschew it."[98]

. . . . .

The moral dilemma, unresolved tension, or aporia between the observance of the rule and its transgression may be seen as intrinsic to Buddhism, or as an unfortunate result of its historical development. The initial rigor was followed by a fundamental ambivalence, product of the philosophical dialectic of Mahāyāna. We are thus faced with a morality of ambivalence: on the doctrinal level (with the Two Truths) and the disciplinary level (with the two types of rule). The rigor of Vinaya, however, seems to go astray from the golden mean and contradicts the example given by the very life of the Buddha. Later Buddhists have always been embarrassed by the apparent laxity of the Buddha, at least with regard to food.[99] Perhaps it is for this laxity that he was criticized by his cousin and unfortunate rival Devadatta, whose misdeeds, if we are to believe a resolutely biased tradition, led him directly into hell. But the "heresy" of Devadatta remained apparently popular in India centuries after the death of the Buddha, according to the testimony of the Chinese pilgrim Faxian (d. ca. 420).[100] Perhaps Devadatta's only offense was to have advocated stricter austerities (to wear rags, to live in the forest under a tree, to observe a strict vegetarianism), and thus to have caused a schism. He may have been in a sense out-Heroding Herod, outdoing the Buddha himself in his asceticism. Contrary to the later tradition, early Buddhism was probably not vegetarian. If the image of an originally "pure" Buddhism needs some revisions on this point, the same may be true, as I will try to show, on other points of this idealized tradition as well.

What seems certain for now is that, with regard to Vinaya as well as to doctrine, Buddhism is characterized by a deep ambivalence, a rather convenient system of twofold truth—since what is true for some is not always so for others. Thus, the Buddha, although he had scolded his disciple Piṇḍola for having shown his powers, was led to perform a miracle in response to the challenge of some heretics. Sensing the perplexity of King Bimbisara, he justified himself as follows: "Great king, this precept applied only to my disciples. . . . I have not proclaimed a precept for myself."[101] And the Buddha compared himself to a king who, when he proclaims a law to prevent people from stealing the fruit in his gardens, is

[98] See *Shasekishū*, in Morrell 1985: 121.
[99] See Arthur Waley, "Did Buddha Die of Eating Pork?" In Morris 1970: 338–49.
[100] See Legge 1965: 21 and 62.
[101] See Burlingame 1921: 38–39.

not subject to this law himself. The king, source of mundane laws, is by nature or convention above them: he does not even have to transgress them. Is the same reasoning valid in the case of the precepts set forth by the Buddha? If these precepts express the Buddhist Law, can the Buddha be above that Law? Or else, if the Buddha and the Dharma are coeternal, is not the Buddha more precisely the *lex incarnata?* The same argument could be made (and was indeed made) by Chan or Tantric masters—as we will see in Chapter Three. For regular monks, however, Vinaya remained important, and was furthermore complemented in China and Japan by an elaborate state jurisprudence, the *Sōniryō* (Rules for Monks and Nuns).

Chapter 3

THE IDEOLOGY OF TRANSGRESSION

> Those who keep the rules are asses, those who break the
> rules are men.
> (Ikkyū)
>
> The road of excess leads to the palace of wisdom.
> (William Blake)

T HE LOGIC of transcendence that characterizes Mahāyāna Buddhism implies, in its very principle, a transgression of all fixed
rules. As Georges Bataille puts it, "The knowledge of eroticism,
or of religion, requires a personal experience, equal and contradictory, of
taboo and transgression."[1] Likewise, according to Michel Foucault, "At
the root of sexuality, of the movement that nothing can ever limit (because it is, from its birth and in its totality, constantly involved with the
limit), . . . a singular experience is shaped: that of transgression."[2] Indeed, transgression constitutes a determining hagiographical motif in
East Asian Buddhist chronicles. There are, of course, different Buddhist
notions of transgression: juridical, disciplinary, ritual, oneirical, literary,
philosophical, and so on. From the philosophical standpoint, transgression derives from a position called antinomianism. We find in Buddhism
two basic types of antinomianism: a naturalist or "spontaneist" tendency, according to which the saint's hubris places him above ordinary
moral rules—as in the case of Tantric or Chan "madmen"; and a systematic ritual inversion of the rule, based on a specific cosmological theory
like that of the yin and yang (for instance, in the Tachikawa school of
Shingon).

In their reaction against the excesses of Indian legalism, some adepts of
the Great Vehicle fell into the opposite excess, advocating a rejection of
all rules. The affirmation of the properly amoral nature of awakening
and the superiority of transgression over the strict (and at times fussy)
observance of discipline finds an expression in the story of Prasannendriya and Agramati. Agramati fell into hell despite his strict observance of the Buddhist precepts, while Prasannendriya, who saw the identity of passions and awakening, became a Buddha. As Rolf Stein points

[1] Bataille 1957: 42.
[2] Foucault 1977: 33.

out, the concept of "pivoting" or "inversion" (*paravṛtti*) seems to underlie the notion according to which, instead of rejecting desire and sexuality, it is better to transmute them through meditation. Without the caterpillar, there would be no butterfly. The logic of transcendence that characterizes Buddhist concentration and wisdom implies, in its very principle, a transgression of all fixed rules. Such an "inversion" is precisely what allows the boddhisattva to consumate the sexual act without being defiled by it. In the *Śūraṃgama-sūtra,* a bodhisattva is shown making love to the daughters of Māra in order to free them, in sharp contrast to Śākyamuni, who resisted temptation by turning them away. The same motif appears in Chinese and Japanese legends about Guanyin (J. Kannon) and various other bodhisattvas.

The figure of Prasannendriya inspired many "biographies" of eminent monks. We are told, for instance, that the Korean priest Wŏnhyo (617–686) did not hesitate to transgress Buddhist precepts by frequently visiting brothels. This attitude could still be interpreted as a form of Buddhist detachment, such as that illustrated in various canonical scriptures like the *Vimalakīrtinirdeśa.* But Wŏnhyo was not merely motivated by proselytism, and he did not stop halfway. Indeed, if he were not such an eminent monk some might even think that he turned back and ultimately fell into Māra's net, the trap of profane life. As the *Samguk yusa* reports, "One day Wŏnhyo saw bees and butterflies flying from flower to flower, and felt a violent desire for a woman. He walked in the streets of Kyongju, singing: 'Who will lend me an axe that has lost its handle? I want to cut a pole that will sustain the heaven!' Passers-by laughed at him, without understanding the true meaning of his song; but T'aejong [King Muryol], when he heard it, said: 'This monk, mad with love, wants to marry a noble lady to beget a wise son. The birth of such a sage would be a blessing for our country.'" Wŏnhyo eventually married a princess, and the son who was born from their union became one of the "ten sages" of the Silla kingdom—justifying ex post facto his father's decision to break his monastic vows.[3]

Buddhism remained ambivalent concerning its condemnation of transgression. In his *Mirror for Women,* the Zen master Mujū Ichien (1226–1312) seems to consider that there are two different standards in this domain:

An ancient said: "Offences committed by a sage are like the iron pot which, however large, does not sink; those of stupid people are like the gravel that sinks, even if it is as light as sand." We know the case of Lady Mallika, who observed the Precepts while taking drugs, and that of Vasumitra, who led a pure life in the midst of debauchery; one cannot deny that these women were

[3] See Ilyŏn 1972: 306.

sages. Although the Buddha Śākyamuni alone is exalted in the Three Periods, and was a Tathāgata since the most distant antiquity, he had three children from three different wives. . . . However, we do not speak of the Buddha as an impure being. The Prince Shōtoku was a manifestation of Guze Kannon, and he appeared in our country in order to spread Buddhism. Nevertheless, he had five children. Furthermore, although he attacked Moriya and committed a murder, we cannot speak of him as an 'immoral prince.' All these actions reflected the elevated behavior of the Bodhisattvas, they were virtuous deeds accomplished in the state of Buddhahood, salvific means to help sentient beings."[4]

In other words: do not judge the apparent transgressions of the buddhas, bodhisattvas, and saints by the same standards that you would apply to ordinary people. As we shall see in the next chapter, this distinction would time and again prove crucial in response to the charge of monastic misconduct.

THE RULE OF ANTINOMIANISM

Because the mind of the sage shows no discrimination, he should not be discriminated against. A paradoxical justification for Buddhist transgression appears in some Buddhist texts: one may kill, steal, and have sex to the extent that one realizes that everything is empty. In the *Jueguan lun* (Treatise on Absolute Contemplation), for instance, we find the following dialogue between a (fictitious) master and his disciple: "Question: 'Are there certain causes and conditions which allow one to indulge in sex?' Answer: 'Heaven covers the earth, the yang unites with the yin; a privy receives leakage from above, spring water flows into ditches. If your mind is like that, nowhere will it encounter any obstacle. However, if feelings produce discrimination, even your own wife will defile your mind.' "[5]

In Praise of Folly

> "Though this be madness, yet there is method in't."
> (Polonius, in *Hamlet* 2.2.223)

Another widespread justification of transgression is holy madness. In many cultures, the sage behaves as a madman or an idiot; he is charac-

---

[4] See Morrell 1980: 57–58.
[5] See Yanagida and Tokiwa, eds., 1976: 94.

terized by an excess or hubris that leads him to deny social norms in order to transcend them. In Christianity, eschatological folly finds its paradigmatic expression with Paul. The true disciple of Christ must appear to be mad in the eyes of the world, by virtue of the principle that divine wisdom appears as folly to men.[6] Next to mystical madness, we also find a simulated or strategic madness. Actually, these two strands are often difficult to differentiate, as they converge within a single tradition or even within a single individual. According to Laozi, the sage is the one who "leaves no track," for he has learned how to "mingle with the dust" and "hide his light." The motif of dirt and refuse ("mingling with the dust") refers also to all that cannot be assimilated, all that remains outside the system or institutional structure—being literally refused. The true Daoist looks like a simpleton because he wants to "suck at his mother's breast," to remain totally dependent on the Dao. Fools "have magical affinities with chaos that might allow them to serve as scapegoats on behalf of order; yet thay elude the sacrifice or the banishment that would affirm order at their expense."[7] In an insane society, only through feigned madness will the sage avoid disaster

In its initial refusal to comply with social norms, Buddhism too implied a kind of "controlled madness," and Confucian critics have not failed to condemn its asocial nature. Insofar as Buddhist "madness" questioned monastic or ascetic norms, however, it constituted as it were a double madness—a madness within madness itself.[8] In the *Lives of Eminent Monks,* one reads about Chinese monks who violate the monastic code with complete impunity: they drink, eat meat, play, fight, and use vulgar language. Much more rarely, however, do they transgress the sexual taboo. Generally speaking, not only do these "crazy monks" know the limits of transgression, but transgression itself seems to be inscribed within precise ritual and social contexts. The Buddhist "madman" is basically a hyperbole of the ascetic: whereas the latter rejects the rules of profane life, the crazy monk, in a typically Mahāyānist move of double negation, rejects even the rules of monastic life. In both cases, it is a matter of a mystical hubris that rejects the *aurea mediocritas* of the conventional Middle Way. Although the two types of transgression remain quite distinct, the affinities between the two figures explain why one finds them side by side in Buddhist hagiography.

Larvato prodeo: the image of the sage "advancing hidden" behind his

---

[6] "If any man among you seemeth to be wise in this world, let him become a fool, that he may be wise. For the wisdom of this world is foolishness with God." (1 Cor. 3:18; see also ibid. 4:10)

[7] William Willeford, quoted in Girardot 1983: 271.

[8] Concerning Japanese Buddhism, see "A Buddhist Paradox: The Aesthetics of Madness," in Marra 1991, ch. 3.

mask of folly is quite popular, for instance, in Chan literature. A case in point is that of Mingcan, alias Lancan ("Lazy Can"), a Northern Chan adept who, upon being invited to court by the emperor, did not even bother to blow his running nose or stop eating his roasted sweet potato to greet the imperial messenger.[9] Lancan's folly was highly praised in Japan by another famous "madman," Ikkyū Sōjun: "How about Lancan turning down the imperial order? / Sweet potatoes locked in smoke in the bamboo stove. / His great activity manifesting itself, this true monk, / On the master's face, throws slop water."[10] Another typical Chan madman was Puhua, the companion of Linji Yixuan (d. 867), the famous Chan Master, about whom Ikkyū wrote the following poem ("Praising Puhua"): "How about if Deshan and Linji traveled along with him? / His mad antics on the street and in the marketplace amazed everyone. / Of all the Zen monks who died either sitting or standing, few could better him. / Ringing in harmony, faintly, the sound of a jeweled bell."[11]

Despite their importance in Chan Buddhism, these eccentrics seem to represent the nostalgia of a lost spontaneity that contemporary imitations made even more distant; for all the lip service, "crazy Chan" was still perceived as a dangerous ideal by (and for) the majority of Chinese Buddhists. Chan madmen have always been an endangered, or at least "protected," species. They serve as an outlet or alibi for a tradition that is at bottom ritualist and hierarchical. Perhaps "madness" was too subversive for a Chan orthodoxy that, by placing the "ex-centrics" at the center of its discourse, always tried to neutralize or exorcize them. As Guifeng Zongmi (d. 841), one of the advocates of this orthodoxy, put it: "Although they are all shadows and reflections of the Chan school . . . , one cannot rely exclusively on them to represent the Dharma of Śākyamuni."[12]

Another feature that needs to be emphasized in the case of Chinese Buddhist tricksters is their function as deities of life. The popular tradition coopted Hanshan and Shide to turn them into "gods of union."[13] A similar destiny is that of Wanhui (d. 711), a monk and thaumaturge whose predictions made a deep impression in the Tang court. His legend turned him into a kind of Daoist immortal who participates in the banquets of the Queen Mother of the West (Xiwangmu). During the Song, he

---

[9] See *Jingde chuandeng lu,* T. 51, 2076: 461c.

[10] Arntzen 1986: 110–11.

[11] Ibid., 112.

[12] See *Chanyuan zhuquanji duxu,* T. 48, 2015: 412c.

[13] Although their friendship may have had homosexual connotations, those connotations are not apparent in the texts. Significantly, Hanshan and Shide (J. Kanzan and Jittoku) are sometimes represented in feminine form in Japanese woodblock prints.

is represented as a disheveled and hilarious buffoon like Hanshan and Shide, with whom he tends to be confused under the name Huohe ("Double Harmony")—sometimes represented in dual form as the gods Huo and He. The tendency to become double in relation to sexual symbolism is, according to Lévi-Strauss, one of the features of tricksters, who are often twins.[14] References to fecundity are also obvious in the case of Budai, the pot-bellied laughing Buddha, often depicted as literally covered with children.

In Tibet also, a certain type of saints, the siddhas, famous for their powers (*siddhi*), have been called "madmen" (*smyon-pa*) because of their paradoxical, nonconventional behavior. There is clearly an analogy between them and the "wild Chan masters," although influences in one direction or another remain to be proved. Milarepa (1040–1123), the "Tibetan Buddha," used to say, for instance, that he was "mad" with the ecstasy of the union with the "Great Seal" (*mahāmudrā*). However, as Rolf Stein points out, this appellation must not "give the impression that these men encouraged an immoral or amoral behavior for ordinary people or that they gave themselves over to excess."[15] Some of them attempted to reconcile the "mystical union" with the need of a strict adhesion to monastic discipline or, to use their own words, to achieve the "merging of the two streams," represented by the Kagyüpa and Kadampa schools.

A particularly famous figure in the history of Tibetan Buddhism is the "madman of Druk," Drukpa Kunle. Although he presents himself, and is worshiped by others, as a paradigmatic "madman," he ridicules the "mad behavior" of some siddhas, at least the kind of demeanor that resorts to violence to achieve the unity of the absolute and the relative: "Who are those people who claim to behave as 'madmen' without observing day and night the behavior of a monk?" Kunle underscores the danger of following this antinomian logic to its ultimate conclusions: "All these people say that everything is the Law, whatever one does, and that one can kill, beat, or tie others; there may be cases where this is true for some, but it is certainly not true for all!" Like Zongmi in his critique of "Chan madmen," Kunle emphasizes that the Mahāyāna notion of emptiness must not lead to a moral relativism: to say that water and fire are fundamentally empty does not amount to saying that they are the same element.[16] Despite the contempt he displayed for the Lesser Vehicle,

[14] See Lévi-Strauss 1974b: 251.
[15] Stein 1972: 9–10.
[16] See ibid., 66.

the Tibetan trickster emphasizes the need, for ordinary people, of a moral behavior inspired by the traditional Vinaya. As far as he is concerned, he rejects both morality and violent madness, chosing instead the spontaneity, the "soft madness" of the buffoon.

According to Georges Bataille, transgression temporarily lifts the interdiction, without suppressing it. This leads us to wonder to what extent Buddhist "folly" is really subversive or transgressive. We find in Buddhism various notions of transgression. During the Tang, for instance, "madmen" flourished in literature and art, particularly in calligraphy with the so-called "mad" cursive. One of the great calligraphers of the time was Zhang Xu (fl. ca. 750), nicknamed "Crazy Zhang" (Zhang dian) because of his eccentric style.[17] The point was to express the spontaneity of Dao, or the buddha nature, without being tied down by social conventions. This technique is reminiscent of the shouts and blows of Linji Yixuan's Chan style. However, the emphasis on simplicity, spontaneity, or even madness became a cultural fashion, thus losing its authenticity and subversive value. In spite of itself, "wild Chan" had attracted a following. In the Tang literature, the term "madness" came to refer to an attitude that was perceived as feigned.[18] Transgression thus revealed its ambivalence, which is to serve to legitimize the norm that it transgresses, like an exception confirming the rule. When one considers that this period of the end of the Tang coincides precisely with the rapid institutionalization of Chan, one could even say that the ideal of the "mad monk," as it developed then in this school, constituted a denial of the reality, an inverted (and therefore ideological) image of the true situation. Far from expressing a mystical summit, it marks the moment of a loss.

Perhaps the point was also to respond to Confucian criticisms by showing that obvious infractions to discipline are not always merely the effect of laxity and corruption, but are sometimes inspired by higher motivations. The threat caused by the anticlerical critique was a real one, since on several occasions imperial edicts forced monks who did not strictly follow the monastic rule to return to lay life. As is well known, clerical corruption justified the great proscription of Buddhism in 845. Sometimes, conversely, monks feigned corruption in order to escape monastic duties and be left alone. A case in point is that of the Japanese monk Genpin, who faked infatuation with women.

---

[17] See his biography in *Xin Tang shu* 202: 5764; and Hsiung 1984. Saints were also represented as inherently eccentric in art: significant examples are those of Damo and the Luohan, "comical eccentrics whose features are decidedly otherworldly" (Brinker 1987: 49). Likewise, the "three sages of Mount Tiantai" (Hanshan, Shide, and Fenggan) are usually shown with Fenggan's tiger "huddled together in deep slumber" (ibid., 76).

[18] See Hsiung 1984: 209.

The Limits of Transgression

In Chinese Buddhism, the characters who resort to simulated madness or eccentricity are often perceived as incarnations of bodhisattvas or arhats, the ideal figures of Buddhism. The most representative case in this respect is probably that of the Chan master Daoji (d. 1209), better known as Jigong, "Master Ji," or Ji dian, "Ji the Madman." According to his "biography," Jigong belonged in the category of "feigned madness": "Understanding suddenly his origin, and fearing to be unmasked, he had afterwards feigned madness, so as to confuse the eyes and the ears of people in this world. Indeed, how could people of this world reach perfect knowledge?"[19] The *Jidian yulu* (1569) paints Daoji simultaneously as an eccentric Chan master and a carefree poet in the style of Li Bai.[20] The main topos here is that of drinking wine (and its corollary, eating meat). We recall that alcohol was prohibited by the Vinaya. As the *Fayuan zhulin* put it: "Now alcohol is a doorway to laxity and idleness. . . . Meat is a seed of abandoning great compassion."[21] But, the text adds, breaking the Precepts entails no offence when it is done for the sake of compassion.[22]

Like some thaumaturges, Daoji's powers seem related to his antinomian behavior: once, when a plague raged through town, he vomited into a mortar, apparently drunk. He covered the vomit and let it ferment, thus producing a potion that cured all who drank it.[23] On one occasion, Daoji appeared to the empress dowager in a dream as a golden-bodied arhat and asked for a donation for the Sūtra Hall of his monastery, the Jingcisi. The next day, the empress visited the monastery and, after surveying the monks, recognized him as the arhat of her dream. When Daoji denied it, she said: "Of course, you would like to remain incognito. But it was you who convinced me to give this cash donation. How do you intend to thank me?" "I am nothing but a mad, destitute, monk," answered Daoji. "I am definitely not an arhat. The empress should not have any illusions about this." The empress, however, would not have it: "As you are mingling with the ordinary inhabitants of this mortal world, it is but natural that you would not acknowledge your true identity. That's understandable. However, I have donated to you 3,000 strings of cash. How do you

---

[19] See Durand-Dastès 1984: 119.

[20] Shahar 1992: 51.

[21] *Fayuan zhulin* 93, T. 53, 2122: 970b–974a.

[22] Ibid. According to the *Chengshi lun* (*Satyasiddhiśāstra*, T. 32, 1646: 300b18), drinking alcohol is not a true wrongdoing in itself, but merely an underlying cause of wrongdoing. Alcohol is allowed as a medicine, but the author, Daoshi (600–683) hastens to add: "Do not take [the above] as a general licence to drink. It is necessary to be really ill and in serious trouble and that you are nearing the end."

[23] Shahar 1992: 63.

intend to repay me?" Daoji said: "I am a destitute monk. The only way I can repay the empress is by doing a somersault. I hope that the empress will learn from this poor monk how to turn somersaults." As he was speaking he turned head over heels and performed a somersault. Since he was not wearing underwear his pudenda were completely exposed. The imperial consorts and palace ladies burst into laughter. The court attendants and the eunuchs, enraged by Daoji's impudence, rushed out of the Buddha Hall to catch him; however, he had already disappeared. The monks, mortified, tried to apologize on account of his madness. "This monk has never been mad," the empress dowager replied. "In fact he is an arhat. His display was intended to show me that I can be transformed from a woman into a man. This is a great Chan mystery, and I should really pay him homage for it. But he has already escaped and I doubt that he would want to come back now. So we must leave it at that."[24] Having thus saved face, the empress returned to the palace.[25]

Interestingly, Daoji's somersaults—his transgression of established order, of hierarchy—is interpreted by the empress as a "pivoting" (*paravṛtti*) that provides her with a model to turn around her female destiny and obtain awakening. But this alleged karmic turnaround is not perfect, since she must be reborn as a man before becoming a buddha. The apparent "reversal" merely reinforces a preestablished—and essentially androcentric—scenario.

Another episode shows us Daoji trying to justify his misbehavior to an offended official: "Now in the houses of courtesans, explaining cause and retribution, madness is not madness! Now in monasteries teaching nuns the Chan stratagems, to knock over is not knocking over! . . . When I sing mountain songs, each note is *prajñā* [wisdom]! When I drink good wine, each bowl is the Cao stream![26] Unable to get used to meditation, on my bed, drunk, I make somersaults; finding it difficult to observe prohibitions, I put meat dishes in my bowl. I pawn my ceremonial robe to the innkeepers, everyone knows the mad monk in love with wine! With my meditation staff I knock over fat women, everyone speaks of the libertine monk! Among the mandarins of the sixteen imperial ministries, there is not one who has not seen me drunk."[27]

[24] *Zui puti*, 10.2b–4a; see also Ono Shihei's Japanese translation in Ono 1978: 188–91; and *Jidian yulu* 11a, in Shahar 1992: 133–34.

[25] Cf. *Jidian yulu* 11a, in Shahar 1992: 133. This episode reminds us of another, concerning the holy man Zōga (917–1003), a master of the Tendai tradition who was renowned for his eccentricities. See *Uji shūi monogatari*, translated by Mills 1970: 362–63. On Zōga, see also Marra 1991: 61–63.

[26] That is, the deep truth of Chan. Caoxi, the "Cao Ford," was the site of the monastery of Sixth Patriarch Huineng (d. 713).

[27] Shahar 1992: 63.

However, Daoji lets the cat out of the bag when he reveals his bodhisattva nature: "In the midst of intoxication, I keep a clear head; in the most extreme agitation, I remain unbound." He even provides a key to his folly: "My madness helps to confuse common people, but I possess the magical force of *samādhi,* through which I help people escape the misery of the world. I have no business reading the Scriptures, but I like Chan devices. Drunk, I shout abuse at the Buddha and insult the heavenly nature." When he is about to die, one of his disciples asks him if he has something to transmit. Daoji then composes the following poem: "With nothing I came, with nothing I go; / If you want my 'bowl and robe,' take this pair of naked balls!" Another significant detail: Daoji's death—like that of Śākyamuni, although the meaning is quite different in the two cases—is preceded by a severe diarrhea.[28]

Daoji liked to parade his talents as a bawdy "nutty" monk. The following poem is representative:

> Every day he indulges in wine and sleeps with courtesans.
> How can the libertine monk be like others?
> His cassock is often stained with rouge.
> His robe carries the fragrance of powder.[29]

However, for all his inflammatory rhetoric, he remains strangely shy when the time comes to put his words into (sexual) action. For here his folly finds its limits. If he finds refuge in wine, it is perhaps to keep sex at bay. Thus, on one occasion, he praises wine to avoid sleeping with a courtesan:

> In the past my parents did this [i.e., indulge in sex],
> Giving birth to this stinking skin-bag of mine.
> But my heart is not like my parents' heart.
> It covets nothing but wine.[30]

After spending a chaste night with a courtesan, he leaves this farewell poem:

> Although I have shared for one night the lovers' bed,
> the Chan spirit does not get along with desire.

On another occasion, he declares:

> [I have] eyebrows like a broom,
> and a huge mouth that cannot lie, but can drink wine.
> Look at my white hair and my often bare feet!
> I have physical form but my mind is free.

[28] *Jidian yulu* 21a; Shahar 1992: 114.
[29] *Jidian yulu* 7b; Shahar 1992: 105.
[30] *Jidian yulu* 8a.

I have sex but I am not attached.
In my drunken stupor I pay no heed to the waves of the worldly sea.
My entire body covered with rags, I act like a madman.
Under the bright moon in the fresh breeze I laugh and sing. . . .
Sitting backward on my donkey I return to the heavenly ridges.[31]

If Wanhui and Hanshan became gods of union and fecundity, such is not the case for Daoji. As the following anecdote shows, he seems to have subscribed, rather, to the antinatalist ideology of orthodox Buddhism. Invited by a friend to spend the night with a courtesan, Daoji finds her asleep, naked, and puts one of her shoes on her pudenda. When she wakes up in the morning, she finds the following poem:

Exhausted by love, the butterfly and the flowering branch
Fall asleep, a spring dream from which it is hard to wake up.
Her silk gown, discarded, is separated from her body.
Her three souls journey to the immortals' abode.
And her seven spirits encircle the islands of Peng and Ying.
Therefore, I used her silk shoe to cover the cave's entrance.
If having awoken she is angry, then she ought to know:
It isn't because Daoji has bad intentions
That he blocked the road of life and death
And shut the gate of being and nonbeing."[32]

Wine, like sex, is hardly more than a cliché in Chinese literature, however. Likewise, the saint in a brothel is a commonplace theme in Mahāyāna literature. The mythic layman Vimalakīrti, remember, visited lupanars and taverns. There is no need to raise a fuss about these apparent transgressions, for, despite all of its discourses on the identity of passions and awakening, the *Vimalakīrti-nirdeśa* remains strangely virginal regarding the behavior of its hero in the alcove. Of Vimalakīrti we are told: "He wore the white clothes of the layman, yet lived impeccably like a religious devotee. He lived at home, but remained aloof from the realm of desire, the realm of pure matter, and the immaterial realm. He had a son, a wife, and female attendants, yet always maintained continence. . . . In order to be in harmony with people, he associated with elders, with those of middle age, and with the young, yet always spoke in harmony with the Dharma. . . . To demonstrate the evils of desire, he even entered the brothels. To establish drunkards in correct mindfulness, he entered all the cabarets. . . . He was honored as a eunuch in the royal harem because he taught the young ladies according to the Dharma."[33]

[31] *Jidian yulu* 18b; Shahar 1992: 116.
[32] *Jidian yulu* 7a, Shahar 1992: 121.
[33] See Thurman 1976: 20–21.

Odds are that Vimalakīrti behaved as properly as Daoji, content with preaching the Law to souls in distress. The brothels described in these texts, therefore, seem to have been revised by pious followers.

Similarly, we may wonder to what extent Daoji's "life" has been expurgated. As it has reached us, there remains of all his real or imaginary transgressions only drunkenness. The fundamental taboo—sex—remains inviolate. Obviously, Buddhist hagiographers intended an image of transgression acceptable to Chinese society, and even beneficial to the clergy. Thus the Chan tradition mentions several similar cases, some of which may have served as models for the characterization of Daoji. One of them is Yixian (922–1009), nicknamed "Wine Immortal" (Jiuxian), after the carefree sobriquet of Libai (Jiuxian weng).[34]

Furthermore, it is not entirely clear whether Daoji is a genuinely rebellious individual who was tamed by the tradition, or merely a literary character whose eccentricity was purposely accentuated. We find in Chinese legends several literary transformations of serious monks, which seem to have little basis in reality: for instance, the Chan master Foyin Liaoyuan (1032–1098), the master of Su Shi (alias Su Dongpo, 1037–1101), is depicted in Ming fiction as an eccentric poet who indulges in wine and likes to flirt with courtesans. We will return to these two figures in the next chapter.

Wang Mengji (fl. 1668) emphasizes the difficulty of distinguishing between true and fake transgression:

> In the lives of the Buddhas, patriarchs, sages, and worthies, the things that need be transmitted [from generation to generation] are those pertaining to body and mind, nature and ordinance, morality and the five human relations. If there was nothing to these worthies but wine-drinking, meat-eating, pointless chatter, aimless wandering, and the random compilation of bad poetry . . . then, everywhere, villainous bald asses would justify [their own wanton behavior] using these worthies' names. The monastic institution would be transformed into a den of rogues and criminals. This would cause the Buddhist school to fall into disarray, and it might even lead to its destruction. How could [such biographies of Jidian] be accepted as standard? When they read fiction or watch plays, the people of the world consider only flowery and erotic pieces to be noteworthy, and they praise [such pieces] as magnificent. They do not care at all whether these pieces have any moral content. Therefore, they would do better to spend three pennies, grab a stool, sit in a circle and listen to a sto-

---

[34] The extraordinary popularity of Daoji—the prototypical "crazy monk"—perhaps has to do with his hometown, Hangzhou, a major economic and cultural center of the time. This provincial capital of Zhejiang is also the setting of many popular stories, such as those of Red Lotus and of the White Snake. On Yixian, see the biography in *Jiatai Pudeng lu* (1204), in ZZ 2, 10/2: 165b–166a. The similarities with Daoji have been pointed out by Sawada 1975: 194–96.

ryteller narrate the *Water Margin* or the *Journey to the West*. Why should they bother to read this *Drunken Ascetic* [i.e., the *Jigong quanzhuan*]?[35]

Wang Mengji also points out the potentially disastrous effects of such stereotypes:

> Pious people everywhere claim that after he had drunk wine Jigong vomited gold, thereby adding luster to a Buddha statue. This is the result of meddlesome people spreading too much gossip. Whoever heard of a wine-drinking and meat-eating monk who vomited gold? If this were the case, then parasitic monks everywhere would use this as an excuse, and spend their entire days drinking wine and eating meat. One would only have to offer them their fill and wait for them to vomit gold. Would not this just make it easier for this villainous lot? The reader ought to consider carefully. Could there possibly be such a thing?[36]

The motif of excrement turning into sacrament often recurs in these stories.[37] As Meir Shahar points out, the gradual apotheosis of Daoji into the trickster Jidian, and eventually into the god Jigong, retains his main characteristic as a mediating figure.[38] Because, as a fictional figure, he bridged the gap between canonical Buddhism and popular literature, the comic relief provided by his transgressive behavior could not entirely overcome the canonical ideal of chastity.

If the legend of Daoji was edited for the Buddhist cause, however, there is still a version that has retained its subversive power. Indeed, this version is at the origin of a medium cult still widespread today among the Chinese in Southeast Asia. According to it, the god Jigong is the "Vagabond Buddha," lord of the dregs of society, who comes to possess his followers during trance rituals. His motto consists of five precepts—to

[35] *Jigong quanzhuan* 27.11b–12a, in Shahar 1992: 158. The author erases the more outrageous traits, namely Jigong's interest in women: his Jigong does not flirt with women, let alone sleep with them. For instance, he omits the episode in which Daoji covers the pudenda of a sleeping courtesan with her tiny shoe.

[36] *Jigong quanzhuan* 32.10a, in Shahar 1992: 156.

[37] See, for instance, the case of another famous trickster, Ikkyū (on whom more later), who had been asked to perform an "eye-opening" ceremony for a statue of Jizō: "Without further ado, Ikkyū climbed right up the ladder, and from the level of Jizō's head he began to piss all over the place. It was like the waterfall of Mount Lu Shan. Soon all the offerings were thoroughly soaked, and as this veritable flood ceased Ikkyū told them, 'So much for an eye-opening,' and set off rapidly toward the east." The locals, mad at him, ran after him, while some lay-nuns started washing the image. They worked themselves into a strange frenzy, and went after Ikkyū to ask him to repeat the ceremony. Instead, he gave them his loincloth and told them to tie it around Jizo's head, because it would cure ills instantly. And so they did (Sanford 1981: 294). This story resonates with folkloric motifs related to rain rituals: it is, for instance, sometimes associated with the failed ritual of the famous rainmaker Shūbin, Kūkai's unfortunate rival.

[38] Shahar 1992: 188.

drink, eat meat, gamble, steal, and fornicate—a parodic inversion of the
Buddhist precepts. One may argue that such a hedonistic motto, characteristic of a carnivalesque vision of the world, has nothing to do with
Buddhism. Unless, of course, it expresses an aspect of popular Buddhism
that is truly transgressive and usually overshadowed—except in some
corners of Tantric Buddhism.[39]

CRAZY CLOUD

Morality is generally preserved, at least in sexual matters, even in the case
of "Chan madmen." However, there is a character who, without being
properly speaking a "madman," was nevertheless quite an eccentric and
rose up against this morality, first on the grounds of the superior freedom
of Chan and then, later in his life, in the name of the blind love that tied
him to a blind female singer named Shin (or Mori). This is the poet-monk
Ikkyū Sōjun (1394–1481), who called himself "Crazy Cloud" (Kyōun).[40] Ikkyū's poetry constitutes an irreplaceable document, although
one often difficult to interpret, on the morals of Japanese Buddhists of the
medieval period. In a poem from his youth entitled "The Calf," for instance, Ikkyū alludes to masturbation as a remedy for a novice's desire:

My naked passions, six inches long.
At night we meet on an empty bed.
A hand that's never known a woman's touch,
And a nuzzling calf, swollen from nights too long.[41]

Later, Ikkyū apparently frequented brothels, if we are to believe the
great number of poems he composed, in a typically Zen vein, to the glory
of prostitutes. In a poem entitled "Portrait of the Arhat at a Brothel," he
alludes to Ānanda's misadventure:

Shaking off dust, that arhat is still far from buddhahood.
One trip at a brothel brings Great Wisdom.

[39] The cult of Jigong spread from Manchuria to Malaysia, and it played a significant role
in the Boxer uprising and in the "Unity Sect" (Yiguan dao), whose founder, Zhang Tianran
(d. 1949), saw himself as incarnation of Jigong. It is also widespread in Taiwan in spirit-
medium cults—possession or spirit writing, *fuji*. Jigong was also worshiped as one of the
five hundred arhats of Tiantai shan. See Shahar 1992: 173; and DeBernardi 1987.

[40] The references to Ikkyū's poems are to Yanagida Seizan's edition of the *Kyōun shū*.
See Yanagida Seizan, ed., *Ikkyū, Ryōkan* (Tokyo: Chūōkōronsha, 1987). I have used the
translations in Sanford 1981 and Arntzen 1986. There is also a partial translation in Covell
1980.

[41] *Ikkyū zue shūi*, quoted in Sanford 1981: 287.

Quite a laugh; Mañjuśrī chanting through the *Śuraṃgama[-sūtra]*
Long gone the pleasures of *his* youth.[42]

We may recall that Ānanda, about to succumb to a courtesan's advances, was rescued in extremis by the bodhisattva Mañjuśrī, acting on order of the omniscient Buddha. In an autobiographical poem entitled "The Heresy of Lust," Ikkyū returns to the same theme:

Whose song carrying over the brothel revelry?
A song of youth that swirls my head,
Then a dawning never seen by Ānanda
A means of enlightenment, this fading autumn moon.[43]

In a poem entitled "On a Brothel," Ikkyū alludes to the games of love (traditionally evoked by the metaphor of clouds and rain) in which he finds pleasure and inspiration:

A beautiful woman, cloud-rain, love's deep river.
Up in the pavilion, the pavilion girl and the old monk sing.
I find inspiration in embraces and kisses;
I don't feel that I'm casting my body into flames.[44]

Elsewhere, he compares prostitutes to monks, to the advantage of the former, in a poem whose title is explicit: "With a Poem about a Brothel, Putting to Shame Those Brothers Who Obtain the Dharma":

With kōans and old examples, arrogant deception grows;
Everyday you bend your back to meet officials in vain.
Proud boasters are this world's Good Friends;
The young girl in the brothel wears gold brocade.[45]

Ikkyū has a number of poems celebrating sexual desire, love, women, and the female body. Comparing himself to the Chinese Dharma master Kuiji (632–682) of Cien Monastery, he writes: "Kuiji excelled in samādhi, but also in wine and meat, in scriptures and in beautiful women. To equal a *zasu* (head monk) with such pupils, in the [Zen] school, there is

---

[42] *Kyōunshū* 255, in Sanford 1981: 156.
[43] *Kyōunshū* 336, in Sanford 1981: 157. Compare with "Pictures of an Arhat Reveling in a Brothel, Two Poems": "The arhat has left the dust, no more desire. / Playful games at the brothel, so much desire. / This one is bad, this one is good. / The monk's skill, Devil-Buddha desire." (no. 255) And: "Emerging from the dust, the arhat is still far from Buddha. / Enter a brothel once and great wisdom happens. / I laugh deeply at Mañjuśrī reciting spells in the *Śuraṃgama Sūtra*, / Lost and long gone are the pleasures of Ānanda's youth." (no. 254) (Arntzen 1986: 135–36).
[44] *Kyōunshū* 144; see Arntzen 1986: 117.
[45] *Kyōunshū* 284; see Arntzen 1986: 138.

only Sōjun."[46] Sexual pleasures seems to have played an important, almost obsessive, role in his life. Here is how, in a self-portrait, Ikkyū boasts of his extravagant behavior:

This kind of madman, who incites to folly,
Coming and going in brothels and taverns,
Which among you, monks with mended clothes, can find him in error?
I indicate the south, the north, the west, and the east.[47]

In one poem whose title is more provocative than its content, "Sipping a Beautiful Woman's Sexual Fluids," he writes:

Linji's followers don't know Zen.
The true transmission was to the Blind Donkey.[48]
Love play, three lifetimes of sixty long kalpas.
One autumn night is a thousand centuries.[49]

The idea that the passion of love will lead to the rebirth of the lovers reappears on several occasions. Ikkyū returns to the theme of "sexual fluids" in another poem concerning Shin:

I'm infatuated with the beautiful Shin from the celestial garden:
Lying on the pillow with her flower stamen,
My mouth fills with the pure perfume of the waters of her stream.
Twilight comes, then moonlight's shadows, as we sing our new song.[50]

It is followed by a variation on the same theme, entitled: "A Woman's Body has the Fragrance of a Narcissus":

One should gaze long at King Chu's hill, then ascend it.
Midnight on the jade bed amid regretful dreams.
A flower opening beneath the thrust of the plum branch,
Rocking gently, gently between her water-nymph thighs.[51]

[46] *Kyōunshū* 161, in Yanagida, ed., 1987: 92. Compare with Arntzen #166, "Praising the Dharma Master Tz'u-en K'uei-chi": "K'uei-chi's samādhi alone was natural and real. / Wine, meat, the scriptures, and beautiful women, / The eye of the abbot was just like this. / In our school, there is only Sōjun." (Arntzen 1986: 120).

[47] *Kyōunshū* 156; see Arntzen 1986: 119.

[48] Allusion to the episode of the transmission of the True Dharma Eye by Linji to his disciple Sansheng. See Fuller Sasaki 1975: 62.

[49] *Kyōunshū* 537 in Sanford 1981: 160.

[50] *Kyōunshū* 541 in Covell 1980: 225.

[51] *Kyōunshū* 542 in Sanford 1981: 167. Different translation by Arntzen, #535, "A Beautiful Woman's Dark Place Has the Fragrance of a Narcissus": "Ch'u's Pavilion, one must regard from afar and moreover climb. / The middle of the night, on the jeweled bed, a bittersweet dream's face, / The flower opens under a branch of the plum tree, / Delicately the narcissus revolves between thighs." (Arntzen 1986: 157)

Another poem, entitled "Taking my Hand to be Shin's Hand," leaves no doubt on his lover's dexterity:

How is my hand like Shin's hand?
Self-confidence is the vassal, Freedom the master.
When I am ill, she cures the jade stalk,
And brings joy back to my followers.[52]

Ikkyū went so far as to have the beautiful Shin appear on his official portrait, something unprecedented in Buddhist annals. At the end of his life, he sings without regret the passion, always renewed:

Although my hair is white as snow,
Desires still sing through my body.
I can't control all the weeds that grow in my garden.[53]

Supplementing his sexual transgression, Ikkyū's literary transgression is a result of his blurring the genres. Thus, in a series of poem entitled "The Scriptures Wipe away Filth," he writes things like "The scriptures from the start have been toilet paper," or "The dog pisses on the sandalwood old Buddha Hall."[54] According to Sonja Arntzen, the title of the series suggests that the poems attack the conventional distinction between the sacred and the profane by resorting to the scatological. These lines "leave the reader with the philosophical, the scatological, and the erotic, the most contradictory of images and ideas juxtaposed and intermingled, impossible to separate."[55] Not surprisingly, the collection of poems that owed him his posthumous fame, *Kyōunshū* (The Record of Crazy Cloud), was not always appreciated by his contemporaries—indeed, it was even censored. Sometimes transgression pays only late.[56]

---

[52] *Kyōunshū* 543 in Sanford 1981: 164. Compare with Arntzen's translation, #536, "Calling My Hand Mori's Hand": "My hand, how it resembles Mori's hand. / I believe the lady is the master of loveplay; / If I get ill, she can cure the jeweled stem. / And then they rejoice, the monks at my meeting." (Arntzen 1986: 158)

[53] *Kyōunshū* 251 in Arntzen 1986: xxx.

[54] *Kyōunshū* 69–71 in Arntzen 1986: 90–95.

[55] Arntzen 1986: 92, 95.

[56] In "Monk Ikkyū," Mushanokoji Saneatsu describes as follows the (fictious) encounter between Ikkyū and a lordless samurai who wants to kill him for his amorality: The samurai accuses him: "You, who are in a position to be looked upon as a living Buddha, drink *sake*, eat meat, kill animals, go to the gay quarters, fool with small boys, commit swindling, and compose poems like indecent pictures." Ikkyū replies: "Why is it bad to go and teach dissolute men and harlots that they can attain enlightenment if only their attitude of mind is good? I like harlots better than a samurai like you who is severe to others." (Hirano n.d.: 35–36) In the *Ikkyū banashi* (1668), Ikkyū's amoral behavior is presented as an example of perfect spontaneity: Ikkyū asks a married woman to sleep with him. She refuses and reports the matter to her husband, who tells her that she must accept. She

Ikkyū's behavior must be replaced in its historical context, that of the growing contestation of established values during the Muromachi period—a phenomenon reflected, for instance, in the so-called *basara* style and the fashion of marginality.[57] Here again, just as in the end of the Tang period in China (or even earlier, for instance with Xikang and the Seven Sages of the Bamboo Grove), eccentric behavior is permitted by a certain decline of central power and societal values.

What about pathological madness? The definition of madness and sanity is cultural, of course, and many phenomena—trance, possession, and so on—which in our societies are quickly labeled as mental illness were admitted in traditional societies as relatively normal. Interestingly enough, whereas feigned madness is often a male strategy, in Japan, paranormal phenomena like trance, but also phenomena described as "madness" [J. *monogurui*], seem to be characteristic of women. The feminine transgression of normal behavior is rejected as utterly alien and alienated.[58]

There is sometimes a fine line betwen transgression, "spiritual folly," and pathological madness. There are obviously types and degrees of obsessive madness. The "soft folly" of Ikkyū—a priest "madly in love"—seems far from the obsessive love of some priests, which causes them to fall eventually into a demoniac destiny and to return as a vengeful ghost that possesses others. However, in his love for the blind singer Shin, Ikkyū comes at times close to the "madness of love." His "madness" needs to be placed against the backdrop of the "free" city of Sakai, where he lived for a long period, and the "unbound" (*muen*) nature of Zen monks (for instance the adherents of the Darumashū). We find in Chan/Zen (as in certain forms of Daoism) a nostalgia for naturalness, a second simplicity in which sexuality would become natural again. This also implies abandoning (in principle) all political ambition, in order to enter the realm of what was called in medieval Japan *muen* (without ties). Amino Yoshihiko has studied sanctuaries where normal social rules would no longer apply and where a certain freedom ruled. These places served as refuges to all those who, for various reasons, had "cut their ties" with or had been rejected by society: gamblers, prostitutes, outcastes (*kawaramono* or *hinin*), actors, and so on. Some of these muen places were Buddhist temples, other were market towns like Sakai.[59] Amino has also

---

returns to see Ikkyū, but he now rejects her, saying that his desire has gone. The husband admires his spontaneity, his free-flowing action like running water; Sanford 1981: 196–97.

[57] See Satō 1995, and Marra 1993b.

[58] On medieval *monogurui*, see Hosokawa 1993: 13–55.

[59] Amino 1978.

argued that, during pilgrimages to some famous cultic centers, women were no longer bound by normal rules of chastity. The communitas in such places implied a certain sexual licence, as well. But in most cases this ideal was to remain wishful thinking as far as sexuality was concerned: in traditional society, sex remains an object of power, too important to be left to individual desires.

Ikkyū appears at a time when, according to Amino, this principle of muen was becoming more self-conscious. Paradoxically, he was himself one of the strongest opponents of certain forms of "wild Zen" and marginality. In his case as in others, however, the feigned madness of the sage is a form of self-protection: it therefore avoids fundamental transgressions, like sex and killing; it is quite different from "Dionysiac" hubris.

When we speak of transgression, sexual or otherwise, and of trickster monks, we should of course always take the historical context into account, lest this ideal type become too abstract. The difference between Chinese and Japanese tricksters is also that of their times. In the case of Ikkyū or of the Darumashū monks who preceded him, we must look at the context of the Kamakura and early Muromachi periods. One phenomenon that stands out is the *basara* phenomenon, which has recently become the focus of Japanese historians. In the divided society of Muromachi Japan, the term *basara* was used to designate both extravagance (luxury, etc.) and "madness" (*monogurui*), as well as the eccentric behavior or artistic effects that seem to break conventions. Everything that was a little strange and unconventional, sometimes perceived as bad taste, was called *basara*. This term, derived from a Tantric symbol, the *vajra* (diamond), became fashionable and emblematic of a new sensibility, that of the "topsy-turvy world" (*gekokujō*) of the late Kamakura and early Muromachi periods. In this context, antinomian monks are no longer so extraordinary, and even their "rugged individualism" can be seen as resulting from their adherence to the zeitgeist.

An interesting case of a basara lord is that of Sasaki Dōyō, military governor of Ōmi province, and a patron of the Ji sect founded by Ippen. Toward the turn of the fourteenth century, he was one of the patrons of the new entertainment arts (nō, renga, tea ceremony, ikebana, etc.). In the company of Ji priests, he organized sumptuous banquets and turned life into a perpetual feast. Like them, he was a severe critic of traditional society, which was then in the throes of civil war and epidemics. He represented the search for new values that denied all authority, the attempt to define a new social order in which "the inferiors surpassed the superiors" (*gekokujō*). These behaviors have to be interpreted against the backround of the rise of the marginals and the excluded, the so-called *kawaramono,* among whom the Ji sect was particularly active. It is significant that Zeami and his father Kan'ami wrote the characters *-ami* (from

Amida) in their name, and came from among these *kawaramono* or *shokunin*. Despite these humble origins, they became the companions of the shōguns and other patrons of the arts, who were able, through their economic support, to reintegrate these unruly elements into high culture, while renewing their own power through contact with their energy. Here again, the transgressive elements are put to the service of the rule.

Another case of medieval hubris is that of Emperor Kazan, who managed to have sex with a lady-in-waiting during the ceremony of enthronement, in the most sacred of all places, the room of the throne itself. Apart from this scandal, Kazan is known for many incidents caused by his indecent behavior, but also for his spiritual achievements, manifested through magic powers and artistic talents. This kind of hubris seems to have become an imperial characteristic, for ideological reasons similar to those which created the Buddhist trickster: not only is the master of the Law (emperor or Dharma master) not bound by the law, but his power to rule over the law-abiding realm (the cosmos, the world of forms and formality) comes from his capacity to strike roots deep in the chaotic realm of the nonform, source of all power. Transcendence, in both cases, is achieved or expressed by breaking through and beyond the rules (*prohibita transcendere*). However, Kazan's scandalous comportment, while bluntly revealing the dark origins of royal power, caused him to lose his throne after only two years of reign. Like that of Ikkyū, his posthumous image remains ambivalent. Despite (or, more fundamentally, because of) his madness, he is praised in the *Ōkagami*. Order, in the end, must prevail: even if his mad behavior was structurally indispensable as a phase preparing this return to order, the mad emperor had to be sacrificed, exiled into institutional madness (that is, he had to become a monk—albeit one renowned for his thaumaturgic powers).

The transgressing priest, once he enters this most troubled and troublesome area of all, the realm of sex and power, is likely to become an evil monk. Perhaps Ikkyū was able to escape this posthumous condemnation (and damnation) simply because he fell in love not with a court lady but with a blind singer, an outcaste. Another paradigmatic case of transgression, often mentioned in Japanese Buddhist literature, is that of Nāgārjuna. We are told that Nāgārjuna, when he was still a commoner, fabricated a drug of invisibility. Together with two companions he penetrated the king's palace and violated all the royal consorts. The latter reported this to the king, who was a clever man: in prevision of the next occurrence, he had powder sprinkled over the palace's floor. When Nāgārjuna and his accomplices reentered the palace, their traces thus became visible. His two companions were killed, and he barely managed to escape by pulling the hem of a consort over his head. Having understood the lesson, he abandoned magical means and turned toward the true teaching of

Buddhism.[60] Whereas his narrow escape led Nāgārjuna to abandon without regret the perilous seductions of the imperial harem and to repent his transgressions, many eminent priests would not be as fortunate, falling into an evil destiny.

TRANSGRESSION — SUBLIME OR SUBLIMATED?

For all its literary importance, madness is only one of the figures of transgression. Antinomianism can also be philosophical or ritual (as in Tantric Buddhism). Halfway between the norm and its transgression, sublimation allows some of the symbolic advantages of the latter without departing from the former. The transition between the two registers is achieved in the Buddhist imagination through the ambivalence of the roles attributed to mythical figures like the Bodhisattva Avalokiteśvara (Guanyin, Kannon). In Tantric iconography, Guanyin appears, for instance, as Senāyaka to tame her brother, the elephant-headed god Vināyaka. When he falls in love with her, she tells him: "I have from ages past been a follower of Buddhism. If you want to touch my body, you must follow the same teaching!" Vināyaka agrees, then embraces her, and achieves Great Bliss [J. kangi, hence his Japanese name, Kangiten].[61]

If the Chinese Guanyin, after his/her enigmatic sex change, becomes a model and a refuge for women who rebel against their procreative role, or to the contrary, try to assume it in the face of all difficulties, he/she constitutes equally a sublimated feminine ideal for the monks. One can, for instance, follow the evolution of the sexual theme in the various stories that present her with the seductive features of "Guanyin with the Fishbasket" or of the "Wife of Mr. Ma" (Malang fu).[62] In the first extant recensions, Guanyin leads men to awakening by adapting herself to their passions, in particular by fulfilling their sexual desire. In later versions, she uses the desire men have for her as a means for their improvement. In the legend of the "Wife of Mr. Ma," for instance, she appears as a young girl who, following a well-known folkloric motif, promises to marry the most worthy of her suitors, a young man named Horse (Ma). However, this is a fool's bargain, as she dies during the wedding night, before their

[60] *Gaoseng zhuan*, T. 50, 2059: 330a-333a. See also Kawaguchi, ed., (1955) 1995: 135–36. The same story appears in Ury 1979: 49–50: "How Nāgārjuna, while a Layman, Made a Charm for Invisibility."

[61] See Sanford 1991b.

[62] The wife of Mr. Ma played an important role in Chan/Zen. See the dialogue of Fuketsu Enshō (d. 973) in *Jingde chuandeng lu* 13, *Wudeng huiyuan* 11 (Sawada 1975: 147). The theme becomes a leitmotif in Chan literature (in Wuzhun Shifan, etc.). See Sawada 1975: 148–51; and Stein 1986. Note also the resemblance between the young Lotus and Malang fu: both die just before their wedding.

union has been consummated. Finally, in the most Buddhistic versions, she simply promises her favors to a monk if he excels in Buddhist practice. However, when the monk thinks that he has reached his goal she reveals her pious trick and denies him his reward. Her image merged with that of the Guanyin with the Fishbasket, praised by Ikkyū:

Red cheeks, blue-black hair, compassion, and love deep;
Wondering at her feelings in the midst of a dream of cloud-rain.
One thousand eyes of Great Compassion; she is looked at but not seen.
A fisherman's wife by the river and sea, one whole life of song.[63]

The *Samguk yusa* tells us that one of Wŏnhyo's disciples, Omjang, obtained rebirth in Pure Land after having received initial guidance from the wife of his deceased friend Kwangdok, a woman who, although she appeared to be only a menial servant at Punhwang sa, was actually a manifestation of Avalokiteśvara.[64] Likewise, in the story of the two monks quoted earlier, the woman who receives hospitality from one of them, after asking him to step with her into the bath, turns out to be another manifestation of this bodhisattva. As the *Samguk yusa* puts it, "The heroine of this story was an incarnation of Buddha in a woman's body," and therefore even the ultimate feminine defilement, childbirth, turned out to be perfectly pure and no hindrance to salvation.[65] A similar story involves Wŏnhyo himself. Going on a pilgrimage to a mountain dedicated by Ŭisang to Avalokiteśvara, he encounters two women: the first one is harvesting rice in a field, and refuses to give him some. The second, however, is washing her menstrual band in a stream, the ultimate act of defilement, for which women have been condemned to fall into the Blood Pond Hell. When she offers some of that contaminated water to Wŏnhyo, the latter, undaunted, gladly accepts. Later he finds out that these two women were manifestations of Avalokiteśvara, who praises him through the song of a bluebird. However, the author seems to have hesitated to push the story to its normal conclusion, unless the following passage is interpolated: we are told that a storm prevents Wŏnhyo from entering the cave where the bodhisattva dwells. This motif seems to echo similar stories in which a woman, defiled by menstrual blood, is prevented by a storm from ascending a mountain and meeting the deity.[66]

---

[63] See Ikkyū's poem, "Praising the Fish-Basket Kannon," in Sanford 1981: 89. The story of Guanyin with the fishbasket is that of a young woman who made love with men on a river bank. After her death, a Western monk comes and opens her grave and discovers her true identity as the "bodhisattva with linked bones." See Sawada 1975: 145–46.

[64] Ilyŏn 1972: 345–46. On this story, see Jang 1996.

[65] Ilyŏn 1972: 242.

[66] See Faure 1994: 185–91.

In a story found in the *Konjaku monogatari shū,* the bodhisattva Ko-kūzō (Skt. Ākāśagarbha) replaces Kannon in this ambiguous role. A young monk from Mount Hiei is surprised by the night during a pilgrimage to Hōrinji, Kokūzō's cultic center on the Western outskirts of Kyoto. He finds shelter in the house of a young widow and falls in love with her. Losing all prudence, he enters her room during the night. Although she declares herself willing to yield to him, she wants before to know whether he is a worthy monk (!). To test him, she asks him to recite the *Lotus Sūtra.* When he proves unable to do so, she advises him to return to Hieizan, and not to come back before learning the scripture. When the monk, having achieved this task, comes to ask for his reward, his pleasure is once again deferred: the lady now asks him to spend three years learning the scriptures in order to become an eminent monk. Having succeeded, the monk returns one last time, only to find out through a revelatory dream that his trials were a skillful means devised by the compassionate bodhisattva Kokūzō to help him overcome his laxity. Although the transgression never actually takes place in this story, swallowing the bait of sexual desire turns out to be the fastest way to salvation.

Despite the progressive watering down of this tale, the erotic element survives in parallel stories. Guanyin, true to her word, or even without any preliminary conditions, gives herself to men as a way to lead them to the ultimate bliss of awakening. In her infinite compassion and her desire to convert beings by adapting to their passions, Guanyin even condones homosexual love, as in the Japanese story of the old monk who, after having lived three years in perfect love with his novice, was stricken with grief at the youth's premature death. During the funerary wake, Kannon appears to him under the guise of the beloved novice, and reveals that he/she had taken human form in order to reward him for a virtuous life (!). Even when she does not fullfil the sexual desires of monks, Guanyin enables their sublimation. In the case of homosexual desire, it is often another figure of the Buddhist pantheon who intervenes: usually, it is the bodhisattva Mañjuśrī, in particular in his manifestation as an adolescent.[67] We will return to this question.

This sublimation can take the form of a rite, but also that of a dream. According to the Vinaya regulations, temptations in a dream (or, more concretely, wet dreams) do not lead to guilt, nor are they contrary to purity. To mention another well-known Japanese example, the monk Myōe (d. 1232) often dreamed of sexual relations with a noble lady, a woman whom he describes as plump and whose appearance he judges "in perfect accordance with the Buddhist Law." We see here again the theme of the bodhisattva as an object of the monk's desire, leading to his

---

[67] It can also be Fugen, Shōtoku, or some lesser figure like the god Jūzenji.

awakening. Myōe sees his dream as a reenactment of the encounter, described in the *Gaṇḍavyūha-sūtra,* between the young Sudhana and his teacher Vasumitra. The latter is a peerless courtesan, who frees men by fulfilling their carnal desire. By merely talking to her or touching her, men enter samādhi and reach awakening. Like the layman Vimalakīrti, these mortals are able to practice meditation while remaining in the realm of the senses. When Sudhana came in presence of the beautiful Vasumitra, she said:

> To all beings . . . I appear in the form of a female of their species, of surpassing splendor and perfection. And to all who come to me with minds full of passion, I teach them so that they may become free of passion. . . . Some attain dispassion as soon as they see me, and achieve an enlightening concentration called "delight in joy." Some attain dispassion merely by talking with me, . . . [others] just by holding my hand, . . . [others] just by staying with me, . . . [others] just by gazing at me, . . . [others] just by embracing me, . . . [others] just by kissing me, and achieve an enlightening concentration called "contact with the treasury of virtue of all beings." All those who come to me I establish in this enlightening liberation of ultimate dispassion, on the brink of the stage of unimpeded omniscience.[68]

Significantly, Vasumitra stops the description of her skillful means at the stage of kissing. Myōe, in some of his dreams, goes one or two steps further. In one of the most famous, he tells us how he discovers a doll of Chinese origin, who is transformed under his eyes (or more precisely, in his hands) into a beautiful young woman. But she is soon accused by another priest to have mated with a serpent. While refusing to believe in these accusations, Myōe wonders whether the young woman does not also have a reptilian form. When he interprets the dream upon awaking, he concludes that she was none other than the Nāga-girl Zenmyō (Ch. Shanmiao). According to legend, this Buddhist Melusine was originally a young Chinese girl who fell in love with the Korean monk Ŭisang while the latter was in China. When Ŭisang embarked on a ship to return to his homeland, she threw herself into the waves, being transformed into a dragon that escorted Ŭisang's ship back to Korea. Then, changing into a large rock, she became the protecting deity of the monastery he had founded. This platonic story had apparently made a deep impression on Myōe, for he returns to it on several occasions. The sexual connotations of this dream have often been noted, but Frédéric Girard denies them in favor of an essentially didactic interpretation.[69] The two types of inter-

---

[68] See Cleary 1989: 146–49. Note in the *Sūtra of Bhādrapala* (T. 13, 417) the association between prostitutes and bodhisattvas. The sūtra compares the experience of visiting various buddhas while in samādhi to visiting various prostitutes in a dream and remaining in love with them after awaking. See Hurvitz, trans., 1956: 851.

[69] Girard 1990a: 329; 1990b: 185.

pretation are not mutually exclusive, and we know since Freud that sublimation or secondary elaboration constitute one of the mechanisms of the dream. In other dreams, Myōe clearly states that that he had sexual relationships with "plump" ladies.

Myōe seems to have identified himself with both the Korean priests Ŭisang and Wŏnhyo. The famous image of Wŏnhyo looking at the moon, for instance, is strongly reminiscent of Myōe's portrait, and for this reason it has sometimes been attributed to the same painter.[70] If Wŏnhyo and Ŭisang are both projections of Myōe, one cannot study Ŭisang alone in relation with Zenmyō.[71] Like Ŭisang, Myōe was described as a "handsome man." He seems to have been in frequent contact with women, and he notes himself that he often dreams of women. After the troubles of the Jōkyu era, he founded a nunnery (named, significantly, Zenmyōji) , and many women came to depend on him. Nevertheless, is is known as a monk who in his whole life never had any sexual relation with women. Here is how he describes himself in his autobiography: "Ever since I was a child, it was my deepest desire to become a worthy priest, and I thought I must remain pure all my life and not commit any sexual transgressions. I do not know what spirit I was entrusted to, but every time I had an opportunity to engage in a sexual act, a mysterious impediment prevented me. I repeatedly awakened myself from my deluded state until I was finally able to realize my aspiration."[72]

Another epoch-making dream is the one experienced by the young Shinran at Rokkakudō, a temple tracing its origins back to Shōtoku Taishi. In 1201, the future founder of Jōdo Shinshū left Mount Hiei to undertake a hundred-day retreat in the Kannon temple. On the ninety-fifth day, at dawn, Kannon appeared to him in the form of Shōtoku, and gave him the following verse:

> Because, due to the retribution of past karma,
> [you,] the practitioner, are involved in sex,
> I will manifest myself as a jade woman so that you can possess me.
> I will adorn your life, and at the moment of death,
> I will guide you to the land of ultimate happiness.[73]

[70] See Brock 1984; and Karen L. Brock, "One Life as Another: Wŏnhyo as Myōe, Myōe as Wŏnhyo" *Bulletin de l'Ecole Française d'Extrême-Orient* (forthcoming).

[71] See Brock 1990.

[72] Kawai 1992: 178.

[73] The *Shinran muki* (Record of Shinran's Dream) continues: "The Bodhisattva Kannon offered this verse to Zenshin [Shinran] and said: 'It is my vow. You shall proclaim the meaning of this vow everywhere, so that every sentient being hears it.' [Shinran] addressed people as ordered by the bodhisattva, and when he imagined that he had come to the end of his address, he awoke from his dream." On this dream, see for instance Inoue 1993, and Kiyomoto 1992.

This verse has embarrassed Shinshū scholars, who have tried to explain it away as apocryphal. But in 1959 an "autograph" copy was discovered at Sennyūji. Other mentions of the dream were found, quoting the *Shinran muki*, in the *Kyōshakumon kikigaki* by Shinbutsu and in a letter by Eshinni, Shinran's wife. The verse is also quoted, without reference to Shinran, in the *Kakuzenshō*. The "jade woman" appears also in the dreams of Myōe and of the Tendai prelate Jien as a metaphor for the *cintāmaṇi*, or wish-fulfilling jewel. This material is perhaps merely a justification for the monks' sexual transgressions and their taking wives. However, Tanaka Takako has argued that the sexual reading of the verse is too superficial, and she shows convincingly that the motif of the jade woman is a complex one. But the fact that other interpretations are possible (in which "jade woman" comes to mean Buddhist relics, and so on), does not invalidate the sexual reading; on the contrary, it makes it richer.

Kannon is not the only Buddhist deity to provide (or promise) sexual gratification to men. Another case in point is that of Kichijōten (Skt. Lakṣmī), an Indian deity of wealth converted to Buddhism. A layman who has fallen in love with the representation of the goddess asks for a woman like her. He makes love in a dream with her, and the following day sees that the image is polluted. However, the story is one of sexual gratification, not of divine salvation, and the lover is not a monk.[74]

We have also mentioned an earlier encounter between a Hieizan monk and a beautiful woman who turned out to be a manifestation of the Bodhisattva Kokūzō.[75] Although in this story there is no sexual fulfillment, the words of Kokūzō to the monk recall those of Kannon to the young Shinran: "I will become father and mother of this person, his wife and his children . . . . I will become the woman he loves, to incite him to study."

Another famous courtesan story is that of the vision of the Bodhisattva Fugen (Samantabhadra) by the priest Shōkū (910–1003).[76] Having prayed for a vision of Fugen, Shōkū has the revelation in a dream that he must pay a visit to a courtesan of Kanzaki. He therefore goes to see her. She is sitting on the side and takes a drum. When Shōkū closes his eyes he sees Fugen, when he opens them he sees the woman. After having paid his homage, he wants to leave, but she follows him and dies before his eyes. The story here does not mean sex between the monk and the courtesan, but the salvation of the monk/man by the bodhisattva/courtesan.

Along the same lines, we find the story of the relationships between

---

[74] See *Nihon ryōiki* 2: 13, translated Nakamura 1973: 178.

[75] See *Konjaku monogatari shū* 17: 33; translated in Frank 1968: 131–38.

[76] See *Kojidan* 3. The same story appears with variants in the *Jikkinshō* and the *Senjūshō*.

Kūya Shōnin and Monju (Mañjuśrī).[77] Kūya (903–972) pays a visit every morning to a sick woman outside the northern gate of Shinsen'en, and buys raw meat at her request. When she gets better, she wants to sleep with him. When, after some reflection, he is about to answer, she turns out to be an old fox of Shinsen'en, and disappears, saying: "The *shōnin* is a true saint." In the *engi* (genealogical story) Kūya realizes that it is Monju who has come to test him. Unlike the *Kūya rui*, the *Rokuharamitsuji engi* emphasizes that the old fox, which under the form of a sick woman had convinced Kūya to sleep with her, was in fact an avatar of Mañjuśrī. Kūya is called a saint (*shōnin*) although (or perhaps because) he—almost—transgressed the taboos against having sex and eating meat.

There are many stories of sexual relations between a man and a she-fox passing herself off as a woman. The fact that the fox in the above story is that of Shinsen'en makes it a divine messenger, like the foxes of Inari or Ise, who combine with Dakiniten and are worshiped in secret rituals of Shingon and Tendai. By 1122, date of the compilation of the *Rokuharamitsuji engi,* the theory of the identity of the fox with Monju was already in existence, and the sexual relations between Kūya and a fox/woman are in fact those between a saint and a deity; the change of Kūya's image in the *Rokuharamitsuji engi* seems to indicate that the motif of the "salvation by an avatar of the bodhisattva"—appearing as a woman—was already established in the twelfth century, as we saw in the cases of Kokūzō, Fugen, and Monju. The vogue of such stories may reflect social changes affecting the Buddhist saṅgha in the second half of the eleventh century, and the greater tolerance for monks having sex with a woman or taking a wife. However, similar stories were already widespread in Tang China.

RITUAL INFRACTIONS

Tantric Visions and Revisions

Another related form of imaginary transgression has to do with visions and visualizations. In the Vajrayāna, for instance, there is a form of ritual transgression that consists in visualizing an incest. In the *Caṇḍa-mahāroṣaṇa-tantra,* we find the description of a form of meditation in which the ascetic must picture his own body as transparent, similar to space. Then he must meditate on Akṣobhya coming out of a lotus and united with Māmakī. Thereupon he must draw near, his thought ab-

---

[77] See *Kūya rui,* by Minamoto Tamenori (d. 1011), and *Rokuharamitsuji engi,* by Miyoshi Tameyasu (1049–1139).

sorbed in Akṣobhya's head, turned toward Māmaki's organ. Then, transformed into spermatic fluid, he must fall into the latter's organ. Thereafter, he must emerge from the organ and kill the father, Akṣobhya, with a sword. Then, he must make love to Māmaki, the mother, whom he visualizes as one of the vajrayoginīs associated with the four vajrayogins.[78] The ascetic then does with these vajrayogins the same thing as he has done with Akṣobhya. Finally, after making love to the four goddesses, he must remove the whole maṇḍala.[79]

According to Filliozat, the *Caṇḍamahāroṣaṇa-tantra* is one of the texts that have given a bad name to "Tantrism." In this text, the emphasis is on sexual union as the supreme realization, especially "when it is practiced in conditions which could set in motion the most violent psychological states, such as the state of consciousness of moral censure (consciousness of incest and of the ignominy of woman) or of repulsion (consuming excrements)."[80] As we can see, the violations remain purely mental.[81]

We also recall the ritual union leading to Tantric *sahaja* ("co-emergence" of preliminary and ultimate bliss).[82] Significantly, this type of union was part of a ritual of royal consecration. In Japan, the relations between sexual ritual and royal consecration were revived during the medieval period, a time that saw the consolidation of the notion of sacred kingship and the emergence of the Tachikawa school of Tantrism. As D. L. Snellgrove puts it, "Indeed it is only in Tantric practice that one may identify a notion of kingship which is in any sense sacral or divine."[83] The originally regal meaning of the consecration was subsequently transformed and the association with kingship became latent.

---

[78] These vajrayoginīs correspond to the emotional states that inspire the violation of the five Buddhist precepts: *moha,* the erring that inebriates; *pisuna,* the calumny that destroys sincerity; *rāga,* passion; *īrṣyā,* envy that incites to theft; *dveṣa,* hatred that impels to kill.

[79] *Caṇḍamahāroṣaṇa-tantra* 4: 16–19; see Filliozat 1991b: 429–31. See also the description given by Strickmann ("L'amour chez les éléphants"): Vajrasattva is surrounded by the Vajra-beings of the Four Defilements: Desire, Pleasure, Passion, and Pride (also called the Five Secret Beings). The orthodox interpretation, according to which the four *kleśa* (defilements) are purified and transformed into virtues by their identification with Vajrasattva is only a pious veil thrown over the sexual symbolism of these "secret beings" who "serve as pretext to an antinomian expression veiled with autogratification by the meditator." Strickmann 1996: 279.

[80] Filliozat 1991b: 429.

[81] In the course of an exercise said to be of "creation" (*bhāvanā,* a psychic creation), the adept imagines, for instance, a god in a terrible form uniting with a goddess who represents that god's energy. He then creates in his mind hatred for the god, love for the goddess, and sees himself killing the god and himself uniting with the goddess in his place. See *Caṇḍamahāroṣaṇa-tantra* 4: 18 ff., 33 ff., Skt. folios 13a, 14b, quoted in Filliozat 1991b: 334.

[82] On this notion, see Kvaerne 1975.

[83] Snellgrove 1959b: 204.

Describing the ritual sequence of the *Hevajra-tantra,* Snellgrove notes, almost incidentally, that in the Secret Consecration (*guhyābhiṣeka*), "the master drops the sacramental *bodhicitta* into the pupil's mouth"— without indicating that this bodhicitta is actually the semen ejaculated during the master's union with a female ritual partner—and in the Consecration of the Knowledge of Wisdom (*prajñājñānābhiṣeka*) he presides over the pupil's ritual union with her.[84] We have no evidence that these rites were ever practiced in Japan outside the Tachikawa school, but it is quite plausible, since their scriptural basis was at the core of Japanese Tantrism. The distance between Indo-Tibetan Tantrism and Sino-Japanese "esotericism" is by no means as great as Japanese scholars, intent on proving the "purity" of mikkyō (esoteric doctrine), would have us believe. This is clear, for instance, from "orthodox" texts like Jien's *Bizei betsu* (Particular Notes on the Abhiṣeka), in which we hear about the sexual union between the emperor and his consort, as Tantric adepts.[85] In Japanese mikkyō, as in Indo-Tibetan Vajrayāna, a number of Buddhist deities were feminized, and the adept had ritual sex with them (or their human substitutes), although the murder of his male divine rivals was not emphasized. However, can one still speak of transgression when the sexual object or partner is a Buddhist deity?

The Tachikawa School

When does transgression becomes inacceptable, and under what conditions is it labeled "heretical"? A rapid examination of the fate of the Tachikawa branch of Shingon may help us anwer these questions. It is in Shingon and Tendai Buddhism that we find for the first time two movements that have been commonly labeled "heresies" (*jakyō*). For all its radical criticism of established Buddhism, even the Nichiren school was not disqualified by this label, and it remained a powerful trend within Buddhism. The Shingon and Tendai traditions, however, tried for centuries to assert a rather problematic distinction between "esoteric Buddhism, or "pure esotericism," and Tantrism (or "mixed esotericism"), that is, a form of Tantrism unexpurgated of its darker magical (and in particular sexual) elements.

The Tachikawa branch is said to have emerged during the Kamakura period, with the teachings of Ninkan (d.u.) and Monkan (1281–1357). It advocated sexual union as the fusion of the two maṇḍalas and as a technique leading to the apotheosis called *sokushin jōbutsu* ("becoming a

[84] Ibid., 216.
[85] See Tendai shūten hensansho, ed., *Zoku Tendaishū zensho,* Mikkyō 3, Kyōten chūshakurui 11: 212–56 (Tokyo: Shunjūsha, 1990).

buddha in this very body"). Certain aspects of the Vajrayāna, which were considered if not entirely orthodox at least acceptable in Tibetan Buddhism, came to provoke strong reactions on the part of conventional Japanese Buddhists. Consequently, the Tachikawa movement was forbidden during the Muromachi period. Despite its formal disappearance, however, its influence lingered and was felt in many places, in the imperial house as well as in Shingon and Zen monasteries.

There is one specific ritual, studied by Noel Péri and James Sanford, which gives an idea of the extent to which transgression can be taken (in principle).[86] It is the "skull ritual." Briefly, the idea is to use a skull in which male and female fluids are poured for a very long period (seven years) to animate it, thereby creating a kind of android that will reveal the mysteries of the invisible world to its master. We are here in the same black-magical atmosphere that surrounds the aghori ascetics in India, who are believed to sit on corpses in cemetaries to acquire power by absorbing the dead's remaining vital principles.[87] Although we may wonder whether such practices belong to the realm of real or imagined transgression, one can understand why such teachings were eventually prohibited in Japan.

Transgression in the Tachikawa rituals finds its limits in the fact that these practices may not have been carried out. Likewise, we have seen that Chan transgression shied away from sexuality while affirming that "passions are enlightenment." Indeed, the most transgressive aspects probably remained a dead letter, as in the case of the skull ritual—when they were not merely the product of the phantasms of the detractors of the Tachikawa "heresy." Furthermore, in the case of simpler rituals involving sexual union, their transgressive nature is legitimized by the fact that they were indeed practiced, if not by everybody at least by a figure as orthodox as the emperor himself. Even when he was ordained as a Buddhist priest, he was apparently exempt from following the rule against sexual union. Like the Buddha, the ruler of the land is not bound by the common laws. Furthermore, the reproduction of imperial power implies sexual reproduction, the production of male heirs in whom the kingship will survive; and the success of this patrimonial enterprise depended to a large extent on the spiritual powers of Buddhist monks. There was at court an interesting institution, that of the "attendant priests" (gojisō), ritual specialists selected among the superiors of the major esoteric temples. These priests were at the service of the emperor and of his heirs. They had to spend all nights in a room next to that of the emperor, performing rituals and prayers for his protection and the prosperity of

---

[86] See Péri 1917; Sanford 1991a.
[87] See Parry 1982.

the country. One of their functions, to which we will return in the next chapter, was to insure imperial fecundity.[88]

One such monk was the Shingon priest Ningai (d. 1046), often described as a transgressive monk, who liked in particular to eat meat.[89] We noted that in many sources there is a strong association between meat consumption and flesh/sex. Sexual transgression is often tied to the transgression of vegetarianism. The drift from one transgression to the other is clear in the case of the "five *m*" (*panca-makāra*) of Indian Tantrism.[90] But we seem to have in Ningai's case a form of what some would call "sacred transgression," because Ningai is said to have had powers almost as great as those of Kōbō Daishi.

In magic rites, obtaining power over the other (through either sex or death—namely, by obtaining the "human yellow") is often only a question of degree: in both cases, one steals the vital energy of the other (partner or enemy).

The power of sexual transgression is implied in a number of stories: we are told, for instance, that the famous hermit of Katsuragi, Kume Sennin, had lost his power when he saw a maiden washing clothes. It might be argued, however, that his true nature was revealed at the contact with a woman. Although he later regained his powers, because of the transgression and the subsequent humiliation he had become a more humane figure.

As noted above, an interesting example of the affinities between imperial ritual and Tantric Buddhism is that of a text written by the Tendai abbot Jien (1155–1225), the *Bizei betsu*. Jien was the younger brother of the regent Kujō Kanezane (1149–1207) and a member of the influential Fujiwara clan, which had risen to power owing to its shrewd matrimonial strategies—by providing wives to generations of emperors. In this text, Jien describes a dream he had, which he interprets as a symbolic representation of the sexual union between the emperor and his consort, called the "jade woman"—one of the seven treasures of the universal ruler (*cakravartin*, "wheel-turning king").[91] He argues that the emperor's enthronement abhiṣeka (*sokui kanjō*) was realized through a sexual

[88] The affinities between royal ritual and Tantric Buddhism have come to light in recent Japanese studies. See, for instance, Abe 1984, 1985. In English, see the forthcoming work of Abe Ryūichi, *The Weaving of Mantra*.

[89] On Ningai as meat eater, see *Kojidan* 3. The text emphasizes that, despite his taste for birds' flesh, Ningai has supranormal powers.

[90] These five transgressions are *madhya* (alcohol), *māṃsa* (meat), *matsya* (fish), *mudrā* (dry grain), and *maithunā* (sexual intercourse). In the *Rudra-Yāmala*, Vāsiṣṭha, son of a brahman, abandons austerities when he sees in China the Buddha surrounded by naked adepts, who drink alcohol, eat meat, and have sex. The Buddha teaches him the true meaning of sexual rites. See van Gulik 1961: 434.

[91] *Bizei betsu*, 231–32. See also Akamatsu 1957: 318–22, and Taga 1980: 421.

union between the emperor and his consort, corresponding symbolically to the first two regalia (the sword and the jewel), and to the Tantric deities Ichirin butchō (Skt. Ekākṣara-uṣṇīṣacakra) and Butsugen butsumo (Buddhalocana). This union creates the third of the regalia, the mirror, corresponding to the Sun Goddess Amaterasu, a manifestation of the Buddha Vairocana. It therefore asserts the status of the emperor as a cakravartin king and the complementarity of royal law (ōbō) and Buddha Dharma (buppō). According to tradition, there was also during the ancient ceremony of enthronement (daijōsai) a part held absolutely secretly, during which an imitation of the hierogamy between the emperor and the deity (Amaterasu herself?) may have been enacted with a sacred prostitute. Likewise, the priestesses of Ise and Kamo shrines, younger sisters of the new emperor, were said to have a solemn sexual union with the kami. The sexual symbolism of the imperial accession ceremony is the same as that of the Tachikawa ritual, although it is not clear which one influenced the other. At any rate, these ideas must have had a wide (if esoteric) currency at the time for Jien to dream about them, and to see them fit to justify the imperial ideology he was hoping to promote. The fact that this ideology was later coopted by Shintō theologians and purified of its Tantric elements should not mislead us. It is not a mere coincidence that this expurgation occurred precisely at the time when the Tachikawa teaching was being turned into a "heresy" and prohibited.

FEMININE TRANSGRESSION

All the motifs of sexual transgression examined above share at least one characteristic: even when the transgressive act requires the participation of a woman, it is essentially performed by a man. For all their talk about breaking the rule, Mahāyāna Buddhists usually show very little tolerance for transgression when it is not male. What happens, however, when the transgression is carried out by a woman? Is not woman in essence (or by accident) transgressive? Because of her yin nature, she is said to belong to the realm of darkness and impurity. Perhaps under Buddhist influence, feminine impurity came to be connected with transgression, as seen in the motif of the goddess banished from heaven. The ambivalent Buddhist attitude toward women was also partly determined by social factors such as the primacy of filial piety and the kinship lineage. Women are also mothers, to whom males (including monks) owe a "milk debt."[92] As spouses, they constitute for the patrilineal system a necessary evil; but once they have become mothers, they become an integral if subordinate

[92] On this question, see Cole 1996. I will return to the status of mothers in Buddhism in *Purity and Gender*.

part of the lineage. Chinese monks, although they had in principle "left the family," remained more dependent than their Indian counterparts on social and familial structures. Eventually, despite some initial reluctance, they became the ideological keepers of Chinese society. With their mortuary services, whose functional ambiguity allowed them to produce with the same ritual gesture ancestors (rightfully inscribed in a lineage) and buddhas (in principle freed from lineage and rebirth), the Buddhists were able to take root in Chinese soil. They came to advocate on the one hand what they denied on the other: the importance of family continuity, and consequently of the procreative role of women, upon which rests the fate of the lineage. Meanwhile, they offered to some women an exit door, a means to escape this role—a particularly unrewarding role in Chinese society—through ordination as nuns. Typical in this respect are the Chinese stories in which a young girl not only transgresses the established social order by refusing to marry but also defies ecclesiastical authority. In Japan, a famous literary case is that of "the girl who loved caterpillars," an idiosyncratic individual who refused to play the game of femininity (wearing makeup, etc).[93] But these forms of transgression of social norms are not specifically sexual. In the case of the courtesan, however, things are different. We have already noted the motif of the female bodhisattva who, like Vasumitra or Guanyin, or the "Jade Woman" in Japanese Tantrism, use sexuality to convert men. Sometimes she brings them sexual gratification, sometimes she scares them. Thus, in the *Da zhuang'yan famen jing* (Sūtra of the Adornment of the Great Dharma Gate, T. 818), the bodhisattva Mañjuśrī brings awakening to a famous courtesan of Rājagṛha, the Lady Golden Light. He then sends her back to her suitors, saying: "A bodhisattva free of defilement, even when associating with impure people, does not risk a bad reputation. . . . When she lays her head on the lap of a noble's son, she manifests herself, owing to her powers, like a corpse in decomposition." Stricken with panic, he realizes the nature of the female body and takes refuge with the Buddha— where Lady Golden Light eventually rejoins him.[94]

Speaking about the different standards that apply to ordinary people and sages, Mujū Ichien seems willing to acknowledge certain female types of trangression: "We know the case of Lady Mallika, who observed the Precepts while taking drugs, and that of Vasumitra, who led a pure life in the midst of debauchery; one cannot deny that these women were sages." Transgression may be accepted in the case of ideal women, but not so well in the case of ordinary mortals.

The emblem of sexual transgression is the courtesan. The Buddhist

---

[93] See *Tsutsumi chūnagon monogatari*, translated in Backus 1985.
[94] T. 17, 818: 831a.

attitude toward the courtesan was from the outset ambivalent, however: she was feared as a temptress, an emissary of hell; had not the Buddha himself, in a former reincarnation as the hermit Unicorn, been shamefully seduced by one of them? Yet the courtesan is also a woman who, in a sense, has "left the world" and can see through its vanity. She has awakened to the (conventional) truth, because she can see behind appearances, through the veil of illusion. She is no longer bound by ordinary social ties and conventional norms, because she can see through men's games. She is not impressed by their social distinctions—priests, commoners, or nobility, all are the same to her—and she can, like a true teacher, manipulate them through her own "skillful means." At the same time, she is perhaps, more than anybody else, prisoner in the net of Māra, bound by the world of desire. Moreover, she plays the evil role of temptress. Māra's own daughters appear to the meditating Buddha as temptresses, skilled courtesans. Equally threatening is the courtesan (or, in some cases, the nun) who, instead of tempting the monk challenges him; although this defiance is not necessarily sexual, the monk eventually takes his revenge by reducing her to her sexuality. The courtesan should also be an object of pity, however, caught as she is in the transiency of things. But Buddhists have preferred to emphasize her abjection, moral and physical. A typical case of a femme fatale is that of the poetess Ono no Komachi, who was made to suffer the karmic result of her past offences by being possessed by the angry spirit of her former lover. She has to be physically degraded while she is alive, as in the nō play *Sotoba Komachi,* where she appears as a hag; but also after her death, when her decaying corpse becomes a memento mori.[95]

As a temptress but also as a suffering being, the courtesan is often attracted to the monk. The figure of another famous Japanese poetess, Izumi Shikibu, reflects well these two aspects. According to tradition, she fell in love with the priest Dōmyō (who turned out to be her own son). According to the *Uji shūi monogatari,* Dōmyō was a man "much given to amorous pursuits," who had an affair with Izumi Shikibu. Once, as he was spending the night at her place, he awoke and began to recite the *Lotus Sūtra.* At dawn, he noticed the presence of an old man and, upon inquiring who he was, he learned that he was the Dōsojin of Fifth Avenue, who had come to listen to Dōmyō's recitation. " 'But I often read the *Lotus Sūtra,*' said Dōmyō. 'Why have you chosen tonight to tell me this?' 'When you have purified yourself before reading the sūtra,' replied the Deity from Fifth Avenue, 'Brahma and Indra and other divine beings come to listen to you and the likes of me cannot get near enough to hear. But tonight you read it without having cleansed yourself first, and so Brahma and Indra were not there to listen. This gave me a chance to

[95] See Waley, trans. (1921) 1976: 114–24.

come and hear it myself, an experience I shall never forget.' "[96] Thus, Dōmyō has been defiled by his lovemaking with Izumi Shikibu, so much so that his usual protecting deities abandon him temporarily—giving a chance to the Dōsojin, a god of sex, to approach him. However, Izumi Shikibu also appears as a pathetic woman in the poem that she writes for the priest Shōkū after being denied an interview with him: "From darkness / Into the path of darkness / Must I enter: Shine upon me from afar, / O Moon above the mountain crest."[97]

The intransigeant attitude of Buddhist monks, emphasized in the canonical tradition, became more nuanced in Buddhist literature—for reasons of proselytism perhaps, but also because Buddhist themes were reappropriated by popular culture, in which love and sexuality were seen in a more positive light. For instance, Izumi and her lover Dōmyō underwent an apotheosis of sorts, becoming the male and female gods of love, an avatar of the dual Dōsojin. A similar apotheosis was experienced by Ono no Komachi and her lover Ariwara no Narihira. Another "illicit" conquest of Narihira is that of the priestess (saigū) of Ise. Here again, the two lovers are eventually deified, and their union becomes that of the yin and the yang: in the esoteric commentaries of the Ise monogatari, a text telling the love adventures of Narihira, he becomes a divine avatar who, through sexual union, guides women toward salvation. The transgressive union between the Ise priestess and the poet has become a hieratic union between the goddess Amaterasu and a divine male. It is the medieval reenactment of the primordial union between the deities Izanami and Izanagi, the "ancestral deities" (Dōsojin), or gods of yin and yang.[98] In other medieval documents, the Ise priestess, instead of being a human manifestation of the goddess Amatarasu, becomes the wife and sexual partner of the kami, now conceived as a male god.[99] The figure of the Dōsojin, on the margins of Buddhism, was instrumental in the acclimatization of transgression in the Buddhist culture of Japan. The Japanese tradition, however, remains ambivalent: at times the transgression is perceived as sacrilegious, and the defiled woman is rejected by the god. At others, as in the case of Izumi Shikibu and Dōmyō, the transgression (in this case a double one, since it is also an incest), is transformed into a positive act through the cult of the Dōsojin, a cult that contributed to the transformation of Buddhism into a doctrine advocating sex and fertility.

We spoke earlier of a double transgression for the Tantric monk, who transgressed the rules of society by "leaving home," and further trans-

---

[96] See Mills 1970: 135–36.

[97] "Kuraki yori / kuraki michi ni zo / irinubeki / haruka ni terase / yama no ha no tsuki." See *Kōchū kokkai taikei* 3 (1927): 64; quoted in Cranston 1969: 6.

[98] On this question, see Tanaka 1996: 112–13.

[99] See ibid.

gressed the moral precepts in the name of a higher, antinomian ideal. In the case of women, Buddhists were much more ambivalent about the first type of transgression to the extent that they came to endorse the social ideology of their time. In some extreme cases they felt compelled to come to the rescue of women who wanted to escape their social and familial bondage, but they were much more reluctant to let women assert their freedom within the Buddhist order. We hear of practically no female tricksters. Women who transgressed the rules or crossed the line were, without exception, regarded as "bad" or "evil" women.

A paradigmatic case is the well-known example of the Chinese empress Wu Zetian. She had been a courtesan and a nun before becoming an empress (or rather, emperor) and a bodhisattva. There are other famous cases of femmes fatales in Chinese and Japanese history. The best known is that of Yang Guifei, who attempted to emulate Empress Wu, but tragically failed, bringing Emperor Xuanzong down with her.[100] Yet, she was redeemed by her tragic end and was even deified later as an avatar of the Bodhisattva Kannon. Her icon can be seen, for instance, at Sennyūji, a Kyoto monastery closely connected to the imperial family.

In Japan, the story of Wu Zetian is often paired with that of Empress Shōtoku (alias Kōken), a woman who also tried to usurp the throne— although not for herself, like Wu Zetian, but for her lover, the priest Dōkyō, whom she promoted as Priest Emperor (*hōō*) in 667. Here again, as we will see shortly, the transgression was later downplayed, in part due to the fact that Shōtoku and her lover became manifestations of the Dō-sojin.[101] However, Shōtoku was condemned for her lust. Her legend sheds interesting light on the way in which lustful women became the topic of sexist discourse. We are told that this lust was the result of her having a very large vagina. This unusual anatomy was itself the result of her bad karma, due to her slandering the Buddha in reaction to the misogyny of the Buddhist teaching. According to the *Keiran shūyōshū,* "When Shō-toku read the *Nirvāṇa-sūtra,* she found the following verse: 'All the passions of the men in the 3,000 worlds do not match the karmic hin-derances of a single woman.' She said: 'Although I am a woman, I have no passions. The Buddha lied.' Then she burnt the scriptures. Because of this sin, her passions were aroused constantly, and her vagina became

---

[100] On Wu Zetian's lover, the monk Xie Haiyi, see the *Sengni niehai,* translated by Huang and Basse 1992: 106–8. This monk is said to have set fire to the *mingtang* ("hall of light") built by Wu Zetian because of his jealousy toward his rival, the imperial doctor Zhen Nanniu. For the historical background of this legend, see Forte 1976.

[101] According to the *Shasekishū,* "This empress was no ordinary person. A story is told of her vow with Amoghapāśa Avalokiteśvara at the Saidai Temple. The things she did were gossiped about, but they were not thought of as precedents. Her actions really should be understood as the actions of a Buddhist incarnation (*gongen*)." See Morrell 1985: xxx.

large."[102] We can see here that her punishment is due to her profanation of the scriptures, but above all to her taking a stand against Buddhism's misogyny. In other words, she has become a scapegoat. All the criticisms against her are collected in the *Mizu kagami,* where she is described as a "lascivious" woman who, by transgressing the Buddhist precept against lust, causes havoc in the world. The *Mizu kagami* also reveals the dirty secret of Shōtoku's death: since Shōtoku's vagina had grown so large that even Dōkyō, despite his robust anatomy, could no longer satisfy her, she resorted to a substitute, a dildo that, when it broke inside her, caused her death.

The criticism against Shōtoku did not entirely originate in Buddhist circles, however, it also reflected the patriarchal and imperial ideologies of the time. Shōtoku had first ascended to the throne as Empress Kōken, succeeding her father Shōmu. As such, she was condemned to celibacy, and to sterility: an empress cannot marry below her rank, or be the servant of any man. The scandal provoked by her affair with Dōkyō was also due to this social faux pas. The *Mizu kagami* suggests that with the rise of Dōkyō, the fragile balance between royal law (*ōbō*) and Buddhist Law (*buppō*) had been destroyed, because Buddhism, instead of remaining subordinated to kingship, came to take precedence over it. This union "against nature" was the harbinger of a "topsy-turvy" world that had to be prevented by all means, and was still conjured long after its demise.

Another woman known for her lust is Fujiwara Kaneko, better known as Kyō no nii (Lady of Second Rank). Because she had been the nurse of Emperor Go-Toba, she enjoyed great power, exerting the same sort of influence at the capital that Hōjō Masako, the widow of the first shōgun Yoritomo, exerted in Kamakura. After the death of her husband, Senior Counselor Muneyori (1154–1203), Kaneko remarried with Prime Minister Ōimikado Yorizane. Like Empress Shōtoku, she acquired a bad reputation among men, and was said to have fallen into a demoniac destiny

---

[102] Similar stories are found in the the *Bishamondō Kokinshū chū* (14th century), or in the *Kokinshū chū nukigaki*—two medieval commentaries on the *Kokinshū.* See Tanaka 1992: 49–50. In later commentaries, the way in which Shōtoku calumniates the scriptures becomes even worse: she does not simply burn them, she wipes her vagina with them. See, for instance, the *Hoki shō* (a commentary on the *Hoki naiden,* an Onmyōdō text) and the *Teikin shiki* (a commentary on the *Teikin ōrai,* in Tenri Library), quoted in Tanaka 1992: 51. The *Mizu kagami,* ca. 1200, describes the incident as follows: "The Saidai Temple was built in 765, and bronze statues were made of the Four Heavenly Kings. Three were successfully cast, but there were seven failures in casting the fourth. Finally the empress made this vow: 'If I can discard my womanly body and become a Buddha through Buddha's virtue, may the next casting be successful as I put my hand into the molten copper. And may my hand be burned off if my prayer is not to be granted.' Not the slightest injury was found on the empress's hand, and the fourth statue was then cast successfully. See *NKBT* 12: 79; quoted in Brown and Ishida 1979: 35.

after her death. According to a tradition, she once met a Miidera monk named Chōgon in front of a Inari shrine. Because of the ragged clothes of the ascetic, she caught a glimpse of his "big penis," and fell in love with him (or it?).[103] In all these stories, we are dealing with women whose "lust," or attraction to erotic pleasures, was seen as a potential threat to social order (these women, like the goddess Izanami in her first flirt with Izanagi, make the mistake of taking the initiative), and to normal sexual (and social) reproduction. Furthermore, they are women who exerted power over men, and sexual defamation has always been (and still is) a convenient way to get even at such women. Along the same lines, we sometimes find another motif: that of the high-ranking woman who is accused of adultery with an eminent monk, in order to discredit her lineage for purely political reasons. For instance, the Somedono empress was accused of having had an affair with the priest Shinzei. The scandal erupted ex post facto, when this priest, having died and become an angry ghost, returned to possess her. We find in the *Konjaku monogatari shū* the following account of the relations of the Somedono empress with the "holy man of Katsuragi" (Shinzei). After exorcizing her (she seems to have been prone to possession—a vicious circle indeed), the priest is asked to stay in the palace for a while: "Since it was summer, the empress was clad only in her undergarment, and the holy man caught a faint glimpse of her. Feeling as he had never felt before, he saw her handsome form, and his heart was suddenly distraught, and his liver went to pieces. He conceived a deep passion for the empress." Eventually, he attempted to rape her, was arrested by the imperial physician, Tajima no Kamotsugu, and thrown into prison. There he made an oath that he should die immediately and turn into a devil, and as long as the empress remained in the world he would have relations with her according to his pleasure. The matter was reported to the emperor, and the ascetic was sent back to his mountain. He starved himself to death, and became a black devil who came to possess the empress. Under a spell, she received him most cordially and led him to her room. When he finally left at sunset, the ladies-in-waiting rushed to the room, where they found the empress, apparently no different from usual but remembering nothing of what had happened. After that, the demon continued to visit her, and she always welcomed him. He then began to possess the sons of the Tamotsugu. Although the emperor called powerful exorcists, the demon continued to possess the empress. Once, he had sex with her even as the emperor was visiting her. The emperor went home, feeling hopeless and miserable. The story concludes: "Therefore, the noble ladies who may hear this should have no

---

[103] See for instance the *Keiran shūyōshū*, quoted in Tanaka 1992: 78–79.

relations whatsoever with such priests."[104] Obviously, the unfortunate Somedono empress is a mere pawn in a political conflict about imperial succession that goes beyond her: she is chosen because she is the most vulnerable link in the adverse lineage. Her (imaginary) rape is transformed into an expression of her lustful nature. In this case, the Buddhist condemnation of feminine transgression becomes a convenient alibi manipulated by a partisan clergy, involved in complex political rivalries.[105]

Feminine transgression remained legitimate in certain cases, however. We have seen that Buddhists were fond of stories in which a bodhisattva appeared as a prostitute or courtesan. In most cases, these images seem to come out of the monks' imagination, and it was perhaps a way to justify their own transgressions. We recall the story of the two Korean monks saved by a manifestation of the bodhisattva Avalokiteśvara. However, such motifs could be read as a legitimization of female transgression as well, and be used by women to justify their own freedom. The courtesan is, to some extent, recognized as a potential bodhisattva. But the motif seems to have developed largely outside of Buddhist orthodoxy. We are dealing here with "ideal" types, of course, and it seems that, except perhaps in the higher strata of society, women had more leeway than we usually tend to believe. Although Confucian ideology was predominant, it was not nearly as monolithic as we generally assume.[106]

We have seen that the Vinaya rule concerning sex refers to "illicit sexual acts." If for a monk or nuns all sexual acts are indeed illicit, at least for lay believers there is a licit sexuality. In the Chinese context, this normal—that is, reproductive—sexuality was not only tolerated but highly recommended, even by Buddhist monks. From this slighty different viewpoint, virginity does constitute a kind of sexual transgression, by default rather than by excess. Buddhists have also been ambivalent about chaste virgins who refused to fulfill their destinies of spouses and mothers. The theme of the "recalcitrant virgin" who refuses to marry, and sometimes prefers death, is a widespread one. Sometimes the Buddhist cloister provided these women with a refuge. But on the whole, Buddhism chose to support social values, and to assert filial piety to the detriment of the particular needs of female individuals. Uncompromising virginity could be somewhat threatening to well-established monks. The case, that of "Loquacious Lotus," a pugnacious girl whose constant bickering causes her in-laws to cancel the wedding, may give the impression that the image of the pure virgin could sometimes draw strangely close to that of the loose woman: indeed, both seem to reject social norms.

---

[104] See *Konjaku monogatari shū* 20. 7, translated in Brower 1952: 496–502.

[105] For a detailed analysis of this story, see Tanaka 1992: 84–152.

[106] On this question, see for instance the recent work of Dorothy Ko, 1994.

Guanyin, the bodhisattva who manifested himself as the virgin Miao-shan, is a good example of how easily signs can be inverted in this domain. As noted earlier, erotic allusions are at the heart of the various legends relative to this bodhisattva, in particular that of the "Wife of Mr. Ma." In some versions, this young girl, like the girl Lotus, dies on the very day of her wedding, but according to other versions, once married, she sleeps with all men and sets them free.[107] In the first case, after her death an old monk comes to collect her bones, which look like golden chains, and he tells people that Mr. Ma's wife was actually a bodhisattva. In the second version, the narrative sometimes merges with that of "Guanyin with the Fishbasket," who slept with men on the river bank.

Another interesting variation on the theme of the bodhisattva manifesting himself/herself as a prostitute is the story of a young woman of Yanzhou, who was loved by all men, to whom she readily gave her favors. After her untimely death, as she had no relatives, she was buried on the roadside. During the Dali era (766–779), a Central Asian monk came to pay homage to her grave and, to the astonishment of the local people, proclaimed that she was actually a "bodhisattva with linked bones." When her grave was opened to test his claim, a skeleton with linked bones—a feature characteristic of Daoist immortals—was revealed. Although in the end her true identity is revealed by a monk, this story, like others of the same kind, could be read as an attempt to emphasize female religiosity, a religiosity shortcutting male hierarchy. In Japan, we find stories like that of the holy man Shōkū who, prompted by a dream, visited a prostitute of Eguchi and realized that her true nature was that of the bodhisattva Fugen (Samantabhadra).

The theme of the woman as seducer also brings to mind the topos of the foxy lady, the she-fox who takes the form of a beautiful young woman to lure an unsuspecting young man. This unnatural conjunction usually leads to the illness and eventually the death of her partner, whose vital essence she steals. But sometimes, for instance in some Japanese Buddhist variants of the story, this illicit sex, actually a form of unconscious bestiality, is redeemed by love, and the Buddhist message of defi-

---

[107] The popular story of Lotus ("Liannu Attains Buddhahood on the Way to Her Wedding") appears in the *Liushijia xiaoshuo* (Sixty-Four Stories, Ming dynasty), by Hong Pian. The only daughter of a devout middle-aged couple, she is actually the reincarnation of a pious old woman who accumulated good karma by reciting the *Lotus Sūtra*. The young girl embarrasses her parents when she begins challenging passing monks with kōan, and then, when they cannot answer her, hitting them in typical Chan style. When her parents decide to marry her to a neighbor's son, she does not resist. However, on the day of the wedding, when the sedan chair carrying her reaches the bridegroom's house, she is found dead inside it. See Hanan 1981: 72.

ance toward female temptation is in the end blurred. Here, it is precisely sexual love that saves the two lovers. The theme of the fox brings to mind the image of the heavenly fox Inari, and that of Dakiniten. In Japan, this Tantric deity came to play an important role in the esoteric sexual rituals performed at the time of enthronement, but also in various magic rituals aimed at obtaining love—or more concretely, at obtaining sex and pregnancy for imperial consorts and other women of the nobility vying for the favors of a husband or an elusive lover.

．　．　．　．　．

The Buddhist discourse on transgression seems reserved to a a few superior men, in a society where women were practically under house arrest, forced to remain at home, and cornered in their role as mothers and wives: spatially and functionally nailed. However, there were some who refused this localization, who kept moving, changing places, changing roles, poaching on men's preserves. The courtesan, particularly in Japan, where she was also to some extent a religous figure, is perhaps the best representative of these women on the move. One may object, of course, that this wandering is still an effect of the structure, that it still belongs to the space of patriarchal ideology and obeys a more subtle form of constraint, and that the courtesans' freedom is of the kind needed, according to Foucault, for power to thrive. Yet, these women are already elsewhere, they do not let themselves be pinned down so easily. Elusive forever, they speak from another space: heterotopy, heterology. They poach on the preserves of official culture. However, since even this transgression, as noted above, remains textual, literary, it is fraught with ambiguity, and we cannot be entirely sure that it overlaps perfectly (if at all) with social transgression. But the virulence with which Buddhists reacted to it suggests that it was perceived as threatening in a very real way. The Buddhist ideology of transgression had backfired, and would backfire time and again, given the proper sociopolitical circumstances.

The "conspiracy of silence" about female transgression can receive at least two readings. In the first reading, this transgression remains irrelevant because women are irrelevant. This is the manifest content. The second reading focuses on the latent content: female transgression has to remain a blind spot because women have to be kept outside of male discourse. Acknowledging female transgression would actually be to permit women to break through the boundaries of male discourse. It would be a kind of performative (albeit passive) discourse—not one that does what it says but one that lets be done what it is talking about. In this model—not exclusive of the first—female transgression *has* to remain invisible or unthought, it has to be made irrelevant, if women are to be kept in a subaltern position. Only male transgression is permitted, because it reinforces the system of male *relevance*. The same can be said about lesbianism: it is not a mere oversight, but an active *omission*. Sexuality without men is properly unthinkable, whereas sexuality with men is thinkable (even if forbidden in the case of nuns), and becomes a privileged object of thought. In this sense, the relative equality, or rather parallelism, between men and women in respect to Vinaya can be said to be mere window dressing.

One may wonder if, when it becomes legitimized by the Mahāyāna teaching, Buddhist transgression still retains its force. The "deep complicity between the law and the violation of the law," as Georges Bataille puts it, sometimes becomes so blatant that the interdict is not only lifted, it is emptied of its meaning. Buddhists knew that "to establish a limit always means to overstep it."[108] Insofar as transgression becomes merely conventional, tending toward a mere aesthetic posture—or imposture—it no longer implies any true reversal of values, and it is no longer traversed by the fascination of danger. It is no longer a true transgression that "exceeds the profane world without destroying it." The thrust toward transcendence is halted, insofar as the inner experience no longer feels the anguish that called for the interdict, nor the desire that led to transgress the latter—nor, consequently, the pleasure that derived from that transgression. By advocating a return to the discipline that had been abandoned by the partisans of a sudden, antinomian Chan, Chinese (and Japanese) Buddhist masters were perhaps merely trying to salvage the symbolic force of transgression. The Chan school, in particular, was held captive in this creative double bind, in which monks had to adhere strictly to the rule while being confronted with the higher model of transgression. This transgression, however, remains a male privilege, and only in their wildest dreams did Buddhist monks allow women to share this privilege with them. In monastic biographies and popular tales, nuns, unlike monks, are always presented as chaste. Within the Buddhist order, there are practically no female tricksters. Even when nuns seems to overstep the limit, as in the case of the two Tiantai nuns who criticized the Chan master Puji, it has to do with authority, not with sexuality.[109] There seems to be no place in male Buddhist discourse for a "legitimate" female transgression. The latter has to come from the outside, from women who, because they refuse to be bound by Buddhist precepts, are not "transgressing" them in the strict sense, although they overstep the limits drawn by monks (the *kekkai* [inner sanctum], etc.). The charisma

---

[108] See Bataille 1986 and Adorno, in Gary Smith, ed., *On Walter Benjamin* (Cambridge: MIT Press, 1991), 4.

[109] Concerning these two figures, see Faure 1997b: 87.

of nuns is usually put in sexual terms. We have, for instance, the case of
Sari and of Emyō's sister Eshun. In the Nara period, the nun Sari was
perceived as a bodhisattva by the people. Her alleged transgression was
minor, since she was reproached by two priests for having trespassed the
limits by participating in a ritual reserved to monks. Her trenchant reply
silenced the priests, clearly showing her superior wisdom.[110] A similar
spiritual power is recognized to both women, but in Sari's case it is associated with her diminished sexual anatomy (she is said to have had no
vagina), whereas in Eshun's case, it is expressed as anatomic superiority:
to a monk who boasted about the length of his penis, she is said to have
spread her legs open and retorted that her vagina was deeper than the
monk's penis. Depending on the context, Sari's singular anatomy can be
perceived as a mark of inferiority (she is not even a woman, merely a
freak) or of superiority (she has the ideal, "closed" body of the bodhisattva). In her case, like in that of Eshun, however, we have typically
misogynistic talk that reduces women to their genitals. Although the
manifest content of their transgression is not of a sexual nature, their
avowed desire to be "on top" is criticized in sexually connoted
fashion—revealing that the latent content of this transgression was perceived in sexual terms.

Do we have a "principle of transgression" operating in Buddhism?
What happens when transgression itself becomes ideological, domesticated? If transgression retains a symbolic force that can be reactivated
under right circumstances, it encounters its limits in reality. We have to
distinguish between social and literary transgression. There is one type of
transgression that is, as it were, internal to Buddhism, and another that is
the result of the encroachment of other types of discourse (literature,
mythology) on Buddhist discourse. A transgression required (and contained) by a literary genre is a safe transgression. Thus, transgression is
fraught with ambiguity, and we must always question whether it is located in the social or the textual realm. Literary transgression can be the
reflection, or the harbinger, of social transgression, but in most cases it
seems condemned to remain a convenient alibi, a theoretical violation of
the law that actually reaffirms the law.

In medieval Japan, desire and transgression tend to become part of a
"dramatic" (yet often comic) dialectical narrative structure, in which
they serve as the impetus to a sequence of events leading to a happy
ending. Such is, for instance, the desire of the priest of Kurama, Saikōbō,
for the daughter of Saemon no jō in the *otogizōshi* (narrative story) *Sasayakitake monogatari*. The result is that desire is perceived more dialec-
tically, if not positively: it loses some of its evil nature, and in some cases

---

[110] See *Nihon ryōiki* 2: 19, translated in Nakamura 1973.

becomes consciously perceived as a necessary condition to enlightenment. The evil monk becomes a mere trickster figure.

Sexuality is caught up in this dialectic of obedience and transgression, of purity and defilement. Becoming a monk is already a transgression of social order, but the Buddhist community, in order to survive, needs to maintain a specific kind of social order. At the institutional level, ordination and confession create order and purity, clear boundaries of the ritual area, the inner sanctum (*kekkai*). However, at the symbolic level at least, transcendence can be reached only through a transgression of social order, of sexual taboos such as incest, of various aspects of purity through defilement (blood, excrement). At the soteriological level, awakening is often described as a conjunction (or inversion) of opposites in which, in some rare cases, women are placed on top. In Tantric Buddhism, the ritual transgression of monastic discipline involves sex with outcast women and sluts, visions of incest and murder. Perhaps the subversive tendencies in Buddhism overlap to some extent with the rise of women in Buddhist communities—or on their margins. Nevertheless, misogyny is fundamental among Buddhist ascetics—always worried about incontinence and the subsequent spiritual impotence—and the "fathers" were always concerned with the cohesion of their male community. Even when women were involved, transgression remained a male prerogative. What happens, then, when women turn the tables on the male rule, when they infringe on the sanctuary and poach on male preserves? This remains to be examined.

There is a regulated transgression—which results, perhaps, from a lowering, a loss of urgency of the constraints: transgression without danger, such as that of the "Chan madmen." Or (but perhaps it is the same) there is the transgression resulting from the interiorization of the constraints. The transgression remains external, and is compensated by a strict inner control of impulses. Perhaps we should see this as a passage to a higher degree of the "civilization process" described by Norbert Elias. (Such is, perhaps, the case of Tantric masters.)

The principle becomes particularly visible at certain times, for instance at the beginning of the medieval period, when Japanese imperial ideology was established through an increasingly marked distinction between "divine" and Buddhist rites. Buddhism participated in this "hieratization" through its solemn ritual, however, which rejects and excludes all marginality. At the same time, Japanese kingship was able to preserve a certain hubris, a sanctity of transgression, by relying precisely on certain Buddhist notions. There is indeed in Buddhism a kind of madness, deviation, which is not always feigned. It is the folly at the heart of reason, the blind spot of the Buddhist vision, which always resists domestication.

In the Vinaya, the sexual taboo is radical. And yet, as we noted above, through its very legalism and casuistics Vinaya produces all sorts of perverse effects, generating at times precisely the offenses that it claims to forbid. Whatever the solidity of its safety net, even when it is King Brahma's net (as described in the *Fanwang jing*), it will always be less tight than that of Māra.

There is a triangular relationship between desire, interdiction, and transgression. The interdiction creates at the same time desire and transgression. According to this schema, desire does not come first, it is itself an effect. In this sense, Vinaya could be read as a device to create desire and guilt. But it is also, and perhaps primarily, a differentiating device. The sexuality of the monk, far from being nonexistent (as Vinaya would have it), is above all of a different type; it distinguishes him from the profane. This explains the emergence of a sexuality specific to monks—in principle, not to nuns, these lesser monks: homosexuality, a form of sexuality that is hardly transgressive in this social context. However, as we will see in the case of Japan, when male homosexuality reached other social layers (warriors, artists, bourgeois), monastic "distinction" had had its day: the next step was to allow monks to marry, and to come back into (family) line. This step would be taken during the Meiji Restoration.

Through its interaction with Buddhism, imperial power seems to have found a legitimization regarding certain forms of transgression. Some forms of ritual transgression were legitimized in particular by Buddhism in the name of the raison d'état, for instance in the case of sexual esoteric rites performed for the emperor, or the enthronement rites (*sokui kanjō*) performed by him. The former rituals were aimed at ensuring a male offspring and the continuity of the imperial lineage. The latter, taking place at the time of the enthronement, also used a strongly sexual symbolism to renew magically the fertility and prosperity of the imperial house and the vitality of the ruler. Although admittedly exceptional, the case of Emperor Kazan having sex with a lady-in-waiting during the accession ceremony reveals a latent tendency. The nature of sex is fundamentally cultural. Its aspect of transgressive force is itself part of the ideology, and can be established only by hiding the dissemblance. A ruler or a lord cannot be spontaneously "weird" (*irui igyō*); this spontaneity has to be carefully staged. However, in Kazan's case the limits of the orthodoxy are revealed. The young emperor pushed the game a little too far, and was rapidly forced to abdicate. The fact that his eccentric behavior was later perceived as a sign of a superior spiritual power does not change this political reality. Transgression may obtain at the textual level or at the level of representations, but it is rapidly checked at the sociopolitical level.

If pleasure becomes legitimate, however, there is strictly speaking no longer any transgression. Yet the Buddhist tradition, even in its most audacious claims, always remained hesitant on this point. If transgression gives access to the sacred, one must preserve the transgressive potential of practice. When transgression itself becomes routine, and anticonformism is just another form of conformism, the profit that was derived from it disappears. At any rate, the ideological evolution leads to a decrease of the negativity of the physical and corporeal realm, but it also allows an exploration of the potential of transgression as such. On the one hand we have a kind of Buddhist humanism, on the other a quasi-Dionysian vision of sexuality. Although they draw on the same motto (the nonduality of passions and awakening), the two movements have radically different motivations.

Chapter 4

CLERICAL VICES AND VICISSITUDES

> Those who hide [their sins] are called monks.
> (Retired Emperor Shirakawa)

> The mosses on Jizō / Spreading like siphylis.
> (Japanese *senryū*)

WE HAVE EXAMINED in the preceding chapters the various normative views entertained in the Buddhist tradition regarding desire and sexuality. Between this theoretical approach and the reality of social practices, the gap is wide at times. The Two Truths theory was often invoked to bridge this gap, for instance by arguing that traditional morality, as expressed in the Vinaya, was only reflecting conventional truth, whereas ultimate truth was beyond good and evil. This argument, which may sound disingenuous to some, reminds us of the words of Hegel at the end of his life, to a natural child who had come to him asking for recognition: "I know that I had something to do with your birth, but formerly I was in the accidental, while now I am in the essential."[1]

However, the Indian Vinaya itself, by looking for the origin of the rules it proclaimed in precise individual acts—errors that, for essentially practical reasons, it was important to prevent from recurring—unwittingly provided the image of a primitive community eroded by human passions. The vision that emerges hardly resembles the idyllic image—nostalgic cliché of a later period—according to which the mere presence of the Buddha in this world was a token of salvation for all those who could approach him. We are told that the Buddha had to confront several cases of insubordination within his own community. Despite the prolixity of Buddhist texts on sexual matters, however, it remains difficult to have access to the reality of practices. Even the most detailed source, the Vinaya, is an essentially prescriptive discourse, and we should be careful when we infer from the existence of the rules the reality of the illicit practices that they claim to remedy.

---

[1] Quoted in Derrida, *Glas: Que reste-t-il du savoir abolu?* (Paris: Denoël/Gonthier, 1981), 10.

Monastic Decline and Anticlericalism

The Buddha was on several occasions accused of having trangressed his own rule—a rule by which, strictly speaking, he was never bound.[2] A well-known episode is one in which a young woman named Ciñcā, after placing a bowl under a dress, accused him of having impregnated her. Her fraud was fortunately uncovered when the bowl fell from under her dress. An even more unpleasant incident is the case of Sundarī, whose corpse, found in the Jetavana (in the city of Śrāvastī), was presented as proof of the Buddha's debauchery and of the excessive zeal with which his disciples had tried to cover up their master's misdeed. Once again, the machination was discovered. This rather dark "report" on monastic life has inspired acerbic comments by critics of Buddhism. Apart from the danger of taking the Vinaya at face value, as if it were a mere reflection of social reality, there is the risk of giving too much credit to a strongly biased anticlerical discourse. Clearly, the Vinaya provides easy arguments to Buddhism's detractors. Our purpose here is not to express full agreement with those critics. One of the questions that will detain us is precisely to what extent the transgression—whether held in contempt, exalted, or simply dreamed of, whether purely incidental, disciplinary, or motivated by "philosophical" choices—may have passed into action and contributed to the supposed decline of Buddhism.[3] This chapter will therefore examine some aspects of the social reality of Buddhism, in contrast to its normative tradition. However, the sources considered remain in various respects normative; they are not simply descriptive. At times, the agenda of the anticlerical critique is not even hidden. We must also keep in mind that the historical vision of a decadent Buddhism—for instance, that of Qing China or Tokugawa Japan—is essentially due to modern reformers, who use an idealized past as a standard against which to assess these periods.

Buddhism was often seen as a threat to society because it undermined the continuity of the family line by taking men and women away. To solve the problem posed by renouncers, Indian society had accepted the notion

[2] See Foucher 1949: 278–80.

[3] Let us note in passing the interesting role played in the Vinaya narrative by Jialuo [Kāla?] or Jialiutuoyi [Garuḍa?], who seems to have been a convenient scapegoat for the early Buddhist community. This monk, otherwise unknown, is accused of every turpitude: not only does he indulge in masturbation, he often invites women to his cell and attempts to seduce them. If he happens to meet a former lover during his begging tours, he does not respect her status as a married woman. On every occasion, he manages to remain alone with beautiful women, nuns, or laywomen, and to tell them saucy stories. The list of his misdeeds seems endless.

of the four stages of life, which allowed a man to abandon the world only after he had fulfilled his familial duties. Women, however, were not given such a choice. In Japan, although we do not find any strong argument against renunciation, most women who became nuns did so after sixty, following widowhood or menopause—that is, when society was no longer interested in them. In China, Buddhism was criticized by Confucianists for its lack of filial piety. Even Daoists joined the partisans of moral order in their criticism of Buddhism. In the *Huahu jing*, for instance, the Buddha is presented as an avatar of Laozi, who advocated celibacy to Western barbarians merely in order to cut off their evil offspring.

The social impact of Buddhism may explain the hostility of conservative forces. It does not justify, however, the specific accusations of immoral behavior leveled at monks and nuns—individuals who were, after all, rejecting sexuality in principle. There is no denying that Buddhist morals have varied considerably across time and place, and alleged immoral behavior justified anti-Buddhist persecutions like that of Huichang (845) in Tang China. "Official" anticlericalism, however, was only the most visible manifestation of widespread scathing anticlerical feelings. Behind the wide range of criticism leveled at Buddhist monastic communities, we find the ideology of different social groups such as the government, intra- and inter-sectarian critics, special interest groups, and society at large. In China, for instance, popular sarcasm found a literary expression in satires such as *Monks and Nuns in a Sea of Sins,* which opens with a vitriolic song entitled "The Happiness of Monks":

Don't tell me that monks are joyous;
strong and violent are what they are!
Wearing the robes,
and with their heads shaven and shiny,
they act as if they are prudent.
But they are bald, on top as below
and the two stones, below and above, are equally shiny.
Bald and naked, naked and bald,
indeed all monks are two-headed.
Their two eyes the eyes of oil-stealing rats,
their two fists the fists of blood-sucking leeches.
Heads protruding, they search for cracks
and summon charming girls,
revealing the true shape of the Buddha's tooth.
Thus the Pure Land becomes a sea of lust,
and priestly robes entangle with rainbow skirts.

They preach in vain that Hell's hard to endure,
for they fear not the judgment of the King of Hell.[4]

The theme of the "monastery of debauchery" was common in Chinese tales.[5] Already in the Northern Wei, the alleged discovery of weapons and evidence of debauchery in a Chang'an monastery was a pretext for the persecution of Buddhism by Emperor Taiwu (r. 424–452).[6] As in Western pornography, monasteries and convents are described as a virtual brothels.[7] Chinese Buddhism found its most severe critics in the popular literature that developed after the Song. The genre of vernacular stories (*huaben*) contains many tales involving Buddhist priests. One such tale is entitled "Chan Master Wujie Has Illicit Relationships with Red Lotus" (*Wujie chanshi si Honglian*). Its protagonists are two Chan priests, Wujie (Five Precepts) and Mingwu (Clear Realization), and a young girl named Red Lotus.[8] Wujie was the abbot of a monastery in Hangzhou, and Mingwu was his disciple. Once, a female baby was abandoned at the gate of the monastery, and Wujie entrusted her to one of his monks. The child, named Red Lotus, eventually turned into a beautiful young woman. When Wujie, who had forgotten her existence, happened to see her one day, he fell madly in love with her. He told the monk to bring her to his quarters, and he subsequently took her virginity. The versified account of the defloration ends with the lines: "What a shame that the sweet dew of *bodhi* / Has been entirely poured into the corolla of Red Lotus!"

But the story goes on: while sitting in meditation, Mingwu saw with

---

[4] See *Sengni niehai* (Taipei: Tianyi chubanshe, 1990), quoted [in Latin!] in van Gulik 1961; see also Levy 1965, 2: 11; Huang San and Basse 1992: 19.

[5] See for instance the seventeenth-century story, "Magistrate Wang Burns the Treasure-Lotus Monastery." In van Gulik's famous Judge Dee (Di) series we find an echo of these rumors.

[6] See *Wei Shu,* translated by Leon Hurvitz 1956: 64–65.

[7] See Robert Darnton, "Sex for Thought," *New York Review of Books* 41 (21) (December 22, 1994): 65–74.

[8] Patrick Hanan distinguishes Wujie from the bad priests caricatured in the vernacular literature. *Wujie chanshi si Honglian* belongs to a class of stories about poet-priests whose death is self-willed and related in some way to sex. In a variant from the Middle Period (1400–1575), "Red Lotus Seduces the Priest Yutong," the priest dies and is reincarnated because of his opposition to a civil official. In the Yuan play *Yueming heshang du Liu Cui* ("The Yueming Priest's Salvation of Liu Cui"), Liu, an arrogant prefect of Hangzhou, dispatches a local singing girl to tempt an old priest, Yutong. By means of a stratagem, she succeeds. When Yutong realizes that he has been tricked, he wills his own death and sends a valedictory poem to Prefect Liu. Yutong is reincarnated as a baby girl born to the prefect's wife. The girl will become a prostitute when her family's fortune declines. See Hanan 1981: 71.

his "eye of wisdom" that Wujie, by defiling Red Lotus, had transgressed the rule against sex and suddenly ruined years of pure behavior. The next day, he invited Wujie to a poetic meeting and chose as his topic lotus flowers in full bloom. His own poem ended with the following lines: "In summer, to admire lotuses is truly delicious, / But can the red lotus be more fragrant than the white?" Realizing that his secret had been discovered, Wujie was so ashamed that he composed a farewell poem, then died while sitting in dhyāna. Realizing that Wujie's karma would cause him to be reborn as an enemy of Buddhism, Mingwu decided to follow him into death. He was reborn as the poet-monk Foyin Liaoyuan (1032–1098), whereas Wujie was reborn as the famous Song poet Su Shi (alias Su Dongpo, 1036–1101), "whose only shortcomings were not believing in Buddhism and abhorring monks."[9] Fortunately, upon meeting Foyin during an excursion to Mount Lu, Su Shi was enlightened and eventually became—somewhat paradoxically—a Daoist immortal known by the name of Daluo Tianxian.[10] As to Red Lotus, we are simply told that she was saved, as well.

The legend of Wujie's reincarnation as Su Shi is quoted, for example, in the *Lengzhai yehua* by the Chan master Huihong (1071–1128).[11] The story of Su Shi's awakening was apparently well known by the time Dōgen visited China, more than one century after Su Shi's death. It is one of Dōgen's favorite exampla, inspiring an important fascicle of his *Shōbōgenzō*.[12] Dōgen was probably unaware of Su Shi's karmic antecedents,

[9] Su Shi is given as the author of a famous anticlerical pun: "If one is not bald, one can't be evil; / if one is not evil, one can't be bald" (*bu du bu tu, bu tu bu du*). See Levy 1965, 2: 45. Su Shi and Fayin also became the pretexts of further buffoonery in a literary genre very popular after the Song, consisting of comic dialogues. In Japan, the comic dialogue between Su Dongpo and Foyin has become a kind of *rakugo* (humorous story). See Sawada 1975: 179–80 .

[10] See *Qingpingshan tang huaben,* ed. (Shanghai: Gudian wenxue chubansha, 1957), summarized in Lévy 1978, 1: 57–60. See also Dars 1987: 425. The story is recited as a "precious scroll" (*baojuan*) by two nuns in the *Jinpingmei* 53; see translation by Lévy 1985, 2: 613.

[11] *Lengzhai yehua*, 7: 5a (ed. Jindai bishu, fasc. 112). The *huaben* (story book) is quoted in other Song works and in later collections of stories such as the *Yanju biji*. A variant appears in the *Jinpingmei* 73, trans. Lévy 1978: 59. See also the huaben entitled "Master Foyin Four Times Composes for Qinniang" (*Foyin shi si diao Qinniang*), in which Foyin, a poet who became a monk because of a whim of the emperor Shenzong, resists the advances of Qinniang, a singer whom Su Shi has hired to seduce his friend and thus force him to unfrock. Impressed by Foyin's example, Su Shi is converted to Chan. In a variant recorded in the *Jinlian ji,* however, it is Qinniang who turns away Foyin. See Lévy 1978, 2: 621–22; and Lévy 1980: 147.

[12] The *Shōbōgenzō* "Keisei sanshoku" (The Sound of the Valley Stream, the Forms of the Mountains) refers to a line of the poem written by Su Shi after his awakening. For more details, see Faure 1987a: 121–42.

since he apparently did not understand colloquial Chinese. The two contrasting images of Su Shi are typical of the selective memory of the "great" and "little" traditions and of the Janus-faced character of their heroes.

The moral decline of the Buddhist clergy during the medieval period has also often been described in Japanese popular literature. Typical is the following tale, in which a priest is asked by credulous parents to change their daughters, aged 18 and 19, into boys. Nothing easier, says the priest, there is a method for "changing women into men" in the sūtras. He has the two girls put into two separate rooms and takes his pleasure with them all day long. Eventually he tells the parents that he has failed, probably due to the girls' karma. When the parents question the girls, one of them says: "Although the monk exerted himself from morning to evening by planting his jade shaft, nothing grew." The other adds: "That's normal, he planted it the wrong way [*sakasama ni,* from behind]."[13]

Many sources argue that the decline of Buddhism increased during the Edo period.[14] This situation is described in the *Usa mondō* by Kumazawa Banzan (1619–1691): "In recent years, from the time of the ordinance banning Christianity, a faithless Buddhism has flourished. Since throughout the land everyone has his parish temple (*dannadera*), unlike in the past, monks can freely indulge in worldly affairs without concern for either discipline or scholarship. . . . The freedom with which they eat meat and engage in romantic affairs surpasses that of secular men."[15]

This anticlerical vision is reflected in the novels of Ihara Saikaku (1643–1693). In *A Bonze's Wife in a Worldly Temple,* for instance, the heroine, a young courtesan, recalls: "In the course of time I urged this one religion [that is, sexual indulgence] on temples of all the eight sects, and I may say that I never found a single priest who was not ready to slash his rosary [that is, break his religious vows]."[16]

[13] See *Ki no wakyō no monogatari,* Koten taikei 100: 88, Ishida 1995: 194.

[14] The point is most forcefully made by Tsuji Zennosuke (1944–1955, 10: 404–89), who quotes in particular the *Yūdoben* (1866) by the Jōdo priest Ryūgyō (ibid., 485–89).

[15] See Watt 1984: 190. See also Kumazawa Banzan, *Daigaku wakumon* (Nihon shisō tōsō shiryō 16: 128); Nakayama Chikusen (1730–1804), in *Sōbō Kigen* 4, "Jiin no koto" (ibid., 6: 515). Ueda Akinari (1734–1804), in the *Tandai shōshinroku,* criticizes the Pure Land schools (*nenbutsumon*), the Darumashū, the Nichirenshū, and the Montōshū (that is, the Ikkō sect). Likewise, the *Seiji kenmonroku* (1816) by Buyō Inshi, ch. 3, "Jisha jin no koto," describes the misbehavior of monks. A similar description is found in the *Tenmeiroku* and in the *Keizai mondō hiroku* by Shōji Kōki (1793–1857). For the latter, the problem comes from the fact that monks have too much contact with laymen, and too many rituals. On all this, see Ishida 1995: 208.

[16] Ihara Saikaku 1957: 149.

Another sharp-tongued critic of Buddhism is Tominaga Nakamoto (1715–1746):

This therefore was Śākyamuni's intention. He only wanted monks not to marry, and said that the monks who had no wives would be able to preserve his intention. However, later generations often found monks taking wives, which meant nothing less than the extinction of the Dharma. Again, the *Shoulengyan jing* and the *Guanshiyin tuoloni jing* . . . both have spells with which one can be released from the sins of passion or from the five sharp vegetables. Those monks of later generations with wives must have made good use of these spells![17]

In the *Kashōki,* we find a revealing argument entitled: "The Monks of This Age Have Deep Carnal Lust." To someone who complains about the current monastic decadence and argues instead that monks should be free of all desires, one of his interlocutors points out, albeit unwittingly, how elitist this conception is: monks of the past were virtuous because they were born from an aristocratic or warrior caste. Of course, "There may be exceptions, like Gyōki Bosatsu or Kōbō Daishi, who were born from a low-caste belly, but these two men were avatars of the Buddha, who took such a form as a skillful means." Contemporary monks, however, like those of the Nichiren and Jōdo sects, or the Ikkōshū, are of common extraction, and this explains their laxity. It would be better to ordain people born from the nobility or the warrior caste "because they do not know the hardships of the lower caste, they are honest in nature, and often mix with good people; because they are familiar with the [Buddhist] scriptures, the Recorded Sayings [of Zen], poetry and literature, they understand the principle and are versed in the meaning." Thus, most of them are good. On the contrary, people born from lower castes tend to be crooked in nature, and they keep dubious company. Thus they look for profit, and are prone to desire. Although there may be cases of stupidity or depravation among people of high extraction, they are still superior to similar cases of low extraction, who become monks to avoid poverty.[18]

In a section entitled "Night Laundry," the same source tells of a priest who kept a young woman in his temple. When a parishioner asked the reason for this, the priest explained: "During the day, I have her entertain the women who come to worship; at night, I tell her to do the laundry." From the medieval period, women often did the laundry for monks. The commentator says ironically: "Speaking of night laundry, I wonder what she could be washing indeed?"[19]

[17] Tominaga 1990: 137–38.
[18] *Kashōki* (1636) 1979: 5, 8: 231–33.
[19] Ibid., 233–34.

Wine-Drinking, Meat-Eating Clerics

As noted earlier, sexual relations were only one aspect of transgression, which also included the breaking of the precepts on alcohol and vegetarianism. Unlike sex, however, the taboo against meat extends to laymen. In the *Sōniryō*, meat and wine were lumped together with sex. Eating meat and drinking wine were regularly condemned. We know, for example, that several monks were implicated in 1409 in a scandal related to eating fish and meat and sent into exile as a result.[20] The Vinaya clause according to which meat and fish could on occasion be used for medicinal purposes lent itself to various kinds of casuistry. The drinking of sake, under the name of "water of prajñā," was also (and still is) widespread. It was strictly forbidden in 1419 at Shōkokuji, one of the major official Zen monasteries in Kyoto. The following year, the prohibition was extended to all Zen monasteries.

Eating meat and fish were on many occasions condemned by Chinese and Japanese authorities as signs of the corruption of the Buddhist clergy—and these regular condemnations reveal the diehard reality of transgressive practices.[21] In China, meat was a particularly dominant feature of social life, just as animal sacrifice was a regular part of religious life. As food, meat had considerable symbolic value as a marker of prestige. Whereas in India the vegetarianism of the renouncers was eventually coopted by the brahmans and became their trademark, exerting through them a major impact on Indian society, it was not so in China. Not all Indian renouncers abstained from meat, of course, and the Buddha himself was perhaps more nuanced in this regard than his successors. Vinaya regulations regarding the prohibition of meat were sometimes contradictory. In the Dharmaguptaka Vinaya (*Sifen lü*), monks can accept meat unless they see, hear, or suspect that the animal was killed for them.[22] The Mahāsaṅghika Vinaya, however, increases the list of taboo foods.[23] In the *Mahāparinirvāna-sūtra*, any kind of meat is forbidden.[24] Among the reasons invoked by the *Laṅkāvatāra* are that eating meat harms compassion toward all sentient beings and gives bad breath. The complexity of the regulations lent itself to casuistry. This point was not lost on Tominaga Nakamoto:

---

[20] Tsuji 1955, 5: 66–67; 6: 330–34.
[21] See Kieschnick 1995: 29–42; Mather 1981; Tsuji 1944–1955, 5: 67–70; 10: 446–93; Wakatsuki Shōgo, "Edo jidai no sōryō no daraku ni tsuite: Sono shorei," *Komazawa daigaku bukkyōgakubu ronshū* 2 (1971): 5–19; Michihata 1979: 275–91.
[22] See *Sifen lü*, T. 22, 1428: 866c, 868b, 872a.
[23] See *Mohe sengqi lü*, T. 22, 1425: 487a.
[24] T. 12, 374: 386.

Thus in the *Sarvāstivāda Vinaya* three kinds of meat are declared pure, and in the *Nirvāṇa-sūtra* there are nine. They both allow these to be eaten. The *Laṅkāvatāra-sūtra* also says: "At times I have taught the prohibition of the five kinds of meat and at times I have made it ten kinds." It should be observed that while both taking and rejecting meat are provided for, only pure meat is allowed. This was how it was originally. However in later times the prohibitions became more severe. The *Laṅkāvatāra-sūtra* says, "In the *Hastikakṣyā*, the *Mahāmeghā*, and the *Aṅgulimālika*, as well as in this *Laṅkāvatāra-sūtra*, I have decreed abstinence from meat." From this we can tell that previous sūtras permitted it.[25]

The ideal of purity was also undermined by the Mahāyāna tenet of nonduality and emptiness, as shown in the following passage in the *Damo lun* (Treatise of Bodhidharma): "The Dharma master Zhi, seeing the Dharma master Yuan in Butchers' Street, asked him: 'Have you seen the butchers kill sheep?' Dharma master Yuan answered: 'My eyes are not blind, how could I have not seen them?' Zhi: 'So you admit having seen them!' Yuan: 'But you, you are still seeing them!' "[26] Seeing animals killed, let alone eating them, is a transgression of the rule and a departure from compassion, but as long as it is done with a nondualistic mind, it is all right.

The Vinaya regulations regarding wine are hardly more straightforward: despite a theoretical prohibition against alcohol, wine was tolerated as medicine, like meat.[27] In China, the difficulty was compounded by the popularity of wine drinking as a literary topos. We may recall the cases of Jigong and other wine-drinking immortals. For once, Tominaga agrees with Buddhist casuistry, and offers a rebuff to the rigorist position represented by Huiyuan:

> When Master Huiyuan was approaching his end, Qide told him to take some rice wine with soya to overcome his illness, but the master replied, "The Vinaya has no statement to justify it." He told him to drink some rice gruel, but the master replied: "The day has passed noon." Then he told him to drink some honey mixed with water, so the master asked him to open the Vinaya to see if it was permitted, but before he had got halfway through the master died. Because [Huiyuan] did not change the rules in a matter of life and death, it must be said that he kept the Vinaya well. Yet how petty it is to say that rice gruel cannot be drunk because the day has passed noon. . . . Well-versed men have determined Vinaya in accordance with time and place, so why should one be restricted to early form alone? Did not Master Yuan know this? Further-

[25] Tominaga 1982: 46, translated in Tominaga 1990: 139.

[26] Faure 1986: 126–27.

[27] On this question, see Michihata Ryōshū, *Chūgoku bukkyōshi zenshū* (Tokyo: Kabushiki kaisha shoen, 1986), 7: 381–542; and Kieschnick 1995: 40–42.

more, if we reflect on the five precepts we see that stealing, adultery, and lying have always belonged to evil, but that taking life and drinking intoxicants have been undetermined. Taking life has been seen as not sinful, while drinking has been considered evil if it leads to a disturbance. The five precepts were originally precepts against evil, yet it is not possible to say that there should be absolutely no taking of life or drinking of intoxicants.[28]

Furthermore, the discrepancy between theory and practice reflected the larger contradiction of East Asian Buddhism, where the ideal of begging remained, even while monks were being lavishly supported by the state and by laymen. There is also a discrepancy between the hagiographical accounts of religious virtuosi, on the one hand, in which monks are beyond temptation, and the "human, all too human" common monks on the other. As John Kieschnick puts it: "Perhaps it is because of this environment of suspicion that one searches the *Biographies* in vain for stories of temptation—the sort of genuine inner turmoil expressed in the *Lives of the Desert Fathers*. . . . Monks in the *Biographies* have no such moments of doubt."[29] Thus, Buddhists may have had extenuating circumstances.

Buddhist Critiques

The above examples are only a sample of the many stories circulating about the Buddhist clergy. It is, of course, natural to suspect the bias of these anticlerical sources. The existence of similar stories in Buddhist sources, however, is more disturbing. As early as the Tang, the Japanese pilgrim Ennin (794–864) described the laxity of Chan monks he happened to encounter during his stay in China. The criticism against "meat eaters and fornicators" is also found among Chan monks themselves. For instance, the criticism of the Song Chan master Puan, which was perceived as still perfectly appropriate in the context of Tokugawa Japan, if we are to believe the Ōbaku master Chōon Dōkai (1630–1682), who quotes him verbatim: "And today there is an empty-minded Zen school, people who, without having the proper awakening, explain that to drink wine, eat meat, or commit adultery is no obstacle for the enlightened nature."[30]

[28] Tominaga 1982: 43, translated in Tominaga 1990: 133–34; and *Xu gaoseng zhuan,* T. 50, 2060: 361a. See also Zürcher 1959: 253.

[29] Kieschnick 1995: 27–28.

[30] See Dieter Schwaller, "Der Text *Mukai Nanshin* des Japanischen Zen-Mönchs Chōon Dōkai," unpublished paper, 1987. As noted earlier, a representative of this trend of Chan during the Song was the "trickster" Daoji (Jidian, Jigong). Particularly significant in this context is the story of Jigong's "encounter-dialogue" with the courtesan Hongjian and its resemblance to the story of Wujie and Red Lotus quoted above.

Such an attitude was apparently widespread in Japan long before the Tokugawa.[31] It seems to have resurfaced in every period, but was perhaps most apparent in the Kamakura period with the development of beliefs about the "final age of the Dharma" (*mappō*). In his *Gukanshō*, the Tendai priest Jien criticizes as follows the antinomianism of Hōnen's Pure Land teaching:

> This strange teaching was embraced by priests and nuns who lacked wisdom and were foolish. But the teaching was very popular and grew rapidly. Among those who embraced it was Lay Priest Anraku who had served under Lay Priest Takashina Yasutsune. Calling himself a "practitioner of the select discipline," Anraku associated himself with a priest by the name of Jūren. . . . Some nuns also became ardent believers in this teaching. The nenbutsu priests went so far as to make such promises as these: "If you become a practitioner of this teaching, Amitābha Buddha will not consider you the least bit sinful, even if you lust after women or eat fish or fowl. If you follow the select discipline single-heartedly, and believe only in [the efficacy of] nenbutsu, Amitābha will certainly come to welcome you [to the Pure land] at the time of death."
>
> While the movement was spreading throughout the capital and the countryside in this fashion, a Lady-in-Waiting at the Retired Emperor's [Go-Toba] detached palace, as well as the mother of the princely-priest of Ninna Temple, became believers. These ladies secretly called Anraku and other nenbutsu priests into their presence to explain their teaching. Anraku seems to have gone with some colleagues to see these ladies, even staying overnight. Anraku and Jūren were eventually beheaded. Saint Hōnen was banished [in 1207] and not allowed to reside in the capital. Although the matter was disposed of with such [leniency], the movement really seemed to have been checked for a while.[32]

Apparently, Jien regrets the "leniency" of the authorities, which forced Hieizan monks to intervene against the Pure Land school: "Because the 'select discipline'—with its permissive attitude toward lust for women and the eating of fish and fowl—had not yet been checked, the priests of Mt. Hiei rose up and forced the *nenbutsu* priests to flee."[33] Jien's criticism seems to have been motivated, however, less by the alleged sexual transgression (in this respect, he was quite broad-minded, as we will see) than by the potential threat to the Tendai school caused by the success of the Pure Land teaching and its antinomianism. This antinomianism was also one of the characteristics of the "Innate Awakening" (*hongaku*) theory, as it found its main expression in Tendai esotericism. It was found in Zen as well, and was denounced, not entirely without sectarian motives, by the Rinzai master Ikkyū Sōjun himself. In a poem entitled "For Stu-

[31] See in particular Ishida 1995.
[32] Brown and Ishida 1979: 171–72.
[33] Ibid., 172.

dents of Pretense," Ikkyū writes: "Sex in the temple, the Zen of demons": "Calling followers in for a 'mysterious *satori*.' / That modern leper, Yōso./ Amidst universal sin, I alone follow nature."[34] Ikkyū sharply contrasts his own "naturalism" with the moral laxity prevailing in Zen monasteries, a laxity that he associates with his codisciple Yōso. Nevertheless, both types of "naturalism" were conflated by the tradition, and the *Kyō-unshū* was for that reason forbidden. We must keep in mind the polemical context of Ikkyū's criticisms. Famous among other things for having in his old age fallen in love with a blind female singer, Ikkyū had also had homosexual experiences in his youth (if not later). Furthermore, we know the name of his "true disciple," that is, his son.

Ikkyū also accused his codisciple Yōso, who had apparently contracted leprosy, of having secretly abandoned the yellow robe of the monks for the orange *katabira* (robe) of the lepers.[35] The orange robe, initially worn by the mountain ascetics (*yamabushi*), symbolized their sacred, "nonhuman" nature. This orange katabira became the emblem of "weird and strange" (*irui igyō*) people in the medieval period. Ironically, Ikkyū's criticism echoes the growing discrimination against these marginals, among whom he himself once lived in Sakai. The Hieizan monks, for instance, criticized Zen monks as being no different from these irui igyō types. A similar criticism is voiced by the priest Eichō in Mujū Ichien's *Shasekishū*:

> Although monks today talk of receiving the precepts, they do not know what it means to observe them. While half-heartedly calling themselves priests, taking alms, and performing services, it is a strange breed of priests which abounds throughout the country, bringing disgrace to the disciples of the Buddha. Some have families and other bear arms, or go hunting and fishing. In these wretched latter days there are those who do not even know the meaning of the word "repentance."[36]

Mujū sees his fellow monks with the distance of irony and never loses a chance to reveal their absurdities. Incriminating worldly monks, he writes:

> Some perform Buddhist services for profit, saying: "I am a disciple of the Buddha. This is what must be done." But when it comes to observing the precepts and correcting their faults, then they say: "I follow the Mahāyāna, not the Hīnayāna." The *Buddha Treasury Sūtra* calls such people "bat-monks" (*chōso biku*). If one says that they are numbered among the birds, they reply that they live on the ground, and go into their holes. But to escape the duties of living on

[34] *Kyōunshū* 351, in Sanford 1981: 135. See also Iizuna 1993.
[35] See *Jikaishū*, quoted in Amino 1993: 132.
[36] Morrell 1985: 189.

the ground, they say they live in the sky. Indeed, they are neither bird nor beast. So also the Law-breaking monk says that he is a follower of the Buddha in order to escape his secular duties. But then he does not observe the precepts, claiming to be an adherent of the Mahāyāna.[37]

Even more scathing is Mujū's indictment of the yamabushi, through the words he puts in Eichō's mouth: "I see one from where I am sitting. I look and ask myself if he is a layman—but he wears a priest's scarf. He is neither adult, child, priest, nor menial. He isn't even shit, but something like diarrhea!"[38] In the *Zōtanshū,* Mujū is more nuanced: "Today, monks are like oxen and sheep wearing monastic robes (*kesa*); some monks may become oxen, others Buddhas, but fundamentally they are neither oxen nor Buddhas. All are only Vairocana."[39]

Sometimes, according to Mujū, the problem is not so much the monks' evil mind or their antinomianism as their stupidity. He illustrates this point with the story of the preacher who tries to explain to his female patron, a widow, the notion of union with the Buddha:

> Now the Great Sun Buddha illumines the great devotion of this lay nun, and feels intimately toward her. If the forehead of the Great Sun Buddha and the forehead of this lay nun were to come together, then hers would assume a golden hue. If the bosom of the Great Sun Buddha and the bosom of this lay nun were to come together, then hers would assume a golden hue. If the abdomen of the Great Sun Buddha and the abdomen of this lay nun were to come together, then hers would assume a golden hue. If the navel of the Great Sun Buddha . . .[40]

At this point, however, the preacher is interrupted by another priest who has overheard and cannot bear to listen further. In another tale entitled "The Nun Who Praised a Preacher," Mujū describes a nun who, wanting to hold a Buddhist service, asks a monk whom she had known since his childhood to deliver the sermon. Finding the sermon to her liking, the nun extols the monk to a group of ladies as follows: "Since I raised him from the time he was a little boy and used to run around with his member hanging out, I was wondering how far he would go. And then he stood erect at the lectern. I had not expected anything extraordinary, but he did very well. As I was thinking to myself how wonderfully he was doing, he pushed forward to the end. I felt as though I had lost my senses." Comments Mujū: "A truly unhappy choice of words!"[41]

[37] Ibid., 141.
[38] Ibid., 189
[39] *Zōtanshu* 1, 3, in Yamada and Miki edition, 52–53
[40] Morrell 1985: 183.
[41] Ibid., 184.

Nevertheless, we must keep in mind Michel Strickmann's remark that the depravity of monks and nuns is part of an eschatological topos and cannot be taken as a mere description of reality (any more than the piety of women, another Buddhist sign of the end of the world!): "The authors of apocalyptic visions put systematically into action the worst fears of Buddhist legislators."[42] Conversely, Jan Nattier argues that the advent of the theory of the final age of the Dharma was triggered as much by anxiety over internal laxity of the saṅgha as by external persecution.[43] At any rate, the Buddhist critique itself should be submitted to an ideological critique. In the context of medieval Japan, for instance, we seem to be dealing with official priests finding fault with marginal monks who are perceived as muen or irui igyō types. Here, the case of Ikkyū is particularly significant since, as a trickster figure, he could be seen as a personification of the muen ideal, while in his criticisms he echoes the dominant ideology.

In Defense of Monasticism

The first Buddhist response to such criticism was denial: bad monks are still better than good laymen. When it does not seem possible to argue that transgression was done in the name of a higher truth, one falls back on a quasi-sacramental conception of the priesthood: the "essence of the precepts," once obtained through ordination, can never be lost. Already in fifth-century China, when the Jin emperor expressed his intention to weed out the saṅgha because of the monks' many transgressions, the Dharma master Huiyuan allegedly replied: "The jade that is extracted from Mount Kun is covered with dirt and grit. The Li river is rich with gold, yet it is also full of gravel. Your Highness must respect the Dharma and value its representatives." The Jin emperor, apparently convinced by this argument, issued a general pardon.[44] In Japan, a similar argument appears in the *Nihon ryōiki*:

> Even a self-ordained monk deserves to be regarded with tolerance, for sages live hidden among ordinary monks. . . . Accordingly, the *Jūrin-gyō* says: "As an orchid, even if it has withered, excels other flowers, so monks, even if they violate precepts, excel non-Buddhists. To talk about a monk's faults such as whether he violates or keeps the precepts, whether he recognizes or does not recognize the precepts, or whether he has or has not faults is a graver sin than that of letting the bodies of innumerable Buddhas bleed.[45]

[42] Strickmann 1996: 98.
[43] See Nattier 1991: 128.
[44] See *Lidai fabaoji*, T. 51, 2075: 179c.
[45] *Nihon ryōiki* 3: 33, in Nakamura 1973: 268–69.

In his *Sanbō ekotoba,* a didactic work completed in 984 for a young princess about to become a nun, Minamoto Tamenori declares:

> I even revere those monks who violate the precepts. In a sūtra it is said that though a monk may violate the precepts, he is still superior to a Wheel-King, and even though he may fall into one of the Evil Realms, he will be a king there. Though the *campaka* flower may wilt, it is still superior to all other flowers in their freshest bloom. The scent of sandalwood incense may burn away to nothing, but still it perfumes countless robes. . . . A bag that has held incense may lose some of its scent, but it still remains fragrant. A monk may have taken vows and then may break one, but still, the Buddha says, he is worthy of reverence. . . . A common man should not use his worldly mind to judge the sincerity of those who follow the path of Holy Wisdom.[46]

Even a purely superficial acceptance of the precepts can provide salvation in the long run, as the story of the nun Utpalavarṇā, quoted by Dōgen, shows:

> In a previous existence I was a prostitute and often uttered licentious words while dressed improperly. One day, however, I put on a nun's robe as a joke. Owing to this good deed, I was reborn as a nun in the time of the Buddha Kāśyapa. My problems did not end then, however. Because of my noble birth and good looks, I became proud and conceited, and consequently I broke the precepts, falling into hell, where I was severely punished. After having redeemed myself and been born in the human world once more, I was finally able to meet the Buddha Śākyamuni and reenter nunhood. As a result I was able to realize Arhathood and become endowed with the six powers for saving sentient beings.[47]

Thus, "in the past an irreligious prostitute laughingly put on nun's clothing as a joke. Although she broke the precepts by that action that belittled the Law, because of the merit she gained from having worn nun's clothing, she was able to encounter the Law in only two generations."[48] Likewise, says Dōgen, though a monk breaks the ten grave prohibitions, he is still superior to a layman who observes the five lay precepts. According to him, Zen in particular cannot be judged by ordinary standards: "Even if a Zen monastery is under the influence of degenerate Buddhism, it is like a fragrant flower garden. Monasteries of other sects can never be its equal."[49]

How did monks and nuns respond to internal purification and external rules aimed at them? Let us first examine the question of male intercouse

---

[46] Kamens 1988: 242.
[47] *Shōbōgenzō* "Shukke kudoku," in Yokoi 1976: 70–71.
[48] Ibid., 74, 75.
[49] Ibid., 83.

with women (*nyobon*), which triggered the repression against the Pure Land school. We have cited above a criticism of the attitude of Hōnen's disciples. In response to this criticism is the *Shichikojō seimon*, a 1204 request in seven points by Hōnen, which amounts to an internal critique of the movement. In its paragraph four, for instance, we find the following: "In the Nenbutsu school, we must silence those who say that there is no practice of the Precepts, and who advocate only love, alcohol, and meat eating, and who tell to those who chose Amida's fundamental vow that they should not fear to commit evil."[50]

Certain nenbutsu adepts seem to have asserted the meaninglessness of monastic discipline, and tolerated sexual relationships. It is against them that Hōnen insisted on the importance of the precepts, arguing, for instance, that the Pure Land patriarch Shandao never looked at women. Hōnen summed up his argument in seven points, saying that those who transgress them are not his disciples but supporters of Māra. He then obtained the signatures of 108 disciples and sent the document to the high priest of Tendai. Among these signatures, one finds the names of Jūren and Anraku, who as we have seen would be later condemned to death for allegedly breaking their vow of chastity with palace women. Hōnen had already responded to a similar charge from Kōfukuji, but his response had not been judged sufficient.[51]

Among the nine points of a petition addressed to the throne by the Kōfukuji monks in 1205, the eighth deals with the depravity of Pure Land monks—their indulging in games like go and sugoroku (a light offense according to the *Fanwang jing*), along with sex, eating meat, and drinking alcohol. Although sugoroku, a kind of betting, was condemned from very early on, the game of go seems to have been fairly popular among monks. Despite their virtuous indignation, however, the entertainment of Kōfukuji monks was probably not limited to innocent go playing. Indeed, the authors of the petition feel obliged to perform their autocritique in a postscript: "Although we do not receive [the precepts] according to truth, and do not observe [these precepts] according to the teaching, we fear this, and deplore it." But the authors of the petition remain adamant in their denunciation of laxity, affirming that "one cannot obtain rebirth [in the Pure Land] through fornicating and eating meat." They claim to part on that point with nenbutsu adepts, who "make transgression their principle."

Although the Kōfukuji monks were not satisfied with the imperial edict issued in response to their petition, they subsequently concentrated their criticisms on Hōnen's disciples rather than on Hōnen himself. Neverthe-

---

[50] See *Hōnen shōnin zenshū*, 788.

[51] See *Kamakura ibun* 3: 1586. Even before this charge from Kōfukuji, there had been others, as can be seen in the *Hōnen shōnin gyōjō ezu* (ch. 31).

less, Hōnen was exiled in 1207 to Sado Island, while some of his disciples were more severely punished—by castration or death.[52] As noted above, Jien, the Tendai zasu, reports in his *Gukanshō* the execution of Anraku and Jūren. A disciple of Shinran, Kawada no Yuien, in a document annexed to the *Tannishō*, mentions two other victims. The same version of the facts is presented by Rennyo, but neither source mentions castration.[53] The *Hyakurenshō* records the punishment of a nenbutsu adept for adultery. It also reports that nenbutsu monks were banished from Kamakura and their temples destroyed after they were charged with eating meat and having sexual relations with women.[54]

The Buddhist clergy tried to improve its image by insisting on the ideal of chastity. In the *Hokekyō kenki,* for instance, we find the case of the priest Jōshō of Saga, who, although he never had sex, happened once to touch a woman's body with a finger, and repented by burning this finger, the cause of the sin, which he then offered to the Three Jewels.[55] Another attempt to deal with the image problem of the clergy was to imply that apparently immoral behavior was only a façade, a way for the sage to "mingle with the dust." Even when a monk behaves in a dissolute way (some will say, especially when he does so), he may turn out to be a thaumaturge. The case of the Chinese monk Jigong, studied above, is already typical in this respect.[56] In Japan, we could mention the case of Priest Eijitsu of Jinmyōji. Eijitsu once went down to Kyushu, where he became very rich by managing secular affairs such as cultivating fields, making an abundant profit in rice and sake. Sometimes he ate fish and fowl and at other times he equipped himself with a bow and arrow. The governor of Higo province slandered him and confiscated his property, saying, "Eijitsu is a precept-violating priest. No one should associate with him." Some time later the governor's wife became fatally ill. When medicinal treatment did not not work, the governor agreed to invite Eijitsu to recite the *Lotus Sūtra*. When Eijitsu finally accepted and began his recitation, the wife was rapidly cured, and the governor apologized as a result.[57] Another significant case is that of the Shingon priest Ningai:

> Long ago, there was a man in the southern capital called the Venerable Ninkai, a priest of the Yamashina-dera. For learning, there was not a priest in the temple equal to him. Now he was suddenly seized by a religious fervour and wished to leave the temple, but the Abbot at the time, the Assistant High Priest

[52] See *Kojiruien,* Hōritsubu 1: 91–92.
[53] See *Shinshū shōkyō zensho* 2:794 and 3:737, in *Shūi kōtoku den* 7.
[54] *Hyakurenshō,* s.v. 1234 (bunreki 1/7/2), and 1239 (En'ō 1/4/13), in *Shintei zōho kokushi taikei;* quoted in Ishida 1995: 111.
[55] See Dykstra 1983: 67.
[56] John Kieschnick has studied a number of similar cases. See Kieschnick 1995: 88–119.
[57] See Dykstra 1983: 89.

Kōshō, was very loath to allow him to leave. In desperation, he entered into a marriage with the daughter of a man in the village to the west of the temple, and his regular visits naturally gave rise to gossip. In order to publicize the affair, he would stand behind his wife at the gate of the house with his arms round her neck, a sight which utterly disgusted and saddened people passing by. His purpose was to convince everyone that he had become a libertine. Yet all the while he lived with his wife, he was never once intimate with her.[58]

Despite his behavior, Ningai was regarded as a saint and was said to have been reborn in the Pure Land. In the *Uji shūi monogatari,* his case follows that of Sōō, as reflecting the standard of the ascetic monk. We know that the image of Sōō underwent some changes, due to his alleged affair with Empress Somedono. The same is true with that of Ningai, whom we have seen described as a meat eater. Despite his chaste relation with his wife, he was also said to have fathered a son, Jōson (1012–1074), who became his "true disciple."[59]

THE DEMONIC PRIEST

As we saw above, the disturbance provoked by Hōnen's Pure Land teaching was reduced to a matter of antinomianism, which led to the sexual scandal in which two of his disciples were directly involved. Jien, who reports the incident in his *Gukanshō,* sees it as an instance of demonic possession:

> According to my understanding of this phenomenon there are two types of demons: the deceptive (*junma*) and the antagonistic (*gyakuma*). Deceptive demons were responsible for such pathetic teaching as Hōnen's. At a time when "the one Teaching of Amitābha" will really increase divine grace, people will certainly have their sins and troubles removed and enter paradise. But before that time comes, and while the Shingon and "eliminate-illusion" (*shikan*) teachings of Tendai are still destined to prosper, no one will be able to achieve salvation by following the teachings of deceptive demons. Pathetic things happen when people think they can!"[60]

Jien implies that "deceptive" demons (*junma,* literally, demons who "submit") are not nearly as dangerous as "antagonistic" demons

---

[58] See Mills 1970: 431–32

[59] See *Kojidan* 3: 71, Koten bunko 60, 279. The story adds that Jōson's mother (who is not described here as Ningai's wife), trying to get rid of the child, made him drink mercury. The only result was that the child became genitally deformed, which is why, we are told, Jōson "never commited an impure act in his entire life."

[60] Brown and Ishida 1979: 173. Jien also discusses the "power and nature of vengeful souls," ibid., 220–21.

(*gyakuma*). He reports how, on one occasion around 1196, the vengeful spirit of Go-Shirakawa was believed to have possessed the wife of a man named Tachibana Kanenaka. Eventually, husband and wife were declared insane and sent into exile because "she really has not been possessed."[61] A few years later, in 1206, a similar incident occurred: the spirit of Go-Shirakawa was said to have possessed the wife of the priest Nakakuni and to have asked that a shrine be built in his honor. Jien declared that this was not a true possession but merely a demonic trick (that is, one caused by "deceptive demons").[62] He manifests here his elitist bias against popular mediums and, more generally, against marginal social categories.[63] He argued, however, that the possessed woman and her husband should not be too severely punished if they had no wrong intent.

This line of thinking leads our discussion to another type of monks that have a bad press. They are sometimes confused with bawdy monks because they fall in love with women. But whether they actually break their vows or not, they are perceived as dangerous because of their magical powers, and they are liable to become angry ghosts because of frustrated love. Significantly, a temple was later built in the memory of the two disciples of Hōnen who had been executed, and this was probably not simply a matter of rehabilitating them for the sake of justice but was rather to appease their vengeful spirits. In most cases, the accounts regarding these demonic priests is another form of anticlericalism or sectarian criticism. Another case in point, mentioned in the *Uji shūi monogatari*, is that of Sōō (832–918), a renowned ascetic, who was called to court to exorcise Empress Somedono. Because of his unusual appearance, Sōō was told to perform his incantations outside the mansion:

> His voice made the Empress's attendants feel that their hair was standing on end, as if he were an apparition of Fudō himself. Presently, the Empress, wrapped in a couple of crimson robes, came tumbling out through the blinds like a ball, and was dumped down on the verandah in front of Sōō. Her attendants were most upset, and cried, "This is very unseemly. You must take Her

[61] Brown and Ishida 1979: 169.

[62] On this occasion, Jien told the emperor: "If Nakakuni and his wife have said what was in their own hearts without being at all possessed by foxes and badgers, they should of course be punished, even with exile." But, he argues, there are also cases of real possession: "That is, some have developed the sickness of possession. But since punishment should not be meted out from above simply because a person is ill, we should place Nakakuni and his wife in isolation and pay no attention to what they say. Then the fox or badger will soon remove itself without a sound" (ibid., 170).

[63] Jien writes: "In reflecting about these developments, I have the feeling that I see crazy people—shamans (*miko*), mediums (*kōnagi*), dancers (*mai*), and comic actors (*sarugō*), as well as coppersmiths and the like, all low-ranking people who served near the deceased Retired Emperor—exerting their influence over this woman [for their own selfish purposes]. The state is now going to ruin!" (ibid.).

Majesty inside and go in with her yourself." "How can a beggarly person like me go into her presence?" said Sōō, and he refused to go inside. He was annoyed at not having been invited in from the first, and so had raised her four or five feet in the air and deposited her on the verandah. In despair the attendants produced some screens, which they stood round the Empress to conceal her, while the inner gate was locked and the place cleared of people. But the Empress was still very much exposed to view. Four or five times Sōō let her drop, and he intoned spells to hurl her inside, so that eventually she was flung back into the room again. Then Sōō took his departure. Though they asked him to wait, he refused to listen, and complaining that his back ached from standing for such a long time, he went off.[64]

After this drastic treatment, the empress was no longer possessed. Sōō was rewarded with a high clerical position, but he declined it. At first glance, the story is that of a saintly if somewhat arrogant priest. The man who, we are told, "wore no cloth which had been sewed by a woman," seems to be the perfect ascetic.[65]

Despite such a positive account, however, the opening section of the tale raises negative expectations in the reader. We learn that Sōō, as a result of his strenuous ascesis under a waterfall, was once transported to the Tuṣita heaven. In the end, however, because he was unable to recite the *Lotus Sūtra,* he could not enter Maitreya's Inner Palace.[66] Thus he turns out to be a flawed ascetic. It should not come as much of a surprise to discover that in some variants Sōō falls in love with the empress. The point is that, because of this impossible love, the priest will after death become a malevolent spirit (*onryō*) who returns to the world of the living to possess the object of his lingering desire. There is a feeling of circularity in this story, because the empress was possessed in the first place by the spirit of another powerful priest, Shinzei (alias Kakinomoto no Ki), who was taking revenge for his own unrequited love.[67]

As a result of vengefulness, Buddhist monks and practitioners of Shugendō often turned (or were turned) into onryō. Sometimes the cause of their resentment was a desire for revenge owing to political circumstances (as in the case of political figures such as Sugawara Michizane or Emperor Go-Daigo). The *Gukanshō* mentions several instances.[68] Sometimes, as in the above examples, love turned into hatred. These cases were well known, as we can see from the words of Emperor Go-

---

[64] See *Uji shūi monogatari,* translated by Mills 1970: 429–30.

[65] See *Tendai Nanzan Mudōji konryū oshōden,* quoted in Ishida 1995: 43.

[66] See *Hokekyō kenki,* translated by Dykstra 1983: 35–36.

[67] See Tanaka 1992: 85–131.

[68] See Brown and Ishida 1979: 70, 87, 124, 220.

Fukakusa to Lady Nijō, after she has told him of her affair with the Ninnaji priest Shōjo Hōshinnō, whom she refers to in her diary as "Ariake no tsuki": "None of this bodes well for the future, for events from the past teach us that passion respects neither rank nor station. For example, the spirit of the high priest Kakinomoto pursued Empress Somedono relentlessly, and it was beyond the power of the Buddhas and Bodhisattvas to prevent her from yielding to his malevolent spirit. The holy man of the Shiga Temple was also smitten by passion, but he was luckily returned to the true way by the sympathy of the lady he loved."[69]

Later, Go-Fukakusa returns to this point:

After thinking about the subject at great length, I have concluded that there is nothing sinful in the relationships between men and women inasmuch as they are usually caused by bonds from former lives and thus defy our resistance. Numerous examples from the past illustrate what I mean, as in the case of the ascetic known as Jōzō and the girl from Michinokuni. To escape from the bond, Jōzō even attempted to kill her, but without success, and finally he yielded to his passion.[70] In another case, the holy man of Shiga Temple was attracted by the Empress Somedono. Unable to endure such passion, he turned into a blue ghost.[71]

Go-Fukakusa had some reasons to be concerned about the effects of Ariake's passion for Lady Nijō. Feeling terminally ill, Ariake tells her that he has begun copying five Mahāyāna sūtras, in each chapter of which he inserted a phrase from one of her letters, with the plea that they might be united in this world: "The sūtras are copied now but not dedicated. I shall dedicate them after we have been reborn together. If I store the more than two hundred chapters in the treasure hall of the dragon king, I will certainly be reborn to this life, and then I shall dedicate them to the Buddha. To accomplish this I plan to take the sūtras with me after death

---

[69] See Brazell 1973: 123.

[70] The same story is told about Tankei, a disciple of Ennin. Tankei is said to have had an affair during his stay in a house where through his prayers he had exorcised the illness of Chūjinkō (Fujiwara Yoshifusa), but we do not have the details. However, the story has a sequel. Tankei had in the past received a dream oracle from Fudō Myōō telling what would happen—namely, that he would find in a certain place a girl whom he would marry. He goes to the place, finds a ten-year old girl, kills her (or so he thinks) and runs away, believing he has thus proven the oracle wrong. But when, much later, he makes love with a woman, he finds that she has a scar on her neck. When he asks her about it, she tells him that when she was young she was once attacked and wounded by someone, but was later cared for and healed. Tankei then understands that his karma, predicted by Fudō, has been realized, and confesses everything. They eventually become husband and wife, after Tankei has returned to lay life and become an official in order to avoid transgression. See *Konjaku monogatari shū* 31: 3, quoted in Ishida 1995: 60.

[71] Brazell 1973: 131.

by having them added to the fuel of my funeral pyre."[72] Ariake died soon after, in 1282, at the age of 36.

Go-Shirakawa seems to have been duly concerned with demonic beings such as *onryō, oni,* and *tengu* (tradition has it that he himself became an onryō). In one recension of the *Heike monogatari,* we find the following passage, in which he receives a revelation from the god of Sumiyoshi:

> The Retired Emperor [Go-Shirakawa] asked: "Regarding the wise men who have become *tengu* [mountain spirits] in the country of Japan, how many are there?" The Daimyōjin [of Sumiyoshi] replied: "Because good priests all become *tengu,* it is impossible to give their number. Priests of great wisdom become great *tengu,* those of small wisdom become small *tengu.* Even among ignorant priests, there is a great deal of arrogance. Thus all fall into the realm of beasts and are stretched out; the horse and cow demons are none other than these. In our land, in the not distant past, there was a renowned sage named the abbot Kakinomoto [i.e., Shinzei], a *hijiri* [ascetic] of miraculous powers. Because of his great arrogance, he has become the number one great *tengu* of Japan. He is known as Tarōbō of Atago Mountain.[73]

As David Bialock points out, demonology functions here both as means for criticizing the retired emperor and as an apologetic for the behavior of the unruly monks. The fact that the "evil monks" (*akusō*) of medieval Japan often added the words *tengu* and *oni* to their name also suggests that the "demonology was widespread enough to become a contested discourse, with the *akusō* deliberately attempting to co-opt, to their own advantage, its capacity to inspire fear."[74]

The Political Context

Clearly, despite its apparent similarity across places and times, anticlerical discourse obeys complex motivations, responding to different historical and political situations. It has a globalizing effect, transforming specific historical cases into as many local manifestations of a persistent tendency, reflecting the evil nature of the monks. Although specific accusations against depraved monks should always be contextualized, this would take us too far afield. We will therefore examine two well-known cases, those of Dōkyō and of Shinzei.

The story of the affair between Empress Shōtoku and Dōkyō is reported as follows in the *Gukanshō*:

---

[72] Ibid., 147.

[73] See *Heike monogatari,* Enkyōbon jō, "Hōō no go-kanjō no koto" (The Matter of the Retired Emperor's Water Consecration Ritual), 223–26, in Bialock 1997: 488.

[74] Bialock 1997: 489; quoting Arai, *Chūsei akutō no kenkyū.* See also ibid., 388.

During her second reign [764–770], Kōken was called Empress Shōtoku. Having fallen in love with Dōkyō, a Buddhist priest, she committed such iniquities as promoting him to the position of Priest Emperor (*hōō*) in 766 and placing other priests in secular positions of state. . . . This Empress was no ordinary person. A story is told of her vow with Amoghapāśa Avalokiteśvara at the Saidai Temple. The things she did were gossipped about, but they were not thought of as precedents. Her actions really should be understood as the actions of a Buddhist incarnation (*gongen*)."[75]

In the *Gukanshō* version, Empress Shōtoku is almost exonerated. This is not always the case, however. The central element in the scandal related to Shōtoku has to do with her love for Dōkyō, the monk with a huge penis. The story of this unseemingly couple first appears in the *Nihon ryōiki*, in a section entitled "On the Appearance of Good and Evil Omens Which Were Later Followed by Their Results." When Shōtoku returned to the throne after expelling the crown prince and murdering all her opponents, anticlerical "children's songs" spread among the people: "It is said that before good and evil events occur they are preceded by some forms of songs which spread throughout the countryside. Thereupon, all the people under heaven hear them and sing them to communicate the message."[76] Some of these songs contained obvious allusions to Dōkyō:

Don't be contemptuous of monks because of their robes.
For under their skirts are hung garters and hammers.
When the hammers erect themselves,
The monks turn out to be awesome lords.[77]

Look straight at the root of the tree,
And you will find the most venerable master
Standing satiated and fat.[78]

The author of the *Nihon ryōiki*, Kyōkai, is very critical of Empress Shōtoku, whom he calls deprecatingly Empress Abe. In case the allusion to "garters and hammers" in the song would not be clear enough, he explains: "In the reign of Empress Abe, in the beginning of the second year of the snake, the first year of the Tenpyō jingo era, Dharma Master Dōkyō of the Yuge family had intercourse with the empress on the same pillow, hearing the affairs of state and ruling over the country together.

---

[75] Brown and Ishida 1979: 33–34.
[76] Nakamura 1973: 276.
[77] Ibid., 277.
[78] Ibid., 278.

The above songs were a prediction of his relations with the empress and his control over state affairs."[79]

In the *Nihongi ryaku*'s biography of Fujiwara Momokawa, we find the following story, taken up at the beginning of the *Kojidan*: Shōtoku, being ill, calls Dōkyō to cure her, but he fails. A nun appears with a remedy (oil to lubricate Shōtoku's sex), but Momokawa sends her away, and soon afterward Shōtoku dies. The same story appears in the *Mizu kagami*. According to the *Kojidan*, the "various things" (*zōmono*) recommended by Dōkyō that caused Shōtoku's death were mountain potatoes (*yama no imo*). Shōtoku, unsatisfied with Dōkyō's penis, is said to have made a dildo with one of these potatoes, which broke and obstructed her vagina. In this version and later, the center of gravity of the story shifts from Dōkyō to Shōtoku. In the biography of Momokawa, it is Dōkyō who recommends the "various things," but in the *Kojidan*, it is Shōtoku herself who takes the initiative. In the first text, Dōkyō is presented as an evil man, whose ambition causes the death of the empress. In the second text, he does not even appear, and the disaster is attributed to the wrongful desires of a lustful empress. For reasons that need further exploration, the critique has shifted from the monk to the empress.[80]

Let us now turn to the possession of the Somedono empress by the "evil priest" Shinzei. The various recensions of the story show a gradual development, from a purely political grudge to a relentless amorous passion. The political context of Shinzei's grudge is clearly described at the beginning of the *Soga monogatari*, in the section entitled "The Succession Struggle between Koretaka and Korehito." We are told that Emperor Montoku had two sons, Koretaka and Korehito. Unable to chose his successor, he resorted to a divinatory contest, decreeing that the throne should be passed on to the one whose side excelled in horse racing and wrestling. To assist him during this ominous contest, each prince had his protector-monk. The rituals on Koretaka's behalf were performed by the Shingon priest Shinzei, abbot of Tōji, whereas those on behalf of Korehito were performed by the Tendai priest Eryō, a resident of Enryakuji. When Eryō heard that Korehito's side had lost the first four of the ten horse races, he decided to adopt drastic measures:

> He turned a portrait of Daiitoku upside down and brought out a three-foot clay statue of a cow and placed it down facing north. When the clay cow changed directions, turning to the west, Eryō placed it southward. It changed directions again, turning to the east, whereupon he placed it westward. Next, he prayed with great intensity, the effect of which was to put him in a frenzy.

[79] Ibid., 277–78.
[80] Tanaka 1992: 31.

While in this state, he smashed his skull with a sharp-pointed vajra. He took some brains, mixed them with poppy seeds and burned them in the hearth, from which a black smoke arose. When he again rubbed the rosary, the clay cow made noises wildly. The image of Daiitoku in the portrait raised its sharp sword and swung it about, whereupon Eryō felt relieved for he then realized that his wishes had been fulfilled.[81]

As a result, Korehito became the crown prince, the future Emperor Seiwa, while his elder brother Koretaka cloistered himself at the foot of Mount Hiei. As to Koretaka's exorcist and the unlucky rival of Eryō, Shinzei, the *Soga monogatari* simply says that he died of disppointment. With the development of the story, however, this disappointment turned into a desire for posthumous revenge on Emperor Seiwa (that is, Korehito), a revenge that struck at one of the weak points in Seiwa's lineage. Shinzei, the priest who could not smash his own skull, now becomes a tengu, who possesses the empress. Somedono's only mistake was apparently to be the mother of Emperor Seiwa, and through her, it was the latter who was aimed at. Toward the beginning of the thirteenth century, the story takes a quite different turn. In the *Hōmotsu shū,* for instance, the possession of Somedono is reinterpreted as an effect of Shinzei's "love" for her. Strange love indeed.[82] The nine-fascicle recension (*kyūsatsu-bon*) of the *Hōmotsu shū* still mentions, as if in passing, the episode of the succession struggle. In later versions, the conflict of succession is no longer mentioned, and only the fateful love of Shinzei for Somedono is described. According to Tanaka, although the focus of scholarship has been the figure of Shinzei, the latter is a mere stooge: given the earlier rivalry for the throne and the resentment it created, there had to be someone, no matter who, who could possess Somedono.[83] And this possession has heavy sexual connotations; it is akin to a rape—and the story of Shinzei's disappointed love sounds like a rationalization. In sum, the "love" of Shinzei is only one of the aspects of his revenge, the rape of Somedono. And he rapes her not only because she is a woman but because she can cause great damage to the imperial lineage. Tanaka Takako points out the essential role of the imperial consort in the transmission of the blood lineage. But Somedono is defiled by her possession. This is all the more serious because her son, Seiwa Tennō, is the origin of an important aristocratic lineage, the Seiwa Genji.

[81] Cf. *Soga monogatari,* in Cogan 1987: 4–6.

[82] In the *Bishamondōbon Kokinshū chū,* a commentary on the *Kokinshū,* the love affair between Shinzei and the Somedono empress is clearly described. Shinzei is exiled for his love for her, expressed in his poems, and he is reborn as a blue-black demon to meet his love again. Quoted in Tanaka 1992: 112.

[83] Ibid., 111, 117.

According to the *Hōmotsu shū,* the cause of Shinzei's fall was not adultery but the crime of lèse-majesté, more precisely the fact of having brought discredit on the imperial lineage and by the same token on Korehito's (Emperor Seiwa's) legitimacy. Although Korehito was born long before the scandal broke out, the stain on Empress Somedono's reputation reached back into the past, before Korehito's birth, leading people to wonder if he was really the son of Emperor Montoku. Although the story of Somedono's possession has apparently little or no factual reality, another scandal, more real, involved her own daughter, Fujiwara Takaiko (Empress Nijō), and the Dharma master Zen'yū of Tōkōji. The rumor had it that Empress Nijō also had sexual relations with Zen'yū's master, Yūsen; and, before entering the palace, with the poet Narihira. According to the *Fusō ryakki,* in 896, the empress was degraded from her rank, whereas Zen'yū was exiled in Izu.[84] Her son, Emperor Yōjō, was also made destitute.

Because of their frailty and of their crucial importance for the perpetuation of the imperial lineage, imperial consorts were particularly at risk, and prone to suffer from the desire of revenge of disgruntled priests. Another case in point is that of Raigō, whose rituals were credited with the birth of Emperor Shirakawa's son. After his untimely request for the building of an ordination platform at Miidera was refused, Raigō became an onryō who caused the death of the crown prince, and later attacked not only the imperial consorts but Emperor Horikawa (Shirakawa's heir) himself.[85] However, unlike Shinzei, he never resorted to sexual attacks.

Priests like Shinzei often belonged to the category of the "protector-monks" (*gojisō*), who protected the emperor and his family through their rituals. These monks had ready access to the palace, and this sometimes gave rise to temptations and scandals—leading to their untimely death and their becoming vengeful spirits. Jien, who distinguished two types of "possessing spirits" in his *Gukanshō,* and who attributed the cause of the scandal of Hōnen's disciples to one of these spirits, was himself protector-monk.

According to the *Taiheiki,* the Tantric master Yixing was exiled to the land of Kara after being accused of making advances to the imperial concubine Yang Guifei.[86] This is clearly an anachronism, since Yixing

[84] Ibid., 121.

[85] The story appears in various sources, including the *Heike monogatari* and the *Gukanshō.*

[86] See the *Heike monogatari* in McCullough 1988: 61–62: "Might it be that even a Buddha incarnate cannot escape unforeseen calamities? In Great Tang, there was once a prayer-monk to Emperor Xuanzong, a certain Holy Teacher Yixing, who was accused of making advances to the imperial consort Yang Guifei. Past or present, great country or small, gossip is a vicious thing. Although there was no evidence to support the charge,

died before the affair between Xuanzong and Yang Guifei, but the episode reveals the Japanese perception of the protector-monks. We have mentioned earlier the case of Dōkyō, who, although not technically a gojisō (the institution became important only in the Insei period), owed his sudden rise to his talent as a healer-monk (*kanbyō zenji*). The institution of the gojisō may be partly responsible for the bad reputation of monks in medieval Japan. These monks not only had free access to the palace but they also lived in a kind of symbiotic relation with the imperial family. The perpetuation of the dynasty depended on them, as the birth of a male heir was believed to depend on their esoteric rituals. Thus they protected the future emperor from before his birth to his enthronement. Through their magic rituals, they took control of the imperial consort's body. Some of these rtuals were quite intimate, for instance a ritual in which bezoar ("ox yellow") was used to rub the genital parts of the pregnant woman at time of childbirth.[87] Male gynecologists have always had a bad reputation, and all the more so when power is at stake. The double-edged nature of the protector-monk institution is well summed up in a later text, "The Boor," an apology for "male love" that projects all the blame on women:

> And the reason that temples exclude women is precisely because they're so fascinating! They arouse deep passion in men's hearts so a scripture says "Priests must not go near the imperial court even briefly. If they do they will surely be soiled with sexual desire." If a monk from Mt. Kōya or Miidera could feel the tender graces of an elegant lady sixteen years of age with a face like a rose mallow clothed like a rain-moistened pear blossom—well then he'd be unable to continue his studies! No matter how resolute the monk! He'd be in danger—and might even demand to return to lay life! That's why Buddha issued his commandment.

The scriptural quotation about the temptations awaiting priests at court seems to imply a reference to the relation between the hermit of Shiga Temple and Empress Somedono. At the same time, we are told that the hermit of Shiga fell in love of his own will.[88]

Amorous passion does not always lead to an evil rebirth. Sometimes a monk is saved by the purity of his voice, which predestines him to recite the *Lotus Sūtra* or some powerful incantations. We have mentioned

---

suspicion alone caused Yixing to be banished to the land of Kara." Chinese sources tell us that Xuanzong remained very close to Yixing and was grieved by his premature death. See Faure 1997b: 79–80.

[87] See Strickmann 1993: 73–74; and Tanaka 1992: 125–31.
[88] Quoted in Leupp 1995: 211.

above the case of Jōzō (891–964), a Hieizan priest renowned as master of *shōmyō* (liturgical chant). Once he was called by a beautiful young woman to perform an exorcism. When Jōzō recited his incantations, the malignant spirit appeared and the illness ceased. Or perhaps it was merely displaced, because Jōzō fell in love with the girl. When the rumor spread, Jōzō took refuge in Kurama to try to forget the young woman, but in the end he could not help himself and returned to see her.[89]

Another famous case is that of Dōmyō (d.u.)., a Tendai monk famous as a reciter of the *Lotus Sūtra*, who is said to have had an affair with the poetess Izumi no Shikibu.[90] In the *Hokekyō kenki*, after Dōmyō's death, a friend sees him in a dream and is told that in spite of all his transgressions, owing to the power of the *Lotus Sūtra*, Dōmyō was able to avoid the evil destinies and was reborn on a beautiful lotus pond, where he could atone for his past offences before being reborn in the Tuṣita heaven.[91] The political context of the amorous passions of Jōzō and Dōmyō need not concern us here, as it seems in both cases to have been overshadowed by the positive image of these two figures as specialists of the *Lotus Sūtra*.

Let us mention one last case (because its tragi-comic nature contrasts with the dark atmosphere of the above cases): that of the bishop Saikōbō of the Kurama Temple, on the northern outskirts of Kyoto. Saikōbō was a revered sixty-seven-year-old ascetic and "a trickster of surpassing cleverness," who convinced a naive couple to give him their only daughter.[92] His transgressive behavior is also reflected in that of his disciples, described as "a band of shameless young priests who regularly caught fish in the Kibune river, or caught pheasants and other mountain fowl to skin and eat."[93] Saikōbō is severely punished in the end, but not before having been made a fool of: while being carried to the Kurama temple, the girl is discovered by a young official, the Chief Advisor, and replaced by a cow, which creates havoc in the temple: "The cow . . . went right on leaping and bucking. Finally the bishop succeeded in catching hold of its tail. 'Although you may not care for me, I have you by the hair. So I have created a bond of love that will endure into the next life, although this be all that binds us in the present one.' Saying this, he tried to embrace the

---

[89] See the *Konjaku monogatari shu* 30, NKBT 26: 218. The same story in a simpler form is found in the *Yamato monogatari* 62, NKBT 9: 259–60. See Ishida 1995: 57.

[90] See *Uji shūi monogatari*, translated by Mills 1970: 135–36.

[91] See *Hokekyō kenki*, translated by Dykstra 1983: 110.

[92] See Kavanagh 1996.

[93] Ibid., 235.

cow. The cow kicked the bishop flat on his back and shook the room with its leaping and bucking."[94] Saikōbō then thinks that the girl must have been transformed into a cow because of her vile temper, and prays for her salvation. "But now he had fallen prey to carnal desires and was unable to restore the cow to its original form." Eventually, the owner of the cow appears and takes it back, leaving Saikōbō dumbfounded and mortified. Saikōbō is finally, literally, struck by lightning, and joins the hordes of demons. His vengeful spirit will, however, be placated when it is worshiped as a guardian deity of Kurama. Furthermore, the character of Saikōbō is partly redeemed when the Chief Advisor donates land to Kuramadera: "Thus the dissolute Saikōbō proved to have laid the foundation for the mountain's flourishing state. It was said that the temple's prosperity was all the doing of the most compassionate Tamonten working through an earthly medium."[95] Retrospectively, Saikōbō's desire is merely an *upāya* (means) of the god Bishamon (alias Tamonten) to bring happiness to his *mōshigo* (heaven-sent child), the daughter of Saemon no jō, and prosperity to the country (through the happy marriage of the girl and the Chief Advisor), and, last but not least, to Bishamon's own temple, Kuramadera. The desire of the eminent priest Saikōbō, who until then had been perfectly pure, was caught up in this network, and duly relativized as part of a larger plot leading to ultimate goodness. In many of these medieval Buddhist tales, the wrongdoing of the evil characters does not prevent them from being deified at the end as ancillary deities (*kenzokushin*).

THE JURIDICAL BACKGROUND

An edict of 1873 declares that "from now on, monks can eat meat freely, take wives, use animal hair, etc." A similar edict for nuns was promulgated the following year. These two edicts were preceded by several others in 1871, which deplored the corruption of the clergy. According to Ishida Mizumaro, the fact that the government decided to promote Shintō as the official religion meant that it chose to leave monks to their degeneration.[96] Knowing the anti-Buddhist atmosphere of the time, however, one could argue rather that the government chose this measure in order to further discredit Buddhism. This situation was the result of a long juridical evolution that I shall outline, taking my cues from Ishida.

The main point is that the inner rule of the Japanese saṅgha was supplemented by the external rule of the Code for Monks and Nuns

[94] Ibid., 236.
[95] Ibid., 243.
[96] Ishida 1995: 212.

(*Sōniryō*). This state legislation was fundamentally ambivalent. It tended to "differientiate the saṅgha," and thus seemed to emphasize its otherness. This essential difference was important: to constitute a source of legitimacy and spiritual protection to political power, monks must be authentic symbols of the Buddha, removed from the secular world. Monastic difference could also be disturbing, however, hence the repeated governmental attempts to curb the saṅgha, to reduce its singularity. Time and again, anticlerical measures were aimed at sending certain categories of monks and nuns back to secular life. To survive, the saṅgha had to become more transparent, obedient to secular values. During the medieval period, various monastic institutions like that of the *monzeki* priest-prince reasserted the values of the clan and lineage, so that the borders between lay and clerical society became blurred. A reaction took place during the Tokugawa period, with the governmental attempt to reinforce specific castes, to emphasize social division, and to prevent social mobility. This evolution led to the consolidation of a rigid schema in which all castes were in principle integrated, unified into one hierarchical system: let the monks be monks, and strictly follow the rule. This ideal system had, of course, very little to do with the reality of social practices.

The Reformation of the Vinaya

We recall how, after Saichō, a new ordination system based on the bodhisattva precepts of the *Bonmōkyō* (Ch. *Fanwang jing*), was established on Mount Hiei, coinciding with the traditional ordination system brought by the Chinese monk Jianzhen (Ganjin), centered on Nara and Tōdaiji. This new form of ordination, however, was to have the unexpected results of lowering the age limit for ordination and allowing nuns into the saṅgha.[97] After Ganjin, the observance of the precepts soon declined, and ordinations became purely pro forma. An effort at reviving the Dharmaguptaka precepts was made by Jitsuhan (d. 1144).[98] In Nara as in the "Northern capital" and on Mount Hiei, however, knowledge about Vinaya remained superficial until the reform that took place at the beginning of the thirteenth century. This reform was accomplished by Jōkei (1155–1213), Kōben (1173–1232), Kakujō (1194–1249), and Eizon (1201–1290) in Nara; and by Shunjō (1166–1227) in Kyoto. In Tendai too, the bodhisattva ordinations experienced a revival with Yuiken (1284–1378) and Kōshū (1276–1350), the author of the *Keiran shūyōshū*.

The reformed Vinaya was, however, more compromising than Ganjin's

---

[97] Ibid., 20.
[98] *Genko shakusho,* in *DNBZ* 101: 291c.

system. In his *Kairitsu saikō ganmon,* for instance, Jōkei, while insisting that ordination requires the presence of ten regular priests, admits exceptions in which ordination can take place with only one or two priests.[99] Jōkei wanted to replace the pro forma ordination that prevailed at the time with an orthodox one but, like his predecessors before the coming of Ganjin, he confronted the problem of finding ten authentic masters well versed in the Vinaya. To solve this problem, it was necessary to bring monks from the mainland or to send Japanese monks abroad.

One of the first Japanese monks to go to China during the Kamakura period was Shunjō, the founder of the Northern Capital Vinaya (Hokkei Ritsu). Shunjō was ordained at nineteen in Dazaifu (Kyushu), then studied Tendai and Shingon.[100] After the death of his master, he went to Nara and Kyoto and studied the Vinaya of the Great and Lesser Vehicles. He left for China in 1199, studying there for over ten years before returning in 1211. In 1217 he entered Sennyūji, where he began to teach the Vinaya commentaries of Daoxuan from a Tiantai viewpoint.[101] The rule set forth by Shunjō for Sennyūji was also influenced by Chan.

Meanwhile, in Nara, the Southern school experienced a first renewal with Jōkei and his disciples, Kainyo and Kakushin. But the scholarly study of Vinaya was not necessarily tied to practice, as shown in the *Shasekishū* section entitled "The gap between study and practice among Vinaya adepts." The disciples of Jōkei continued to keep young boys (*chigo*) and to break the vegetarian taboo. The true revival of Vinaya in Nara had to wait Kainyo's successors Kakujō and Eizon.

At Saidaiji, Eizon's main disciple was Ninshō, who became active in Kantō (at Kōsenji in Hitachi). On the occasion of a visit from his master in 1262, he is said to have conferred the bodhisattva precepts on several thousand people.[102] Whatever the truth of this, the revival of the Ritsu with Eizon and Ninshō was spectacular. These massive ordinations, often motivated in the case of lay people by the belief in the magical efficacy of the precepts, did not necessarily translate into ethical behavior. According to Mujū's *Zōtanshū*, "Hardly fifty years have passed since Ritsu monks and Zen monks have become many in the world. . . . Ritsu monks are particularly numerous; however, rare are those who are in accordance with the Dharma, many are those who are dissolute, or so I have heard."[103]

---

[99] *DNBZ* 105: 13c.
[100] See Ishida 1972: 411c.
[101] See *Ritsuon sōbōden,* in *DNBZ* 105: 228c.
[102] See Ishida 1995: 92.
[103] *Zōtanshū,* 1973: 248.

The dominant trend, the so-called Vinaya of the Southern Capital, was derived from Eizon's teaching at Saidaiji, and it eventually absorbed that of the Northern capital (based on Shunjō's interpretation). The bodhisattva precepts were conferred on all kinds of people, even prostitutes.[104] In some cases, their reception was laden with restrictions. An interesting case is that of Retired Emperor Kameyama and his consorts, who received in 1276 the ten strict precepts, except the one against sex. Furthermore, it was decided that, although he should avoid sexual relations with his consorts, he could still have sex with other women or with boys.[105] The ordination according to Eizon could therefore turn into casuistry to take imperial resistances into account.

The progressive changes in Ritsu monasteries soon became obvious. Thus in 1212, in Kaijūzanji, a temple restored by Jōkei, the age for the ordination was raised from 16 to 20 in an attempt to return to Nanzan Vinaya.[106] In the rule of Shōmyōji in Arima, declared by Shinkai in 1283, the Vinaya observance became even stricter—a rare case.[107] Likewise, in the *Keidoin kishiki* set forth in 1292 by Kakushin, the strict observance of the ten major precepts of the *Bonmōkyō* was affirmed, along with a prohibition against lodging men, children, or women overnight.[108] The restriction of women's entry reappeared in many temple rules. In this troubled period, however, these internal rules were often transgressed due to external circumstances. Similar changes took place in Zen monasteries, for instance at Tōfukuji, where Enni Ben'en decreed a new set of rules.

In the Pure Land school too, the accusations of immoral behavior leveled at Hōnen's and Shinran's disciples—many of whom, following Shinran's examples, were married—led to a reform attempt. In 1285, a seventeen-article rule for nenbutsu practitioners was issued by Zen'en. It prohibited adultery and emphasized in particular that male and female followers were not allowed to sit together during the nenbutsu. It also prohibited drinking alcohol and gambling.[109] There were also individual initiatives, like the "pledge letter" of the *shuto* (priests) of Senjuji in Bizen in 1262, which is a promise not to lodge women.[110] Likewise, the vow

---

[104] See *Kongō busshi Eizon kanjin gakushō shiki*, s.v. 1285 (Kōan 8/8/13); and *Saidaiji Eizon denki shūsei*, 61, quoted in Ishida 1995: 112.

[105] Ishida 1995: 112.

[106] See the *kishōmon* (written pledge) of Jōkei for Kaijūzanji in 1212, the prohibition for Anryūōji in 1223, and the last instructions of Ryōhen for Chisokuin of Tōdaiji in 1251, all in Ishida 1995.

[107] See *Kamakura ibun* 10: 388, 20: 138a.

[108] Ibid., 23: 229; quoted in Ishida 1995: 117.

[109] See *Shinshū shiryō shūsei* 1: 1009, in Ishida 1995: 121. The same interdictions are found in the rules of Jōkōji (d.u.), ibid., 983c.

[110] *Kamakura ibun* 12: 204.

(*ganmon*) of the *shami* (novice) Son'e in 1286, in thirteen articles, is a resolution to suppress any desire toward women.[111] Further reforms took place during the Muromachi period, initiated by monks of Tōshōdaiji, Tōdaiji, and Saidaiji in Nara, and by heirs of Shunjō at Sennyūji in Kyoto, but none of them had a lasting impact. After the Ōnin civil war, another attempt was made to revive Vinaya in every school, but the main impact was to come from the state.

The Evolution of State Legislation

After the Taika governmental reform of 645, monastic control was entrusted to a system of ten masters, and a series of codes appeared.[112] Only a few articles of the *Sōniryō* (Regulations for Monks and Nuns) of the Taihō era (701) dealt, in fact, with sexual matters. The first article lists the four *pārājikā* of the Dharmaguptaka Vinaya, but merely holds that sexual offense can cause temporary exclusion and can be amended through confession. Articles 11 and 12 forbid women to spend the night in a monastery, or men to do so in a nunnery, and declare that they will be punished appropriately if they break that rule.[113] The code also forbids drinking alcohol and eating meat and the five stringent (supposedly aphrodisiac) aliments for monks. It seems in this respect to have been influenced more by the *Bonmōkyō* than by the Dharmaguptaka Vinaya. Significantly, the three rules against alcohol, meat, and the five aphrodisiacs were grouped as the "three precepts" (*sankai*). The strict interdiction against eating meat, while at first glance unrelated to sex, was indeed perceived as a precaution against "carnal" desire.

In 780, after the "Dōkyō incident," an imperial edict pointed out that the acts of monks are not different from those of lay people, and required that the entire clergy perform a self-examination. This, however, did not have much effect, as can be seen from several subsequent edicts that deplored the laxity of the Buddhist clergy. Too often, the major motivation to become a monk was to avoid taxes and corvées, and it had very little to do with renunciation. This type of monk was usually self-ordained and continued to live a rather secular life. Thus, the *Sōniryō* had some reason to be concerned with the issue of "self-ordination" and to insist that this practice had to be stopped. However, this was by no means easy, because

[111] Ibid., 21: 101b. For other examples of self-imposed discipline, see Ishida 1995: 127.

[112] On regulations for monks and nuns in pre medieval Japan, see Hori 1975, 2: 262–81.

[113] Thus, for one to four nights, ten days of punishment; for more than five nights, thirty days; for more than ten nights, one hundred days. See Ishida 1995: 10. This article recalls the fourth of the ninety *prāyaścittika* rules, concerning staying under the same roof with a woman, or the fourth of the 178 equivalent rules in the Vinaya of the nuns—offenses requiring confession.

self-ordination had been until then commonly admitted in Japan. Even after the establishment of an official ordination system, or rather because of it, such practice continued and contributed to make this system inefficient.[114]

At any rate, the authorities—clerical as well as secular—do not seem to have taken their role very seriously, if we are to believe an edict of 812, which reproaches the clergy for its tolerance toward monastic laxity. The same year, as if to manifest their lack of trust toward monastic jusrisdiction, the government severely punished two monks who had commited an offense. But these bursts of legality, limited to extreme cases, were unable to control the general laxity. Thus in 825 several Nara monks were exiled from Tōtōmi province for adultery. But punishment for adultery seems to have become increasingly rare, provoked only by extraordinary circumstances. We hear, for instance, that in 896 the Dharma master Zen'yu was exiled to Izu for allegedly having had an affair with an imperial consort, who was demoted from her rank. Some were concerned with this state of things, and petitioned the throne about it. In 914, an address to the throne by Miyoshi Kiyoyuki describes the degeneration of Buddhism.[115]

The Vinaya renewal at the beginning of the thirteenth century took place in the context of a major sociopolitical change, the rise of warrior rule. Although the monastic rule did not change, the *Sōniryō* established secular laws regulating the behavior of monks and nuns. The *Jōei shikimoku,* issued in 1232 (Jōei 1), constituted the first element of the penal system established by the Kamakura Bakufu. Among its fifty-one articles, only one (article 34) deals explicitly with illicit sex: punishment for adultery or sexual relations in public ("at crossroads"). It states that "in the case of Dharma masters, the crime must be punished according to circumstances."[116] What is new in this code is that the activities of monks and nuns, and more precisely their misdeeds, which in the past had been tolerated, are now seen as falling into the domain of secular jurisdiction. Even so, the law seems remarkably tolerant. Thus article 34 concerning adultery gives the example of a priest who, upon encountering a woman at a crossroad at night, attempts to rape her. Alerted by the cries of the woman, people catch the priest, tie him up, and take him to the police station. After questioning the protagonists, the policemen, while recognizing the aggression, eventually acquit the priest. Ironically, they call the people brigands for having captured the priest, and put the woman in jail because, by walking alone at night, she has provoked

---

[114] Ishida 1995: 40.
[115] *Honchō monzui* 2, in *Kokushi taikei* 29b: 44, 52.
[116] *Chūsei hōsei shiryō shū* 1, 20, 1, quoted in Ishida 1995: 95.

evil.[117] We can readily see that there is no intention here to find fault with the monk. In a typical instance of blaming the victim, it is the woman who is judged responsible for the desire she provoked in the monk, and therefore for causing her own misadventure. In a similar circumstance involving a layman and a woman, the man would probably have been found guilty of attempted rape or assault. There is no record indicating what would have happened in the case of a nun being raped. Two standards are applied here, depending on the gender and the lay or clerical status of the person. Ishida argues that the monk was probably turned over to monastic jurisdiction and thus the decision was left to the saṅgha—but nothing in the text seems to confirm this interpretation. Significantly, the code hardly mentions—and then only in an annexed section—the question of clerical responsibility. The reasoning behind the application of secular laws to monks and nuns is not entirely clear. The level of harm needed for secular jurisdiction to intervene varies drastically over time. It seems that the threshold for intervention was more easily crossed when the misdeed was perceived to affect society at large rather than individuals.

Soon the Bakufu became conscious of the insufficiency of the *Jōei shikimoku,* and it gradually added "annex laws," the last of which, dated 1235, aims at nenbutsu adepts, who were said to transgress monastic rules and live a dissolute life (eating meat, drinking alcohol, having sex with women).[118] Thus, referring to the specific "case of the nenbutsu practitioner"—a man who allegedly "ate fish and fowl and invited women, associated with evil people, and self-indulgently enjoyed wine and banquets"—one article ordered the destruction of the culprit's house and his eviction from Kamakura.[119]

A similar criticism regarding Pure Land adepts is found in the *Azuma kagami.*[120] Even after the exile of Hōnen and his disciples, this article 75 can be said to foreshadow the interdiction of exclusive nenbutsu in the Gennin and Karoku eras. In the annex law 386, too, nenbutsu adepts are mentioned, as well as their aggressive behavior regarding women.[121] The change of language shows that they were suspected of sexual relationships—encouraged by the promiscuity of nenbutsu assemblies. They were certainly not alone in drinking alcohol nor eating meat and fish, as we can see in these "annex laws," in the section on "New

[117] See *Gosei hai shikimoku chū,* in *Zoku zoku gunsho ruijū* 7: 224a; quoted in Ishida 1995: 26.

[118] See *Chūsei hōsei shiryō shū* 1: 96.

[119] Ibid.

[120] *Azuma kagami,* s.v. 1235. See *Kokushi taikei* 33: 162.

[121] *Chūsei hōsei shiryō shū* 1: 272.

Rules of Kantō" (*Kantō shinsei jōjō,* 1261), and in the annex law 377 on the interdiction of nonvegetarian banquets in monasteries.[122]

The *Kuge shinsei* (1263) provides a rule for monasteries quite different from the previous ones.[123] Under the rubric "Kenmitsu monks in all temples and mountains must observe the law of the precepts," it is said: "Nowadays, [monks] often like to drink and eat, and furthermore, they collect wives and concubines, failing to observe integrally the four strict rules (*pārājikā*) and to respect the ten precepts. Not only do they muddle the ultimate truth, but they transgress the fundamental laws of the state." However, the evolution is such that, faced with monastic laxity, the secular jurisprudence too increased its degree of tolerance toward the monks. Despite variations, the tendency seems to have been a general one.[124]

Prohibitions for specific temples were also issued, like the one pronounced by Hōjō Sadatoki for Engakuji in 1294, prohibiting access to all women—except for certain periods.[125] Around the same time, in 1285, an edict of emperor Go-Uda reminds monks that they cannot "become husbands."[126] Attitudes have therefore changed regarding tolerance for married or sexually active monks. In the *Kenmu shikimoku* of 1336 there is no attempt to control the actions of monks. At the end of the Muromachi period, regional laws appear that basically repeat the previous law that prohibited women from entering temples.

The *Kōshū hattō no jidai,* a series of laws proclaimed by Takeda Shingen in 1547, approaches the question from a more pragmatic angle. Rather than forbidding monks to marry, a method that had proved its inefficacy, it tries to sever the ties monks have with the donors who support them: "One must not give offerings to monks who have wives and children. Those who go against the spirit of this law, masters and donors, will not escape prosecution. However, if [these monks] repent their past offences, and abandon their wives, they will not be punished."[127] In keeping with this pragmatic approach, Takeda Shingen also allowed Nichiren monks to marry under the supervision of a magistrate, to whom they had to pay an annual tribute.[128]

---

[122] Ibid., 210. Note in the text of that law the presence of children at these banquets—which evokes the pederasty of monks. The expression "to replace meat with fish" might be a veiled allusion to heterosexual and homosexual practices—because if the point was only to prohibit meat eating, the mention of children would be superfluous. See Ishida 1995: 98–99.

[123] *Kuge shinsei,* in *Zoku zoku gunsho ruijū* 7: 182c.

[124] Ishida 1995: 27.

[125] *Kamakura ibun* 24: 108c–109a.

[126] See *Kamakura ibun* 21: 6, quoted in Ishida 1995: 100.

[127] *Chūsei hōsei shiryō shū* 3, 198, quoted in Ishida 1995: 102.

[128] Ishida 1995: 102.

By contrast, the laws promulgated by the emperor continued to hold monks to a higher standard. Thus, in 1285 an imperial edict aimed at lay people states that a woman cannot take a monk as husband.[129] In the *Meihō jōjō kanroku* (1267), the question of the recognition of such illegal marriages is discussed in light of juridical precedents. The texts are in conflict, since the *Ryōgige* declares that these marriages must be recognized, whereas the *Sōniryō* argues to the contrary. This leads to the following dialogue:

> Question: "When a monk or nun takes a spouse and has children, and they already have private property, if the monk or nun dies, how should one dispose of it?" Answer: "The fact that a monk or nun marries and has private property is in transgression of Vinaya and [also] violates the Codes. If this question arises while he or she is still alive, it must be dealt with according to existing laws. However, if the monk or nun is already dead, although it is contrary to the law, the wife and children must be taken into account. Thus, the property must be given to them."[130]

The commentary (*gige*) clearly considers the marriage of monks to be illegal, since such an act is contrary to both Buddhist law and secular jurisdiction. However, it also takes it as an established fact, and choses to focus on the practical matter of succession rights.

In the Edo period, rules promulgated by the Bakufu, the *hattō* or ordinances, came to complement the inner reforms of the clergy. Several *hattō*, like the *Kantō Jōdoshū hattō*, strictly forbade the admission of women in monasteries—except in the case of pilgrimages—as well as promiscuity between men and women during rituals like the *jūya-e* (Ten Nights Assembly). Prostitutes were also banned from plying their trade in front of temples.[131] In the *hattō* for Saidaiji, likewise, nuns were forbidden to remain alone with a monk or to enter a temple in the evening. Even in Jōdo temples, where women and eating meat had traditionally been tolerated, admission became restricted. However, despite the general tendency, all these rules were not systematically unified or enforced. Thus in 1742 the *Gyoteisho hakkō jō*, the basic juridical text of the Edo Bakufu issued under the shōgun Yoshimune, lists according to monastic status various punishments for adulterous monks, from exile on an island (in the case of an abbot) to exhibition in a pillory (*sarashi*), imprisonment, or crucifixion.[132] Other punishments include exclusion from the monastery, removal from the registers, solitary confinement, and so on. These kinds of edicts and punishments appear in many documents.

---

[129] See ibid., 103.
[130] *Kokushi taikei* 22: 99, quoted in Ishida 1995: 103–104.
[131] Ishida 1995: 154.
[132] See text in *Kujikata gyoteisho*, quoted in Ishida 1995: 155.

The Edo period is thus marked by a radical change in the penal system. Although the corpus delicti (sexual offense) and the way to prevent it (prohibition of women from temples) remain practically the same, the rigor of the punishments and the systematic nature of their application are quite different from the earlier period. The margin of tolerance that surrounded monastic offense has disappeared. What was considered a misdemeanor (except in some cases where imperial lineage was at stake) has become a criminal offense, falling entirely into the domain of secular jurisdiction, and subject to harsh (often capital) punishment. The radicalization of the penal system might also reflect the consciousness of the extent to which monastic society had been pervaded by secular values.

NYOBON

Whereas the Bakufu law remained adamant in its denunciation of married monks, affirming that "the unrepentant priest who violates the [Buddhist] precepts shall be punished [according to the seriousness of his crime] by either death or banishment," the Meiji government found it convenient to allow marriage as the best way to undermine the remaining prestige of monks. In 1872, an order issued by the Ministry of State declared: "Priests may do as they wish regarding the eating of meat, marriage, and the cutting of their hair. Moreover, they need not be concerned about the propriety of wearing commoners' clothing while not performing official duties."[133]

Illicit Sex

We recall that ritual sex had become licit in at least one line of Buddhism, the Vajrayāna. This type of sex, it is true, was not precisely the kind of hedonistic exercise favored by Western imagination—but neither should it be too much idealized, as is often the case.[134] In other forms of Buddhism, sex remained theoretically prohibited, object of the cardinal pārājikā rule. Nevertheless, the *Fanwang jing* and other Mahāyāna texts allowed a more flexible redefinition of what constitutes an offense, arguing that the "essence" of the precepts, once obtained, could never be lost.

Although the ritual conception of sacred sex as a *coincidentia oppositorum* found its way into Japanese Buddhism, the monastic conception of sexuality in Japan, as reflected for instance in the use of the term

---

[133] See Order #1339, fourth month of 1872 (Meiji 5), quoted in Ketelaar 1990: 6.

[134] See for instance Shaw 1994. According to Tibetan Buddhists themselves (for instance, Drukpa Kunle), the ritual union with a "secret mother," although controlled in theory by meditation, did sometimes degenerate. See Stein 1972: 115.

nyobon (literally "assaulting" or "forcing" women, although it came to lose some of its violent connotations), remained basically androcentric and inegalitarian. Although nuns were often suspected of similar behavior, the term nyobon does not have a gynocentric equivalent. In this respect, Indian Vinaya was more egalitarian, insofar as it mentions cases of nuns raping a monk. Although typically a male offense, commiting *nyobon* was seen (and in a sense partly justified) as the unavoidable male reaction to temptation from women. Consequently the first (and often the only) measure taken to prevent it was to deny women access to monasteries. Promiscuity could never be entirely avoided, however, particularly in famous pilgrimage centers.[135] The popular perception of what could happen during periods of incubation (*komori*) is described in a story of the *Zōtanshū* (1306), in which an aged monk whispers to a young woman and her wet nurse as they doze off during their vigil, telling them to follow his instructions. He wants the woman to be his. The story recalls the Chinese topos of the "monastery of debauchery." In the same anticlerical vein, one could probably argue that it explains why the sterile women who practiced incubation retreats in such cultic centers would often have "auspicious dreams" in which a male figure (usually perceived as a manifestation of the Bodhisattva Kannon) appeared to them and granted them a child (*mōshigo*).

What seems reasonably certain is that sexual relationships and marriage became increasingly common for Japanese monks.[136] Already in the Heian period many monks were married. One of the first cases recorded is that of an anonymous monk who, after being married, was ordained on Hieizan and spent ten years at Miidera. Eventually he returned to his province of Bizen, and resumed living with his wife.[137] According to the *Kōfukiji bettō jidai,* the *bettō* (administrator) of Kōfukuji, the former *daisōjō* (high priest) Gaen in 1218 recommended his own daughter to be the consort of Emperor Go-Toba.[138] In 1101, in a text requiring judgment from the *mandokoro* (chancellery), we find mention of a Dharma master Tokuman, a former resident of this temple, who ran away from his wife.[139] In 1146 a monk of Enmyōin, a branch temple (*matsuji*) of Hosshōji, was involved in a lawsuit with his wife's brothers.[140] According the *Konjaku monogatari shū,* the wife of the bettō of Kokuryūji in Inaba province ran away with another man. We

[135] On this question, see Amino 1993: 77–94.
[136] See Ishida 1995, and Tsuji 1944–1955, 6: 330–34.
[137] See the *Honchō hokke kenki, Nihon shisō taikei* 7: 130, quoted in Ishida 1995: 45.
[138] See *DNBZ* 124: 30c, quoted ibid., 46.
[139] *Heian ibun* 4: 1402 a–c.
[140] Ibid., 6: 2184a.

also learn from the same source that the bettō of Daianji was married to a nun, and they had a beautiful daughter.

Sometimes, these stories are apologetic. In his diary, Fujiwara no Munetada notes what a monk of Miidera named Keizen told him about the Hōjōji priest Ryūson and the *ajari* (teacher) Jōsen: "For many years, Ryūson has transgressed the precepts and, with the help of his wife and children, has directed Hōjōji."[141] Likewise, Jōsen "transgressed the precepts, having wife and children, and lived in the capital."[142] Munetada indicates that the two men were adepts of nenbutsu and were certain of their rebirth in Pure Land. According to the *Shūi ōjōden* by Miyoshi Tameyasu (1049–1139), the monk Jungen of Anrakuji in Chinzei was a lazy man who, after the death of his wife, married his own daughter. When his disciples reproached him for this, he answered that ancient priests had various attitudes: some of them married their sister, others their daughter. Furthermore, since Japan is an outlying country, there is no need to regulate one's behavior. In the same work, we find a monk from Higo who practiced austerities and "contemplation of the principle," and who, past the age of fifty, took a wife. Tameyasu also compiled, as supplement to the *Shūi ōjōden*, the *Goshūi ōjōden*. In this work he mentions the case of a monk from Enryakuji, Ryūsen (1057–1117), who at first practiced meditation, then went to the capital, took a wife, and dedicated himself to the nenbutsu—which he recited 130,000 times a day.[143] However, in the *Sō Myōtatsu soshō chūki*, we find several stories about monks who have fallen into hell for abusing the generosity of donors, taking a wife, and transgressing the Vinaya.[144]

The author of the *Hōmotsushū*, Taira Yasuyori (1157–1195), summarizing the question of adulterous monks, says that the situation is well known, and mentions the cases of the Dharma master Jōzō who made his own son his disciple; of the retired emperor Kazan who "fell [to the rank of] a wet-nurse's son"; of the *sōjō* (high priest) of Izumi who had an affair with the Higashi sanjōin empress; of the Vinaya master Meitatsu, who had incestuous relations with his mother; and of the Dharma master Jungen who married his own daughter. He is referring, of course, to stories as he knows them through tales (*setsuwa*), and the historicity of the events described remains problematic.

According to the *Chōshūki* by Minamoto no Morofusa, three "Dharma masters" had slept with ladies-in-waiting of the empress. Despite their protestations of innocence, the three women were sent

---

[141] See the *Chūyūki*, s.v. 1120/2/11, quoted in Ishida 1995: 47.
[142] *Zōho shiryō taisei* 13 204a–c.
[143] *Goshūi ōjōden*, in Nihon shisō taikei 7: 668c.
[144] See *Zoku zoku gunsho ruijū* 16: 306a; quoted in Ishida 1995: 50.

away.[145] The *Hyakurenshō* reports the imprisonment in 1175 of the monk Ensai after the murder of an official named Tametsuna.[146] The trial revealed that Tametsuna had an affair with a young woman. But this woman also slept with her brother-in-law, a man named Taira no Moritaka. To make things worse, after the death of her father, Ensai became her protector and he started sleeping with her, as well. Eventually, two of these three men sharing the same woman, Ensai and Moritaka, joined forces to kill the third, Tametsuna. It was Moritaka who commited the murder, however, and was therefore condemned, whereas Ensai, who as a priest was supposed to be exempt from adultery, escaped punishment.[147]

We have already mentioned Shinran's dream of Kannon at Rokkakudō, a famous Kannon temple. Kannon's oracular verse was recorded by the young Shinran.[148] The verse is also quoted, without reference to Shinran, in the *Kakuzenshō*.[149] Hirata Atsutane uses Shinran's dream as proof of Buddhist decadence, and criticizes the poem itself: "Can Kannon . . . be as unlettered as this?"[150] We recall that a "jade woman" also appeared in the dreams of Jien. But whereas in Jien's case this figure symbolized the prosperity of the imperial lineage, in Shinran's case she legitimized the sexuality and marriage of monks. The verse given by the Bodhisattva Kannon to Shinran became the ideological justification of the Shinshū domestic community, and the source of a monastic blood lineage.[151]

Shinran's dream was the result of a ninety-five-day period of incubation at Rokkakudō. Ritual incubation (*sanrō*) was frequent in Kannon temples, where men and women slept in the same place.[152] As noted earlier, there was a lot of promiscuity during these vigils, and they were therefore forbidden by an edict of Go-Uda: "During the worship in front of the treasures and during the night vigil (*tsūya*), men and women must not stay together."[153] Amino Yoshihiko wonders whether, until the Kamakura period, the place of incubation was not a place of sexual li-

---

[145] *Chōshūki*, s.v. 1111, in *Zōho shiryō taisei* 6: 32c.

[146] *Kokushi taikei* 11: 91–92.

[147] Ishida 1995: 64.

[148] Not surprisingly, this poem has embarrassed Shinshū scholars, who have preferred to see it as apocryphal. It was believed to have been copied by Shinbutsu, the founder of the Takada branch. But in 1959 an "autograph" copy was discovered in the Sennyūji collection.

[149] See *Kakuzenshō*, quoted in Tanaka 1989: 95.

[150] See Ketelaar 1990: 35, who inadvertently attributes the dream to Hōnen.

[151] See Endō 1992.

[152] See *Ishiyamadera engi emaki*, quoted in Amino 1993: 86.

[153] *Iwashimizu monjo* 1: 9, quoted ibid.

cense.[154] In liminal places like the Buddha Hall, the usual constraints no longer obtained, possibly leading to free sex. In the *Nihon ryōiki* and similar works, one often finds grizzly tales of divine punishment for this kind of profanation. We are told, for instance, of the immediate retribution that befell a licentious scripture copier on a rainy day: "The temple was cramped by those who took shelter from the shower, and the copier and the [female devotees] were sitting in the same place. Then the scripture copier, driven by lust, crouched behind one of the girls, lifted her skirt, and had intercourse with her. As his penis entered her vagina, they died together embracing each other." And, as if to warn female devotees, the texts adds that "the girl died foaming at the mouth."[155] In the *Konjaku monogatari shū,* a monk who was reciting the *Lotus Sūtra* is punished for having sex with a maidservant, and dies.[156]

We also have the case of the "letter of grief" sent in 1268 by the *shuto* (monks) of Jissōji in Suruga (a Tendai temple that later became Nichiren), complaining that the abbot ate fish and fowl and killed silkworms. During monthly ceremonies, the rules against eating meat and admitting women were constantly transgressed. Again, in the Fudō-dō constructed by Hōjō Masatoki, banquets including women were organized, causing grief to monks.

A particular type of documentary source called *rakusho* is made of anonymous complaints against monks and nuns. One example, dated 1463, criticizes the "impure" deeds of a Tōji priest, Jūzō. Another such document, the "Tōji rakusho" (dated 1504), complains about a monk who sleeps with a woman and about whom, even after the denunciation, nothing has been done.[157] The rakusho may take the form of a letter from a monk.[158] Letters dated between 1487 and 1532 complain that nothing has been done to put an end to the relations between a monk named Chōsō and a nun, mother of a child named Gorō.[159]

In the *Kanmon gyōki* by the imperial prince Sadafusa, one also finds many stories of adulterous monks. For instance, in 1418, a monk from Narutaki is killed because of an affair he had.[160] In 1427, a lady-in-waiting of the shōgun is investigated and discovered to have had sexual relations with monks and practitioners, who are beheaded as a result.

[154] Amino 1994.

[155] See Nakamura 1973: 245–46. The same text, however, mentions the lustful love of a man for the goddess Kichijōten, who responds with extraordinary signs. See ibid., 178.

[156] See *Konjaku monogatari shū* 14: 26.

[157] Nihon shisō taikei 22: 349a.

[158] See *Tōji Hyakugō komonjo* 115, in *Kojiruien,* Shūkyōbu 2, 28: 694.

[159] *Tōji rakusho,* ibid.: 349a–c, quoted in Ishida 1995.

[160] *Zoku gunsho ruijū,* hoi 3, quoted in Ishida 1995: 133.

The severity of the punishment here, as in the case of Hōnen's disciples, seems to have less to do with the sexual transgression in itself than with the fact that it casts a shadow on the shōgunal lineage.[161]

According to the *Oshoki saikyō chō* (1671), a man named Shūzen who practiced at Zenkōji had sex with a nun and was denounced by her disciple. He was taken to Edo and crucified in Asakusa.[162] Another case is that of a Jōdo monk of Teramachi in Kyoto, who seduced the daughter of a parishioner and ran away with her to Sakai, where he passed himself off as a doctor. Later, when he was recognized, he was brought back to Kyoto and interrogated. Because he now had long hair, he was asked whether he had returned to lay status, which would have provided him extenuating circumstances. He denied having become a layman, arguing that he had taken the girl away to protect her from her stepfather. However, when it was established that he had had sexual relations with her, he was condemned and executed in 1671.[163]

The *Getsudō kenmonshū* (1718) mentions the exclusion of all women, nuns and others, from Kyoto monasteries, because "from the headquarters to the branch temples there have been cases of promiscuity (*ofure*)." In Kyoto, according to the *Shiojiri shūi*, the Honkokuji was investigated, and several women were found hidden there.[164] Nichiren monks in particular were accused of seducing young girls, because they had closer relationships with their parishioners. For the same year, the *Getsudō Kenmonshū* mentions the arrest and crucifixion (*haritsuke*) of the Shingon monk Hōshakubō for having sexual relations. The punishment was extreme, perhaps because the offense was judged extreme, too.[165] In the *Kyōhō tsūgan* (Penetrating Mirror of the Kyōhō Era), a strange case is reported, in relation to Honnōji. In 1720, the corpse of a twelve-year-old acolyte was found in a field. The parents and the temple tried at first to cover up the affair. But the inquiry took a new turn when a search of the temple revealed the existence of hidden rooms, where priests' wives lived.

---

[161] See *Manzai Jungō nikki*, s.v. Ōei 34/6/24 (1427), in *Zoku gunsho ruijū*, hoi 1, quoted in Ishida 1995: 133.

[162] See *Kojiruien*, Hōritsubu 2: 971.

[163] Ishida 1995: 158

[164] See *Nihon zuihitsu taisei* 3, 18: 213; see Ishida, 1995: 159. According to other accounts, young girls called Myō (an abbreviation for myōhō, the Wonderful Law of the *Lotus Sūtra*, the scripture of the Nichiren sect—but also a character whose two components could be read as "young woman") were found at Honkokuji and other Kyoto temples. The case is also mentioned in Hirata Atsutane's anti-Buddhist work, *Shutsujō shōgo*. See Tsuji 1945–1955, 10: 467. Tsuji also quotes the *Getsudō kenmonshū*, s.v. 1718, according to which, after inquiry of some Kyoto temples, all women (including nuns) were expelled from them.

[165] See *Kojiruien*, Hōritsubu 3:118–19.

The woman whom the priest kept cloistered was disguised as a novice (*wakashu*). It was apparently to prevent the novice from speaking that he had been killed. Eventually the monks were sent into exile and the temple closed. The motive of the murder was not established.[166]

After the *Gyoteisho hyakko jō* (1738), crucifixion becomes the standard punishment for adulterous monks. In the *Kajōruiten*, for instance, a magistrate of Echizen, addressing the issue of "transgressing monks," requests various punishments including crucifixion.[167] One such monk is Jōnyo, a disciple of Tannyo at Nishi Honganji, who became the sect leader and committed many offenses—such as hunting, womanizing, and criminal activities. Eventually his ten disciples were sent into exile, and he ended his life in reclusion, while his name was removed from the list of the sect leaders.[168] Again in 1797, according to the *Ruisetsu hiroku*, a monk named Ryōhen was condemned to exile on an island. But as there was no island in this domain, he received a life sentence in prison, whereas the nun who was his accomplice was jailed for one month.[169] The growing frequency of relegations *in insulam* calls to mind Tacitus, "plenum exiliis mare": the seas were covered with people exiled and relegated to islands.

According to the *Wagakoromo*, because in past years Buddhist priests' wives (*bonsai*, lit. "brahmanic wives") had become numerous in temples, a severe prohibition was proclaimed in 1788; as a result, the abbot of Sōninji was jailed.[170] In 1791, according to the *Kiki no mani mani*, the abbot of Anrakuji was exiled to an island for adultery.[171] In 1796, several monks were exiled, others put on the pillory (*sarashi*) for three days at Nihonbashi for "not conforming to the Dharma" (that is, for committing nyobon).[172] In the summer of 1796, after a police raid, more than seventy monks were caught returning from Yoshiwara and other redlight districts. They were bound and displayed for three days at the Nihonbashi crossroad, their offense written above them, before being banished.[173] It was the first time that so many people were put on the pillory together; usually there were only one or two. The text gives their full names and sectarian affiliation. Practically all sects of Japanese Buddhism are represented, but the largest number of monks come from the Jōdo (26)

---

[166] See Ishida 1995: 160–61.
[167] *Kojiruien*, Hōritsubu 2: 2–3.
[168] Ishida 1995: 167.
[169] See *Kojiruien*, Hōritsubu 3: 271.
[170] See *Wagakoromo* 1b: 242, s.v. Kansei 1, quoted in Ishida 1995: 170.
[171] See *Mikan zuihitsu* 6: 74, in Ishida 1995: 174.
[172] See *Tenmeiki mon*, in *Kojiruien*, Hōritsubu 2: 277b, quoted ibid. 171.
[173] See *Hōreki genrai shū*, Zoku zuihitsu taisei, bekkan 6: 126.

and Nichiren sects (15).[174] Similar raids took place in the Kyoto-Osaka area in 1830 and again in Edo in 1851.[175]

In 1803, according to the *Ichiwa ichigon*, the Nichiren monk Nichidō of Enmyōin was executed for having sexual relations with several women, one of whom he had impregnated and convinced to have an abortion. Nichidō was not the only person implicated; several women went to jail, and another man was put to the pillory.[176] This affair was the talk of the town and appears in several sources, for instance in the *Kyōwa kuchō* by the poet Kobayashi Issa, who was living at the time in Edo. Issa also tells how, in 1804, the monk Kyōdō of Engakuji in Kamakura was pilloried at Nihonbashi.[177]

In 1813, according to the *Bunka hihitsu*, the wife of a carpenter had an affair with a monk of her neighborhood temple (*dannadera*). When the wife of another parishioner was buried in the temple, the monk exhumed her corpse, took it to the carpenter's house, and set fire to the house. He then took his lover with him and hid her in the temple. During the seven-day funerary ritual, the carpenter went with his child to the temple. At one point, hearing her child cry, the mother could not resist and came out of hiding to console him. The child told his father that he has seen his mother, and the lovers were eventually arrested and punished.[178]

In 1824, four Nichiren monks of Myōhonji were pilloried at Nihonbashi. Two years later, several other Nichiren monks were arrested, including the abbot of Hōjōji in Osaka, on the charge of seducing women through their prayers and incantations and causing them to be possessed by foxes, in order to steal from them and rape them.[179] We recall that an edict to control monks was issued in 1829. This created a great tumult among monks. According to the police, they could not arrest all of the offending monks because of the latter's great number. In Osaka, only six temples were found innocent of such violations.[180] At Zentsūji, women were allegedly raped and stolen from. At Isshinji too, many offenses were supposedly committed, said to be even worse than taking "brahmanic wives," while the abbesses of nunneries were often found to be the mothers of several children.[181]

---

[174] Ishida 1995: 171.

[175] See Tsuji 1944–1955 (reed. 1984), 4: 96–101; quoted in Ketelaar 1990: 232.

[176] Ishida 1995: 173

[177] See Nihon koten bungaku taikei 58: 489. Significantly, Issa makes a reference to the story of the Somedono empress and her alleged passion for (and possession by) the priest Shinzei. He says: "To love sex is in human nature, those who do not like it are rarer than the *kakurin* [a mythical animal]."

[178] See *Mikan zuihitsu* 4: 277a, in Ishida 1995: 175.

[179] Ibid., 177.

[180] See *Ukiyo no arisama*, in Seikatsu shiryō shūsei 11: 62, quoted ibid.

[181] Ibid., 178.

Significantly, this grave situation was blamed on the deleterious influence of Ōshio Heihachirō (1793–1837), whose rebellion had just been crushed. About thirty temples were investigated in Osaka, and their abbot were arrested on grounds of "eating meat and having a wife." The same thing happened in Kyoto, at monasteries such as Chion-in, Honganji, Kurodani, Nanzenji, Myōshinji, and Tōfukuji. As a result, many monks were sent into exile, and one of the abbots of Chion-in was put on the pillory at the Sanjō bridge.[182] The event repeated itself in 1836 and 1839.[183] In 1836, too, a scandal took place at Kannōji, one of the great temples of Edo. The abbot was arrested and the temple destroyed. In the same year, another scandal struck at a Nichiren temple, Hokkekyōji, in the village of Nakayama in Shimotsuke. The same source mentions that a Jōdo monk, Chidō, was put on the pillory, then expelled from Edo for having sexual relations with the daughter of a parishioner. In the same year, more than two hundred monks of the Hokke sect were investigated and received various punishments. In 1842, after a severe investigation in Osaka, many cases of adultery were revealed. The Nichiren sect was forbidden, in particular in the domains of the Mito clan, and its temples were given to the Jōdo sect. All this was supposedly because an imperial favorite, an illegitimate child born at Kannōji, had used her influence to build temples and organize orgies in them.

Cases of monks visiting the red-light districts of Edo, passing themselves off as doctors, are regularly reported. For instance, in 1739, a monk of Banryūji in Asakusa was exiled to an island after provoking a scandal in a brothel.[184] In 1721, a monk named Chōen was put on the pillory for three days after a failed "double suicide" with a prostitute. The same source speaks of monks executed (*gokumon*, "[having one's head exposed at the] prison gate") in 1729 after one of them had sexual relations with the daughter of a villager in the village of Kurihara in Bushū. The worst criminals were dragged through the city before being executed.[185]

Married Monks

Married monks, now a characteristic feature of Japanese Buddhism, are also found in various other places such as Tibet, Korea, and Southeast Asia. Nuns, however, remain celibate. In Tibetan Buddhism, some monks of non-reformed schools married, whereas others chose celibacy, which

[182] Ibid., 179.

[183] See *Ukiyo no arisama*, quoted in ibid., 180.

[184] See *Gyoteisho hyakkojō*, quoted ibid., 184.

[185] In Edo, the places of punishment were Kozukahara in Asakusa and Suzukemori in Shinagawa.

became the rule for reformed schools. As in Korea, the mingling of married and unmarried monks was never easy.[186] A particular case is that of the Sakya princes, who were married and had families but were also the highest dignitaries of the Sakyapa school. Their palaces, built not far from the Great Temple founded in the thirteenth century, were for all practical purposes (except one) organized like monasteries. Many village priests were also married. Thus Marpa, in the eleventh century, had as his principal spouse Dakmema but also had, according to tradition, eight secundary spouses, who were his partners in Tantric rituals. Drugpa Kunle (1455–1529), who had been married against his will and who was known for his transgressive attitude, was nevertheless very critical of monasteries in which married monks "held up as a flag their monastic robe and prepared offerings only for their wife and children, without thinking of the Buddha's disappointment." Even in celibate orders there were some failures. Thus the great Gelugpa (lit. "Virtuous") master Sangye Gyatso (1653–1705), regent of the fifth Dalai Lama, had several mistresses and a number of children, and was succeeded by one of his sons.[187] In Cambodia, too, the celibate Theravāda tradition of the Dhammayutika, founded in 1829, coexisted with the older tradition of the Mahānikāy. The latter, influenced by Tantrism, were perhaps derived from the Arī cult of Burma, whose adepts were known to drink alcohol and not to respect the rule of chastity.[188]

For early Japan, we have no indication in the Sōniryō that such conditions existed, and we remain in the realm of suppositions. However, we find a little later in the Nihon ryōiki a monk who has a wife and a daughter at the time of Emperor Genmei (r. 707–715).[189] At this early stage, the tendency to interpret marriage as nyobon and to condemn it as an offense was apparently not yet widespread. There was also a category of practitioners called shami or nyūdō (novices), who were usually self-ordained and often married.[190] Despite this fact, they were perceived as holy men.[191] But soon, with the appearance of rules to restrict private

[186] On Korean married monks, see Buswell 1992.

[187] See Chayet 1993: 201–9.

[188] See François Bizot, Le figuier à cinq branches: Recherces sur le bouddhisme Khmer (Paris: Ecole Française d'Extrême-Orient, 1976), 1–44.

[189] See Nihon ryōiki 70: 327.

[190] The term appears in the Shoku Nihongi, under the dates 756 and 777. In the Nihon ryōiki, one finds several references to "self-ordained novices" (jido shami)—most of whom seem to have a wife. These shami usually received the ten precepts.

[191] Thus, in the Nihon ojō gokuraku ki, in the notice of Shōnyo (781–867), there is mention of one of his shami named Kyōshin, who announces his own rebirth in Pure Land, as well as Shōnyo's. Kyōshin was a poor married shami, and after his death his corpse was eaten by dogs, but the village people respect him and call him Amida-maru, because he recited the nenbutsu day and night. He also appears in the Konjaku monogatari shū 15: 26.

ordinations and the marriage of monks, first outside Buddhism with the enactment of the *Sōniryō,* then within, references to these figures diminish. After mentioning one such case, the author of the *Genkō shakusho* comments: "Among the lay people of this country, although they cut their hair, those who do not observe the entirety of *brahmacārya* [chastity] and who take wives are called *shami,* despite the fact that they are laymen."[192] We also find fully ordained monks (*bhikṣu,* Jap. *biku*) taking wives. According to his own testimony, Kyōkai himself, the author of the *Nihon ryōiki,* was one of them:

> Ah! What a shame! Born in this world, I know no way to make a living. Because of karmic causation I am bound by the net of lust, enveloped in cravings, combining death and life, running in all directions, and burning my body alive. Remaining in the secular life, I have no means to support my family and am without food, salt, clothes, or firewood. My mind is never at rest, worrying about the things I need. As I am hungry and freezing in the daytime, so at night I am hungry and freezing. For in my previous lives I did not practice almsgiving. How mean my heart is ! How low my deeds are![193]

Kyōkai was probably a self-ordained monk at the time, but he was correctly ordained later, before residing at Yakushiji and obtaining a monastic rank. The *Nihon ryōiki* gives other examples of married monks. Kyōkai seems divided between his criticism of monks who like sex and his respect for saints who live an apparently worldly life, like Kanki (d. 782).[194] The argument in favor of a monk having a family is laid out in the *Shasekishū*'s anecdote of "The monk who had children":

> A monk's having children is not without precedent. The monk Kumārāyana of India was transporting to China the sandalwood image of the Buddha made by King Udyāna, the original of the Śākyamuni at Seiryōji in Saga. Then the king of Kucha joined Kumārāyana to his daughter in marriage, and from that union Kumārājiva was born. Kumārājiva went to China and had four children: Shō, Chō, Yū and Ei [that is, Zhu Daosheng, Sengzhao, Daorong and Sengrui]. They collaborated with him in translating the *Lotus Sūtra.* Although there were instances of such behavior among the sages in antiquity, they were men of such parts that their children were also wise and distinguished. But today, when the father is foolish, how can a son amount to anything?[195]

---

[192] *Genkō shakusho, DNBZ* 101: 341a.
[193] See Nakamura 1973: 279–80.
[194] See also the cases of Myōichi, a Tōdaiji monk (d. 798) and Jibō of Gangōji (d. 819), in *Genkō shakusho* 2, who are the object of Kokan Shiren's praise. *DNBZ* 101: 163; Ishida 1995: 38.
[195] Morrell 1985: 143–44.

Here the distinction between disciples and children is all but forgotten, and the metaphorical expression of lineage found in the Chinese texts is taken quite literally, transforming famous Chinese monks into an Indian missionary's sons. Mujū, however, feels that the rationale for a monk's begetting children is often lacking in Japan, where "worthless monks are also called 'bald householders' (*kafuro koji*), and 'thieves wearing surplices' (*kesa wo kitaru zoku*).'"[196]

Mujū also tells the story of a paralyzed monk who encouraged marriage for one's care in old age: "Get yourself a wife right away! . . . I feel that if I had a wife and children I might not have come to such a bitter pass. Now, when you are just the right youthful age, get together with someone."[197] But Mujū links this story with that of a monk whose young wife tried to kill him after falling in love with a young ascetic. And he comments: "When we consider such an incident as this, it is hard to follow the advice of the monk with paralysis. We should weigh the options carefully."[198] As usual, he concludes with a malicious tale:

> A monk of Shinano province had three children, each by a different woman. When the mother of the first child brought it to him, the monk had doubts since he had been very circumspect in his affair with her. So he named the child "Unexpected" (Omoiyorazu). Since the mother of the second child used to visit him secretly from time to time in his quarters, there was little doubt that the child was his. So he called it "Probably" (Samoaruran). He had maintained the third woman in a house, so there was no doubt that he had fathered her child. He called it "Unquestionably" (Shisainashi).[199]

In the *Zōtanshū* by the same author, we find the story of a Ritsu nun who has a child with a Zen monk. Mujū jokes: to which sect does this child belong? To the Ritsu sect if he looks like his mother; to the Zen sect (Darumashū) if he looks like his father. But someone argues that, because giving birth is hard for the mother, the child belongs to the Nanzan school (that is, Ritsu; pun on *nanzan*, difficult childbirth). Mujū continues: because he is the child of a saint, he will certainly be someone respectable. One of his interlocutors objects: if the child looks like his father, an adulterer, how can he be respectable? Mujū then points out the paradox: if this is so, only the child of a saint who never sinned during his whole life, resembling his father, would be respectable.[200]

The most visible examples of married priests are the retired emperors. This status presupposed their reception of the ten precepts or of the

---

[196] Ibid., 144.
[197] Ibid., 145.
[198] Ibid., 147.
[199] Ibid., 143.
[200] Ishida 1995: 138.

bodhisattva precepts, but it seems often to have excluded the rule about sex. According to the *Fusō ryakki*, Retired Emperor Uda became a monk in 899 under the name Kongōkaku (Adamantine Awakening), after receiving the ten precepts from the Shingon priest Yakushin. Later on he was ordained at Tōdaiji, and in 904 he also received the bodhisattva precepts on Hieizan from Zōmyō. It is said in the *Nihon kiryaku*, however: "The tenth prince Gamyō was made an imperial prince (*shinnō*). Actually, he was one of the princes born after the ordination of the Retired Emperor [Uda]."[201] However, "He was made a child of the present emperor (that is, Daigo)." Interestingly, the name of Gamyō Shinnō, who died in 932 at the age of ten, appears twice in the *Honchō kōin shōunroku*, where he is first listed as a younger brother of Emperor Daigo, then as one of his ten sons, adopted after the ordination of Emperor Uda.[202]

Retired Emperor Kazan was ordained at nineteen under the religious name Nyūkaku. Soon after that he received the title of *hōō* (Dharma Emperor), and was ordained again on Hieizan. His ordination had perhaps been a little premature, and he was soon involved in sexual scandals.[203] He had four sons, two of whom became imperial princes (*shinnō*), while the two others became Buddhist prelates. Because they were all born after his ordination, the matter had to remain secret. Emperor Shirakawa abdicated at forty-four after the death of his wife and became Retired Emperor in 1096.[204] The *Kojidan* reports, however, that he had a secret affair with Empress Taikenmon'in, the wife of his grandson, Emperor Toba.[205]

There are many examples of men who had wives and children prior to being ordained as monks, and who continued to live with their families afterward, or of monks who married after ordination.[206] Married monks appear in testaments, when they bequeath land to their family: see, for instance, the will of Kakusen in 1202, and of Genshin in 1208.[207] There are also examples of *shindei*, "true disciples" (in other words, sons), like the Vinaya master Shinkai, "true disciple" of the priest Shūzen. Apparently, the Ninnaji tradition was to transmit the temple to one's own son.[208]

---

[201] See *Nihon kiryaku*, s.v. 921/12/17 (Enki 21); in *Kokushi taikei* 11: 24.

[202] *Gunsho ruijū* 3: 424–26; Ishida 1995: 54.

[203] See *Heike monogatari*, in *Kokushi taikei* 75: 156.

[204] See *Hyakurenshō* 5, in *Kokushi taikei* 11: 43.

[205] See *Kojidan* 2: 55, Koten bunko 60: 168; quoted in Ishida 1995: 55. Shōshi, who received the name Taikenmon'in when she took the tonsure in 1124, was the adopted daughter of Shirakawa, and the daughter of the Senior Counselor Kan'in Kanezane.

[206] Ishida 1995: 128.

[207] See *Kamakura ibun* 1: 58, 369.

[208] In *Ninnaji sho inke ki*, quoted in Ishida 1995: 130.

This transmission from master to disciple, which is at the same time a blood transmission, is characteristic of Japanese Buddhism. In the *Kichi no ki*'s entry for 1185 there is mention of the priest Chōken, a famous preacher, who had wife and child.[209] His elder son was Shōkaku, himself an excellent preacher. In the *Hōnen Shōnin gyōjō ezu*, it is said: "The 'Dharma seal' (*hōin*) [priest] Shōkaku of Aki was the grandson of the *nyūdō* [lay priest] shōnagon Tsūken, and the 'true disciple' of the *hōin daisōzu* [head priest] Chōken." In the *Enkō Daishi gyōjō yokusan*, the term "true disciple" is glossed as follows: "When one takes one's true son, born from one's own flesh and bones, as a disciple, one speaks of a 'true disciple.' In this biography, there are many such cases." "The son of Shōkaku was Ryūjō, that of Ryūjō Kenjitsu, that of Kenjitsu Kenki. At court, they were loved for the beauty of their talents. . . . At that time, all preachers took a wife, so I have heard."[210]

In the *Genshō shakusho*, too, there is mention of the Dharma master Chōken and his lineage: "At the end of his life, he did not respect the Vinaya, and gave birth to several children. His heir was the elder son, Shōkaku . . . Shōkaku gave birth to Ryūjō, Ryūjō to Kenjitsu, Kenjitsu to Kenki. . . . The court appreciated these preachers, and their lineage flourished more and more."[211] Thus, in the oral tradition of Tendai, one sees the emergence of a system of succession based on the transmission from master to disciple and from father to son, and this is the characteristic of this oral transmission of the *kechimyaku* (transmission chart, lit. "blood lineage").

As we will see, monastic *paideia* often meant pedophily in the Japanese Buddhist context. One may even wonder whether the tolerance for priests marrying women was not to a certain extent a compromise in order to reduce pederasty and other types of semi-clandestine loves such as those described by Ihara Saikaku. One of the most famous cases of a monk taking a wife is that of Shinran. However, marriage was legally forbidden for monks until Meiji, although monks often entertained female servants or concubines.

An interesting case, found in the *Hosshinshū*, is that of a monk living at the foot of Mount Kōya with many disciples. He calls one of them and says that he his thinking of taking a wife to prevent the loneliness of old age. The disciple finds him a woman of about forty, and all goes well for six years, unbeknownst to anyone. But one morning, the woman comes in tears and tells the disciple (who has replaced his master as abbot) that the old monk has died the night before. When he asks her details about their

[209] See *Kichi no ki*, s.v. 1185, in *Zōho shiryō taisei* 30: 145c.
[210] *Hōnen shōnin gyōjō ezu*, in *Jōdo zenshū* 16: 281a–c.
[211] *Genkō shakusho*, DNBZ 101: 488a.

life, she speaks of a life of chastity dedicated to nenbutsu. Marriage, for this old monk, had been a pretext to live as a recluse and practice nenbutsu in secret.[212]

The question of married monks is related to the importance of hereditary succession in Japanese society, particularly in early Japan, where Buddhist temples were clan temples (*ujidera*). As early as the *Engishiki* (10th century), we find mention of monks who transmit the *bettō* office (*bettō-shiki*) from generation to generation. This type of transmission was apparently recognized legally. It is a transmission not only within the same clan but from father to son or between brothers. Heredity was the principle of succession not only for bettō offices, but also in ujidera such as Hōryūji, Kōfukuji, and Tōdaiji.

The author of the *Shasekishū* complains: "In this Latter Age when the Dharma has decayed, it becomes rarer each year to hear of a priest who does not take a wife. The retired Emperor Go-Shirakawa said, 'Those who hide it are the priests, those who don't do it Buddhas.'. . . These days there are few priests who even bother to hide it; rarer still are those Buddhas who don't do it."[213]

As is well known, the Ōtani Mieidō, the grave site of Shinran, was transmitted through the lineage of descendents. At Honganji too, only the descendents of Shinran become *monshū* (head of the school). The same hereditary succession prevailed at Kōyasan, at Hakusan (after the thirteenth century), and at Kinpusen, after the eleventh century. "Monastic houses," like houses in the profane world, have a succession from father to son, from brother to brother, between members of a same lineage, or between disciples, and take the form of a succession of blood lineage—that is, they constitute a fictitious lineage.

The cases of succession from a monk to his wife or to his children, as they are found in donation letters and contracts after the twelfth century, are too many to be listed. Their number is higher than that of successions from master to disciple. At the peripheries of great monasteries, monks had their private property, their private house; the wife lived there and administered this property, and this is where the children's education took place. By contrast with the *sato no bō*, dwellings of the monks at the foot of the mountain, their pied-á-terre in the capital, during ceremonies ordered by the nobles at the palace or in the "vow temples," were something like branch offices in the capital. For instance, near Hosshōji, which was the vow temple of the retired emperor Shirakawa, were inns named Shirakawa-bō for the monks of Hieizan, Miidera, Kōyasan, Ninnaji, Kō-

[212] See *Hosshinshū* 1.2, quoted in Ishida 1995: 68.
[213] Quoted in Kawai 1992: 173.

fukuji, Yakushiji, or Hōryūji. Women stayed there, and we know that these houses were intimately related with the profane sphere. It is probably no coincidence that these places are today populated with "love hotels." These monastic inns had yet another function: they were used by women of the nobility as places for childbirth.

The development of the Japanese saṅgha in the medieval period was achieved through an inclusion of the "house" [J. *ie*] of the patriarchal system. The ordination of a new monk, far from being—as Confucians had argued (and as the expression "leaving the family" implied)—an abandonment of his familial duties, was in fact perceived as a warranty of familial prosperity and better rebirth for his relatives. This conception was probably not specific to Japan, but here, in the background of the monk there is always a number of dependents. The monk became the representative of his village, often maintaining very close ties with it. The saṅgha takes responsibility not only for the family (parents), but also for the lineage.[214]

Kyōkai, the author of the *Nihon ryōiki,* became an important monk at Yakushiji but continued to live a profane life, supporting wife and children in his native village in Kii province. In his work he speaks of a series of calamities that have fallen on him and his family. It is clear that even after becoming a monk of Yakushiji he was still deeply concerned with secular life. In the *Nihon ryōiki* many privately ordained and married monks appear, and they hardly differ from Kyōkai even though marriage and private property were forbidden in the Codes. Many stories of married monks are also found in the *Hokekyō kenki* and the *Konjaku monogatari shū.*

A particular class of married priests were the *rokubu* (abbreviation of *rokujūrokubu,* pilgrims who offer copies of the *Lotus Sūtra* in the sixty-six shrines). By the Tokugawa their practice had declined, as well as their reputation. As one witness describes them in 1813: "From their pilgrim's basket they take out fish and meat, and when they don't have enough they go buy some at the fish seller. They eat this at the three meals. . . . Furthermore, they bring with them their wife, whom they call 'my sister.' This is a deplorable situation, impossible to describe. It is horrifying!"[215]

Apart from Shinshū, a school famous for its antinomian tendency, married priests were particularly common among Shugendō adepts, whose ancestor, En no Gyōja, was described as a lay practitioner (En no Ubasoku, "En the *upāsaka* [layman]").[216] On their part, Shinshū scholars tried to respond to their critics. In the *Shinshū ryūgi mondō* we

[214] For similar examples, see Ishida 1995.
[215] Rotermund 1983: 176.
[216] On monks taking a wife, see Hori 1953.

find a series of refutations in twelve points; for instance: 6. to forbid the love of women and to like the love of men is like avoiding fire to die by drowning instead; and 9. married and meat-eating monks have existed since the time of the Buddha, as the scriptures clearly show.[217]

The *Chaten mondō* points out that in the *Dazhidulun* various bodhisattvas have wives. The same was true of Fu Dashi in the *Hufa lun,* Yuanjue in the *Avataṃsaka sūtra,* of Nāgārjuna and Kuiji, Shōtoku Taishi, and a whole list of famous Indian, Chinese, and Japanese monks. The *Nikushoku saitai ben* provides a similar list, including priests like Jōzō, Shōken, and Dōmyō, and gives several contemporary cases of "temples with priests' wives"—for instance Gion shrine and Kiyomizu temple in Kyoto, or Chūsonji in Hiraizumi.[218]

Yamaori Tetsuo discusses the emergence in Jōdo Shinshū of a "blood lineage" (*kechimyaku*) that is no longer a metaphor for the Dharma lineage (*hōmyaku*), but an orthodox hereditary lineage. Kakunyo's *Kudenshō* was an attempt to show that the "blood lineage" of Shinshū was transmitted from Shinran to Nyoshin (the grandson of Shinran, through his disavowed son Zenran) and the nun Kakushin (a half-sister of Zenran). Thus, whereas Nyoshin was Shinran's grandson through a male line, Kakunyo was his great-grandson through a female line (Shinran—Kakushin—Kakue—Kakunyo). The Honganji community, centered on Kakunyo and Rennyo, became the keeper of the Ōtani mausoleum and of Shinran's grave. The kechimyaku had become a biological reality. Rennyo is said to have had thirteen sons and fourteen daughters from three women, and these blood ties played an important role in the establishment of his power.[219]

ORDER OR FREEDOM

What do we learn from this rather tedious series of "facts"? And what are the assumptions in this collection of documentary "evidence"? First, the evidence in question is not as obvious as we have been led to believe. There is a certain naïveté in taking these facts at face value, as if these data, and a fortiori their listing, were not constructed. Historians are "hunting" for facts, not simply "gathering" them. And the most neutral-looking document is already a narrative, with all the problems attendant to narrativity. In some of the last examples mentioned, it is easy to see that Buddhist monks and their temples were framed as opponents by

[217] See *Shinshū taikei 59,* quoted ibid., 368–669.
[218] Ibid., 369–70.
[219] Yamaori 1973: 327–44.

political forces, and that sexual offenses were a ready-made pretext to curb them.

One of the underlying assumptions of the discourse on Buddhism has been that discipline equals a certain moral purity that is the very essence of Buddhism, whereas antinomianism, even if it has some philosophical legitimacy, breeds laxity and decadence. The construction of the two series, discipline within the monastery and the penal system outside, however, has revealed their convergence (and parallelism—contrary to classic geometry), their deep complicity: they share the same language and perhaps the same goals. This was explicitly formulated during the medieval period, with the notion of the interdependence of Buddhist Law and secular law. This interdependence is not quite an equivalence: Buddhist Law remains subservient to secular law. When monastic discipline is strong, secular law does not intervene—unless, of course, the social or political interests it seeks to protect are at stake. When it loses ground, however, secular law attempts to make up for this deficiency. The fact that we are dealing with a society in which the legislative power is not independent, and therefore plays a political role, alerts us to the ideological and political functions of monastic discipline, as well. It is indeed disciplinarian, in the Foucaldian sense of *Discipline and Punish*. It is an ideological discourse that does not aim primarily, if at all, at individual deliverance. It does not even aim only at the survival of the monastic institution itself, but is always enrolled in the service of political power.

Consequently, the schema of Buddhist degeneration, promoted by governmental authorities and by some Buddhist reformers (whether they are sincere or not does not really matter), must be seen for what it is: a political device, a propaganda effort, aimed at maintaining the power of a ruling caste over society, privileging obedient groups, and scapegoating others—not only some Buddhist temples but also groups like the outcasts (*hinin*) and the "artisans" (*shokunin*), all those belonging to the spheres which, according to Amino, were qualified by the terms *muen* ("without ties"), *kugai* ("public"), or *raku* ("blissful").[220] The Buddhist ideal of individual freedom resurfaced in front of these forces whose goal was to "discipline and punish," and the Buddhist clergy was also one of them. Like European popular culture in the classic age (according to Bakhtin and Foucault), this Japanese and Buddhist world of muen was crumbling with the advent (and advances) of the Tokugawa age, and enclaves of freedom tended to disappear. This process, according to Amino, was a slow one, an erosion that had already begun in the medieval period. Even if at times, for instance during the Kenmu Restoration of Emperor Go-Daigo, the central power attempted to channel the energy of these mar-

[220] See Amino 1978.

ginal groups, it was always a temporary measure. We should not, for all that, idealize the freedom of these marginals, as Amino and other historians tend to do. Teleological schemas, whether of progress or of decline, have little to tell us.

Buddhism was "domesticated" (also in the sense that it became a familial affair): this "domestication," by first making Buddhists more homologous as a group with civil society, had a paradoxical effect. It made a better instrument of social control, coterminous with family and society; but it also blurred the traditional hierarchy, opening the Buddhist institution to a multiplicity of private interests and diminishing its discipline. To further domesticate Buddhism and transform it into a state apparatus, it had to be, in turn, paradoxically stripped of its domestic features and severed from all relations with legal or illegal forms of sexuality. If beheading means castration, as Freud argues, the beheading of monks during the Tokugawa period was an eminent symbol for the castration of Buddhism that was taking place.

Interestingly, the two schools most often attacked by the Bakufu seem to have been the Jōdo Shinshū and Nichiren schools. There were at least three other schools in the Muromachi period that had a strong liminal quality about them, however, namely, the Zen, Ritsu, and Ji schools. Despite their very different doctrinal backgrounds, priests belonging to these three schools played an important role in the performance of funerary rituals, and this brought them closer to the margins—margins between life and death, but also the margins of society, where the hinin, other funerary specialists, lived. Amino has argued that the importance of Zen and Ritsu priests was due to their muen quality, a quality recognized by the shōgunate itself, which used them as mediators. Zen monks in particular, because as "public individuals" (*kugaisha*) they were said to have "neither enemies nor allies," often served as emissaries between fighting daimyōs during the Muromachi and Sengoku periods. However, with the "Tokugawa peace," when the control of the daimyō over individuals became stricter just as the muen places began to shrink, the "free" activity of these monks became increasingly difficult.[221]

By virtue of their muen quality, some temples also served as sanctuaries. A case in point is the *enkiridera,* a refuge for women who were searching for a divorce, which could be obtained after three years of service as a nun. The number of these nunneries was drastically reduced during the Edo period.[222] *Enkiri* is a synonym of muen: in both cases the

---

[221] Ibid., 79–80.

[222] Two of these, Tōkeiji and Mantokuji, were protected by the Tokugawa. Tōkeiji was a branch temple of Engakuji, directed by women of the Kitsuregawa clan. Mantokuji was a Jishū temple, branch temple of the Jōjōkōji in Fujizawa. See ibid., 24. On the institution of the enkiridera, see Takagi 1992.

emphasis is on cutting all social relationships.[223] The term *muen* can refer to someone who has "no relations" (and therefore no family ties). But for monks, who had left the family, the fact of living in a muen area came to mean just the opposite: a departure from the "ties" of discipline, and a release into a kind of communitas. This community was not only the familial community of the *sato no bō,* monastic villages on the edges of great monasteries. The *monzen,* agglomerations that developed in front of the temple's gates, were strange places indeed. For some people at least, the "cutting" of social ties was not voluntary: in these muen places were found all those who had been rejected by society: prostitutes, gamblers, *kawaramono* (outcasts), actors, hinin. The other side of this ghettoization was a certain freedom, for instance from fiscal and juridical pursuits. Women were numerous and played an important social role in these places.[224] Probably because of their muen nature, their perceived closeness to the otherworldly, they were associated with Zen and Ritsu monks in the *Kenmu shikimoku.* Because they lived in such places, Zen and Ritsu monks fell into the category of the *geinōmin* ("artists," in the broad sense of marginals), together with yamabushi ascetics, masters of "linked verse" (*renga*) or tea ceremony, artisans of all kinds, and so on.[225]

In the Kamakura period, Eizon and Ninshō of Saidaiji worked on behalf of the hinin, whom they considered to be "incarnations of of the Bodhisattva Monju." The same is true for the Ritsu school of the Northern capital, where Sennyūji specialized in funerals and social activities closely connected to the hinin. Likewise, Jishū monks, although they had no fixed temples or cemeteries, followed warriors on the battleground, gave the Buddhist extreme unction and disposed of the corpses.[226]

Zen monasteries became, on the other hand, a kind of inn for travelers. In the thirteenth century, however, violent criticisms were leveled at these Zen, Ritsu, and Ji priests, criticisms that verge on discrimination. And these criticisms were usually expressed in sexual terms. For instance, the

[223] The term *muen* also has a Buddhist origin: it means, for instance, "unconditioned," like compassion. But this term, already widely used long before *kugai* and *raku,* takes on the connotations of *"en,"* dark connotations deriving from its association with poverty, hinin, hunger. See Amino 1978: 128. Compared to kugai and raku, the affirmation of a positive ideal does not seem very obvious in the case of muen. But these Buddhist terms, emerging from popular life to designate an ideal of peace, freedom, and equality, reveal to what extent Buddhism had become popular. This ideal disappears quickly, however, when one enters the Edo period; ibid., 129.

[224] See, for instance, at the beginning of the fourteenth century, the quarrel over the inheritance of the nun Myōen, between her daughter and her daughter-in-law, in relation to shops, stores, and land (in *Gion shūgyō nikki*); ibid., 202.

[225] See the comments of Jien, mentioned above, in Brown and Ishida 1979: 170.

[226] See Amino 1978: 157–58.

Tengu zōshi, in its denunciation of Ji and Zen monks, argues that the former, when they recite the *nenbutsu,* become restless like monkeys or horses and do not even hide their pudenda, while the latter no longer even shave their head; they wear hats, forget zazen (meditation practice), and wander on the roads like madmen, uttering crazy words. Likewise, the *Nomori no kagami* attacks Ippen's disciples, whom he labels "bandits of the kingdom, vermin of the eight sects." The *Chiribukuro* even uses the expression *eta* (outcasts) with regard to them.[227]

Not everyone shared this opinion, however. On the contrary, monks such as Eizon even received imperial favors. With him and his disciples, the Ritsu sect spread throughout Japan, with the protection of the shōgunate. The same thing happened to Zen with the emperors Hanazono and Go-Daigo. We recall that Monkan, Go-Daigo's favorite, was initially a Ritsu monk of Saidaiji. Even the Bakufu of Muromachi, which, in its code of Kenmu (*Kenmu shiki*), criticized Ritsu and Zen monks, in practice protected their monasteries and judged them to be important.[228] Although attempts to "discriminate" against the hinin were not entirely successful and the world of the muen retained in the fourteenth century its vitality and its power of opposition, it became progressively organized and repressed by the rulers.[229] The reorganization of the Buddhist church at the beginning of the Tokugawa rule, and the severe condemnations of some of its members for sexual crimes (actually, misdemeanors in the worst cases), are the two faces of this new moral order.

There was a deep ambivalence in these sects—or a fault line running through them. On the one hand Ritsu monks such as Eizon were close to the hinin, and were themselves often muen individuals; on the other hand, they obtained imperial favors and contributed to "reforming" not only monasteries but society as well—to the profit of central power. More than the "marginal" nature of the Zen monks, it is precisely their ties with the court and the shōgun that brought criticism such as that of the *Nomori no kagami.* The shogunate was actively trying to absorb and systematize the energy of the muen, through the mediation of the Ritsu and Zen monks who, on the pretext of their muen status, became closer to the center of power.[230] The Ritsu monks of Saidaiji, by establishing close ties with the Bakufu, built branch temples which they turned into "temples of the imperial vow" at the terminus of the great roads. Conversely, the Hōjō, rulers of Eastern Japan, used Ritsu monks to extend their rule to the west. In the same way, Go-Daigo attempted to organize muen Ritsu monks like Monkan to consolidate his power. Likewise,

[227] Amino 1993: 159–60.
[228] Ibid., 161.
[229] Ibid., 162.
[230] Ibid., 173.

the activity of Zen monks developed thanks to their ties with the Hōjō, the Southern court, and the Muromachi Bakufu. The opposition between the positive tendency to protect these activities, and the negative tendency to repress them, constitutes one axis of the political history from Nanbokuchō to Muromachi.[231] This trend, however, merely reflects (and to some extent contributes to) broader societal changes. In the Kamakura period, the yamabushi, Zen monks, and nenbutsu monks had not yet lost their sacred nature, and the basara (unconventional) style of the irui igyō people was still considered a positive quality. But after Muromachi, marginality and difference became increasingly negative, and the term *irui igyō* acquired very pejorative connotations. On the one hand, yamabushi and Zen monks became increasingly perceived as vulgar, and lost much of their prestige; on the other, social discrimination against marginals became stronger. In the Edo period, these "weird people" lost their "silver lining," their stronghold on the people's imagination.[232]

The words *irui igyō,* usually used together but also sometimes separately, were first applied to spirits or demons, but they came to refer to people, as well. Between Kamakura and Nanbokuchō, the expression does not imply social discrimination, but rather a certain fear. It appears frequently, for instance in the *Taiheiki,* without any apparent negative meaning. Later on, in the *Tengu zōshi* for instance, the irui igyō people are compared to the tengu, and the term now has a clearly pejorative connotation. The "dancing nenbutsu" (*odori nenbutsu*) of Ippen, the Ikkōshū, and the freak Zen masters (*hōge no zenji*) "who let their hair hang, wear hats, forget the meditation mat, and roam on the roads," are severely criticized in the *Tengu zōshi* and in the *Nomori no kagami.* Ippen has become the "leader of the Tengu" (*tengu no chōrō*), and we are told of a nun collecting his urine to use as medicine.[233] Thus, the *Tengu zōshi* describes the irui with a strong sense of discrimination. In 1344, the monks of Mount Hiei also accused the nenbutsu followers and Zen monks (in particular Musō Soseki) of belonging to the category of the irui igyō. In 1368, wanting to defeat Nanzenji, they also accused the Chinese Zen monks of being "Chinese *irui,*" allies of the Mongols."[234]

The *Yūzū nenbutsu engi emaki* represents all the irui igyō together. Although it is not a polemical text, the very gesture of gathering these people already points toward exclusion. Even monks like Ikkyū, who had

[231] Ibid., 174–75.

[232] See Hermann Ooms, "Status in Tokugawa Revisited" (unpublished paper).

[233] This practice, reflecting the belief in the thaumaturgic powers of the holy monk's body, is well attested in the Edo period, for example in the case of the nenbutsu ascetic Tokuhon (on which see Bouchy 1983).

[234] See *Yasaka jinja monjo* 1939–1940, quoted in Amino 1993: 137.

been themselves labeled *irui,* now used the term as an insult against their enemies (like Ikkyū's co-disciple Yōsō). Soon courtesans and prostitutes would also be included into that category. Thus, the social discrimination of the Edo period is no longer limited to eta and hinin, but includes all these irui igyō. The tendency had already become stronger in the Muromachi period, and in this sense Nanbokuchō constitutes a turning point. Amino has pointed out that, after Nanbokuchō, the sacred hinin and prostitutes became despised outcasts, which no longer had a privileged access to the emperor, the buddhas, and the kamis. In the Edo period, such discrimination was systematized, and the groups in question were relocated in *buraku* (settlements) and red-light districts.

· · · · ·

Despite all attempts to curb the monks however,—repeated interdictions and drastic punishments like pillory, banishment, crucifixion, and beheading—their transgressive behavior persisted. How can we explain this resilience? Whereas Ishida has focused on the legalistic aspect of the problem, examining the fluctuations of monastic discipline in relation to the mundane ambitions and political involvement of the monks, Hori Ichirō has pointed to a broader variety of social and cultural factors. The sexual elements in Japanese Buddhism are related to the "shamanistic" nature of monks and nuns, the latent presence of sexual magic in shamanism, and the social demand for ritual experts like the yamabushi and Zen priests. The question of married monks and the transformation of monastic lineage into blood lineage are aspects of the larger question of the house and family in medieval Japan. The importance of domestic values explains, for instance, the emergence of *sōbō,* or monastic households, on the margins of the *kekkai* (sacred area). As a result of this, the transmission of *ujigami* (clan) shrines, and that of the lineages of all kinds of religious specialists, were without exception blood-line transmissions. Likewise, the priests of the *ujidera* (clan temple) affiliated to these shrines were always members of the clan, and their lineage tended to become hereditary. The same is true for the priests of the Buddhist temples (*jingūji* or *bettōji*) placed in these shrines. Finally, the involvement of monks in secular matters is a response to the expectations of society and the state regarding them, and a consequence of the privileges accorded to them in return for their magical expertise.[235]

We have examined "hard realities," in contrast (and yet in resonance) with anticlerical discourse. Actually, even in the case of "documentary" evidence, we are still dealing with texts that are in various respects nor-

---

[235] Hori 1953: 374–75.

mative or polemical. If we can easily discern the (not so) hidden agenda of anticlerical critique, in a more subtle fashion the vision of a decadent Buddhism—whether in Qing China or in Tokugawa Japan—is essentially the work of modern reformers (Buddhist or anti-Buddhist), who use the previous period as a foil. From this statement, we may either deduce that early modern Buddhism was not as degenerate as we were told, or that it was at least not more morally corrupt than the Buddhism of earlier periods—or than most other religions, for that matter.

Thus, the degeneration of Buddhist monasteries during the Tokugawa might have been somewhat exaggerated. A good part of Tsuji's evidence is provided by anti-Buddhist tracts and by the accounts of Christian missionaries.[236] Even though it may have some basis in fact, his account of a degenerate Tokugawa Buddhism, which became the accepted opinion among Japanese historians, is too close to the official interpretation of the puritan Meiji ideologues—intent on offering Buddhism as a scapegoat—not to raise a few questions.

It is also based on an uncritical acceptance of the Tokugawa records, full of punishments: it is not that monks in that period were more immoral but that their behavior, which had previously been accepted, was now criminalized and severely punished. This is the result of several factors: a general growth of intolerance in society at large and in the Bakufu (after the Christian rebellion); and the political expediency of using politically recalcitrant monks and monasteries as scapegoats.

The criticism leveled at Jishū monks and "mad" Zen monks in texts like the *Nomori no kagami* and the *Tengu zōshi* must be taken with a grain of salt. We have here a conflation of sectarian attempts (by other Buddhist schools, for instance Hieizan monks attacking the Darumashū, or denouncing Hōnen's disciples), and a growing impatience on the part of political leaders with these representatives of a free, "unruly," muen subculture. As Amino has shown, the Sengoku and Edo periods marked the end, or at least the domestication, of these "free spirits." The Zen and Ritsu sects were themselves divided. Even as they themselves expressed this spirit of freedom, and benefited from it, when they came under attack they were quick to find scapegoats within their own ranks (as when Yōsai and Dōgen criticized the Darumashū), and eventually used their aura of freedom (muen) to get closer to the center of power (the emperor, at the time of Go-Daigo; and the Bakufu).

We should therefore be careful, and not hasten to accept the criticism of Zen monks vis-à-vis their own sect's moral degeneration as a proof that this was truly the case. This apparent auto-criticism remains a criticism of others (like Ikkyū vs. Yōsō), and in this sense it does not differ

---

[236] See Tsuji 1944–1955, 10: 404.

fundamentally from the anti-Buddhist (Confucian, Christian) criticism of Buddhism.

Likewise, the juridical evidence presented by Ishida needs to be examined more closely. Although its terseness stands in sharp contrast with a manifestly rhetorical or literary document (lending itself to a hermeneutic of suspicion), an imperial or shōgunal decree is anything but ideologically transparent. Many historians have accepted the view that Buddhist monasteries, because they became a refuge for all kinds of outlaws and produced warrior-monks, were morally decadent and politically corrupt. This view rests on a notion of Buddhism as a pure and otherworldly teaching, uncontaminated by the ways of the world. Such a Buddhism probably never existed or, if it did, it probably went out of existence very quickly and could never had become the social movement called by this name. Furthermore, we must realize that this view of monasteries as so many "cours des miracles" or dens of thieves is very elitist, representing the ideology of "law and order." In this legalistic utopia, freedom would have no room.

The same movement that brought Buddhism back in line in the Edo period (after destroying its pockets of resistance—Hieizan, Honganji, and so on), while accusing it of moral decadence, no longer able to tolerate the freedom that had been until then accepted, and even encouraged—this same movement turned hinin and other marginals into eta, victims of social discrimination, and drastically lowered the status of women, locking wives and daughters at home, while it turned courtesans into whores and locked them up in red-light districts (not surprisingly, the famous red-light districts in Kyoto and Edo were a strategy of Hideyoshi). We have here something very similar to the "great enclosure" described by Foucault. Anticlerical discourse is part and parcel of this ideology.

This is not to deny that there was corruption within Buddhism or that there were monks for whom the ideal of purity was merely rhetorical, and others for whom the cause of "freedom" was only a pretext for selfishness and corruption. But purity and corruption, as always, can be found on both sides of the fence, with the partisans of a strict rule and with the representatives of the antinomian spirit.

We have therefore to revise our conception of Buddhist monasteries as places of decadence. It is true only from the standpoint of the rulers, who cannot impose their power to the monks. The "outlaw" nature of some monasteries was only the other side of their freedom, which made them places of asylum. This freedom would be lost in the Edo period. However, it is because they were so free that they could elaborate their own culture, which was in many respects a counter-culture.

This aspect of Buddhism, as a utopia "without ties" (*muen*) with the profane world, counterbalances the repressive tendencies (such as sexism) of an institution at the same time pervaded by patriarchal ideology. However, just as we cannot locate sexism exclusively in Buddhism (which only reflects larger societal trends), we cannot attribute to Buddhism all the merit of this libertarian spirit. It is because Japanese society in its entirety tolerated these enclaves of freedom that temples were authorized to assume the function of asylums. Whether Japanese Buddhism was politically correct or not, it was never autonomous, even in its freedoms.

Chapter 5

BUDDHIST HOMOSEXUALITIES

> In brief, know that all were clerks,
> And great men of letters and of great fame,
> In the world defiled by the same sin.[1]
> (Dante)

THE NEW SODOM

> Sots d'hommes, égaux morts.
> (*Jacques Prévert*)

W E HAVE examined the accusations leveled at Buddhism in matters of sexuality. The strongest case for the moral turpitude of Japanese Buddhists, from an European perspective at least, was "sodomy," a term designating, in this case, the type of sexual relations commonly described nowadays as "homosexuality." Despite their contrasting evaluation of Chinese and Japanese Buddhism, Jesuit missionaries in China and Japan agreed in their condemnation of the moral depravity of Buddhist monks—and more precisely, in their denunciation of the "sin of intellectuals and clerics."[2] They were reminded of the old dictum: "Pedagogus ergo sodomiticus." What we will refer to

---

[1] "In somma sappi, che tutti fur cherci, / e literati grandi et di gran fama, / d'un peccato medesmo al mondo lerci." (Dante, *Inferno,* song XV: 106–8)

[2] Ariès 1982: 95. See also Charles Quint's edict (1532): "If someone commits an impurity with a beast, or a man with a man, or a woman with a woman, they have forsaken their life and will be condemned, according to custom, to death by fire" (quoted in Brown 1986). According to John Boswell, this intolerance can be traced back to the twelfth century and in particular to the influence of Thomas Aquinas, who defined sodomy as a sin against nature. Before that, homosexuality was not stigmatized in Western societies. See Boswell 1980: 269–302. Legend has it that all sodomites died when Christ was born. See also Bleys 1996. The Jesuit discourse on the sin "against nature," however, can be inscribed in a long tradition that can be traced back to Plato. Speaking of Zeus's mythical seduction of the handsome Ganymede, Plato writes: "We must not forget that this pleasure [of sex] is held to have been granted by nature to male and female when conjoined for the work of procreation. The crime of male with male, or female with female, is an outrage on nature and a capital surrender to lust of pleasure. And you know it is our universal accusation against the Cretans that they were the inventors of the tale of Ganymede; they were convinced, we say, that their legislation came from Zeus, so they went on to tell this story against him, that they might, if you please, plead his example for their indulgence in this pleasure too." See Plato, *Laws* 636d, in Edith Hamilton and Huntington Cairns, eds., A. E. Taylor, trans., *Collected Dialogues of Plato* (New York: Pantheon, 1961).

as "male love" (J. *nanshoku*), often a euphemism for pedophily, seems to have been widespread among the Chinese and the Japanese. It was not an object of social reprobation and repression as in Europe, where it had been strongly condemned by the Church since Thomas Aquinas and was punishable at the stake.[3] Throughout European history, homosexuals were subjected to the same persecutions as Jews and other minorities.

Francis Xavier was horrified by the "abominations of the flesh" he discovered in Japan, and deplored the fact that "great and abominable sins are held in such slight regard." Homosexuality, or rather "male love," was not, in premodern Japan, the "love that dare not speak its name." Matteo Ricci gave a similar description of the Chinese, and strongly condemned the "Hanlin style":[4]

> In China there are those who reject normal sex and indulge in depravity, they abandon sex with women and instead they corrupt young males. This kind of filthiness is not even discussed by wise men in the West, for fear of defiling their own mouths. Even the wild animals only make their bonds between female and male, none of them overturn the nature heaven gave them. Men who are like this never blush for shame, how sinful these men have become. The members of my humble society retain all their seed, and do not plant it out in the fields. If you doubt the wisdom of this, how much more should you question throwing it away in a ditch or a gutter.[5]

But if homosexuality was widespread in Chinese and Japanese societies, the situation seems to have been even worse in Japanese Buddhism:

> They are fewer sins among the laity, and I see that they are more subject to reason than those whom they regard as priests, whom they call *bonzos,* who are inclined to sins abhorrent to nature, and which they confess and do not deny; and this is so public and manifest to all, both men and women, young and old, that they do not regard it as strange or an abomination, since it is so very common. . . . We frequently tell the *bonzos* that they should not commit such a sin, and how much they offend God; and everything we tell them amuses them since they laugh about it and have no shame when they are reproached about so vile a sin. These *bonzos* have many boys in their monasteries, sons of *hidalgos,* whom they teach how to read and write, and they commit their corruptions with them; and this sin is so common that, even though it seems an evil to them all, they are not upset by it.[6]

---

[3] In Manila, Chinese homosexuals were burned alive by the Spaniards at the end of the sixteenth century. See Spence 1984: 227; and Boswell 1980.

[4] Ricci fails, however, to point out that the famous Hanlin Academy was not a Buddhist institution but a Confucianist one.

[5] Spence 1984: 229.

[6] Schurhammer 1982: 84.

Xavier's successor, Torres, discussed this point in his controversy with Zen monks: "They said that this might be so with respect to women, but it would not be so with respect to boys, since there is no consequent shame to their relatives, and still less to the boy, when one commits sodomy with him, since he has no virginity to lose, and sodomy is not a sin."[7] The Jesuits' reprobation was all the more necessary, since they were themselves suspected of behaving "against nature."[8] However, the term "sodomy," in their mouth, was first of all an insult addressed generically to heretics of all kinds. It was also used by Protestants when speaking of Rome, a "cistern full of sodomy." Often paired with circumcision in Western imagination, "sodomy" is one of these categories that define primarily the "Other."[9] As Jonathan Spence points out, the practices designated by this term were ordinarily associated with the paradigmatic Other, Islam, although Luther had given a broader extension to the term "Sodomites," by which he meant "Turks, Jews, papists and cardinals."[10] Thus, we cannot rely entirely on Jesuit testimony to decide the extent to which homosexuality was widespread in Buddhist monasteries.

But Jesuit indignation finds echoes among the Buddhist themselves. According to the *Ōjō yōshū* (Essentials for Rebirth) by the Tendai monk Genshin (942–1017), "homosexuals" fall straight into hell. A similar position was already expressed in a Chinese text dating from the sixth century.[11] Although no great attention is paid to male homosexuality in the Vinaya, some scriptures such as the *Saddharmasmṛtyupasthāna-sūtra* describe a "Hell of Many Rains" where those who committed homosexual acts are attracted to "a man of flame who burns them with his embrace."[12]

The strongest case for the persuasive and deleterious influence of male

[7] Ibid., 287.

[8] See Spence 1984: 225.

[9] A few decades before Xavier, for instance, Alfonso Zuazo, in a letter dated November 11, 1521, not long after Mexico's fall, wrote that the indigenous priests "are almost all sodomites," and that, "before approaching the altar or making a sacrifice, each takes his young boy, the younger among those serving in the temple, and do with them what those of Sodom wanted to do with the Angels, and despite this they are never blind." Quoted in Michel Graulich, "La fleur défendue: interdits sexuels en Mésoamérique," in Marx, ed., 1990: 115.

[10] Spence 1984: 222. Originating in the Bible, where it applies to the behavior of the men of Sodom, the term "sodomy" refers as much to the type of heterosexual intercourse said to be "against nature"—or rather, against "human" nature (*more canum*)—as to male homosexual intercourse (*masculorum concubitus*) proper. See Ariès 1982: 84. Ironically, the notion of an act "against nature" seems to derive from a passage in Plato, an author known for his homosexual inclinations. See Boswell 1980.

[11] See Eberhard 1967: 63.

[12] See Matsunaga and Matsunaga 1972: 112.

love in Zen monasteries has been made by Tsuji Zennosuke.[13] As evidence, besides the letters of Jesuit missionaries, Tsuji quotes a number of official edicts. For example, in 1303, the regent (*shikken*) Hōjō Sadatoki (1270–1311) promulgated an edict forbidding the admission of *kasshiki* (novices) in all monasteries. Ashikaga Yoshimochi (1368–1428) also decreed that, in the rules of Shōkokuji, shami and kasshiki novices were forbidden to wear silk robes, white powder, and lipstick. The *Inryōken nichiroku* reports that in 1436 the interdiction was extended to all the kasshiki of the Five Mountains. These documents show that the custom of keeping mignons had become widespread, and that there was much competition among monks to get the beautiful adolescents. Such a custom was also in part due to the relations between monks, warriors, and the nobility. The edicts of the Bakufu against homosexual practices were aimed not only at monks, as male love was a common practice between daimyo and retainers. The Bakufu itself was not beyond criticism. If homosexuality became common in major Zen monasteries like Shōkokuji, it is because these were places where the shōgun held his parties. According to the *Inryōken nichiroku*, in 1463, "when the practice of the whole monastery was perturbed because of a kasshiki of Chōtokuin named Shōkō, an edict ordered the latter to be transferred from Chōtokuin to the distant Kenseidō."[14] A Tenryūji record dated 1458 indicates that the abbot of this monastery was held responsible for a disturbance provoked by a kasshiki.[15] And the many love letters and poems recorded—if not in the Gozan literature, at least in diaries such as the *Hekizan nichiroku,* written by a monk of Tōfukuji—bear witness to the role played by kasshiki in Zen monasteries.[16] Likewise, nanshoku (male love) developed in Shingon monasteries such as Ninnaji and Daigoji, places related to the institution of the *monzeki* (Buddhist temples governed by an imperial prince).

A case worth mentioning is that of Shūshō, the monk who restored Tōdaiji in 1260. Earlier in life, in 1235–1236, Shūshō had made some interesting vows: "During my stay at Kasagidera, I must practice assiduously during seven days, twice seven days, three times seven days, etc. Apart from the period of rest, I must refrain from drinking alcohol and from having sexual relationships, and I must abandon all chance games like go or *sugoroku*."[17] In other words, while one is not practicing, one can drink, make love, and gamble. This notion that there is a time to play and a time to work can be found even today in Zen monasteries. Ten days

---

[13] See Tsuji 1944–1955 6: 335–37.
[14] Tsuji 6: 336.
[15] See ibid., 6:326.
[16] Ibid., 5:70.
[17] *Kamakura ibun* 7: 184a, quoted in Ishida 1995: 113.

later, Shūshō reiterated his vow not to drink alcohol, except as medicine, during a period of thousand days. In 1237, he drew a wish-list of five points, among which were: (1) to live as a recluse at Kasagidera until he was forty-one; (2) not to go beyond a hundred partners till then (he has already had relations with ninety-five at the time; and (3) not to keep any boy with him, except for Kameōmaru.[18] We therefore learn that Shūshō, in his thirty-sixth year, had already had ninety-five (apparently all male) sexual partners, that he planned to live as a recluse at Kasagidera until he turned forty-one, and did not intend to have more than a few partners until then, with the exception of a young boy named Kameōmaru (King of Turtles, perhaps a nickname with a sexual double-entendre). We seem to have here a representative example of a monk who, despite a few regrets, liked wine and boys and could not really dispense with either.[19]

Some Zen masters were adamant in denouncing the degeneration of their school. According to Manzan Dōhaku:

> It is said in the *Kudoku enmangyō* that "The monks of the final period [of the Dharma] will indulge in concupiscence and adultery (*inyoku*) will flourish; day and night they will rape young boys. Although their outer appearance will be that of monks, inwardly, they will not differ from heretics." There may be a difference between men and woman, but what they think, as a karmic cause, is the same thing. When I consider those who dwell in the monasteries of the world, I see those who keep novices and young boys and who will not avoid [the punishment] mentioned by this sūtra. Even if you must keep relations with these monasteries, consider carefully what they teach you. If you have to approach these people, be careful not to catch their stink.[20]

Ikkyū too, in an allusive poem entitled "The Strife about the Shami and the Kasshiki of Shōkokuji," laments the events that have brought the ruin of the monastery.[21] In several other poems, he comments on the scandals provoked by male love in Zen monasteries, and he admonishes monks against lewdness and promiscuity.[22] However, he himself seems to have practiced male love in his youth, and his relation with homosexuality was complex.[23] Let us, for instance, quote a series of *renga* (linked

[18] Ibid., 7: 361c–362a, quoted in Ishida 1995: 116.

[19] Ishida 1995: 116. See also Leupp 1995: 39.

[20] See *Manzan hōgo*, quoted in Kagamishima Genryū, ed., *Manzan; Menzan* (Tokyo: Kōdansha, 1978), 100.

[21] See *Kyōunshū* #279, in Yanagida, ed., 1987: 157. See also Covell 1980, #265: "Shōkokuji's Younger Priests in Turmoil."

[22] See *Kyōunshū* #284, #285, #286, #343, #350, in Yanagida, ed., 1987.

[23] The tradition of Ikkyū's homosexuality is reflected (and explained away) in a modern piece by Mushakoji, "Monk Ikkyū," where we find the following exchange between the master and a lordless samurai: "Lordless samurai: 'Why is it good to fool with small boys?'—Ikkyū: 'It is not good to fool with small boys. But it is a good thing to take back a

verses) composed by the Shingon priest Sochō (1448–1532) and seven others under Ikkyū's auspices at Shūon-an in 1523:

Is it a boy or a girl	chigo ka onna ka
Sleeping there? The morning after	nete no akatsuki
On my hand that gropes	mae ushiro
before and behind, the light	saguru te ni tsuki no
of the moon at dawn	ariake ni
People's emotions	hito no nasake ya
Are concentrated in a hole	ana ni aruran
A woman's letter:	onna fumi
"That's the place, that's it!"	kashiko kashiko ni
Carelessly dashed off.	kakisutete
The young man I counted on	tanomu wakazō
was oh so very chilly	amaru tsurenaya
Grappling with him	hikkonde
I would like to thrust my sword	sashi mo ireba ya
And die from his thrust![24]	chigaeba ya

The translator, Donald Keene, has chosen to emphasize the indecent meaning, but each link is full if wordplays that make possible quite respectable utterances. For instance, *hito no nasake ya / ana ni aruran* could also be translated as: "people's emotions / reach their peak in wonder." Likewise, *onna fumi / kashiko kashiko ni / kakisutete* could be rendered as: "A woman's letter / carelessly signed, / 'Very respectfully.'" There is a wordplay based on the familiar expression *ana kashiko,* exclamation of awe and wonder; *kashiko* = "with awe," but also "that place": the double entendre alludes to homosexual relations with *chigo* (young novices).[25]

One might distinguish two kinds of Buddhist critique. The first one is an indictment against all forms of sexuality, including homosexuality, as tied to desire. The second may be a lament not about homosexuality per se, but about the decline of the "way" of male love, its increasing commercialization. Monks no longer entertain chigo, they go to brothels to

boy who is followed by bad men. I could not bring myself to play with the poor little boy. But I believe I can make a splendid man out of child even as I play with him.' " Hirano, n.d.: 36.

[24] *Hōchō shuki,* 655–56. As Leupp points out, this verse is one of the very few that suggest that the poet could assume both the active and passive roles. The author is a married priest, father of two children. See Leupp 1995: 178.

[25] See Keene 1977: 274–75.

buy themselves young prostitutes, male or female. This critic is somewhat reminiscent of Minakata Kumagusu's distinction between pure and impure "male love." By "pure" is not meant simply male friendship: the relation may be sexual but it is not merely venal, it involves affection.

If the "Hanlin Way" was perceived in China as a Confucian characteristic, in Japan the traditional view was that the way of "male love" developed first in Buddhist monasteries; it spread among the samurai and the "artists" after the Kamakura period, and eventually among the merchant class in the Edo period. The later stages of this evolution are well described in Ihara Saikaku's novels.

In what follows, we will place Buddhist "male love" (and its elusive female counterpart, never named as such—"female love" is usually understood to mean "(male) love of women"—in its cultural contexts, before examining what might have been specific to it (and different from other forms of homosexuality) in the case of Japan.

The assimilation of male love to sin, as found in Genshin, seems to represent a minority voice. According to the Buddhist tales known as *chigo monogatari* (Tales of Chigo), for instance, it does not seem that homosexual relationships were regarded as a moral issue in and of themselves. To be sure, they were condemned as moral transgressions or worldly attachments, but their gravity was apparently less than that of heterosexual relationships. Perhaps, as Louis Althusser once noted in the modern Western context, inasmuch as women meant defilement, by rejecting women—even if for young boys—monks thought that they were rejecting defilement.[26]

We have discussed earlier (in Chapter 2) the canonical treatment of homosexuality in the Buddhist Vinaya. However, Japanese Buddhist homosexuality offers a particular case, one that deserves close scrutiny. It poses a problem precisely because of its euphemization of exploitation and its glorification of the pederastic relationship as an elevated form of *paideia* (education). Between the Kamakura and Edo periods, the nature of the Buddhist discourse on male love changed. Whereas the language was romantic before, it became now satirical. Of course, there are numerous cases, for instance among the work of Edo writers like Saikaku or Chikamatsu, in which a text can belong to both genres. It would be too easy to trivialize this claim itself, to dismiss as "false consciousness" the love of the monk for the chigo and its tragic nature. The periodization cannot be too rigid here: an early text like the *Chigo no sōshi* (1321) has been defined as a "ribald masterpiece."[27] Already in the medieval period,

---

[26] See Althusser 1992: 265: "Many priests believed that they were refusing defilement by rejecting women and 'buying themselves a boy.'"

[27] Leupp 1995: 40.

different types of documents or literary genres give very different images of male love: we will contrast, for instance, the idealized image of these relations in the so-called *chigo monogatari* and the rather crude image emerging from temple documents.

Most historical accounts of the phenomenon reduce Buddhist homosexuality to the prostitution of the Edo period (a little as if courtly love were seen simply as a moment in the history of prostitution). Although it is undeniable that prostitution and child abuse were rampant, can we refuse to hear the pedophile's plea? Or can we, in this case, keep to a kind of middle way that would hold together the phenomenological and ideological levels of interpretation? How can we avoid taking sides? Is condemnation merely a refusal to understand, or conversely, is any attempt to understand the phenomenon a way to condone it?

Terminology

According to John Winkler, "scholars of recent sex-gender history have asserted that pre-modern systems classified not persons but acts and that 'the' homosexual as person-category is a recent invention." The *kinaidos* (socially and sexually deviant male), to be sure, is not a "homosexual" but neither is he just an ordinary guy who now and then decided to commit a kinaidic act.[28] The same can be said of the category of effeminate individuals called *paṇḍaka* in India. We may recall how the Buddhist Vinaya attempted to deal in a piecemeal fashion with various phenomena that we would perhaps today subsume under the word "homosexuality." In the Vinaya, the line was not always clearly drawn between the act and the agent. Vinaya texts usually denounce various acts judged harmful to the community (and only secondarily to the individual). However, they also came to define the paṇḍaka negatively. Thus, even if this notion of paṇḍaka covers a broad semantic field, the texts seem to run against the argument about the modern specificity of the notion of the "homosexual." The paṇḍaka are often confused in translation with "eunuchs." As is well known, eunuchs played an important role in premodern and early modern China, whereas they were conspicuously absent in Japan. Eunuchs are impotent, and at the same time powerful and transgressive, because their desire turns into ambition, and because they have access to women's quarters. In many cases, however, sexual desire remains.

The Chinese Chan master Rujing (1163–1228) warned his disciples not to be intimate with "eunuchs, hermaphrodites, and people of that kind."[29] Sexual identity can be modified as a result of good karma, how-

28 Winkler 1990: 45.
29 See Kodera 1980: 120, 174.

BUDDHIST HOMOSEXUALITIES 215

ever, as we recall from Dōgen's story about the eunuch who saw his male functions restored after saving a herd of bulls from castration.[30] Here, sexual identity is seen as part of psychophysical integrity, and no person of the "third kind," whether paṇḍaka or "eunuch," can enter into the Buddhist heavens. We are told that the Buddha fathered a child with his wife before abandoning her only to prove his virility.

It is in Japanese Buddhism that male love became most visible and came to designate a certain type of discourse and of sexual relationships, as well as an ideal of man (and not simply a type of act). If homosexuality is culturally bound and socially constructed, one could argue that nanshoku (male love) is specifically Japanese. Is the same true, then, of Japanese Buddhist homosexuality? Minamoto Junko, for instance, contrasts nanshoku with Western homosexuality, but she focuses on power relationships and downplays what we could call the "platonic" element. She argues that in the Japanese case we do not find, as in the West, love between consenting adults. But Buddhist homosexuality is not limited to relationships with paṇḍaka, and conversely, the Buddhist rejection of paṇḍaka-type individuals is by no means a rejection of homosexual relationships per se.

The use of the term *homosexuality* (or even *pederasty*) in the Japanese context raises obvious problems: it remains somewhat anachronistic and too vague. Anachronistic because the term presupposes a certain discourse on "sexuality," and various authors, since Foucault, have noted that this discourse did not yet exist in premodern societies. It is only toward the end of the Meiji period, when a few scandals suddenly revealed the prevalence of lesbian relationships among college girls, that the term *dōseiai* (literally, "same-sex love," a term patterned after "homo-sexuality," itself coined in 1892 by Charles Gilbert Chaddok) came into existence in order to "express an erotic relationship between two partners of the same sex, since the existing terms, *nanshoku* and *keikan,* applied only to men."[31]

The term *homosexuality* is too vague because it masks the fact that Buddhist nanshoku is essentially age-structured rather than gender-structured. This Buddhist form of pedophily is at times rather different from the kind usually encountered in the West. This term also tends to mask the absence of lesbianism in the Buddhist discourse. Unlike Indian Vinaya, which refused to name the reality that it claimed to legislate, and Chinese culture, which grasped this reality under the cover of crude or

---

[30] *Shōbōgenzō* "Sanji gō," T. 82, 2582: 275a. The text has *Kōmon,* "yellow gate," i.e., paṇḍaka.

[31] Furukawa 1994: 115.

refined metaphors, Japanese culture had a clear awareness of the phenomenon, which it designates more straightforwardly with the term "male love" (*nanshoku*, love of males by males), or, in an even more specific manner, with the expression "way of the ephebes" (*shudō*, in reference to *wakashū*, temple youth).[32] The terminology makes it clear that women are entirely out of the picture as sexual subjects (lesbianism), and appear as sexual objects only as foils or phantasms. *Nanshoku* (Ch. *nanse*), by opposition to *joshoku* (Ch. *nüse*), refers to the "[love of] male beauty." As Giovanni Vitiello points out, "We are dealing here with a diagram of sexuality whose referent point is a male individual. *Nüse* and *nanse* constitute the two optional spheres of a man's sexuality."[33] It is therefore practically impossible to retrieve a genealogy of female homosexuality because, as in Western culture, there never was a clear perception of the phenomenon, let alone a discourse about it.

Female homosexuality, unfortunately, was never the object of a similar "way" and is therefore much more difficut to assess.[34] Although a number of Vinaya rules point to its widespread existence among nuns, there was no single rubric or convenient terminology to locate it, make it thinkable, and discuss it. We have here the same situation as in the West, as described by Judith Brown and (*cum grano salis*) by Sinistrari d'Ameno.[35] As Freud put it, "Homosexuality in women, which certainly is not less common than in men, although much less glaring, has not only been ignored by the law, but it has also been neglected by psycho-analytical research."[36] Minakata mentions, in the Dharmaguptaka Vinaya, the case of a woman who was punished for having dressed as a male to commit an impure act with another woman, but he offers no Japanese anecdotes similar to those of the Buddhist priests he was so conversant with. If Buddhist commentaries, unlike Christian ones according to Judith Brown, do not betray "a fundamental ignorance of what women could do together," they do not differ fundamentally from the former in their

---

[32] The term "gay," used by Boswell, also seems anachronistic in this context, or at least ill-adapted to Buddhist realities.

[33] Vitiello 1994: 29–30.

[34] See Brown 1986.

[35] A fascinating discussion of female "sodomy" as distinct from "Tribadism" is found in Sinistrari d'Ameno's *De Sodomia*. Although the work seems to be the forgery of a nineteenth-century bibliophile, the material gathered by this genial fraud is not entirely irrelevant. We know that sexual penetration was the only criterion used by the Inquisitors to define "sodomy." As James Saslow points out: "In Spain, two women were merely [*sic*] whipped and sent to the gallows for sex 'without an instrument,' but the penalty for penetration with a dildo was burning, suffered by two fifteenth-century nuns"; Saslow 1989.

[36] See Freud 1924: 202.

"total incapacity to classify these acts under well-established sexual rubrics and in recognized criminal categories."[37]

The question of lesbianism between nuns is raised by Kuroda Hideo in his analysis of an image in the *Tengu zōshi,* representing two nuns walking together, one having her arm over the other's shoulder, and holding hands. This text expresses a strong criticism of the monks and nuns of the Jishū, "who don't even hide their pudenda, etc." One sees indeed in another scroll, the *Mabutsu ichinyo e* (Pictures of the identity between Māra and the Buddha), nuns urinating or defecating in public, but not in the *Tengu zōshi,* where we only see monks eating. The attitude of the two nuns suggests a lesbian relationship. They wear a *zukin,* the typical headdress of the nuns. In another scene of the scroll, a nun collects Ippen's urine in a flacon. In order to emphasize the sexual promiscuity which, according to him, characterizes the Jishū, the author of the *Tengu zōshi* chose to show lesbianism: normal male-female promiscuity was too common in medieval society, and male homosexuality too common in Buddhist temples. But in this context female homosexuality appears as a transgression worse than heterosexuality, not to mention nanshoku. Given the hypercritical (and perhaps also hypocritical) tendency of the *Tengu zōshi,* this image in all likelihood does not simply express friendship between two nuns. It has to be more significant.[38]

The term *homosexuality* also masks the diversity of relationships between men and youth—idealization of boys (which sometimes led to seeing in them not simply novices to initiate to sexuality but potential initiators, divine avatars), relationships of friendship, of confidence, of protection—all that Minakata covers under the term "pure love": platonic love (but we know that the love of Plato for Alcibiade was not so platonic); but also relationships of power, reinforced by the ecclesiastical hierarchy and age differences, and sometimes covering situations that amount to institutionalized rape.

In Japanese sexuality, distinctions between male and female, or between homosexual and heterosexual, are perhaps less relevant than that between active and passive.[39] The "passive" category refers not only to women; it also includes young boys, chigo. In the Buddhist context in particular, male love—more precisely, "love of youth" (*amour des garçons*)—designated a pederastic-pedagogical relationship. In a strictly hierarchical society in which women occupied the lowest level, homosexuality encouraged misogyny, and conversely.

[37] Brown 1986: 20. Brown quotes a passage of Brantôme's *Les femmes galantes,* which shows that lesbianism was only perceived as a preparation for heterosexual relations. In Buddhism too, it seems that it was perceived as such.

[38] Kuroda 1986: 18–23.

[39] See "Entretien avec Foucault 1982," in Foucault 1995, 4: 286.

With these caveats in mind, we will nevertheless continue to use the term *homosexuality*, together with *nanshoku* and its equivalents. For lack of a better Western term, and because I feel unable at this point to adjudicate the question of the cultural/historical specificity or universality of the phenomenon; but also to indicate a certain continuity (despite changes) between premodern nanshoku and modern Japanese homosexuality.

Despite the abundance of documents, the study of "male love" is sometimes obscured by the use of "secret words," or at least euphemisms related to male homosexuality.[40] Some of these "secret words" are well known. For instance, the word *kiku*, "chrysanthemum," found in many poems, was not only an imperial emblem but also a metaphor for the anus (and by extension for male love).[41]

Japanese Buddhist nanshoku was often called *shudō* (abbreviation of *wakashū dō*, the "way of male adolescents"), and these adolescents were known under a variety of names, such as *chigo* (boy, acolyte), *kasshiki* (novice), *terakoshō* (temple page), or *monju bosatsu* (in reference to their patron, the Bodhisattva Mañjuśrī). Chinese literary euphemisms or metaphors, such as the "cut sleeve" or "half-eaten peach," were also commonly used. The first term refers to the story, found in the *Han shu,* of an emperor who, called to a meeting while lying with his young lover, cut off his sleeve so as not to wake up the boy. The second refers to the peach that another emperor shared with his protégé.[42]

Typology

Another more recent Chinese and depreciative borrowing is *keikan* (Ch. *jijian*), "sodomy," literally, "chicken lewdness," written with the character *ji,* "chicken," according to the belief that domesticated chickens would behave in this "unnatural" way. The term often appears in the

[40] See Hirazuka 1987: 32–35.

[41] According to Pflugfelder 1996: 63, "The monastic culture of male love possessed a set of conventions and specialized vocabulary that were not always familiar to those who lived beyond its walls, so that the youths in several of Anrakuan's stories are hardpressed to explain to their parents the meaning of such terms as *nyake* (referring to an anus) or *suban* (signifying a particularly narrow orifice). The term *kawatsurumi* appears in the description of Uzumasa' Ox Festival, in the *Ujishūi monogatari,* where it designates *nanshoku.*"

[42] See Hinsch 1990: 53; and *Jakushōdō kokkeishū, DNBZ* 149: 257b. Interestingly, the story of the "cut sleeve" appears in a quite different context: "'Tis true, a Dog is counted an obscene and nasty Creature by them [the Turks] . . . but they nourish a cat as a chaster and modester Creature in their Judgments. This custom they received from Mahomet . . . who was so much in love with a Cat that, when one of them fell asleep on his sleeve, as he was reading at a table, and the time of his Devotion drew near, he caused his sleeve to be cut off, that he might not awake the Cat by his going to the Mosque." A. G. Busbequius, *Travels into Turkey* (London, 1744), 140; quoted in Minakata 1973, 10: 184–185.

post-Meiji period but tends to be superseded by the more "medical" but equally pejorative *hentai seiyoku* (sexual perversion). The changing perception of homosexuality after Meiji is clear from the so-called sodomy ordinance, drafted by the Ministry of Justice in 1872. This ordinance, enforced until 1881, punished all "sodomites" with ninety days in prison.[43] This criminalization of male homosexuality was introduced from China and found its source in Qing codes, but it was soon abolished under the influence of the French model. In the end, however, homosexuality was medicalized as a kind of illness: the focus was now on the physical act itself, but it shifted eventually to the psychological identity of the individual behind it, disregarding the spiritual elements that had long been associated with nanshoku. Despite this, nanshoku also remained equated in public perception with manliness and the samurai code, a martial tradition that would lead to Mishima Yukio.[44] Furukawa Makoto contrasts the various codes: in the *keikan* code, the act only is deviant, but the actor is not yet identified as a "sodomite," let alone as a "pervert." The hentai seiyoku code, on the other hand, goes from "sexual perversion" to a "sexual pervert." It does not stop at the act. The nanshoku code too internalized the roles as determinant of an identity but, unlike the hentai seiyoku code, it valued this identity positively. The persistence of this nanshoku code explains the more positive image of homosexuality in modern Japan. Furakawa describes two sub-codes of nanshoku: samurai and *kagema* (male prostitute). He forgets Buddhism. Although the priestly nanshoku code is said to have been the source of the samurai nanshoku code, it remains different and deserves to be studied on its own ground.

If the modern discourse on "homosexuality," in the case of Japan, goes back to the 1920s (Furukawa), the traditional discourse on nanshoku emerged from two different periods: the late medieval (Muromachi) and premodern (Edo). Much of the recent research has been based on the epoch-making work of Ihara Saikaku, in particular *The Great Mirror of Male Love,* which combined the various strands of nanshoku—of the priests, nobles, military, artists, and merchants. His work, however, represents a time when nanshoku has changed drastically (even if we may not want to qualify, like Minakata, this change as a decline). In this new context, the specificity of the Buddhist discourse on nanshoku tends to be lost, and the spiritual (or ideological) dimensions of the phenomenon disappear behind its more obvious commodification. Thus, in order to emphasize this specificity, we need to go back to the earlier medieval period, while still drawing extensively on Saikaku's work and on the research of our predecessors.

[43] Furukawa 1994: 108. For the following account, I am indebted to Pflugfelder 1996.
[44] Mishima was both homosexual and an adept of a martial ideal and cult of the body.

In the prevalent teleological view, Buddhist nanshoku is usually glossed over as a mere preliminary stage for later developments (Leupp). Even when it is discussed in more detail (Schalow), it is usually from Saikaku's perspective. On the other hand, the work done for the previous period (Childs) on chigo stories tends to idealize the phenomenon and to adopt a purely literary perspective, while downplaying its ideological and mercenary elements.

A recent work by Gary Leupp examines in detail the widespread tolerance of male love during the Tokugawa. Although he has an introductory chapter on Buddhism, Leupp is interested primarily in the "commodification" of homosexuality in the urban centers of Japan. Gregory Pflugfelder examines the shifts in perception for the later Meiji and Taishō periods. In both studies, as in Japanese histories of nanshoku, Buddhism plays only a prefatory or marginal role. I want here to focus on the specific development of homosexual ideology within the Japanese Buddhist context.

We find in the medieval period a constellation of different elements defining Buddhist nanshoku, some of which are internal to Buddhism whereas others are external (such as the influence of literature, arts of entertainment, and so on). Minakata Kumagusu emphasizes the distinction between pure and impure male love, between the "love from the heart" (or "from the brain") and the "love that comes from sex, lewdness," and he complains that in Japan the two are often confused, as they are indeed juxtaposed in his works.[45] This distinction may be a product of the Meiji era, but it also inherits a long tradition of Buddhist and warrior nanshoku.[46] He argues that in Chinese works like the *Pinhua baojian*, the two forms of male love are clearly distinguished. The kind of male love practiced in contemporary Japan is, according to him, clearly

---

[45]Minakata had himself, in his youth, fallen in love with a young boy, who died while he was in the United States, and the memory of this pure love never left him. He married only late in life.

[46] On Minakata, see Pflugfelder 1996: "Born in 1867 in Wakayama domain, Minakata had heard firsthand accounts of monastic sexual practices on nearby Mt. Kōya from those who had served as acolytes there in the waning years of the Edo period. Likewise, as a student in early Meiji Japan, Minakata was no stranger to 'roughneck' eroticism. Through his prolonged residence and travel abroad, Minakata also became one of the first Japanese to acquire an extensive knowledge of Western literature on male-male sexuality. In his largely epistolary writings on the subject, dating from the 1890s until shortly before his death in 1941, Minakata thus combined a command of native sources that few educated after the Meiji period could claim with a cosmopolitan erudition that enabled him to consider these in broader cross-cultural and transhistorical perspectives." See also Nakazawa Shin'ichi, "Kaidai: jō no sekusoroji," in Nakazawa 1991–1992, 3: 7–57.

of the second type.[47] Even if the two forms of male love were never as clearly distinct as Minakata argues, he is right in pointing out that the second half of the seventeenth century (and more precisely the Genroku era) marks a turning point, with the rapid and irreversible commercialization of nanshoku. Another consequence of this change, according to him, was the fact that monks "returned to women."

As Pflugfelder notes, the "beautiful boys" appear in popular writings in one of two guises. The first is that of the acolyte or chigo (alternatively, *terakoshō* or "temple page"), an adolescent male, technically a layperson, often sent to serve in a temple or monastery in order to receive an education. The figure of the acolyte had played a central role in medieval writings on male-male eroticism, ranging from the "Book of Acolytes" picture scroll to such didactic treatises as *Chigo kyōkun,* to the genre of the *chigo monogatari,* in which a priest's infatuation with a youth, in many cases the incarnation of a Buddhist deity, leads him to attain enlightenment. In popular discourse of the Edo period, however, priest-acolyte relations were less likely to occasion spiritual salvation than earthy humor, whether in such forms of comic verse as *senryu* or in the pages of the anecdote book *(hanashibon).* Acolytes feature prominently in *Seisuishō (Rousing Laughter,* completed in 1623), one of the progenitors of the latter genre, whose author, Anrakuan Sakuden, had gathered such stories over many decades of monastic life. Sakuden depicts the acolyte as an often less-than-willing sexual partner to the senior inhabitants of the temple: one youth, for instance, curses the "hateful" *(niku ya)* Kūkai for bringing such a "bothersome" *(nangi)* thing as *shudō* ("way of the ephebes") to Japan.[48]

In his "Notes and Queries," Minakata, among the various meanings of the suffix *maru,* includes the "chigos, or infants." He explains that they "originated in the Buddhist system of keeping in the cloisters the young novices with unshaved heads, who became the sincere attendants of their instructors. Thence, down to the commencement of the present regime,

---

[47] Minakata becomes quite critical of Yanagita Kunio when it comes to the discussion of Japanese male homosexuality. In a letter to Iwata Jun'ichi dated July 17, 1935 where he tries to explain the distinction between chigo and kasshiki, he writes: "When Mr. Yanagita speaks of *kasshiki* literature, he is, as you saw clearly, someone who, while assuming the air of knowing everything, has not understood much." Iwata had complained to Minakata that Yanagita did not distinguish between chigo and kasshiki. Yanagita speaks of *kasshiki bungei (kasshiki* fine arts) in Yanagita (1969) 1990: 3. Minakata, quoting a passage according to which "in the holy way one says *chigo,* in the Zen forests *kasshiki,*" concludes that by the Genroku era the two had already become confused; Nakazawa 1991–1992, 3: 534.

[48] Anrakuan Sakuden, *Seisuishō,* in Hanashibon taikei, 1975–1979, 2: 133.

they acted as inveterate corrupters of clerical morals."[49] This seems to be an instance of "blaming the victim." He also refers to

> a curious anthology, *Zoku Mon'yō Wakashū,* dated 1304, preserved in Hanawa's "Collection," wherein not a single poem occurs either composed by or addressed to the fair sex, its place being throughout occupied by the chigos, whose verses, together with those of the prelates and priests, make up the whole contents. And I find in it the names altogether of forty-nine boys, suffixed with *maru* without a single exception, which indicates amply how the spread of the honorific word went *pari passu* with that of the *vice italien.*"[50]

With the development of pedophily, within and outside the temples, the chigo were eventually supplemented by another category of youths in the monks' affections—namely, the male prostitutes (*kagema*). The monks were no longer content to stay inside the monastery and to enjoy intramural love: they discovered the attractions of the entertainment districts and of commercialized shudō. In the *Great Mirror of Male Love,* Saikaku complains about the inflation caused in the shudō market by these wealthy newcomers.[51]

Names such as *terakoshō* and *kasshiki* referred to functions usually performed by minions. The term *kasshiki* is specific to Zen and designated in Zen monasteries the young boys (from seven to fifteen) charged with announcing mealtime etiquette in the refectory; they were postulants beginning training in reading and chanting Buddhist and Chinese classics and learning ritual under supervision of an abbot.[52] Like the terakoshō, they had long braids, wore makeup (white powder on the face, stylized eyebrows and lips colored in red), and lavish silken robes.[53] We know, for instance, that Nanzenji had 130 shami (novices) and kasshiki for 700 monks. Although Mujaku Dōchū, in his notice about kasshiki in *Zenrin shōkisen,* does not elaborate on the specific problems raised by this category of novices, apparently kasshiki often became causes of sexual rivalry among monks.[54]

---

[49] "Notes and Queries," s.v. "Maru," *Minakata Kumagusu zenshū* 10: 148–52. Minakata quotes various Western sources on Japan, and concludes with a remark from Voltaire's *Philosophical Dictionary*: "Monks who are in charge to raise the youth have always been somewhat addicted to pederasty. It is the necessary consequence of the celibacy to which these poor people are condemned."

[50] Ibid., 150–51.

[51] See Ihara Saikaku 1990 and Pflugfelder 1996.

[52] See Collcutt 1981: 245–47, 322.

[53] See Takahashi Ryūzō, "Rinzaishū kanji no seidō," pt. 1, in *Kokushigaku* 23 (May 1935): 9–43; 24 (Oct. 1935): 12–30.

[54] See *Zenrin shōkisen* 1909: 341. Another of Mujaku's works has a rubric "homosexuality" (*nanshin*), but significantly all the references are to non-Buddhist Chinese texts. See Mujaku, *Saiseki kijishū,* vol. 3 (unpublished ms.).

One also finds the term *warawa* (youth), written sometimes with the character meaning "concubine," or *ako;* as well as allusions to the love between Benkei and Ushikawamaru (that is, Yoshitsune as a youth). With the development of male prostitution in the Edo period, the term *kagema* came into wide use.[55] These kagema, originally kabuki performers, were the male equivalent of courtesans, and they plied their trade in kagema teahouses. The development of the kagema marks a radical change (and according to some, like Minakata, a decline) in the way of "male love." It is no longer, as it was within the Buddhist monastery and among the samurai, an idealized relationship between an adult and an adolescent, an elder and a younger brother. As Furukawa points out: "In contrast to the samurai model, in which the homosexual relationship involved a difference in age, the kagema model can be said to have been based on gender differentiation: the beauty of the kagema, specifically, was compared to that of a courtesan: it trespassed on heterosexual ground."[56]

Most authors agree that male love was well accepted in premodern Japanese society, even more than in ancient Greek society, to the extent that the passive role does not seem to have carried negative connotations. After the Muromachi period, it became widespread among the warriors and in the artistic world. Homosexual stories are found in various types of literature: in the Japanese case, for instance, we find genres that are anecdotal (like the *otogizōshi*), romantic (like the *chigo monogatari*), practical, esoteric, juridical, and so on. There seems to be general agreement that male love was at first essentially a "way" reserved to monks and aristocrats, which gradually extended to warriors and artists and, with the urbanization of early modern Japan, eventually spread among commoners (merchants, and so on). With this gradual extension, it became increasingly commodified and debased. There were in Edo seven areas of masculine prostitution. However, male love remained a dominant feature of Japanese monastic life. It was seen by many as a kind of compensation for the prohibition against the presence of women in monasteries, a prohibition particularly reinforced under the Tokugawa rule. According to Hirazuka Yoshinobu, its transgressive nature diminished with time, so that it came to be perceived as a privilege of the monks—a

---

[55] According to Minakata, the word *kagerō*, used as a synonym of *wakashū* (ephebe), is an abbreviation of *kagema yarō*, referring to a youth who is in the *kagema* (or *kagenoma*), a place in temples where the sexual act often took place, near the latrine, where monks undressed. After the act, the wakashū went to the latrine to wash himself (otherwise, it was believed, he would get hemorroids, *ji,* homophone and homograph of *ji*, temple, composed of the two graphic elements "illness" and "temple"—hence the association with "temple illness"). The term *kagerō* also evokes an insect, and the fact that the wakashū's beauty was ephemeral. The transiency of the chigo beauty, like that of fireflies, may have inspired Saikaku's witticism: "Fireflies also work their asses at night." See Saikaku 1990: 246.

[56] See Furukawa 1994: 100.

privilege that eventually extended to other social categories. The central position of homosexuality in Japanese Buddhism thus deserves fuller treatment.

If Buddhist male homosexuality was at times repressed, it is therefore not because of some "sinfulness" of the homosexual act in itself, but for its social consequences—in particular for the disturbances it caused in monastic life. It was seen by some of its critics as a side effect of Buddhist misogyny, both a cause and a sign of spiritual degeneration.[57] This characterization, perhaps more accentuated in Japanese Buddhism, may have been if not provoked, at least to some extent justified by alleged misinterpretations of the "innate awakening" (*hongaku*) theory and the corollary notions that "this very mind is the Buddha" (*sokushin ze butsu*) or that "defilements are awakening" (*bonnō soku bodai*)—in other words, by the transgressive spirit that was perhaps the most valuable but also the most dangerous element of Mahāyāna, in particular in its Tantric and Chan/Zen variants. Besides illustrating the problems resulting from the literal interpretation of "naturalist" or antinomian theories and the negative effects of the collusion of elite Buddhism (Zen, Mikkyō) with the ruling classes, the question of Buddhist (homo)sexuality has revealed some of the gaps in Chan/Zen traditional discourse. Contrary to Daoism or Tantrism, Chan/Zen never considered the sexual act (or the sexual organs) as a gate to a higher reality—despite a possible influence of the Tachikawa teaching on that school.

A number of senryū or satiric poems deal with the topic, for instance the following: "The handsome woman goes to the city, the handsome man to the temple." As if following the biblical precept, Buddhist monks usually chose the "narrow gate"—with a few exceptions, as suggested in the following senryū: "From where he finds himself / Too cramped / The Priest / Has taken a dislike."[58] In such cases, monks woud leave the "narrow gate" for the "flaccid gate": widows, concubines, or prostitutes. But more often, "When hungry / The priest borrows / The pot of his cooking boy."[59] In "A Bonze's Wife in a Worldly Temple," Saikaku's heroine remarks: "Now this period was the very 'noonday of

[57]One is reminded of Melford Spiro's "phobic" characterization of Buddhist monkhood: "[Monks] are willing to pay this price [renunciation] because, at least for many of them, celibacy is not really a price. . . . Monks are characterized by (among other things) latent homosexuality and an above-average fear of female- and mother-figures. . . . The monastic role permits a person characterized by fear of women to lead a life of female-avoidance, and the all-male monastery permits the sublimated expression of a latent homosexuality." Spiro 1982: 342–43. In the Japanese case, however, renunciation is not truly at stake, and homosexuality is not simply latent.

[58] *Suetsumu hana* 2: 23, in Cholley 1996: 31.

[59] *Senryū fuzoku jiten*, (Tokyo: Seiabō, 1962): 156, in Cholley 1996: 30.

Buddhism'—and indeed even at noon the priests disported themselves with their temple pages."[60] In a letter to Iwata, Minakata points out that, judging from the number of anecdotes and legends regarding chigo, male love flourished from the Ashikaga period to the Genroku era (1688–1704).

Although most of the Buddhist materials deal with Shingon and Tendai Buddhism, the situation may not have been drastically different in Zen monasteries, as the popularity of figures such as *nawa* ("rope," because his robe is made of rope) Monju, Mañjuśrī as a youth, or Jizō, seem to suggest.[61] The figure of the pot-bellied Hotei, who as a god of fertility was often represented with children, lent itself to misinterpretation. Even Bodhidharma, the stern founder of Zen, was not only shown as cross-dressing but more crudely represented as an old insertee type. As one senryū puts it: "The overripe persimmon / looks like Daruma / with a rotting asshole."[62]

Leupp characterizes the homosexuality of premodern Japan by the existence of two distinct homosexual traditions, monastic and samurai, traditions "that 1) emerged largely as the result of the lack of women; 2) were age-structured and seen as contributing to the younger partner's education or maturation; and 3) often required the younger partner to assume a female-like or androgynous appearance." Leupp further argues that "heterosexual desire was evident in the construction of sexual objects made up, coiffured, and dressed much like women." This may be true of the kagema, but the chigo was not simply "feminized" but rather often continued to be perceived as male. The difficulty in distinguishing between nuns and chigo in the *emaki* (illustrated scrolls) is due to the fact that the nuns, by shaving their head, have lost their most visible sexual characteristic and joined the chigo in this intermediate, androgynous realm. We are reminded here of Lévi-Strauss's description in *Tristes tropiques*: "This placid femininity, as if freed from the conflict of the sexes, is also evoked by the bonzes of the temples, confused because of their shaved heads with the nuns in a kind of third gender, half-parasite and half-prisoner."[63] The absence of women is not sufficient to explain the emergence of monastic nanshoku: women were never far away, even when they were barred in principle from the temple precincts. Their relative scarcity of women is only one among many factors, ranging from the

[60] Waley (1921) 1976: 148.

[61] See Guth 1987: 13–16. Mañjuśrī shares a number of features with Skanda (Ch. Weituo, J. Idaten), represented as Kumāra, a handsome youth. Before becoming a protecting deity in Buddhism, this child of Śiva was originally a demon-child who kidnapped and tormented children. See Strickmann 1996: 273–76.

[62] Leupp 1995: 181.

[63] Lévi-Strauss 1974a, 488.

most negative (misogyny) to more positive ones, such as the child mystique. The educational element was an aspect of the homosexual relation, but it should not obscure the belief that the elder partner was also at times initiated, regenerated, or redeemed through love.

One of the recurrent motifs in the first encounter between the monk and the chigo is the question: "Was it a woman or a chigo?" The gender of the partner is not clearly defined, but he is characterized by his femininity. The chigo is, as it were, the perfect sexual companion (without the usual womanly flaws). In samurai stories, however, the chigo, although not yet a man, is clearly perceived as male. It seems that his feminization, when it occurred, had something to do with social class and power. A child from a good family, promised to a future as warrior or official, was more likely to retain a certain maleness, whereas a chigo of low extraction was more likely to be made into a feminized sexual object. Finally, the overreliance on Edo-period sources might lead us to a utilitarian, merchant-class view of nanshoku. In this sense, recent work on Japanese homosexuality would be well inspired to read Minakata again. As Pflugfelder points out:

> Idealized though it may have been, Minakata's vision of *nandō* was intended to suggest that male-male sexuality, instead of merely constituting an "obscene act," had once formed—and might perhaps still form—part of a larger "way" or discipline interlaced with such positive social values as friendship, education, and spirituality. To simply dismiss such traditions as "filthy" or "immoral," he insisted, was to misunderstand the meaning they had carried for their participants in the context of their time. In this way, Minakata not only relativized the moral absolutes of Meiji Civilization but was also able to resist the totalizing impulses of the medical model of male-male sexuality that had become so influential during the second half of his lifetime.[64]

This idealized version of nanshoku seems to have been more prevalent during the Muromachi period, but in the Edo period, too, the development among townsmen of a more mercantile form of nanshoku in the kabuki theater as a form of boy prostitution produced a reaction. As Schalow notes, "The townsman's appreciation of youths was crude by samurai and priestly standards, and elitist *kana-zōshi* writers in Kyoto were stirred to defend their spiritualized practice of male love. Their defense involved creating, and claiming for their own, a historical past. It was a de-eroticized past, meant to serve as an antidote to the eroticized version of the 'way of the youth' practiced in theater districts."[65] It is for such a purpose, for instance, that the anthology *Iwatsutsuji* was com-

---

[64] Pflugfelder 1996: 230.
[65] Schalow 1992a: 3.

piled. Clearly, both the idealized and the derisive approach remain shallow and fraught with ideological motives. We must try to walk the "narrow path to the deep" (Bashō's *oku no hosomichi*, another homosexual metaphor?), by paying attention to both the ideal and the material reality of nanshoku.

THE SOCIAL AND CULTURAL CONTEXT(S)

We know not how the Southern Mode began
And women's travail was bequeathed to men:
Face to back, opening the firmament,
For lack of a woman, making do with a man.

(Li Yu, *Silent Operas*)

Male love was seen as part of a civilizing process (departure from nature), hence as a borrowing from China (or, in a nativist reaction, a native custom of Japan traced back to the *Kojiki*). As noted above, the term *nanshoku* (Ch. *nanse*) itself is a borrowing from the Chinese.[66] As Leupp points out, many societies have regarded homosexuality as a foreign importation, a defining characteristic of foreign cultures. "In all these cases," he writes, "homosexuality was linked with rival or enemy cultures."[67] In the Japanese case, however, nanshoku, because of its association with China—both a rival and a model culture—and with Buddhism, was aestheticized as a "way" or teaching (*dō*). It had powerful credentials, since most Chinese stories on the subject deal with relations between rulers and their favorites: for instance between the Duke Ling of Wei (534–493 B.C.E) and his minister Mizi Zia; between Prince Zhongxian of Chu and Pan Zhang; or between Prince Ai of the Wei and his minister Long Yang (fourth century); between Emperor Ai (r. 6 B.C.E–1 C.E.) of the Western Han and Dong Xian.[68] Homosexuality occupies a special section in the *Shiji* (Record of the Grand Historian): "It is not women alone who can use their looks to attract the eye of the ruler; courtiers and eunuchs can play at that game as well. Many were the men of ancient times who gained favor in this way."[69]

In China, however, the relation could be between consenting male adults of equal status: see for instance the case of Xi Kang (223–262) and the poet Yuan Ji (210–263). Many other Tang and Song poets and scholars, including the most famous (such as Li Bai, Bai Juyi, and Su Dong po) were known for their homosexual tastes, and by the Qing the

---

[66] See Ruan and Tsai 1987.
[67] Leupp 1995: 12.
[68] See Hinsch 1990: 44–46
[69] Watson 1961, 2:462.

so-called *Hanlin feng* (style of Hanlin academy) had come to designate this form of consensual homosexuality. Leupp observes, however, that "generally, homosexual relationships were class-structured and trans-generational; the 'active' partner was the social superior or, at least, the older partner."[70]

Similarly in Korea, we find the case of the *hwarang* or "flower boys," an elite class of warrior youth in the Silla dynasty, who also performed ritual (and probably sexual) functions at court. Kakhun argues that the love of King Chinhung for his "flower boys" was not, like that of Emperor Ai of the Western Han, motivated only by lust.[71] But, as Leupp points out, the comparison can be drawn only against the backdrop of an association between the hwarang and homosexuality. Several later sources talk about the *namsaek* (from the Chinese *nanse,* "male love") tradition. Monastic homosexuality was less developed in Korea than in Japan, but not entirely absent, as implied by the (real or feigned) indignation of a Korean ambassador to Japan at the time of the shōgun Yoshimune, about the fact that noble and wealthy merchants kept beautiful young men "like flowers": "I have never seen such a thing in other countries!"[72]

Certain sexual habits considered "against nature" by the Christians may have been encouraged by the antinomian teachings of Mahāyāna, but they must also be placed in their institutional, social and cultural contexts. Was "sodomy" as prevalent in China and Japan as missionaries claimed, or was it, as in Europe, merely "the sin of intellectuals and of clerics"? For China at least, opinions differ widely.[73] Traditionally, it has been associated in China with the southern province of Fujian, "where homosexuality was supposedly so prevalent that an euphemism or metaphor for male homosexuality was the 'southern mode' (*nanfeng*)."[74] Per-

---

[70] Leupp 1995: 17.

[71] See Ayukai 1932, 4: 36; Lee, trans. 1969: 70; and Ilyŏn, 1972: 234–36.

[72] Watanabe and Iwata 1989: 88. See also Stevens 1990: 139–40.

[73] For a recent synthesis, see Hinsch 1990. Sodomy in the "technical" sense does appear in Chinese literature. In the *Jingpingmei,* for instance, Ximen Qing, as condition for buying a beautiful dress for Fan Jinlian, sodomizes her.

[74] Ng 1987: 68. Li Yu remarks: "The practice is prevalent in all parts of the country, but especially in Fujian." See Li Yu, "A Male Mencius's Mother," in Li 1990b: 101. So widespread was it indeed that in Fujian "even such insentient creatures as plants and trees have become infected and take delight in it" (ibid.). This is shown by the case of the banyan tree which, "if there is a sapling nearby, will actually lean over and try to seduce it" (ibid.). See also Minakata's description of the origins of the "rabbit-child" god in China. Toward the beginning of the Qing, a man of Fujian named Hu Tian'ai had fallen madly in love with a handsome regional inspector and followed him everywhere. When the official found him hiding out in the toilet to sneak a look at his buttock, he became furious and had Hu executed. Hu appeared in a dream to the people of his village and complained that he was only guilty of loving. Therefore, the lord of the underworld had taken pity on him and given him the title of "god of the rabbits" with the function of promoting male love. Hu asked the

haps it is the other way around, since *nan,* south, is homophonous with *nan,* male: thus homosexuality becomes the southern mode, whereas heterosexuality becomes the northern mode. According to Li Yu (1610–1680), "We do not know when the mode began or who invented it, but isn't it strange that it now competes with the Way of Man and Woman as created by Heaven and Earth?"[75]

Li Yu complains that the southern mode (homosexuality) lacks three things found in the way of man and woman (heterosexuality): complementarity in physical terms (the obvious yin-yang complementarity in male/female anatomies); mutual pleasure in emotional terms; and offspring in terms of effects. He then addresses the physical act in a way that is strongly reminiscent of the Jesuits (could he have been influenced by them?): "Beside, that sinkhole was created to eliminate bodily wastes, because the foul matter and rank odours produced inside the five organs needed somewhere to drain away. The Creator, in first endowing us with physical form, was afraid that men and women might mistake this orifice for the other one during intercourse, and so he situated it at the rear. Why then, after it had been segregated to emphasize its inferior status, did men wilfully cross the alps and seek out this remote spot for their clandestine purposes?"[76] Li Yu justifies his condemnation by resorting to natalist arguments:

> The reason is that this practice is not one of those universal principles created by Heaven and Earth but an unnatural development by certain ancients who travelled a deviant path. When the practice is carried to extremes, therefore, it conflicts with ethical relations. I urge everyone not to follow this deviant path but to save a little essence and apply it where it will do some good. How beneficial it would be to increase the population for the Court's sake and to continue the family line for your ancestors! Why pour this essence, precious as molten gold, into that sordid place? There is a poem that bears witness:

> Semen forms offspring everywhere;
> North or South, there's an embryo.
> Don't say that catamites can't conceive—
> In the rear courtyard maggots grow.[77]

---

villagers to erect a temple to him. This temple became a place of wonders, where all prayers were answered. According to Minakata, the "god rabbit-child" was a kind of androgynous animal related to the hare. The "god of rabbits" thus became a patron of homosexuals. See *Zi buyu,* "Confucius Never Talked about It," by Yuan Mei (1716–98) (Shanghai: Shanghai guji chubanje, 1986: 458–59; Vitiello 1994: 81–82, and Minakata, in Nakazawa 1991–1992: 543–44.

[75] Yu 1990: 99–100.
[76] Ibid., 100.
[77] Ibid., 133–34.

However, Li Yu goes on to the story of a wonderful love between a man and a youth, who later castrates himself out of love for his companion. He becomes the man's wife, and the adoptive mother of his son. After his "husband's" death, he takes such good care of the child, passing himself off as a woman, that Li Yu's praises him in the title of his novel as a "male Mencius's mother"—a reference to the famous story of Mencius's mother, who moved her house three times to provide the best education to her son.[78] Li Yu concludes: "If all the world's catamites were as chaste as You Ruilang, the southern mode would be worth enjoying. And if all the world's lovers were as fond as Xu Jifang, young Ruilang would be worth emulating. But I fear that there are no others like Ruilang and Jifang. Men waste their essence and ruin their conduct to no purpose, which is why I consider the practice deplorable."[79]

Li Yu's condemnation was apparently to no avail. According to the supposedly "objective" testimony of the medical doctor J.-J. Matignon, an observer of China who wrote at the turn of the century, "pederasty is extremely widespread in the Middle Empire. All classes of society give themselves up to it, and all ages, youth as old people, are fond of it."[80] However, in his ground-breaking (but sometimes flawed) study of Chinese sexuality, Robert van Gulik thinks that it is difficult to credit the affirmations of many foreign observers, according to whom China would have known, in the eighteenth century and at the beginning of the twentieth century, "an unrestrained display of homosexuality and pederasty."[81]

Opinions also differ as to how homosexuality was perceived by the Chinese. Angela K. Leung concludes that China, during the sixteenth and seventeenth centuries, "tolerates homosexual practices and considers them as 'normal.'"[82] Homosexuality was not perceived as a sin or a moral failure. Although it was condemned in Christianity for its *malizia*,

---

[78] See ibid., 99–134; and Vitiello 1994: 129.

[79] Li 1990: 134. See also *Bian er chai* (Wearing a Cap but also Hairpins), late Ming edition, Palace Museum, Taipei (Taipei: Tianyi chubanshe, 1990). This is a Hangzhou collection of stories about homosexual love affairs (hence the title) between an older sophisticate and a younger innocent. The older man is always of the scholar class. The author argues very seriously for the validity of homosexual love. Langxian, on the contrary, emphasizes the unnaturalness and comic absurdity of homosexuality. It is "academicians' love." But it is also treated with condemnation. Yet the dominant note is of idealized romance and humor; Hanan 1981: 137.

[80] Matignon 1898: 255.

[81] Van Gulik 1961: 78.

[82] Leung quotes J.-J. Matignon's remarks that homosexuals have never been persecuted in China—at least until the twentieth century—and that the only reproach addressed by public opinion to pederasty is that it had a baneful influence on eyesight; Leung 1984: 662–63.

its violence against nature and God's plans, there was no notion of such acts as "counter-nature" in China.[83] Like other nonprocreative practices, it was judged merely on social grounds. The situation seems to have been somewhat similar to that in Roman antiquity described by Paul Veyne.[84] However, the active/passive opposition stressed by Veyne in the Roman case did not play as significant a role in Chinese culture, where the yin/yang complementarity, which could be invoked in a male-male relationship as well, involves relationships of equality.[85] Nevertheless, as in Rome, the moral judgment passed on a particular homosexual relationship had essentially to do with the social positions of the partners involved and with the potential social disorder that might result from "excesses." As a Ming juridical manual makes clear, "A man must abstain, as much as possible, from having relationships with handsome youths and from having female servants, so that everything works all right in the conjugal bed."[86] Van Gulik notes that, according to the *Gaiyu conggao* by Zhaoyi (1727–1814), in the Northern Song there was a class of men who earned their living as male prostitutes. In the Zhenghe era (1111–1117) of the Northern Song, a law punished them with a hundred bamboo strokes, in addition to a monetary penalty, but their activity continued. However, Zhaoyi also points out that this marked the apogee of homosexuality in China.[87] Van Gulik argues that the rise of puritanism under the Qing drastically modified the situation. Vivienne Ng mentions several cases recorded in the *Xingan huilan* (Conspectus of Criminal Cases), "involving the seduction of young boys or young men by their Confucian teachers, and seduction of neophytes by Buddhist monks."

[83] On the history of Western homosexuality, see Boswell 1980. The notion of "counter-nature" is illustrated by the rooster burned at the stake by Christians for laying eggs.

[84] See Paul Veyne, "L'homosexualité à Rome," in Ariès and Béjin 1982: 41–51.

[85] Leung 1984: 660.

[86] Ibid., 665; quoting Huang Zhengyuan's *Record of Ming Juridical Cases* (Taibei: Academia Sinica, 1979), 933.

[87] Van Gulik 1961: 210. See also *Duan xie bian*, in *Xiangyan conshu* (Collection of Writings on Perfumed Elegance), 9th series, vol. 2 (Shanghai: Guoxue fulun she, 1909–1911). Bai Xingjian (d. 826, younger brother of Bai Juyi), in his *Tiandi yinyang jiaohuan dale fu* (Poetical Essay on the Supreme Joy of the Sexual Union of Yin and Yang and Heaven and Earth), in *Shuangmei ying'an congshu*, edited by Ye Dehui (repr. Hong Kong, n.d.: 7b-8a), gives a survey of sexual life, with a section on hetero- and homosexual relations in Buddhist monasteries; see Hinsch 1990: 84. Male prostitution was popular under the Song, according to works such as the *Records of the Extraordinary* (*Qing yi lu*) by Tao Gu: "Everywhere people single out Nanhai for its 'Misty Moon Workshops,' a term referring to the custom of esteeming lewdness. Nowadays in the capital those who sell themselves number more than ten thousand. As to the men who offer their bodies for sale, they enter and leave places shamelessly. And so prostitution extends to the hive of alleys and lanes, not limited to the Misty Moon Workshops themselves." *Qing yi lu*, Chen shi kangxian zhai kanben (n.p., 1875), 10b, quoted in Hinsch 1990: 92.

Analyzing a case of male rape in 1815, she concludes that "male homo-sexuality was being punished as well as the crime of rape. The harsher punishment for the unchaste victim suggests that perhaps homosexuality was regarded by the Qing government as a worse evil than female un-chaste behavior. Iconoclastic men were more subversive to the state than immoral women."[88] Attempting to explain what she sees as Qing homo-phobia, Ng suggests an analogy with Europe, where "the onset of homo-phobia in the late Middle Ages coincided with the rise of absolute government."[89]

In his study of monastic life in modern Chinese Buddhism, Holmes Welch argues that monasteries were relatively free of sexuality—a far cry from the Japanese situation: "Monks were forbidden by their vows to have any form of sexual outlet. If detected, it meant a beating and expul-sion for the monk and discredit for the monastery."[90] His informants told him in particular that homosexuality was very rare and was consid-ered "low taste" (*xialiu*). Welch notices that the monastic diet contrib-uted to the reduction of sexual desire, and that a light was kept burning in the meditation hall and other dormitories to discourage "laxity." And he concludes, perhaps hastily: "Given their diets and beliefs, it seems more likely that the monks of China were able to adjust themselves more easily to continence than their counterparts in Europe."[91] But the evi-dence he cites could lead to precisely opposite conclusions. It is also pos-sible that, under such circumstances, homosexual attraction often found an outlet in some kind of platonic love.

The missionary description of the moral depravity of Chinese Buddhist monasteries may have been somewhat exaggerated *ad majorem ecclesiae gloriam*. To be sure, there were many anticlerical stories circulating among the Chinese people in which corrupt monks were giving them-selves over to homosexuality or paedophily. But in most of these stories the monks, once discovered, are severely punished, and this may reflect the fact that, as van Gulik and Ng argued, the Qing rule marked a drastic change in the public perception of male homosexuality. In short, al-though the case for male love could be made in China from the fact that the models were found in the higher strata of society, with the emperors, the spread of the phenomenon and its social effects, in particular the development of male prostitution after the Song, paved the way to crimi-nalization of male homosexuality.

[88] See Ng 1987: 69; and M. J. Meijer, "Homosexual Offences in Ch'ing Law," *T'oung Pao* 71 (1985), 109–33.

[89] Ng 1987: 68.

[90] Welch 1967: 116.

[91] Ibid., 118–19.

THE QUEST FOR ORIGINS

The situation in Japan, at the beginning of the premodern period, provides an interesting contrast with that of China. Ironically, "male love," although imported from China (like Buddhism), fares much better in the Japanese environment than in its country of origin (again, like Buddhism). The comparison between Li Yu and Ihara Saikaku would be revealing in this context. In the Edo period, male love became widely accepted and does not seem to have been considered a crime. The only law against sodomy dates from the Meiji period, and it was adopted under the influence of Chinese law, only to be abandoned a few years later in light of European (more specifically, French) law. It may be too early to pass judgment, as studies on how homosexuality was treated in Japanese juridical codes are just beginning to appear.[92] There are, however, many fictional accounts of the love life of the Japanese (including Buddhist monks), a number of which deal explicitly with male homosexuality.[93]

Perhaps one of the most striking features of Japanese "male love" is its self-definition as a "way" (*wakashudō*) and its emphasis on the question of origins—whether Chinese and/or Buddhist, or purely Japanese. In Japan, a compromise between the Chinese and Buddhist origins of nanshoku is found in the story of the love between the legendary King Mu and his young lover Jidō, to which I will return in the next chapter.

The Two Ways

Certain texts argue for bisexuality or the harmony between the "two ways." According to a source quoted by Hirazuka, for instance: "The kasshiki are novices, young men. Since Heaven and Earth were produced, among the animals and vegetals there is Yin and Yang. In the way of the flesh too, there is love of women and love of men. Through the harmony of these two ways the world comes into being."[94] Here we see how the yin/yang symbolism, instead of being used as an argument for heterosexuality (as in the case of Li Yu, quoted below), becomes an argument for the coexistence of two incommensurable ways, those of male love and of heterosexuality.

The definition of male love as a "way" has a polemical element, as

[92] See in particular Pflugfelder 1990a and 1990b. Earlier studies include those of Iwata Jun'ichi and Minakata Kumagusu.

[93] See Saikaku 1990.

[94] Hirazuka 1987: 16. See also *Koji ruien*, Shūkyōbu 2: 1217, for a description of the kasshiki of Myōshinji.

apparent in the many tracts arguing for the superiority of male love over "female love" (that is, heterosexuality, not lesbianism). It is significant that the discussion about the origins of male love and about its relative merits compared to heterosexual love came to occupy so prominent a place in the Japanese discourse on homosexuality.

According to the preface of the *Nanshoku yamamichi no tsuyu*, "To stop at cherry blossoms when one thinks of flowers, or at women when one thinks about 'form,' such a one-sidedness is due to one's ignorance of the unique and ultimate path of equality."[95] Thus, Buddhist nonduality was invoked to justify bisexuality. The double-entendre about "form" (*shiki*, also meaning "sex") was frequently implicit in the quotation of the famous passage of the *Heart Sūtra*, "Form is Emptiness, Emptiness is form" (J. *shiki soku ze kū, kū soku ze shiki*), to the point that the term *Kōya shingyō* (The *Heart Sūtra* of Mount Kōya) came to be used as a euphemism for homosexuality. The advocacy of shudō, whether among the clergy or the warrior class, was often associated with a misogynistic attitude.

In his *Iwatsutsuji* (Rock Azaleas, 1667), a collection of homoerotic poetry and prose whose title is inspired by a poem of the Shingon monk Shinga, Kitamura Kigin (1624–1705) argues that: "To take pleasure in a beautiful woman has been in the nature of men's hearts since the age of male and female gods, but for a man to take pleasure in the beauty of another man goes against nature. Nevertheless, as relations between the sexes were forbidden by the Buddha, priests of the law—being made of neither stone nor wood—had no recourse but to practice the love of boys as an outlet for their feelings. Just as the waters that plummet and flow below the pass as Tsukubane form the deep pools of the Mino river, so this form of love has proved to be deeper than the love between men and women."[96]

In a tract entitled *Denbu* (The Boor), a discussion about the respective merits of normal sex and male love takes place between two men: "the boor" advocates heterosexual relationships, and "the refined one" is a partisan of homosexuality. Despite their nicknames, which seems to indicate a prejudice in favor of the homosexual standpoint, the discussion ends abruptly, after an apparent victory of the heterosexual position. In fact, most of the argument revolves around women and normative sexuality. Buddhism seems to provide arguments on both sides of the issue: its blatantly misogynistic description comforts the homosexual's contempt for women, whereas its affirmation of married life and social values gives reason to the heterosexual.

---

[95] Quoted in Hirazuka 1987: 50.
[96] Schalow 1992a: 222.

According to the boor, Buddhist priests practice homosexuality for lack of women. Note that this argument, which can also be found in the work of scholars such as Iwata Jun'ichi, and amounts to denying the biological reality of the homosexual drive, comes from the strong supporter of heterosexuality:

> True, it's said that priests prefer [the love of youths], but this is only because when priests take up their calling renouncing attachments to this world they give up all hope of having children. Even so the very fact that the Way of Women is more attractive than the Way of Youths has recently led even priests to lose themselves in relationships with women. Of course, if priests firmly adhere to the Way of Buddha and avoid this tempting Way they'll probably avoid disaster. But if their desire [for women] is denied by the society around them what on earth can they do [but turn to boys]? Since priests must avoid the Five Deadly Sins they lack freedom; they shave their heads, don surplices and priestly robes and abstain from fish and fowl. So how can they avoid the so-called "forbidden way"? The proverb says "Cattle follow cattle, birds follow birds." But it would be best for these people to hurry up and follow a way more suitable to human beings![97]

The homosexual interlocutor ("the refined one") answers that the Buddha despised women, and asserts that homosexuality has good credentials, since not only the Buddha but Confucius also practiced it. The relation between the Buddha and Ānanda, or between Confucius and his disciple Yan Hui, become homosexual ones. He mentions several reasons for women's inferiority, most notably the blood defilement of childbirth that makes them fall into the Blood Pond Hell, and the prohibition against women's entering sacred space (*nyonin kekkai*). In addition, women are progenitors, giving birth to children who will become impediments to the man's practice. And the temptation that arises in men at the sight of seductive women causes them to lose the benefit of their ascesis. He mentions as examples Ikkaku *sennin* (the ascetic Unicorn) and Kume *sennin*, two variants of the same topos.

> I still can't understand how you can suggest that the Way of Youths is wrong. It's precisely because of the excellence of this Way that Buddha had Ānanda, Confucius Yan Hui, Su Dongpo had Li Jietui. If the Way of Youths were wrong would Buddha and Confucius have enjoyed it? Buddha despised women. One of his Five Commandments forbids [monks to have sex with them].[98]

It's said that men infatuated with women are reborn in hell when they die. It's also said that women who die in childbirth sink into a sea of blood. As the *Ten*

[97] Leupp 1995: 210.
[98] Ibid.

Kings' Sūtra explains, "In one day ten thousand people descend into hell." Seven or eight thousand of these are women, two or three thousand are men. That's why the founders of Japan's Buddhist sects despised women and forbade them to visit the holy mountains and temples. But I've never heard of anyone despising *men*![99]

The boor points out that fearing female temptation is not quite the same thing as despising women. But he undermines his own argument by emphasizing that women are indeed very tempting, and monks should never be allowed to come near them. The boor also points out the importance of procreation: even the Buddha and Shōtoku Taishi were married and became fathers. He also emphasizes filial piety, resorting to famous historical examples. Thus, homosexuality is seen as lacking in filial piety and undermining social order. He continues by showing the importance of women in Japanese mythology and literature. The refined one replies by pointing out the many cases in which women have been the cause of social troubles. Much of the argument revolves around the merits and demerits of women, rather than those of male love. Relationships with women last long, and women can watch over the family property, whereas love of young men is ephemeral, cooling as soon as the youth grows; and the lineage remains neglected. Many historical examples are given to show that homosexuality has led to social and political trouble.

Mythological and Legendary Origins

> On Kōya the mountain
> Where women are hated
> Why does the maiden-pine grow?
> Yet even if the maiden-pines
> Were all rooted out,
> Would not the stars of love
> Still shoot through the night?

More fitting than pine, than plum or willow is the minion cherry, the temple page, for his is the way of Monju the Minion spread by the Great Teacher, the love of fair youths respected even by the laity: this is the home of the secrets of pederasty.[100]

---

[99] Ibid., 210–11.

[100] Donald Keene, trans., 1961: 132. Keene's commentary: women are prohibited on Mount Kōya; therefore, the argument runs, the "maidenpine" *(mematsu)* should not be allowed to grow there either. But it does, and even if it were rooted out, fleshly indulgence ("night-crawling stars") would continue.

Far from remaining "hidden from history," Japanese male love has looked for credentials in high antiquity. Thus, one tradition traces the origins of homosexuality as far back as Japanese mythological times, with the legend of the two friends Otake no mikoto and Amano no mikoto. Another mythological tradition goes back to ancient Chinese mythology. A third is purely Buddhist. A compromise between Chinese and Buddhist elements can be found in the legend of King Mu, who received from the Buddha a magical stanza, which he later transmitted to his young lover to protect him from harm when the latter was sent into exile.[101]

Homosexuality was perceived as a Buddhist characteristic, however, introduced from China. In the *Jakushōdō kokkei zokushū*, in a section on "The Rise and Prosperity of Male Love" (*Nanshoku no kōjō*), it is said that male love prospered from China to Japan: "Since a certain epoch, it is practiced openly in monasteries, and finally one comes to forget that it is a sin against chastity and compassion."[102] A prevalent tradition attributes the origin of male love in Japan to the founder of Shingon, Kūkai: "Since the time of Kanmu Tennō, when Kōbō Daishi [Kūkai] returned from China, homosexuality has flourished. In the monasteries of Kyoto, the five mountains of Kamakura, the four great temples of Washū and Kōshū [Yamato and Edo], and in all the temples of the capital, homosexuality (*shudō*) has become widespread. Later on, not only the Buddhists, but also the nobles, the warriors, and all, without distinction of rank or wealth, have become familiar with it."[103] As a senryū puts it: "Kōbō enters the back gate, Shinran the front." We will not try to solve the following chicken-and-egg problem: is it because of Kūkai that Mount Kōya became a stronghold of male love, or because Kōya turned into such a center that the origins of male love were traced back to Kūkai? According to the *Iwatsutsuji*, it was a poem about "mountains of evergreen" attributed to Kūkai's disciple Shinga in the *Kokin wakashū* that first revealed, "like plumes of pampas grass waving boldly in the wind, the existence of this way of love, and even serious people came to know and practice it."[104]

According to the *Yakeiyu shamisen* (1628), "the love of women is the mystery of the Way of the kami, the love of men is the mystery of the Buddha Dharma."[105] Another common saying has it that Jizō prefers the

---

[101] For a detailed discussion of this story, see Itō 1981, Abe 1984, and next chapter.

[102] *DNBZ* 149: 257a–c.

[103] See Georg Schurhammer, "Kōbō daishi," in *Zeitschrift für Missionswissenschaft Münster* 12 (1922): 89; and his "Die Yamabushi," ibid., 206–28.

[104] Schalow 1992a: 10.

[105] See Hirazuka 1987: 39. The noted parallelism between *nanshoku* and *joshoku* has

"love of women" (*joshoku*), Yakushi the "love of men" (*nanshoku*).[106] Yet the most important patron of Japanese Buddhist homosexuals is not Yakushi but the handsome Mañjuśrī (due to a pun on his Japanese name, Monjushiri, *shiri* meaning "buttocks"). In Saikaku's "The Almanac Maker's Tale," the heroin Osan tells Mañjuśrī: "You may indeed, Lord Monju, understand love between men, but so far as womanly passion is concerned, you cannot have the slightest knowledge."[107] According to a variant of Kūkai's legend, homosexuality was revealed by Mañjuśrī in India, and by Kūkai in Japan. The pair formed by Monju and Fugen is often presented as a symbol of a homosexual relationship (although apparently not a pederastic one), in which Fugen is said to play the dominant role.[108] The same was probably true of their Chinese manifestions, Han-shan (J. Kanzan) and Shide (J. Jittoku).[109] According to the *Kōbō Daishi ikkan no shō,* "What is called *shudō* began in antiquity when Kōbō Daishi had a conjunction with Monju. . . . When one looks deeply into the basis of *shudō,* the three holes are the extreme of pleasure (*rakugoku*). To have the chance of being born as a man and to ignore the secrets of *shudō* is truly sad. Kōbō Daishi appeared to the author and revealed these things to him."[110]

Another story, found in Hiraga Gennai's *Nenashigusa,* tells how King Yama has decided to forbid homosexuality, when one of the Ten Kings, the "King Turning the Wheel" (*tenrinnō*), defends it by arguing that it is less baneful than heterosexuality. In the first chapter of *Nenashigusa,* a young monk who has, because of his love for the famous *onnagata* (an actor playing feminine role in kabuki) Kikunojō, wasted the fortune of his monastery, falls into hell and must eventually confront King Yama. The ruler of hell, who is said to "execrate the vice of the monks," is about to condemn him when the monk shows him a portrait of the actor. The beauty of the image is such that Yama himself is fascinated. Having fallen in love, he wants to enter the human world to find the actor, but is finally convinced by the other kings not to leave. There is only one remedy for

---

suggested the translation "love between women," but it is more accurately a (male) love of women. We are probably not dealing with lesbianism here.

[106] Here again, the terminology reflects the typical male view that prevails in Japanese literature, since *nanshoku* refers clearly to "love between men," whereas *joshoku* seems to refer to a man's attraction to women.

[107] Ihara Saikaku 1956: 95.

[108] See Strickmann 1996: 274.

[109] Significantly, these two trickster figures, who were deified in China as "gods of union," are sometimes represented in Japan as a couple of young lovers. See, for instance, the *ukiyoe* by Suzuki Harunobu (Musée Guimet) representing the pair as a couple of Japanese lovers, in which the rather effeminate young man reads a long love poem to his lover.

[110] Nakazawa, 1991–1992, 3: 422.

appeasing his longing: to cause the death of Kikunojō, if possible in such a way that he arrives "intact" in the world of the dead. First, a *kappa* (water spirit) is sent to capture the actor during his participation in a nautical feast on the Sumida River. However, the kappa himself falls in love and cannot complete his mission. In the end, Yama's impatience is rewarded.[111] Thus, beauty and love are stronger than death, although in this case they precipitate death. The homosexual connotation of Yama derives perhaps from the fact that, in Japan, he was perceived as an avatar of Jizō, a bodhisattva who is usually represented in the form of a young androgynous monk, or even as a child. Another avatar of Jizō was the Hieizan deity Jūzenji, who appeared to Saichō. Kūkai himself is often represented as a chigo, as well as Shōtoku Taishi.

Despite its more frequent association with the monks of the Shingon sect, it seems that the phenomenon was also quite common in Zen and Tendai. Mount Hiei, the Tendai headquarters, was a *haut-lieu* of male love—if we are to believe the words of the chorus in the Nō play *Shuten Dōji*: " 'First the temple youths, / then the Mountain King' [Sannō]— monks hold the temple boys much dearer / than they do the gods themselves!"[112] There was on Hieizan a specific homosexual tradition associated with the god Jūzenji.[113] As we will see in the next chapter, this god was closely associated with the chigo and often represented as one.[114]

[111] See Maës 1970. In one of the stories of the *Longyang yishi* (The Forgotten Tears of the Lord of Longyang), a collection of tales on male love by Zuizhu Jushi, Yama forgives a boy who commited suicide after being abused by the jealous wife of the man who bought him out of a brothel, and makes him his attendant. Quoted in Vitiello 1994: 79.

[112] Shuten dōji, the Wine-Drinking Lad, is a demon exiled from Mount Hiei by Saichō. He invites two samurai, disguised as monks, to drink with him. At night, when he is asleep, the two men kill the demon. See *Ōeyama* (The Demon of Ōeyama), translated by H. Mack Horton, in Brazell, ed. 1988: 158.

[113] In the *Heike monogatari*, we find the following anecdote. Some monks stop in front of Jūzenji shrine. They want to take the abbot away. "An eighteen-year-old youth named Tsurumaru, the servant of the Mudōji monk Master of Discipline Jōen, suddenly took leave of his senses, writhing and perspiring. 'The Jūzenji god has possessed me,' he announced. 'Whether this is the latter end of the Law or not, I could not recover from the grief, no matter how many times I might be born in new existences. It is useless for me to stay at the foot of this mountain if such things are to happen.' The boy shed floods of tears, with his two sleeves pressed to his face." The monks feel skeptical. They ask for a proof and are convinced when the boy returns. See McCullough 1988: 60. On Jūzenji as an expression of the Three Truths of Tendai, see *Keiran shūyōshū*, T. 76, 2410: 865a.

[114] Another mythological figure sometimes associated with male love is the god Ebisu. As the saying goes, "Ebisu is nanshoku." According to Minakata, this has merely to do with the fact that Ebisuchō was famous as a gay quarter. Iwata suggests that Ebisu here designates beriberi, and refers to the belief that homosexuality cured this illness. Minakata, quoting from Hippocrates and from the *Kōbō Daishi ikkan no sho*, suggests that this may have to do with the fact that penetration warms up the intestines and was used as a recipe for longevity. See Nakazawa 1991–1992, 3: 535.

. . . . .

Buddhist homosexuality (like Buddhist sexuality in general) is at the point of convergence (or overlap) of several heterogeneous discourses (on the body, society, kingship, mythology, art, power, salvation). The principles that organize this into a more or less coherent (and sometimes *extravagant,* in the etymological sense, "erring outside") discourse are external to it. We thus have several crisscrossing discourses: for example, that of the Buddhist institution, on the danger of desire and on the importance of endogeneity; that of the medieval royal ideology, searching in sexuality (including homosexuality) for a source of legitimacy; a psychological and androcentric discourse, on the superiority of male love and males in general, and so on. We will therefore adopt here several approaches: the first is broadly cultural and sociological, in that it considers the Chinese and Japanese cultural backgrounds and examines the old (but unconvincing) idea that advocacy for homosexuality is a kind of "sour grapes" argument from men uncomfortable with the other sex, or at best a second best for monks deprived of women. A second approach, while still sociological, focuses on the Buddhist institution and considers Buddhist homosexuality as the manifestation of an esprit de corps (where *corps* is understood in both senses of male body and male saṅgha). It is the approach that we have underscored earlier in our discussion of the Vinaya rule. A third approach, moving temporarily away from the sociological mode, focuses on the literary and mythological record and examines the medieval Buddhist discourse on the chigo. While trying to avoid reducing everything to ideology, it remains alert to the ideological nature of this discourse, and considers without complacency its trivial and repressive aspects. For that purpose, the further debasement of homosexuality in Edo discourse is revealing, although it too must not be taken entirely at face value. On the other hand, as Schalow argues, it is significant that the monastic tradition of nanshoku (and in particular Kūkai's legend) was rediscovered, or rather reinvented, in the seventeenth century as "a social heterodoxy legitimizing the sexuality of men in the urban merchant class," at a time when Confucian ideology discouraged personal visions of self and society.[115]

[115] Schalow 1992a: 228.

Chapter 6

BOYS TO MEN

> The teacher of the seven Buddhas is a boy five feet tall
> Whose hair hangs down to his shoulders like clouds.
> (Godaichi Shōgaku)

THE LITERARY TRADITION OF THE CHIGO

WHAT differentiates medieval Japanese Buddhist discourse on male love from other homosexual traditions is its fascination for the chigo. The range covered by chigo literature is vast. From the Heian period onward, the chigo appears in many love poems.[1] However, the most interesting genre is formed by a series of tales called *chigo monogatari* or *otogizōshi*.[2] In these texts, the sexual element is often downplayed, and the narrative unfolds around the concept of friendship between a priest and a youth. This notion of male bonding was preserved until Saikaku, who gives many examples of idealized friendship between chigo and monks and contrasts the chigo with the wakashū or kagema, objects of prostitution. Saikaku further elaborates the notion of youth as an "idealized role not contingent on the reality of youthfulness."[3] This evolution was particularly important in kabuki; after the banning of boy actors from the stage in 1651, it led to the redefinition of the "youth" as a role played by actors outside the stage. This was not entirely new, however, since we find, as early as the Muromachi period, an oxymoronic type of "adult youth."

According to Margaret Childs, "*Chigo monogatari* seem to have been grouped together because of a modern view towards homosexuality as aberrant and hence the most significant characteristic on which to base classification."[4] Reacting against this tendency, Childs wants to focus on the religious elements in an effort to reevaluate the genre—while admitting that some of them lack a religious import. She rejects the idea that

---

[1] See, for instance, the *Goshūi wakashū* compiled by Fujiwara Michitoshi in 1086, or the *Kokon chōmonjū* by Tachibana no Narisue (1254); Nishio and Kishi 1977.

[2] The *chigo monogatari* genre traditionally includes eight representative works: *Aki no yo no nagamonogatari* (A Long Tale for an Autumn Night, ca. 1377), *Genmu monogatari* (The Tale of Genmu), *Ashibiki, Hanamitsu, Matsuho ura monogatari, Toribeyama monogatari, Saga monogatari,* and *Ben no sōshi.*

[3] Schalow 1989: 126

[4] Childs 1980: 128.

these tales were artificial contrivances designed to exonerate the priests from the charge of sexual offence, and sees their message as one about the transiency of life.

The *Aki no yo no monogatari* is representative of the genre. It describes the love between Keikai, a Hieizan monk, and Umewaka, the young son of the *sadaijin* (Minister of the Left) of Hanazono. Because of a tragic misunderstanding, this love leads to a conflict between Enryakuji and Miidera and the subsequent destruction of Miidera. But not in vain: after the suicide of the youth, Keikai, having realized the truth of impermanence, becomes a hermit and eventually reaches awakening. A little before the end of the story, the god Shinra Myōjin appears in a dream to the Miidera monks, and tells them that the chigo was an avatar of Ishiyama Kannon. In the conclusion, the whole affair is presented as a— rather costly and convoluted—*upāya* of the bodhisattva Kannon to bring about the monk's salvation.[5] Thus, the negative elements—the suffering and death of the chigo (an apparent death, since he is actually an avatar of Kannon), the destruction of the temple, and the death of the monks— are finally transformed into positive elements, namely, the conversion and subsequent holiness of the priest. Therefore, the tale is not simply, as Childs argues, a parable for impermanence, with the destruction of Miidera.

In most chigo monogatari, Buddhist morality is preserved. In one of them, however, the *Chigo Kannon engi*, we find a rather interesting twist. In this tale, the bodhisattva Kannon appears as a young novice to reward the devotion of a monk and bring him salvation. We recall stories in which Kannon (Guanyin) appeared as a prostitute to save men, but sex was then an upāya, not a reward. In this case, the reward is short-lived, since the novice dies after three years. To alleviate the priest's sorrow, however, he reveals his true form, that of the eleven-faced Kannon. According to Childs, this text suggests a kind of sanctification of homosexual relationships within the Buddhist community.[6] Even if this is the case, it does not necessarily mean that the text was written merely to justify the monks' homosexual whims. The chigo literature is complex, and we should not be too quick in explaining it away as a mere indulgence on the part of the monks—although it may also be that. In particular, as we will see, textual and mythological constraints are also at play.

---

[5] Ibid., 129; Guth 1987: 18.

[6] See Margaret H. Childs, "Sexuality and Salvation," paper presented at the annual meeting of the Association for Asian Studies (1987). Things did not always end as well, however. In Ueda Akinari's *Ugetsu monogatari* (1776), for instance, we have the story of an anthropophagous monk. After the death of the adolescent whom he loved, the bereaved monk ate his lover's corpse and, having acquired a taste for human flesh, thereafter began to murder travelers to devour them.

Another widespread chigo monogatari is *Ashibiki,* the work of a scholar-monk of Tendai.[7] The story is that of a monk of the Eastern pagoda of Enryakuji, Gen'i, who, after seeing in the vicinity of the Shira-kawa a young lord from Nara, Minbugyō no Tokugyō, falls in love with him, and is loved in return. After all sorts of incidents, the two men end up practicing on Kōyasan, and die after reaching awakening.

Admittedly, these chigo monogatari, despite the tantalizing historical elements they seem to provide, cannot simply be used as documents describing the social reality of homosexuality in medieval Japan. One must first pay attention to their literary nature, and argue that they are liable to a literary critical approach. They are above all "tales," which have, as such, their own logic—which is not the "practical sense" of social actors in the "real" world. This textual logic, as we will see, is at least twofold: literary and mythological. These texts have to be placed first in their literary context, and not read as transparent historical documents. One cannot simply transpose their passages dealing with male love into another literary discourse, that of history, without respecting certain protocols.

Let us raise some preliminary questions. Can we assume that, in various literary genres, we are dealing with the fragments of a discours amoureux, a homogenous discourse on (homo)sexuality that would penetrate all these different genres and be differently refracted through each of them? Can we assume that this discourse would be itself the expression of a social reality? Or rather, is it not that each field, each genre, produces, according to its own structural laws, narratives that would merely have a "family resemblance," without any common ancestor? It would then be an error—or at least a kind of constructive theology—to try to gather all these excerpts (whose meaning was entirely dependent on their literary context) into a unified discourse, which would supposedly explain and help to recover a social reality.

The sufferings of the child in these tales respond above all to a narrative necessity. They are the dramatic devices of a theatrical plot. At another, more philosophical level, they also express the dialectical nature of transgression. Only a naive historicism could take them at face value. Chigo are narrative actors, playing the same narrative function in the tale as the young heroine in traditional love stories. If we try to retrace the genealogy of these written texts, we may encounter other texts, written or oral: namely, their mythological sources. We would thus move from the literary stories (*monogatari*) back to the Buddhist tales (*setsuwa*) and to folklore or myth (*shinwa*). It is doubtful, however, or in any case rela-

---

[7] The title derives from the expression "Ashihiki no (to koso)" used in literature as *makura kotoba* ("pillow-words") of the "Moutain" (*ashihikino*), that is, Hieizan.

tively irrelevant, that we encounter hard-core sociohistorical realities along the way. Such would be the formalist argument.

And yet—and this is the double bind of any interpretation—who would deny that there is a sociohistorical reality framing these stories? Even if their referentiality cannot be taken for granted, there is sufficient evidence to suggest that the social reality of the time was not significantly different. But although, as far as we can tell, at times this reality bears an uncanny resemblance with our texts, one cannot jump to conclusions and decide that the texts simply mirror the reality. We could probably just as well argue that this reality itself is structured along the same fault lines as our texts, or that it is the myth that is mirrored by the reality. Or all of the above. Here again, a superficial resemblance does not necessarily entail a direct influence. A case in point is the story of "the two chigo," for which we have both the "literary" and the "sociological" versions. We will return to this account.

Although these stories have their own structural (literary) dynamics, and that may be the case with the sociohistorical narrative itself, we can still argue that they were used in (or that their dynamics was reinscribed into) specific strategies of power and of ideological justification, in attempts to present an inverted, sublimated, or euphemized image of social relationships. Furthermore, we know that all elements in a narrative are not always equally well integrated into its main plot, and the discrepancies between its subplots may help us to deconstruct this ideological attempt.

In conclusion, the tension between the two types of interpretations—the formalist and the positivist—cannot be simply resolved either by idealization or by a reductionism, let alone by a rather cynical commodification (of the *eroguro* type, aimed at titillating curiosity for the erotic or the grotesque). As Dominick LaCapra points out, "There is . . . no autonomous realm of signification of either literary or documentary language. In brief, formalism is as questionable as positivism."[8] Texts are not mere transparencies through which one could see reality, but neither are they mere opacities. We have to see through them as "through a glass darkly." Before trying to get at the "practical sense" that characterizes social behavior, one must first "be attentive to the fact that all one has are texts that must first be read."[9]

One of the first questions to ask in our case is that of the genre of the chigo monogatari. On the one hand, as Childs has noted, this genre,

---

[8] LaCapra 1989: 19. LaCapra characterizes positivism as "a reductive equalization of all texts and artifacts into a homogeneous body of documentary 'information' or constative statements as well as disavowal of any transferential relation to the object of inquiry" (ibid., 16–17).

[9] Ibid., 72.

despite the common chigo element, seems quite heterogeneous. At any rate, a text can be inscribed in different genres and function in different ways. It always "exceeds or falls short of the expectations genre create."[10] Abe Yoshirō and Hasegawa Masaharu, on the other hand, argue for the inclusion of these texts into the larger monogatari genre, and find that they share many common features that were not seen by Childs.

The few tales mentioned above might provide sufficient formal characteristics—a structure or a plot—to define the chigo monogatari genre. This structure is often theatrical and at times paradoxical: it not only exaggerates the suffering of the hero in order to emphasize the happy ending, it also shows how errors and transgressions can lead eventually to redemption. The general atmosphere is, to use categories that may be inappropriate, tragic and romantic. It recalls the tragic love stories between an emperor and his concubine.

Hasegawa contrasts monastic tales of male love and traditional love stories. In the case of monks, the traditional love plot has been redirected from women to boys. The theoretical symmetry, according to which the transgression is the same whether a monk has sex with a woman or with a boy, is belied by the style and the structure of the stories. If love between a monk and a chigo provides appropriate material for a monogatari, the same is not true in the case of a monk and a woman. Whereas the male love story unfolds in a romantic atmosphere and often ends in tragedy, the heterosexual love affair is usually treated with disrespect, in a comical fashion. The chigo monogatari is paradoxically a story of ascesis, in which the monk eventually sees the light and amends his ways; the female love story is presented as a case of debauchery, which leads to the "defeat" of the luxurious monk. Despite the argument that monks merely replaced women with chigo, the dynamics of the chigo tales, owing to their symbolic and mythologic associations, is very different from that of tales involving female heroines. There is a desire to see the divine in the child. The same is sometimes true in the case of courtesans. But whereas many tales about chigo love turn into full-fledged monogatari, such is apparently not the case of monks falling in love with a woman. The tragic element is usually lacking in the latter stories, which remain at the erotic or comic (sometimes grotesque) level. A case in point is that of the *Sasayakitake monogatari,* mentioned earlier. Whereas the love of the priest for the young girl is met only with derision and punishment, the romantic element is reported on the love of the young official for the girl.

The setsuwa literature about depraved monks having affairs with women, for all its erotic and grotesque elements, is essentially didactic;

---

[10] Ibid., 76.

by ridiculing the depraved monks, it tends to reinforce social and religious norms. In contrast, the case of the chigo stories is more ambivalent. Religious values are indeed asserted, in the sense that the monk usually achieves some sort of insight. But this insight is achieved through the homosexual relationship, a feature that seems to imply a subversion of social norms. Both the setsuwa and the medieval monogatari obey their own dynamics, and their goal is not the same. Thus, homosexual stories are presented ultimately as narratives of ascesis and redemption, whereas heterosexual stories are often narratives about sensuality and spiritual failure. As noted earlier, the gravity of the sexual act is determined as much by the genre of the partner as by a spatial metaphor: whereas the woman is entirely Other because she lives outside the monastery bounds, the chigo is a relative Other—the other within, a familiarity that at times makes him uncanny (*unheimlich*). Thus, sex with a woman not only breaks the Vinaya rule but transgresses the spatial boundaries, threatening the community in a way that chigo love, in principle, does not. In practice, however, we recall that chigo and kasshiki were the source of desire and discord in medieval monasteries.

If the *chigo monogatari* can be read as a description, not simply of a platonic love but of the sexual relations between the chigo and the monk, they also have a significant mystical aspect, which seems at first glance to add little to the sexual plot. The chigo is often perceived as a manifestation of Fugen or Kannon, or of a kami. In many cases, the narrative ends with the conversion or awakening of the main protagonist, the priest.[11] The *Saga monogatari*, however, leaves the reader with the impression of increasingly deeper relations between the monk and the chigo. We have here a tale that does not represent the chigo merely as an object of sectarian or political rivalries but seems to reflect a widespread mythological pattern, that of the relations between the young god and his protector.

Clearly, the chigo monogatari do not always follow the expectations of the genre. In the *Matsuho ura monogatari*, for instance, the usual morality is entirely absent. The chigo of this tale is a more positive and active hero, who embarks on a journey to search for his lover, a monk exiled at Matsuho no ura. After describing the reunion between the two lovers, the tale concludes with a kind of "and they lived happy ever after," without even mentioning any religious awakening. There is no sense of guilt here, let alone of redemption. Furthermore, the perspective has radically changed, since the story is told from the viewpoint of the boy and not that of the monk. The chigo, usually a passive figure both sexually and narratively, assumes now a more active role. In this story he is no longer a

---

[11] See, for instance, *Aki no yo no monogatari,* or *Toribe monogatari,* in *Gunsho ruiju* 14, 311.

mere object of desire, and a cause of disputes between monks or between monasteries.

The chigo monogatari is actually a mixed genre, derived in part from Heian love literature but also from legendary literature (*engi, setsuwa, honji*) and, at another level, from folklore and mythology. The influence of these "mythological" genres contributed to giving a more positive, yet at the same time ambivalent, image of the chigo and of his relationship with the monk. We find, for instance, in *Matsuho ura monogatari* a narrative development structurally similar to that found in another genre, the *honji monogatari*, or tales about the *honji*, that is, the buddha or bodhisattva who is the "true nature" of a local god. It seems that some of these chigo monogatari were influenced by contact with the medieval honji monogatari, even if the two genres remain perfectly distinct. As to the reason behind the production of these tales, Hasegawa, far from seeing these chigo tales as an attempt at self-justification on the part of monks, thinks that they were produced as a "prayer to the chigo," seen as a manifestation of a buddha or kami.

In Japanese folklore, too, the chigo was a familiar figure. The legend of the chigo stone, for instance, tells how a chigo, upon receiving a letter from his lover, went to the evening rendezvous at some distance from the temple, and waited there all night long, despite the falling snow. In the morning he was found dead with a strange smile on his lips, holding a large stone in his arms. Villagers buried him there, and on his grave they placed the stone, which became known as the chigo stone. Another legend has to do with the chigo pine, a pine that was planted on the grave of a chigo, who had died during a pilgrimage. Minakata Kumagusu, by pointing out that the chigo's death was allegedly caused by his giving birth, argues that he was actually a girl disguised as a boy.[12] There are also *chigo-zuka* (chigo funerary mounds) for novices who died before being ordained as monks, and who could not be buried within the temple, so were buried instead on a roadside under a tree.

The Suffering Child

The themes of monogatari can thus often be traced back to mythological motifs. The emergence of a "chigo narrative" appears to have developed from the medieval motif of the "suffering god" in the so-called honji monogatari. The sufferings of the child may be interpreted as the "pas-

---

[12] There are many cases of transvestism in Japanese legend, for instance that of Yoshitsune's lover, Shizuka, who in the *Gikyōki* disguised herself as a chigo to enter Heisenji, a Shugendō center at the foot of Hakusan. See Abe 1989b.

sion" of a god in one of his former lives as a human.[13] However, we seem to witness only the positive aspect of the god, who reveals his true nature after (and as a result of) experiencing all kinds of hardships in his previous lives, and the theme of sexual love—a leitmotif of the chigo monogatari—is absent.

The same structure is also found in otogizōshi such as "Tada Michinaka." In this tale, Michinaka sends his son Binyo Gozen (literally "handsome girl") to Chūzanji to study. Binyo finds interest only in martial arts, however, and does not learn a single line of the scriptures. His father becomes enraged and orders his vassal Nakamitsu to kill the child. Nakamitsu substitutes his own son Kōshumaru, however, and brings the latter's head, pretending that it is that of Binyo. This Kōshumaru was the perfect chigo, handsome and diligent, loved by everyone, in sharp contrast to Binyo.[14] He represents the classical form of the chigo in the monogatari. Thus, his cruel death is not an accident but the expression of the vicarious suffering that is the destiny of these divine chigo. Furthermore, Binyo too eventually becomes a kind of wandering chigo, abandoned by his parents. The tale thus spreads the suffering of the chigo over two "actants." However Binyo, not too surprisingly, meets Jūzenji on his way. Thanks to the god, he finds refuge with a priest, Eshin sōzu, who ordains him as a monk under the name of Engaku. Some time later, Eshin goes with his disciple to the village of Tada, and preaches Michinaka while the child reads the scriptures. Owing to this, his mother, who had become blind for crying too much over her lost son, is cured, and the reunion between parents and child takes place in joy. In order to perform services in the memory of Kōshumaru, a temple is founded, Shōdōji (Temple of the Child), whose *honzon* (object of worship) will be the chigo Monju (Mañjuśrī as a child). Thus the story, while telling the origins of this temple, shows a chigo (monk) converted by Jūzenji. The suffering and death of the chigo Kōshumaru, which served as the prerequisite for the salvation of the other protagonists, seem to be part of Jūzenji's design.[15]

These stories, first developed as tales about the origin of certain Tendai temples, made their way into the chigo monogatari. The motif of the sufferings of the chigo was included to express the theme of the hierophany at the sacred place. In the tale of Aigomaru, for instance, the nature of the god Sannō Gongen is revealed through the ordeals of a youth named Aigomaru. The youth is punished after being accused by his stepmother of having sold a precious object belonging to his father. In his exile, Aigomaru receives help from a monkey, from a weasel who is none other

---

[13] Hasegawa Masaharu has also shown the progressive shift from stories about children given by the gods (*mōshigo*) to chigo tales. See Hasegawa 1987.

[14] Abe 1993: 308.

[15] Ibid., 309.

than his late mother, and from marginal people living in the mountain. However, mistaken by his uncle for a tengu, he is driven away from the mountain and beaten to death by an old woman. Seized by remorse, all the protagonists, beginning with his parents, kill themselves. They come to be worshiped as the kami of the 108 shrines of Sannō. We find in this tale many elements of the chigo monogatari connected to the genealogical story (*engi*) of the god. The death of the scapegoat brings a catharsis and prefigures the rebirth of the god. The source of the chigo's misery, namely, the illicit love of his stepmother for him, brings to mind the love of the monks for the chigo. This love, which was in the chigo monogatari both a source of disaster and the distant cause of the god's hierophany and of salvation, has now been transferred to the folkloric motif of the illicit love of the stepmother.[16]

THE "DIVINE CHILD" MYSTIQUE

The figure of the child was idealized and sometimes perceived as a youthful incarnation of bodhisattvas like Kannon, Monju, or Fugen. The same feeling of love and respect was addressed to the figures of Kūkai and Shōtoku Taishi as chigo. Until the Insei period they were represented as adults, and it is only from that time onward that they came to be represented as children. Shōtoku himself was widely perceived as an avatar of Kannon, and it is significant that, for a ritual that took place at Hōryūji in 1069, his representation as a seven-year-old child was chosen as honzon instead of Guze Kannon.[17] The image of Shōtoku as the "incomplete emperor"—who had ruled Japan as crown prince—became, paradoxically, the ideal of the perfect emperor, and this image seems related to the changes that led, during the Insei period, to the "infantilization" of puppet emperors under the rule of retired emperors. It is also toward the same time that one sees the emergence of the cult of the *wakamiya,* or young gods. Not too surprisingly, the Fujiwara elites who sponsored such cults were also known for their taste for young boys. Another related phenomenon is the fashion of unisex clothing or cross-dressing. Whereas men began to shave their beard and their eyebrows and to wear makeup,

[16] Although this is nowhere explicit, Aigomaru also seems to become identified with the god Jūzenji. The fact that a monkey accompanies him everywhere perhaps reveals the nature of this chigo. We will see that the monkey is the emissary of Sannō, and the *suijaku* (manifested trace) form of Daigyōji. It is said in the *Keiran shūyōshū* that "Jūzenji became a monkey to preach to the monkeys and to save beings." From the standpoint of the chigo monogatari, Aigomaru is thus none other than a figure of the chigo as a manifestation of the sacrality of Hieizan. See Abe 1993: 310.

[17] See Matsuoka 1993: 265.

female dancers called *shirabyōshi* took on male attire, paving the way to the gender inversion that would later characterize nō and kabuki.

According to Matsuoka Shinpei, this attraction for adolescence and ambiguous gender can be connected to changes in the imperial system. With the dissolution of the Ritsuryō system and the ascendency of the Fujiwara regents, the emperor had lost his political power but had gained instead symbolic prestige, through the image of the "child-emperor." The return to power of the retired emperor in the Insei period did not revert this tendency; on the contrary.[18] There is therefore a symbolic equivalence between the chigo of the Buddhist temples (as avatars of the kamis or of bodhisattvas like Kannon) and the emperor. This equivalence would be played out in the chigo *abhiṣeka* (*chigo kanjō*), as it developed in Tendai as a Buddhist replica of the imperial accession rite (*sokui kanjō*).[19]

All these figures inherit features from the cult of the divine boy in Japanese folklore. Folkloric motifs regarding the child cover a wide range, from the suffering god to the recalcitrant child. The child is not always as passive and silent as in classic chigo tales. In the *Seisuishō*, for instance, we find the story of the chigo of a priest on Mount Hiei, who was ill with smallpox and secluded himself for seven days to pray to the Healing Buddha, Yakushi, but received no auspicious sign. In anger, he composed a poem to express his resentment to Yakushi. No sooner had he read it, than the buddha's voice was heard from the outside, answering his poem with another. The fact that a similar story is often told about the the courtesan Izumi Shikibu suggests a kind of functional equivalence between chigo and courtesans.[20] Izumi Shikibu and Ono no Komachi represent a type of women who, due to their poetic talents, were able to achieve a certain degree of independence.[21] We often encounter the theme of the scholar or priest defeated by a woman or a chigo.[22] In

---

[18] Yoshimura Shigeki has calculated that sixteen was the average age of accession during the fourteen imperial generations of the Regent period, from emperors Yōsei to Goreizei, whereas the average reign was a little over fifteen years. During the twenty-three imperial generations from the beginning of the Insei period until the reign of Go-Daigo, however, the average age of accession was slightly lower than nine, and the average reign ten years. See Yoshimura 1955, quoted in Matsuoka 1993: 267. As Matsuoka points out, the ten years of reign of these adolescent emperors overlapped precisely with that of their chigo status.

[19] Matsuoka 1993: 267.

[20] See Yanagita 1990c: 377.

[21] On this question, see Faure, *Purity and Gender,* forthcoming.

[22] To give just a few examples: the dialogue between Confucius and the child (in Soymié 1956); the dialogue between the Chan monk Deshan and the old woman, in *Biyan lu,* T. 48, 2003: 143c; Saigyō and the *modoshi-matsu* ("Pine Tree of Returning," for instance near Zuiganji in Matsushima), in Yanagita 1990a: 504.

medieval Japan, as elsewhere, truth is found in the mouths of children. Was not the chigo, living in an institutional and sexual limbo, also the embodiment of a certain quasi-divine freedom (which may be just the other side of his powerlessness)? The chigo's status was not clearly determined and, as a lay person in a clerical environment, straddling childhood and adulthood, he enjoyed some of the privileges of the trickster, or of a mediator between the sacred and the profane. This aspect of the chigo also reflects the status of the child in medieval Japan.

This image of the child as it developed in the chigo stories provides us with one of the bridges—an unsecure footbridge, really—between fiction (legend or literature) and social reality. Let us examine briefly the socio-historical evidence as it has been derived from another artistic genre, painted scrolls (*emaki*). The fact that many playing children appear in the emaki has prompted some scholars to claim that children were extremely free in premodern Japan. Such freedom was due not only to their lack of responsibility but to a kind of inherent sacredness.[23] Amino Yoshihiko mentions, for instance, several juridical cases at the turn of the twelfth century, in which children were arrested for participating in violent acts (throwing stones, arson, and so on). In one instance, the case of a child suspected for having set fire to the Hachimangū, Emperor Shirakawa himself intervened and declared that because of his youth the child could not be questioned. This suggests that the authorities' handling of children was different from the way they handled adults. Because of their special status, children also came to play a significant role in the political scene. Taira Kiyomori, for instance, was using groups of youths to implement his strategies. According to the *Heike monogatari*:

> Kiyomori had hit on the notion of recruiting 300 messenger boys, from 14 to 16 years of age, whom he sent ranging over the city in page-boy haircuts and *hitatare*. If anyone chanced to speak against the Heike, nothing happened if none of those youths heard him. Otherwise, the boy would alert his comrades, and a gang of them would burst into the person's house, confiscate his belongings, and march him off under arrest to Rokuhara. . . . The very words "The Rokuhara Lord's page-boy cuts" were enough to make horsemen and carriages swerve from their paths. There was no question of demanding a boy's name if

[23] On what follows, See Amino 1993: 52–67. Miyamoto Honjō even speaks of the "sacred child" (*shinseina dōji*). See also Kuroda 1986b: 217–30. Kuroda argues that the buddhas and kami appear as children, old men, and women. See also Tanabe Miwako, "Chūsei no 'dōji' ni tsuite," *Nenpō chūseishi kenkyū* 9 (quoted in Amino 1993), who follows Miyamoto, while showing that the plaints of *warawa* (adolescents) were well accepted, and that the children were seen as very close to the gods and buddhas.

he went in and out of the imperial palace gates; the officials seemed to avert their eyes.[24]

According to medieval standards, a person became responsible at fifteen. As the saying goes: "Above, sixty; below, fifteen."[25] These ages marked the limits between which male individuals were taxable and subject to corvée and criminal punishment. Various rites of passage socialized the child into gendered adulthood. At seven, for instance, children began to work. A child who died before that age received no funerary rites, and his corpse was merely abandoned in a bag.[26] The major rite was the coming-of-age ceremony (*genpuku*), by which a male adolescent exchanged his child's name for an adult's name, and adopted a hairstyle that would clearly indicate his gender. Before that ceremony, children were not yet officially gendered, and thus they remained close to the gods: "Until seven, child of the kami." This proximity to the divine explains their role as mediums.

The sacred character of the child is particularly evident in divination. The medieval custom of using young male and female children as *yorimashi* (mediums) to summon kamis and demons in ritual exorcisms seems to originate in the Tantric rite of *āveśa*.[27] A famous case was the ritual performed by Vajrabodhi with two seven-year-old girls to attempt to cure a daughter of the emperor Xuanzong. Here is how Zanning describes this event: "The ritual of the Five Division Maṇḍala, in order to summon demonic entities, must make use of the medium of young lads and virgin girls. [If this is done,] expelling illness and doing away with misfortune is a simple matter. People of recent times have attempted to use the ritual for physical and material profit, and so it has had little effect. Hence, in our time the ritual is held in contempt. Alas that the Correct Law has been diluted to this extent!"[28] Kūkai's master Huiguo also performed a divination ritual in front of the emperor with eight young boys. Many of these rites of āveśa, in which a god or demon possessed the child and spoke through his/her mouth, were placed under the authority of Guanyin/Kannon. Likewise, the Ennen no mai, or "life-prolonging dance," was danced only by boys (*dōji*).[29] In the *Fukū ken-*

[24] See McCullough 1988: 28. *Hitatare* is a kind of blouse worn by nobles and warriors in the Kamakura period.

[25] These limits varied with the period. In the Heian period the adult age was from twenty-one to sixty, whereas in the medieval period it was from fifteen to sixty. On this question, see Kuroda 1986: 218–221.

[26] Ibid., 223–226.

[27] See, for instance, *Hōbōgirin*, vol. 1, s.v. "abesha"; and Strickmann 1996: 216–21.

[28] See Zanning's addendum to Vajrabodhi's biography in *Song gaoseng zhuan* T. 50, 2061: 711c.

[29] See, for instance, Honda 1969: 1045–49 and passim.

saku shinpen shingon kyō, for instance, a dragon, through the power of mantras, turns into a boy and gives the "sweet dew" that prolongs life to the practitioners.

Puer Ludens

Whereas the children used for divination were usually under seven, the older chigo had often lost some of their childish innocence. In the world of the monasteries, the chigo was a kind of artist, an indispensable presence in all banquets and poetical contests, and often the object of infatuation on the part of his admirers.[30] The *Jikkinshō* contains the exchange of *waka* (poems) during the cherry-blossom festival of Daigoji, where an adolescent dance (*warawa-mai*) is described, and the priest Sōjun falls in love with the youth who performed it, sending him a love poem on the next day.[31] Likewise, in the *Kokon chōmonjū*, Suke no hōin, a priest of Ninnaji, sees an adolescent during the cherry-blossom festival of Daigoji and composes a poem. The adolescent dances of Daigoji during this festival are described in the *Tengu zōshi,* and were the occasion for the blossoming of love. There was apparently an association between the beauty of the chigo and that of the cherry blossoms, both transient. At any rate, the medieval love for the chigo had, in its depths, a religious background.[32]

The chigo spent much of his time in artistic performance, and it seems that his activity was perceived as a religious activity, a form of "sacrality." We find, for instance, in the *Bizei betsu,* a booklet of oral traditions left by Jien, a section on the four maṇḍalas that contains a passage on the chigo and their "play" (*asobi*). Jien notes that the thirty-seven worthies of the Dharma maṇḍala are represented as women, and he sees some deeper meaning in this. Such meaning, which must remain hidden from common people because it would merely confuse them, is that awakening is inseparable from attachment to sensual desire. The passage is followed by this comparison: "Like the children and adolescents who erroneously apply their mind to banquets, archery, and so on, as well as go, sugoroku, and so on, in the same way this spirit of play turns to reading Buddhist and non-Buddhist texts, performing lectures, arts, ceremonies, and discussing commentaries. Thus, they become experts. With a mind fiercely

---

[30] In the works of Prince Shukaku (second son of Emperor Go-Shirakawa, 1150–1202) from Ninnaji, there is a text entitled *Uki,* which explains Shingon to the profane. The first part, in particular, explains the etiquette for chigo in monasteries. In twenty-five rubrics, it describes the appropriate behavior during banquets, attitude vis-à-vis alcohol, makeup for poetic gatherings, and so on. The emphasis is on elegance in all details—not only dressing—and it reflects the extreme popularity of chigo in the feasts of the time.

[31] See *Jikkinshō* 10; and *Kokon chōmonjū* 5, quoted in Nishio and Kishi 1977.

[32] Abe 1993: 298.

burning with error, one can know the mind fiercely burning with awakening."[33]

Thus, in the same way that chigo immersed themselves in play, they could also plunge themselves into study. Likewise, those who could concentrate on all Buddhist practices, as if "just gaming," would naturally obtain the way. Admittedly, the chigo plays only a metaphorical role here, but this metaphor is closely related to other elements in Jien's thought. The play of the chigo provides a necessary preliminary to understanding the nonduality between profane and sacred. In Jien's mind, the image of the chigo at play becomes tied not only to the idea of (homo)sexual desire but also to the study and the awakening of the monks. For him, the love for the chigo is inseparable from the realization of the sacred. We see in this secret confession of Jien that the chigo played an essential role in the monasteries, and his play is more than a metaphor.[34] Whereas the "literary" chigo was represented as a passive victim, the development of his divine nature in Tendai genealogical tales (*engi*) leads to a more dynamic and ambivalent figure in which the sexual element becomes more visible.

Jūzenji

The well-known line, "First, the chigo, second, Sannō" (*ichi chigo, ni Sannō*) is often interpreted as a cynical comment on the fact that Hieizan monks were more interested in boys than in their protecting deity, Sannō.[35] In the Tendai tradition, however, the interpretation of this passage is somewhat different. In his *Gonshin shō* (1414), the Tendai priest Enshun distinguishes, for instance, between two forms of the deity: the fundamental Sannō, who dwells on the top of the mountain, and his manifestation or "trace" (*suijaku*), who dwells at its foot. He continues: "When the fundamental master [Saichō] climbed for the first time on the mountain, he first met a chigo, then Sannō. 'First a chigo' means Jūzenji, 'then Sannō' means Ōmiya Gongen. This passage deals with the 'great event' (*daiji*) of the Chronicles, the arcana of the *abhiṣeka*, and I cannot say more."[36]

The *ichi chigo, ni Sannō* constitutes here the essential aspect of the story of Saichō climbing on Mount Hiei, one of the secrets that were transmitted during the kanjō or abhiṣeka ritual. We find the same "mystery" in the *Sanke yōryaku ki*, a collection of stories about Hieizan com-

[33] See *Bizei betsu*, in *Zoku Tendaishū zensho*, Mikkyō 3, Kyōten chūshakurui II, edited by Tendai shūten hensanjo (Tokyo: Shunjūsha, 1990), 229.

[34] See Abe 1993: 299.

[35] See, for instance, Leupp 1995: 38.

[36] *Gonshin shō*, in *Zoku gunsho ruijū* 49: 642a.

piled toward the end of Kamakura by a "chronicler" (*kike*) named Gigen. In a recension of this text dated 1315, we find a section about Saichō's climb to Hieizan in 785. At that time, we are told, the sky became dark, lightning struck, the earth shook. Saichō explored the mountain until the third month of the following year. Then comes a section on his "encounter with Jūzenji":

> In the forests of the northern ridge, [Saichō] met a divine youth and asked him who he was. The youth replied: "I am the divine child of the warp and woof of heaven and earth. I am the god Dōshōjin who controls the fundamental destiny of beings. I have three names: (1) Dōshōten, because I am the god through whom all beings are born alike; (2) Yūgyōjin, because I govern the revolution (*yūgyō*) of the fundamental destiny of beings; and (3) Jūzenji, because I give to the beings of the ten (*jū*) directions the food of bliss of dhyāna (*zen*), and I am the master (*shi/ji*) who ties their karmic affinities for the future and who can teach them."[37]

Then the god gave Saichō a verse.

The *Gonshin shō* gives the following etymology for the name Jūzenji: he is an avatar of Ninigi, a grandson of the sun-goddess Amaterasu, and it is at the tenth (*jū*) divine generation that he received (*zen*) a divine body and came down to this world. His coming thus marks the beginning of the imperial lineage. The *Yōtenki* gives yet another etymology: there was once at Kōshakuji in Yokawa a group of ten dhyāna masters (*jū zenji*) of great virtue, endowed with both wisdom and practice. The mountain god Sannō manifested himself as one of them, who therefore took this name.[38]

Jien and Jūzenji

Jien's interest for the chigo is documented in a text of the later Hieizan tradition, the *Rō no miko ki* (1603), in which female mediums of the Hie shrine—namely those of Ninomiya, the shrine dedicated to Jūzenji—tell the story of their origins.[39] In particular they attempt to trace their origin back to Jien through the "miraculous birth" of a god named "August child of the corridor" (Ro no miko).[40] Here Jūzenji assumed the form of a chigo and served Jien for two years. The text mentions the *saihai (saiwai) no mono* left behind in the Hieizan valley as a result of their encounters, and the term seems to refer to semen. This

---

[37] Quoted in Abe 1993: 304.

[38] *Zoku gunsho ruijū* 49: 642a; 48: 587b.

[39] See Yamamoto 1995: 23.

[40] Note the similarity with the birth of the legendary Izumi Shikibu from the semen of the hermit Unicorn; and of the birth of the *kawaramono* at Tiantongsi. See Faure 1996: 21.

"leftover," without passing through a female womb, grew into a child, who was subsequently worshiped as Daigyōji Gongen, a subaltern deity of Hieizan. The fact that the abandoned child, avatar of Jūzenji, is no other than the chigo himself, seems clear from another passage. We know that children played a central role in Jūzenji's revelations. The manifestation of Jūzenji as a chigo is obviously related to these child-mediums. Thus, we must keep in mind that they are the form used by the narrative imagination to explain the source of the oracles, that is, of the god as chigo. The basic elements that are found in the chigo tales (the relation of the chigo and the monk, the abandonment of the chigo, his manifestation as "sacred being") also circulate in our story. The sacredness of Hieizan is also revealed in the comments added in 1737 by a monk named Chūzen to the *Rō no miko ki*: "Reverend Jichin [that is, Jien], as he was too deeply immersed in debauchery, found it increasingly difficult to stay on the mountain, and he was thinking of leaving [Hieizan]. Sannō took pity on him and, in order to make him stay for a long time on the mountain, Jūzenji took the form of a chigo. Every night, perched on the shoulder of a monkey, he came to comfort the heart of Jichin."[41]

These texts are admittedly the products of a later period, but we know that Jien did indeed worship Jūzenji, and that the dream oracles or predictions received by Jien during several years toward the time of the Jō-kyū War (1221) were given by Shōtoku Taishi or Jūzenji Gongen.[42] Also, the *ganmon* (vow) addressed by Jien to Shōtoku Taishi in 1224 was addressed again later to Jūzenji. Thus, both figures seem to have been indissociable for Jien. Furthermore, Jūzenji seems to have symbolized the sacredness of Hiei Sannō as a whole, and Jien performed many ceremonies for him until the end of his life.[43]

In the medieval period, according to the Sannō maṇḍala, Jūzenji manifested himself as a young monk—because he was perceived as an avatar of Jizō. In the texts of Sannō Shintō, too, he is often a monk, but we also find descriptions of him as a youth (*dōji*), probably because of his nature as giver of oracles. The image of Jūzenji preserved at Enryakuji depicts him as a chigo worshiped by two monkeys. Why is this god who appears principally as a monk also represented as a chigo? These two forms express the two complementary aspects that constitute his sacredness. For instance, in the relation that causes the monk to obtain awakening owing to the chigo, or the instance where the chigo appears as "sacred" near the monk, doesn't Jūzenji show his function as a god? In short, the legend of

---

[41] See Abe 1993: 301–2.
[42] See Yamamoto 1995: 29–30.
[43] Abe 1993: 302.

the love between Jien and the chigo, avatar of Jūzenji, tells us that sacrality is revealed in its essence through the sexual relationship between monk and chigo.[44]

The image of Jūzenji as chigo was perceived by priests like Jien as that of a medium-child. However, another image seems to have emerged, that of a mystical chigo having sexual relations with eminent monks and bringing them to enlightenment. This is probably a manifestation of the double nature of the god who reappears as chigo. When Jien considered the "deep play" of the chigo to be the preliminary condition to the awakening of the monk, or claimed that (sacred) sex is the secret gateway to sacrality, he probably just expressed the deep structures of medieval religiosity. Jūzenji, as *wakamiya* (divine child) of Sannō, was related to the chigo who symbolized the flourishing vital force of youth. Since Jien himself gives the spirit of desire as the driving force of his awakening, it is clear that salvation through sex with a chigo was in accord with the will of the tutelary deity of Hieizan, Sannō Gongen, and it seems that Jien had interiorized the secret tradition of medieval Tendai.[45]

Perhaps Jien himself was not always, as the legend seems to indicate, an active partner in his relations with the chigo. At least in his dreams, the roles were sometimes inverted. In 1210, he reports that in a dream he had sex with Emperor Go-Toba, "like husband and wife." This dream, in which he plays the female role, recalls another dream in which he saw in symbolic fashion the sexual union of the emperor with his "jade woman." In the first dream, it is Jien himself who takes on the role of the "jade woman," sexual initiator of an emperor who is twenty-five younger than he is. Go-Toba was at the time a young man in his twenties, and could almost have been a chigo. For monks like Jien, it seems that the trivial aspects of the sexual relationship could be dissolved by the rhetoric of nonduality, which led to a kind of sacralization of daily life.

On the basis of Jūzenji's story, the association between Sannō Gongen and the chigo became common.[46] This meant that the chigo of Hieizan were not perceived as ordinary chigo but as avatars of the god. Saichō himself is credited with a vow to be reborn as a chigo on Hieizan, and furthermore with a request that Hiei monks do not beat the chigo. These stories were taken up by the "chroniclers" (*kike*). In the *Sannō ekotoba*, a collection of prodigies of Sannō, a revelation from Ōmiya Gongen explains that Jūzenji protects children who have left their family in order to come to Mount Hiei. The text gives several other stories illustrating this function of Jūzenji. One of them is that of the priest Chūkai, a member of

---

[44] Ibid., 303.
[45] Tanaka 1989: 114. See also Yamamoto 1995.
[46] See, for instance, *Shokoku ikkenshō monogatari,* quoted in Abe 1993: 305.

the Taira family. When he was young, his father went to the Hie shrine to pray to Sannō, and received an oracle requesting him to consecrate his son to Jūzenji. After the Taira defeat, Chūkai was made a prisoner and was condemned to death. One night, he dreamt that a monkey tied to his sleeve a flower whose light illuminated his body, then became the light of the lamps in the Main Hall of Enryakuji. That same night, Jūzenji appeared in a dream to Yoritomo in the form of a young monk, and asked him to spare Chūkai. Yoritomo obeyed him.

In another story, a governor of Sanuki named Senkō was returning to the capital when a typhoon sank his ship. Everyone died except for a three-year-old child who was miraculously stranded on the shore. His cries attracted a big monkey who then fed him roots and fruit. For five years the child was nourished by the monkey, until a yamabushi discovered him and took him home. At the age of ten the child fell ill, and a female medium of the post-station (*shuku*) of Tadaguchi was called. The spirit of the child's father manifested itself and revealed that the post-station's owner was the child's very own mother. The spirit also revealed that the child had been saved by Sannō, and was therefore to become one of the god's attendants (*kenzoku*). After the patron of the post-station recognized the child as her own son, another oracle from Jūzenji declared that the child, because of his karmic affinities with the god, was to be sent to Hieizan to become a priest.[47]

These two legends revolve around the help brought to a priest of Hieizan by Jūzenji. The function of Jūzenji as a protector of children is made clear. However, to protect these children, the god requires their prior suffering.[48] Jien's devotion to the chigo as avatar of Jūzenji—that is, Jizō—is not very different from the devotion to the chigo as avatar of Kannon, as we saw it in the *Chigo Kannon engi* and other related texts. The buddhas and kamis appear in the form of a chigo and, through his devotion to the child, the monk receives the protection of the god and eventually obtains salvation.

The Legend of Jidō

The chigo, with their intermediate status between the sacred and the profane, also played an important role in the medieval elaboration of Japa-

---

[47] Ibid., 307.

[48] Another feature of these two legends is the presence of a monkey. In the second case the monkey appears as a foster parent. The monkey is usually represented as an emissary or an avatar of Sannō in Tendai literature, but here it seems associated with Daigyōji, one of the acolytes of Jūzenji at the Ninomiya shrine. This deity is represented as a layman with a monkey's head. We have also seen that in the *Rō no miko ki*, the chigo had been nurtured by the offerings of both Daigyōji and Jūzenji. Thus, through the figure of the monkey, Daigyōji seems functionally similar to Jūzenji.

nese imperial ideology. The most important aspect of the conscious "mythologization" of (or reinscription of the literary theme and of its origins into) the chigo tradition is probably the legend of Jidō. This legend appears in many texts of the Tendai tradition, such as the *Tendai sokui hō,* and in the nō tradition with plays like "Makura Jidō." Although its variants are often significant, we can only give its outline here. The story is located in the distant Chinese mythological past, opening with the reign of King Mu. This king had received eight heavenly horses, with which he roamed through the world. He happened to visit the Vulture Peak at the time when the Buddha was preaching the *Lotus Sūtra.* The Buddha entrusted him with an eight-line verse that would help him rule his kingdom. This verse, centered on the Sanskrit name of the *Lotus Sūtra,* became a secret formula to be transmitted only at the time of the enthronement of a new ruler. Now King Mu (or in a significant variant, the first Chinese Emperor Qing Shihuangdi) was in love with a youth named Jidō (Compassionate Child). Unfortunately, Jidō committed a serious breach of etiquette by stepping over or breaking the emperor's pillow, and thus he was sentenced to death by jealous ministers. The ruler was only able to commute this sentence into exile. Fearing that Jidō would not survive the dangers of the wilderness, he transmitted to him a section of the secret verse, ordering him to recite it daily for his own protection. Jidō followed his instructions, and in order better to remember the lines he wrote them down on the leaves of chrysanthemums, in the desolate mountain which had become his abode. Due to the supernatural protection of the *Lotus Sūtra,* he eventually became an immortal, known by the name of Pengzu (actually an avatar of the bodhisattva Kannon). Having reached the age of six hundred years, he transmitted the verse to another ruler, Emperor Wendi of the Wei. The water of the river by which he lived, sanctified by the leaves of the chrysanthemums that had fallen in it, became a water of life, bringing longevity to the inhabitants of the town downstream. This "crysanthemum water" (*kikusui*) became the source of the Chrysanthemum Festival, a festival still celebrated in Japan on November eleventh each year.[49] More impor-

---

[49] Here is how a "Pillow Book" of the Edo period, the *Onna Imakawa oshiebumi,* describes the "Union of the Chrysanthemums": "On the ninth day of the ninth moon occurs the union of the chrysanthemums, after a banquet during which many wines are served: one celebrates that day by practicing the way of the youths. In China, Emperor Mu, during the Zhou period, used to take the crysanthemum seat (*kikuza*) of the youth Jidō, a delight of particular taste whose pleasure is said to last seven hundred years. It is a felicitous example of entertainment, and this is why one calls young boys 'chrysanthemum seats.' On the ninth moon, the moon of the chrysanthemums, one takes the seat of similar name, and it is reported that this ensures a long life. Based on that precedent, one has spoken since of the union of the chrysanthemums." See Cholley 1997: 48.

tantly perhaps, the verse transmitted to Jidō, and then from him to Emperor Wendi, became the core of a rite of enthronement performed in medieval Tendai.

According to Matsuoka, the legend, by reiterating the motif of the transmission of Buddhist legitimacy to the emperor, first in the "world of light" (from the Buddha on Vulture Peak to King Mu), then in the "world of darkness" (from Jidō/Pengzu to the Wei emperor), shows not only the complementarity between Buddhist Law (*buppō*) and imperial law (*ōbō*), and the superiority of the former over the latter, but also the fact that the Tendai teaching, present in both worlds (of "light" and "darkness"), transcends them both. Matsuoka underscores the symbolic equivalences between the phases of the legend and those of the enthronement ritual. The first transmission, that of the eight verses of the *Lotus Sūtra* from Śākyamuni to King Mu on Vulture Peak corresponds to the transmission on Hieizan, in the "world of light," from the Tendai high priest to the emperor. Several Buddhist legends reinforce this identification between Hieizan and Vulture Peak. The transmission of the two verses from Jidō, now Pengzu, to Emperor Wendi corresponds to the transmission from the chigo, taking place in the "world of darkness," also on Hieizan.[50]

Again we are confronted with the motif of the suffering of the divine (or immortal) child. However, the sexual element has become more conspicuous. This may be due in part to the influence of the hongaku theory and its assertion of the identity between passions and awakening. The sexual act committed by the king (or the priest) with a youth perceived as an avatar of Kannon becomes in itself a sacred act—one that will sanctify (and be sanctified in return by) the enthronement ritual. The point that the enthronement rite appeared through the intermediary of sex (and more precisely homosexual sex) is elaborated in the *chigo kanjō*, a ritual of the Eshin branch of Tendai.[51] Similar sexual interpretations of ritual can be found in the Genshi kimyōdan ritual of the rival branch of Tendai, the Danna-ryū, as well as in the Tachikawa branch of Shingon.[52] Shihuangdi's transmission of the secret verse to Jidō is perceived as both a Buddhist anointment (*abhiṣeka*, that is, an ordination) and an imperial enthronement: the chigo is thereby raised (ideally) to the status of a king or emperor. This rite also legitimizes the love between monks and chigo, emphasizing its sexual aspect: "The love and affection of this emperor [Shihuangdi] came from his having sex with males (*nanbon*)." Further-

---

[50] Matsuoka 1993: 271–72.

[51] This ritual is described in the *Chigo kanjō shiki,* Shinnyozō, Hieizan Collection, unpublished.

[52] On this question, see Faure, *Erecting Obstacles,* forthcoming.

more, "All the boys who become chigo in the Latter Period [of the Law] are avatars of Kannon."[53]

According to the *Chigo kanjō shiki,* the purpose of this *abhiṣeka* ritual is to introduce the chigo into the compassionate realm of Kannon and to achieve his identification with this bodhisattva, through his becoming an "ideal" chigo. After the preliminaries, the chigo is introduced into the sacred area by the officiating priest (*ajari*), where, the upper part of his body naked, he will receive initiatory mudrās, before putting on makeup. He then ascends the hight seat, and is treated as an emperor. In a sense, he is a double of the adolescent Shōtoku Taishi, who was both the ideal ruler and a manifestation of Kannon. The figure of Shōtoku Taishi sums up the two aspects, the compassionate bodhisattva and the compassionate ruler, which are spread in the Jidō legend over two narrative actors, King Mu and the youth Jidō.[54] Through this initiation, the ephemereal chigo, whose "flower" will so soon fade with the advent of puberty, acquires an eternal youth. He is now an ideal chigo created and fixed for eternity in his youthful splendor by the ritual. Like the king or the emperor, the chigo has "two bodies"—and actually the everlasting imperial body is that of a chigo. Thus, the everlasting youth of Jidō is also that of the emperor.

The *Chigo kanjō shiki* adds an interesting comment: it is precisely because the chigo has become ritually identified with Kannon that he can be "forced." Following the hongaku notion that "defilements are awakening," sexual transgression with a chigo involves no culpability, provided that the chigo has duly received the abhiṣeka, that is, that he is Kannon. As we recall, having sex with an avatar of Kannon transmutes desire into deliverance, whereas having sex with an uninitiated chigo, a profane body, will cause one to fall into the three evil destinies. Avatars of Kannon were relatively rare in China and pre-Kamakura Japan, however, whereas in medieval Tendai they were created ritually. The self-serving aspect of this reasoning is all too obvious. False consciousness or not, the fact remains that the identity between the chigo and Kannon or other bodhisattvas and kamis had become part of the medieval Japanese imaginary. As Matsuoka points out, the chigo whom the priest rapes is at the same time a potential savior, and the priest rapes him while worshiping him as an avatar and a double of the emperor.[55] Surely, this heightened sense of transgression must have increased the pleasure.

[53] *Chigo kanjō shiki,* quoted in Abe 1984: 50; Matsuoka 1993: 276.

[54] In the *Sokui hōmon* by Zonkai, a monk of the Eshin-ryū, we find an explicit identification between Jidō, the Tendai patriarch Nanyue Huisi, and Shōtoku Taishi. See Matsuoka 1993: 277, and Abe 1984: 24.

[55] Matsuoka 1993: 279.

The Tendai enthronement ritual finds its equivalent in the Shingon tradition with a ritual traced back to the legend of Kamatari (614–669), the founder of the Fujiwara lineage. According to this tradition, the youth Kamatari was abducted by a fox (a manifestation of Dakini, that is, of the Kasuga deity, and in last analysis of Amaterasu). After having had sex with the fox, he received from it the magic formula and the insignia of power, the scythe (*kama*) that became part of its name.

The relation between youth and immortality was a commonplace in Chinese legend, where immortals are often represented as children. In Japan too, many stories present the chigo as an immortal but, as noted earlier, these stories characteristically insist on the sufferings of the chigo. Another recurring motif is that of the chigo who is abandoned by his lover and who subsequently becomes an immortal. A case in point is the legend of the chigo of Matsumuro Chūsan, a scholar-monk of Kōfukuji. Chūsan, having fallen in love with a chigo of Ryōgon-in on Hieizan, kidnapped him and took him to Nara. After a while his love wore off, however, and he became increasingly distant. The child, feeling rejected, disappeared into the mountains, where he read sūtras and fasted for several months. After some time he became an immortal, but when Chūsan eventually came to see him, he could not approach him.

The Jidō legend weaves together several distinct (Daoist and Buddhist) representations of the youth as a Chinese Immortal or as an avatar of kamis and bodhisattvas like Kannon, Fugen, Monju, or Jizō (Jūzenji). The transition from one type of representation to another is apparent in various recensions of the *Chigo Kannon engi* (including the emaki version): some elements of the earlier recensions, for instance the apparition of the immortal child on the branch of a pine tree, have disappeared from the later versions, which emphasize the power of Kannon and of the *Lotus Sūtra*.

The most striking narrative elements in these chigo stories, however, are the love between the monk and the handsome youth, and the description of the latter's sufferings. From the narrative viewpoint, the sacrality of these chigo, like that of Jidō, is revealed through love and suffering. As the narratives become increasingly literary, these two elements or mythic structures are magnified with the influence of medieval imagination. This mythical structure appears clearly in the story of Hakke Gongen in the *Shintō shū*. This engi consists of two parts. The first part recounts the founding and later destruction of two mountain temples, Funaodera and Sekiganji. The second part tells the origins of the god Hakke Gongen. The connection between these two distinct parts is not that of a mere geographical coincidence. The same narrative elements that we found concentrated on one figure (the chigo) in the chigo monogatari are here spread across two "actants" (a young girl and a chigo) and two separate tales.

The first story revolves around Senju no mae, the daughter of a *chōja* (rich householder). After hearing stories about the capital told by the chōja's adopted son Tōji Ieyasu, she began yearning for the flowers of the capital. She soon died, dreaming of flowers that she had never seen. She then appeared to Ieyasu in a dream, singing and dancing under cherry blossoms. When her coffin was opened, she looked as if she were sleeping, and her face was ornamented with flowers. Later Ieyasu became a monk and founded Funaodera, a temple dedicated to Kannon, whereas the girl's parents founded Sekiganji.[56]

The tale continues with the story of Tsukisae-dono, the handsome child of the provincial governor. This child became a chigo at Funaodera, and the priest was extremely fond of him. However, one day he was kidnapped by a tengu and, after vainly searching for him, his servants as well as his mother and his wet-nurse all killed themselves in despair. When the father, wanting to join them in death, ascended the mountain with his army, he was mistaken for an enemy, and the two temples were eventually destroyed in the battle that ensued. When the child was released among the ruins, he became mad with grief. He was subsequently divinized, together with his relatives, and worshiped as Hakke Gongen.[57]

The suffering of Tsukisae-dono and his final apotheosis, as well as the destruction of the temple and the death of those dear to him, have a latent relation with the tale about the founding of the temple after the death of Senju no mae. The vision of the girl (first in a dream, then in her coffin) suggests that she was an avatar of Kannon.[58] This episode leads to the creation of a Buddhist temple, a place dedicated to the bodhisattva Kannon. And when this sacred place is destroyed, it is to give birth to a new god. The connection between the two stories suggests that Hakke Gongen himself is an avatar of Kannon. It also shows the theatrical versatility of the sacred beings called bodhisattvas, who can embody a local sacrality that is no longer strictly Buddhist, reflecting as it does the complex narrative moves of medieval Japanese imagination. As Abe points out, the chigo is one of the most developed forms of such imagination. While clearly inheriting elements from mythological images of the divine child (*mikogami, wakamiya, ōji*), the chigo can no longer be reduced to them. Through the presence of Kannon, in particular, a new form of sacrality, typical of medieval literature, has been achieved.[59] This sacrality, which reveals itself in many ways (through rites of enthronement,

[56] See *Shintō shū*, edited by Kishi Shōzō, Tōyō bunko 94 (Tokyo: Heibonsha, 1967), 168–70.

[57] Abe 1993: 293.

[58] One detail here (the fact that the coffin is on the branches of a tree) recalls earlier stories of immortals appearing on the branches of a tree.

[59] Abe 1993: 294.

conversion, rebirth, immortality, divinization), is initiated by the love of the monk for a chigo. But it seems to be achieved only through a process leading to the sacrifice of the chigo and the destruction of his world. The love, death, and destruction caused (unwillingly—"over his dead body") by the chigo, now perceived as a mythological structure, constitutes a fundamental and necessary process leading to a new (or renewed) sacrality.

Another interesting story is that of Kakunyo, a chigo of Hieizan. Rumor of the beauty of this boy reached a priest of Miidera, Jūchin, who eventually kidnapped him. The new life of the boy was spent in banquets and all kinds of games, in which he excelled. Another priest of Kōfukuji named Shinshō also fell in love with him, however, and in turn eventually abducted him. But Shinshō died without having had the time to enjoy the chigo, and the latter came to serve Shinshō's disciple, Kakushō. The chigo eventually became a monk under the name of Kakunyo, and later became the third-generation abbot of Honganji and a leading figure of Shinshū. It is therefore significant that this eminent monk was abducted twice in his youth. But is that a fact? We are told that the first abduction almost caused a war between Miidera and Hieizan, a story strangely reminiscent of the *Akiyo no nagamonogatari*. One could, of course, argue that the chigo monogatari itself was based on this real event, but it seems more likely that the compiler of Kakunyo's biography made use of the monogatari of the time. The point remains that biographies of chigo had become indissociable from the monogatari.

In the *Kokon chōmonjū*, we find stories of the two chigo of Ninnaji, Senshu and Sansen, minions of Kakushō shinnō, both experts in entertainment arts (flute, imayo, and so on). Senshu was at first eclipsed by Sansen, but managed to become Kakushō's favorite again, and Sansen disappeared, leaving a poem behind. The story is reminiscent of that of the dancing-girls (*shirabyōshi*) Giō and Hotoke Gozen, favorites of Kiyomori. The shirabyōshi too disguise themselves as men. Their imitation of the chigo constitutes a similar transvestism and inversion of sexual roles. As we can see, the chigo and the shirabyōshi are the two sides of the same phenomenon.[60] Note also that these stories revolving around Omuro (that is, the abbot [*monzeki*] of Ninnaji) and Kiyomori—figures who are at a level close to that of the king—overlap in the sense that the shirabyōshi and the chigo are first favorites, then abandoned. It is once again the story of their suffering which expresses the upcoming "sacredness," and their salvation. We find here the same paradoxical structure as in all chigo monogatari.

According to Abe, these legends elucidate the mechanism of the partic-

---

[60] Abe 1993: 297.

ular religious worldview symbolized by the figure of the medieval chigo. At a deeper level, we find a paradoxical structure, namely, the fact that precisely because of the passionate attachment for the chigo (an attachment normally repudiated by Buddhism) a hierophany takes place. The medieval chigo, whose enactment of sexual inversion made him a central figure of entertainment arts (*geinō*), and who was also at the center of monastic ritual, came to embody this paradox. His passions (in the psychological sense) led to his "passion" (in the religious sense). His sufferings resonated with the medieval topos of the "suffering god" and made him a most appropriate tragic figure.[61]

HEAD OR TAIL

In actual practice, things were rarely as beautiful as the chigo monogatari paint them. Like Childs, we may hesitate between reading these texts as Buddhist sermons or reading them as love stories. But this interpretive alternative may not be sufficient. We may also see them as a rather crude ideological cover-up for a kind of institutionalized prostitution or rape. Therefore let us leave the high spheres of "pure" love, and consider for a moment the trivial or base aspects of male homosexuality. A type of euphemization that may seem at first glance relatively harmless is the comic representation found in writers like Saikaku or Chikamatsu. In the latter's work, we find the figure of the candid chigo Hananojo. Upon hearing one of his companions declare that "a page in a temple is just like a wife in the lay world," Hananojo asks:

> Does that mean that the High Priest and I are man and wife? Then my father and mother back home must be liars. They told me that on the mountain I'd have to pretend when I ate bean curd that it was sea bream, and that parsnips were lamprey, because priests aren't allowed to eat fish. They said I should make believe that yams were eels and that the High Priest was my father. That was all they told me. I never heard anything about being the High Priest's wife. But come to think of it, at the festival the day before yesterday I sat next to the High Priest at dinner and I ate thirteen bowls of rice dumpling soup. I wonder if that made me pregnant. Look how swollen my stomach is!"[62]

Hananojo's candor may not be as candid as it seems, as it eventually reveals his companions' moral turpitude.

[61] Ibid., 311.
[62] See Keene, trans., 1961:136.

Debasement

This aspect of male love, however, is more crudely described in a number of manuals that provide abundant information on the technicalities of male love. The *Kōbō Daishi ikkan no shō* describes the hand signs of the chigo and his appearance, and the various ways of penetrating him.[63] Similar instructions are given in the *Onna tairaku hōkai,* a parody of *Onna daigaku* (The Great Learning for Women).[64] The *Instructions for the Wakashū* is an anonymous text that claims to be an illustrated version of the *Hyakunin isshū* but gives only about twenty images accompanied by "crazy verses."[65] They are followed by instructions to get into bed (*sokoiri no kokoroe*), and to prepare for penetration (put on some powder to avoid hemorrhoids), warnings for the wakashū (how to avoid women or keep a close watch on one's relations with them), advices for hygiene (go to the latrine before going to bed, wash your anus well, your hands, your mouth), a description of the act itself, and additional advice for hygiene (avoid bad smell, go quickly to the latrine afterwards—again to avoid hemorrhoids). Finally, latrines should not be too close, lest the fall of the "water of luxure" be heard by others.[66] Homosexual sex is also depicted in pillow pictures. In Utamaro's *Michiyuki koi no futozao* (Trysts of Big Penises), we find the scene of a boy, apparently a shop apprentice, being raped by the master of the store.[67] The act is, however, euphemized by its ribald context.

Jokes are also revealing: "An old priest went into a bamboo garden and he was taking a great shit when his ass got pierced by a bamboo shoot. The novice who was looking on clasped his hands (in reverence)

[63] Nakazawa 1991–1992, 3: 423–28; see also Schalow 1992a.

[64] Nakazawa 1991–1992, 3: 443.

[65] Ibid., 403.

[66] Ibid., 403–5. Note in passing the importance of the intercrural space (*kōkan, matama*). Minakata mentions, for instance, the following story: in a place where there were few women, one could marry youths called *warawazuma* (lit. boy-spouse). Although the ceremony was quite regular, the husband had to avoid the relatives of his spouse and he was forbidden from performing anal penetration: the act had to take place in the intercrural space. On Kōyasan, says Minakata, this practice was as important as sodomy (letter to Iwata Jun'ichi, dated December 5, 1932). One of my informants, who will remain anonymous, tells me that a similar practice is also well known among Tibetan monks. Another technique described (and even illustrated) by Minakata is the following: "On Kōyasan, when someone wants to take a boy frontally, in the orthodox style, one joins as in the above image three things like a *futon* (one has put cotton in a *birōdo* [a kind of velvet]), one pushes one's sex in the lying position, and with four threads one ties it between the thighs. In France too, and in other countries, this device is used. It is probably the most useful instrument for male love. . . . Without it, one could not make love frontally." Nakazawa 1991–1992, 3: 495.

[67] Minamoto 1993: 109.

and said: 'Amida Buddha, it's Heaven's reward.'"[68] Amida (rather than Monju) seems to have been invoked often in these circumstances: in another anecdote, a priest seduces his young disciple and "sweet feelings arose, but the young disciple's penis got larger and [semen] oozed out. The priest grasped it with his hands and sighed, saying: 'Oh Amida Buddha, it's pierced through.'"[69] Likewise, in the *Jinpingmei*: "Once a priest and his disciple went to a benefactor's house with some religious papers. When they reached the door, they found that the disciple's belt had come loose and the papers had fallen out. 'It looks as though you had no bottom,' said the priest. 'If I hadn't,' returned the disciple, 'you wouldn't be able to exist for a single day.'"[70] In this last story, we find a rather unexpected symbolic use of vegetarianism: "One night the Venerable Master spoke to an acolyte, saying: 'Tonight we ought to do it the vegetarian way.' 'What do you mean by the vegetarian way?' 'I won't use my tongue [to lubricate the penis].' They did it that way but the youth felt extremely pained so he cried out, 'Master, I can't stand it any longer, let's go back to a meat diet.'"[71] These stories are more complex than it may seem: on the one hand, they allow the voice of the dissenting chigo to be heard and depict the priest in a rather unpleasant light; on the other hand, the fact that they are perceived as jokes weakens their social criticism considerably.

It is tempting, and perhaps too easy, for the historian to commodify male love, replicating the moves of his Tokugawa predecessors and of modern scholars like Minakata (despite the latter's nostalgia for a golden age of "pure" nanshoku). All this talk about chigo may have the paradoxical effect of covering their voice. I have not myself completely escaped this tendency when quoting the above stories. Although I do not intend to dwell on this confessional mode here, it is clear that such an attitude makes one an "accomplice of silence." However, these are Tokugawa texts, dating from a time when nanshoku has become increasingly trivialized. What about medieval exploitation?

Exploitation

As noted above, the unruliness of the medieval youths may be read as a sign of their quasi-sacred nature. However, just as the sacred can be (and often is) manipulated, so were these boys. For all their apparent freedom, they were not leading an independent life: they were actually a kind of

[68] Levy 1973: 233. See also Hinsch 1990: 112.

[69] H. Levy 1973: 233.

[70] Hinsch 1990: 103, quoting Clement Egerton's translation, *The Golden Lotus* 2: 124 (London 1939).

[71] Levy 1973: 234.

servant, and were often sold by their parents. Their role went beyond that of ordinary servants, however, for instance at the time of *matsuri* (festivals). In temples, too, the children served as sexual objects and appeared in matsuri, "wearing nice makeup and riding a horse or a palanquin." In some cases, we find adults assuming the appearance of a youth. It seems that they were men who, being sexual objects, were forced to keep this childish appearance all their life. This "institutionalization of liminality" seems to be a Japanese characteristic: it is apparently not found in China and Korea, despite the existence of a Korean form of "male love."[72] The cowherds, too, although adults, bore children's names and kept the appearance of youths. The oxen drawing carts were fierce animals, and in order to control them, one was perhaps expected to have the magical power of the youth. There was some relation between the childish appearance and the control of these half-wild beasts (oxen, falcons, and so on). At any rate, one can say that the youths, or people looking like youths, were believed to have extraordinary, divine powers. Like the *basara* (flamboyant individuals), they wore splendid clothes, and were objects of taboos, really more like hinin than like servants.[73] Likewise, the so-called *kyō no warawa* were youths who participated in matsuri, and whose freedom was also reflected in their sharp criticisms of the rulers.[74] Although it was said that these youths were close to the hinin, we cannot simply assimilate them with despised lower castes. The hinin, too, played a critical role. If these people who looked like children came to be despised socially, it was probably after Muromachi, when the discrimination toward hinin and beggars increased. It was also at that time that the *warawa* almost lost their sacredness, and gradually became mere "children."[75] Admittedly, these unruly youths were quite different from the boys sent to the temple to accomplish their education, but their case reveals the changing status of children in medieval Japan.

In Japanese legends, the kami appears as an old man (*okina*), but also as a woman and as a child. The three share a common characteristic: they are not autonomous individuals, and they remain on the margins of the social hierarchy in the Middle Ages. The old man, like the child, is close to the kami. It is because they are structurally marginal that they are close to the divine—the closest of the three being, perhaps, the old man. But in the medieval world, to be close to the divine also means to be close to death. The "child" (*warawa*) in premodern Japan risked starvation or

---

[72] See Minakata, *Minakata Kumagusu zenshū* 3: 511–12.

[73] Amino 1993: 66.

[74] These figures appear in documents like the *Chūyūki*, the *Kojidan*, or the *Utsubo monogatari*.

[75] Amino 1993: 66.

being sold into slavery, or being turned into a kind of subaltern figure, like the oxherds (*ushikai-warawa*) or the hall attendants (*dō dōshi*), lower groups that are called *warawa* and assume a childish appearance.[76]

Stories of children abducted and/or sold are common in medieval literature. We have already encountered some examples of child abduction in the chigo monogatari. Others are found in nō plays like *Katsuragawa* and *Sumidagawa*. In *Sakuragawa*, the child Sakurako sells himself to alleviate the misery of his mother. Three years later, he has become the chigo of Isobedera in Hitachi, and together with his master he goes to see the cherry trees. They encounter the mother, who has become mad. She explains to the priest that her child had been called Sakurako after the name of the *ubugami* (deity of childbirth) of her village, Konohana Sakuyahime. The priest, who has realized the situation, reunites mother and child. Another example of mother-child reunion is *Miidera,* a play revolving around the boy Senman and his mother. How did these children sold to a merchant find their way to a temple? In the case of Sakurako, one can think that it was the temple who bought him.[77] In the story of the *hanami* (flower-viewing festival) of Isobe at Sakuragawa, which serves as a basis to the nō *Sakuragawa,* the priest of the Isobedera, struck by the beauty of Sakurako, asks to buy him from the merchant. This suggests that the monks of Isobedera were buying chigo.[78]

Minakata mentions the case of a chigo sold to monks as early as the Heian period.[79] Another well-documented case is found in a letter through which Jinzon, priest of Daijōin, acquired in 1467 the total rights of property over his favorite, Aimitsu-maru, from the latter's father Kasasagi no Yushirō, a drummer of *sarugaku*.[80] These stories are all the more significant when we recall that Zeami himself, under the name of Fujiwaka, had been the chigo of Yoshimitsu.[81]

In the Nō *Tsunemasa,* the *shite* (main actor) is the young Taira no Tsunemasa, who died in battle and was a biwa specialist. The *waki* (acolyte) is the priest Gyōkei, who served the Hōshinnō Shukaku. Shukaku was the sixth abbot (*monzeki*) of Ninnaji, and the second son of the cloistered emperor Go-Shirakawa. Tsunemasa served at Ninnaji as a chigo and this is where he obtained his famous biwa, called "Seizan." In

---

[76] See Amino 1993; and Kuroda 1986: 30, 227–29.

[77] See Hosokawa 1993: 43–45.

[78] Ibid., 46.

[79] See *Minakata Kumagusu zenshū* 9: 47–48, letter to Iwata, dated Shōwa 6/8/25 (1931).

[80] See *Zoku zoku shiryō taisei,* "Daijōin jisha zatsuji ki 4" (Tokyo: Rinsen shoten, 1978).

[81] Hosokawa 1993: 47.

the play, following Shukaku's request to perform a service in the memory of Tsunemasa, Gyōkei deposits the biwa in front of the Buddha and performs a ritual. In the middle of the night, when the flames of the torches create a mysterious atmosphere, the spirit of Tsunemasa appears, and tells his life to Gyōkei, then plays the biwa. But soon Tsunemasa, who has become an *asura* (demon), is tormented by the flames, and he asks that the torches be put out.[82]

The above story illustrates the fact that the children of courtiers and warriors served as chigo, becoming the favorites of monks and studying the entertainment arts until the coming-of-age ceremony (*genpuku*).[83] We find in the *Kokon chōmonjū* an interesting anecdote on the homosexual relations between priests and chigo. Kakushō had a favorite named Senju, very handsome and gifted, who played the flute and sang *imayo*. But another chigo, Mikawa, came to serve Kakushō, and in turn became his favorite. Senju left the Gosho of Omuro. One day, during a banquet at Ninnaji, Kakushō asked his disciple Shukaku to fetch him for a recital, but Senju pretended to be ill. After several requests, however, he had to comply. Asked to sing an imayo, his song moved everyone, and Kakushō embraced him and took him to his room. In the morning, Kakushō found a poem from Mikawa, who had left to become a monk on Kōya.[84]

The relations between Kakushō and Tsunemasa were probably homosexual, too. This love for the chigo included study and performance of musical arts (waka, imayo, biwa, flute, etc.). Tsunemasa, after his genpuku ceremony, returned to profane life. As noted earlier, the age of responsibility in medieval society was usually fifteen, and this was the age at which a chigo often became a monk. However, there were chigo older than that, who were called *ōchigo* (older chigo, in contrast to the *kochigo*, small chigo).[85]

In the nō *Kagetsu*, the kasshiki Kagetsu has gone far beyond the

---

[82] The source of this nō is chapter 17 of the *Heike monogatari*, "Tsunemasa miyako ochi," in which Tsunemasa, at the time of the loss of the capital by the Taira in 1183, takes refuge at Ninnaji and, while returning to Shukaku the biwa "Seizan" which he had received the year before, takes leave of his former master Gyōkei. We learn that he had served at Ninnaji from 8 to 13, until the age of his genpuku ceremony. The story also appears in the *Sa no ki*, Shukaku's diary, and seems real. However, according to this source, the personage whom Tsunemasa served as chigo was not Shukaku but his predecessor, the fifth monzeki of Ninnaji, Kakushō hōshinnō (fifth son of Shirakawa). Tsunemasa had therefore received this biwa from Kakushō, and after keeping it many years, went back to Ninnaji in 1183 to return it to Shukaku. Kakushō was himself a biwa expert, from whom Tsunemasa learnt his art.

[83] Hosokawa 1993: 61.

[84] Ibid., 62. See also Watanabe and Iwata 1989: 39–41.

[85] See, for instance, the *Seisuishō* edited by Suzuki Tōzō, 1986, 2: 7–37.

fifteen-year limit as ōchigo. A monk of Hikosan, who had lost his seven-year-old son, finds him again as kasshiki of Kiyomizu, and learns that he had been kidnapped by some tengu. He had lived on various sacred mountains before landing at Kiyomizu.[86] These tengu are probably a metaphor for slave merchants, who often appear in nō plays—or perhaps he had been abducted by some yamabushi of Hikosan.[87] It seems likely that the man of the Kiyomizu gate, who was the interlocutor of the monk/father of Kagetsu, was both the pimp and the manager of Kagetsu—as artist. And Kagetsu's father, although he does not know that he is the boy's father, buys him from the "friend" in question as a sexual object. After having been kidnapped and sold, Kagetsu has thus become an artistic and sexual entertainment for the tourists of Kiyomizu. We must therefore keep in mind that the young "artist" Kagetsu has been sold over and over again. To see there only the aesthetic side is to forget the other side. This Kagetsu, surrounded by "friends" who are lovers and pimps, has hardly any prospect for a happy future.[88] Thus, apart from the cases of chigo who, like Tsunemasa, become adults through the genpuku ceremony, we have those who, like Kagetsu, are bought and sold, remaining sexual objects their entire life. The two literary cases of Tsunemasa and Kagetsu find their counterpart in social reality with the instance of the two favorite chigo of Jinson, a priest of the Daijōin at Kōfukuji.

These two chigo, Aichiyomaru and Aimitsumaru, allow us to understand the different destinies of Tsunemasa and Kagetsu.[89] In Jinson's diary, it is said that Aichiyomaru was taken as chigo at the age of sixteen, and received a stipend from Jinson in 1475. He was the son of Kishida Kamonnojō, who resided in Sakai toward 1480. In the same year that his father became a hermit, he went through the genpuku ceremony, taking the name of Sashidakyūrō Nobutsugi. In 1481, he was nominated to the position of *gesu* (manager) of Nikinoshō in Yamato, a domain of the monzeki of Daijōin, and he went to do business in Sakai. He was there-

---

[86] See Hosokawa 1993: 62–65.

[87] See, for instance, *Sakuragawa, Sumidagawa, Miidera,* or *Jinen koji.* In the *Azuma kagami,* for instance, evil monks of Kumano, during a battle with Seki Nobukane of the Taira clan at Ise and Shima, burned the houses of the people of Futami-ga-ura, and took away more than thirty-three women and children on their boat, withdrawing to Kumano Bay. See *Azuma kagami,* s.v. Jishō 5/1/21 (= 1181); quoted in Hosokawa, 1993: 66.

[88] Ibid., 67–68.

[89] Jinson's two chigo have already been studied in relation with Zeami by Tokue Motomasa, "Zeami dōkei kō," in *Muromachi geinō shiron kō,* quoted ibid. With regard to Aimitsumaru, we know that his father, Kasasagi no Yushirō, was related to the *sanjomono* [= kawaramono]. See Miura Keiichi, "Chūsei goki no sanjo ni tsuite," in *Nihon chūsei senmin shi no kenkyū,* Burakumin kenkyūjo, 1990, quoted in Hosokawa 1993: 69.

fore of samurai status, in the class of shōen administrators. In 1498, at the age of thirty-seven, he killed himself for an unknown reason. His career resembles that of Tsunemasa, member of the Taira clan.[90]

By contrast, Aimitsumaru was taken by Jinson much earlier, in 1461, at fifteen. His father Yushirō was a *genin* (menial) of Ueda Yukiharu of Tateno in Yamato, and after buying back his genin status, he became a *sanjomono* ("marginal," dweller of a liminal area) under the jurisdiction of Ryūshun Hōgen, a priest of Kōfukuji. At the end of 1461, Jinson asked Yushirō, through the intermediary of Ryūshun, to give him his son Aimitsumaru as acolyte. Five days later, a man named Mijirō escorted Aimitsumaru to Jinson's temple. The sanjomono are low-status individuals, like artists. However Yushirō, Aimitsumaru's father, was nominated drummer of Sarugaku at Kōfukuji the following year (1462).

The love of Jinson for Aimitsumaru was very special. In 1467, he was able to obtain from the father a letter giving him rights of total ownership (*mibiki jō*) over Aimitsumaru. The latter was thus bought as chigo, sexual object, losing his status of sanjomono. This Aimitsumaru also killed himself at twenty-eight, after serving Jinson fourteen years. His destiny is very similar to that of Kagetsu of Kiyomizu. Aimitsumaru, who was the favorite of Jinson and had studied linked verse (*renga*), passed the age of genpuku without changing status. He remained until 1472, that is, until he was twenty-six, an "older chigo" with long flowing hair. This same year, without having reached the "adult age," he withdrew from the world, under the precept master Hibō Kaishun, taking as religious name Jōami. But soon after, he fell ill (mentally?) and put an end to his life. He had reached an age where he could no longer preserve his identity as a chigo.

To those who, like Inagaki Taruho (and to a lesser extent Minakata), discuss the decline of the beauty of the wakashū from an esthetic viewpoint, we must recall the sordid and abusive nature of the relations between a powerful monk and a vulnerable chigo like Aimitsumaru.[91] It was a one-way relationship between a free and active (penetrating) adult and a vulnerable (penetrated) adolescent. Jinson exerted real power on Aimitsumaru, as shown by the transfer letter written by the child's father. These relations could sometimes break the inner self of the passive subject, when he could no longer preserve his adolescent identity. Jinson had kept his love for Aimitsumaru, however, giving him fairly important funerals at Byakugōji, building a stūpa built for him at the south of the

---

[90] See the *Daijōin jisha zōji ki*, s.v. Bunmei 12/9/10 [= 1480], quoted ibid., 70.

[91] To give just one example, in his *Shōnen'ai no bigaku* (The Aesthetics of Adolescent Love), Inagaki Taruho discusses pedophily as a form of dandyism, and he says in particular about Kagetsu: "Perhaps we must add [to the turbulent life of Kagetsu] the memory of hemorrhoids." Quoted ibid., 67–68.

Mandara-dō of Gokuraku-bō, and composing a poem for the occasion. His feelings for a chigo of low extraction are perhaps relatively exceptional. Nevertheless, Jinson could not have him ordained as a monk of Kōfukuji, or let him undergo the genpuku ceremony, like Aichiyomaru, let alone turn him into an administrator. He let him grow older as a chigo, and then let him simply leave the world as a hermit. In the nō, Kagetsu has a bow and arrow, but no sword, which was the symbol of the adult independence in medieval society. This is because Kagetsu is a childish-looking *kugaimono* ("public individual"), who has no enemies, and cannot defend himself.[92]

We noted above that various scholars have argued that chigo were perceived as sacred beings, avatars of the deities.[93] Even Abe, however, who emphasizes the mythological and ideological contexts of the chigo kanjō (unction), admits that it was probably merely a superficial legitimization for the sexual desire of monks, in a monastic society forbidden to women. These scholars have, however, tended to rely too exclusively on literary documents, and to neglect temple documents (*monjo*). But the attitude of the monks toward the chigo was sometimes rather casual, especially given their divine nature. In the *Nanajūichiban shokunin uta awase,* for instance, we find a poem in which a "Dharma master of the mountain" (that is, Mount Hiei) complains of freezing alone in his bed, without a chigo. Likewise, according to the *Genkō shakusho,* the priest Jōkei, frustrated by a chigo's frivolity, decided to become a hermit, leaving the following poem: "Although I think of you every time I shit, I am not even worth a fart in your eyes."[94]

These are exceptions in the elevated love poetry addressed to chigo. In the rules of the temples, however, the chigo appear stripped of any mystique, as sexual objects. Thus, in a code (*shikimoku*) dated 1355, for Gakuenji in Izumo, a branch temple of Shōren-in on Hieizan, we read that although women under sixty, even parents, are not allowed, the same is not true for the chigo. The reason given is that not only they are the ones who transmit the Dharma lamp but, more cynically, that they alleviate the coldness of lonely nights.[95] We have noted above that sometimes the chigo were the cause of feuds among the monks.[96]

---

[92] Hosokawa 1993: 71–74.

[93] Among studies on this, apart from Iwata 1974, see Matsuda 1988 and Inagaki 1973b.

[94] In the *Shasekishū*, Jōkei enters reclusion with six monks. When one of them breaks his fast and shares his cell with a chigo, Jōkei scolds him, but the monk replies: "Haven't you yourself come to the Way because of a youth?" See *Shasekishū, NKBT* 85: 154–55; and Morrell 1985: 130.

[95] Hosokawa 1993: 77.

[96] See, for instance, the *Kishōmon* in five articles written by Jōkei for the monks of

There are also cases where monks leave the capital to take refuge in mountain temples, after the murder of a chigo. Thus, in 1275, the Kegon monk Sōshō of the Sonshōin in Tōdaiji, leaves Nara to take refuge at the Hannya-in of Kasagidera.[97] As he himself points out, the cause of his departure was the murder of an innocent chigo, Rikimyōmaru, who lived with him near Kōfukuji. We see that the chigo were often victims of violence. Although in all the medieval legends, at the end of their sufferings they appear as deities, in reality they were often sacrificed on the altar of male love, and their redemption remained a pious wish (or a pious lie).[98]

In a letter to Iwata dated Shōwa 8/1/6, Minakata, quoting the *Yōshū fushi*, writes:

> The chigo shrine is on the west of Hirosawa Pond. According to tradition, Kanchō of Henchōji ascended once [temporarily] to heaven, and no one knew where he was. His attendant chigo, suffering from the separation, threw himself in the pond, and died. A shrine was built, where he was worshiped. The stone of Kanchō's ascension to heaven still exists today. It is said that this chigo was an avatar of Monju, who always protected Kanchō, and after his death, entered the water and left.[99]

We seem to have here a suicide turned into sacrifice, a kind of Girardian scapegoat. We have heard repeatedly about the tragic destiny of the chigo. Does not their divinization perhaps simply reflect the fact that they served as victims? The chigo became stakes of personal rivalries, but also political rivalries. To give just one example, because the tradition of artist chigo had become the hallmark of Ninnaji, Emperor Go-Uda, by reaction, came to forbid the chigo in Daikakuji, the monastery he had just restored in 1321.

Kenko Urabe, author of the *Tsurezuregusa,* describes the excesses of the banquets at Ninnaji.[100] Go-Uda was perhaps aware of this, because in an edict of 1324, he forbade all banquets and promulgated a few rules relating to the chigo.[101] He prohibited, for instance, the keeping of chigo under fifteen, age of the ordination at Daikakuji. He also forbade music within the limits of the *kekkai* (sacred area), except in the context of

---

Kaijūzanji in southern Yamashiro. The fifth article, "About the need to stop fighting in monasteries," shows that the chigo were a source of trouble; likewise in 1349, at Kannonji in Ōmi, a center of shugendō.

[97] See Hosokawa 1993: 78.

[98] See ibid., 79.

[99] *Minakata Kumagusu zenshū* 9: 165.

[100] *Tsurezuregusa* 54: "There was at Omuro a handsome chigo." See the translation by Porter 1974: 47.

[101] See *Daikakuji monjo,* vol. 1, 1980, quoted in Hosokawa 1993: 80.

ceremonies. He seems to have wanted to avoid reproducing the situation of Ninnaji at Daikakuji. As can be seen in the *Ninnaji goden,* at the end of Kamakura, after Shōnin Hōshinnō, fourth son of Go-Fukakusa, entered the religious life, the princes of the Jimyōin-tō line began to succeed each other as abbots of Ninnaji. The Ninnaji was dominated by this party of the monzeki—which Go-Uda, of the Daikakuji party, criticized. The temple regulations of the time reflect this opposition between the two parties.[102]

We have to come to terms with the fact that every sexual relationship, insofar as it is based on desire, may involve a certain form of predation, hence of violence and power. From the Buddhist viewpoint, desire and power always make two victims: the subject, or consumer, who becomes dependent on the sexual object and is consumed by desire; and the object of desire, who is consumed (and consummated). Thus, homosexuals (or gays) were not always the victims (as John Boswell argues). They could at times be quite oppressive. The ageless (and age-structured) question raised by pedophily is both that of the (often unwilling) seduction of the old by the young, and that of the predation or exploitation of the young by the old. Power as determined by age and social status is here more important than gender, and the same exploitation can be found on both sides of the homo/hetero divide. Thus, the expoitative aspect of pedophily is by no means specific to homosexuality. Child abuse, related to sexual desire, was and remains institutionalized in many traditional societies, where young girls were given to marriage at a very tender age. However, their situation is not exactly symmetrical to that of the chigo, since this institutionalized child abuse often leads to an official status as wife.

One may wonder which is worse: the euphemization of exploitation through a mystical discourse (as in the medieval chigo tradition), or its euphemization through derision and laughter (as in Edo)? The fact remains that *shudō* was in the medieval period a way to power (in particular royal power) and/or salvation. This characteristic seems completely lacking in the Western tradition.

The chigo stories also reflect the medieval (and modern) interest in liminal existences. The chigo is only one of the figures of the child, but it influenced considerably the medieval perception of children. In the emaki of the medieval period, it is often difficult to determine if some figures are women or chigo. In these emaki, women wear straw sandals called *igege,* but chigo also wear them. This shows how close women and chigo were in their clothing, and also in their use of makeup. Note, however, the fan: men usually hold a fan outside, whereas women hold it inside the house.

[102] Hosokawa 1993: 81.

It must therefore be chigo who appear in these emaki, because some of them have a fan.[103]

The *Hōnen shōnin eden* and the *Kitano tenjin engi* show many images of chigo. In the first emaki, in the crowd of Hōnen's disciples we find three figures with their head covered, and their gender is not clear: they may be chigo. The *Kitano tenjin engi* or the *Ishiyamadera engi* show similar silhouettes with their head covered. From their clothes alone, it seems impossible to determine whether they are women or chigo. The covered heads and *kāṣāya* (surplice) are probably those of chigo. The chigo are usually ranked behind the monks, and it is only when they have their head covered that they are sitting in front. Thus covered, these novices turn into monks. But through their clothes—and on the sentimental plane as well—they are still almost women. By covering his head, the chigo, this pseudo woman, can participate in rituals where they would normally not be admitted.[104]

. . . . .

From all the above it should be clear that the notion of male love in the Japanese Buddhist context covered a broad diversity of phenomena. One is therefore justified in speaking of Buddhist homosexualities. The pure and the sordid, the spiritual and the physical, paedeia and pederasty, child-love and child-abuse, were intimately intertwined to form a complex reality—as if to illustrate Buddhist nonduality. Buddhist homosexuality is also the manifestation of what we could call an esprit de corps, an attempt to protect the monastic body from all intrusion, a cause and effect of Buddhist misogyny. Monks found in the youths their ideal, their alter ego, represented by figures like the Bodhisattva Jizō. As Aline Rousselle puts it regarding the Western context, "Homosexuality in that period [the Roman Empire] represented the attractions of the world, and at the same time the love of something close to oneself, for women were so different, so far removed from men's thoughts and eyes."[105]

The youth will become a warrior who, like Yoshitsune, is actually stronger than his lover and bodyguard, the monk Benkei. Although the feminization inherent in male love could at times lead to transsexuality

---

[103] See for instance, in *Kasuga gongen kenki e*, where women/chigo are mixed with the warrior-monks; or in *Hōnen shōnin eden*, *Ishiyamadera engi*, *Kitano tenjin engi*. Sources: *Emakimono ni yoru Nihon jōmin seikatsu ein*, Heibonsha; *Nihon emakimono zenshū*, Kadogawa shoten; *Nihon emaki taisei*, Chūōkōronsha; *Zoku Nihon emaki taisei*, ibid. All quoted in Kuroda 1986a.

[104] See ibid., 45.

[105] Rousselle 1988: 3.

and threaten gender differences, hermaphrodites were not valorized. On the contrary, they were considered to be inferior beings, inferior even to women. We may recall that the early Buddhists believed in the transient nature of gender differences. This belief probably partly justified the practice of cross-dressing and blurring genres, paving the way to the evolution that led from the chigo to the *kagema* (male courtesan). It is clear, at least, that "sexual variation was not invested with the aura of social heresy it acquired in the West."[106] In the medieval tradition, however, transvestism was not merely a feminization of the boy. Things are a little more complicated, as can be seen from the fact that the shirabyōshi, or dancing-girls, usually dressed as boys. Thus, transvestism cuts both ways. It is above all a gender transgression.

We recall how the early Buddhist Vinaya legislated homosexual acts only to the extent that they might threaten the borders of the monastic community by blurring sexual difference. In Tokugawa Japan, similar attempts were made by the authorities to enforce a strict social hierarchy, but Japanese society had been (and still remained to a large extent) open to notions such as *muen,* and fence-straddling was still widely practiced by a large segment of the population, institutionalized marginals. The chigo were such liminal figures, but they could play with sexual difference only as long as they remained clearly male. Transsexual, yet male. Had they become totally feminized, as the later *kagema* or *onnagata* of kabuki, they would have been perceived as mere *paṇḍaka,* losing their mystical quality as mediators between the sacred and the profane.[107]

All chigo did not have the chance of becoming monks or samurai, that is, to change roles from penetrated to penetrator (the child abused often becomes a child abuser). Some would remain stuck in this kind of sexual liminality, condemned to eternal youth (at least as long as they were sexually attractive), to remain "artists" like Kagetsu, the chigo of Kiyomizu, whose story became the subject of a nō play. As in the modern period, tourism and pilgrimage went hand in hand with male and female prostitution. Those who did not find the sister-soul at Kiyomizu could always, for a fee, find sex there.[108] Monks were sometimes themselves accomplices to this form of slave trade whose raw material were the chigo.

The estheticism of Buddhist monks (and of modern scholars like Inagaki) covers up rather sordid realities, and sets little store by the devastated lives and psychological harm caused by this practice. The euphemized violence is characteristic of the chigo monogatari and artistic

[106] Schalow 1989: 121.

[107] There are well-known cases of such female impersonators in the artistic milieux of the Edo period. Let us simply mention the Shitennō onnagata, four famous transvestites, one of whom interiorized his feminine role so completely that he was said to menstruate.

[108] See Hosokawa 1993: 65–67.

representations of the divine child. Were these what Childs calls "love stories," or Hasegawa "prayers to the chigo"? Whatever the case may be, this idealization is not sufficient to redeem the massive child abuse.

We have described the importance of the chigo in the medieval monastic discourse on male love. There are two theses regarding the interpretation of these chigo stories. According to the first, such tales are a mere justification of the monks' desires. According to the second, they are the expression of a frustrated religious yearning, a vision quest through the avatar-chigo. The two are not necessarily incompatible and could, for instance, be described as representing two different levels—the phenomenological and the ideological level. There is no need to deny systematically the good faith of the monks. We recall the case of Jinson, who maintained his lover in a liminal chigo status even after the boy grew up, but who was deeply affected when the latter killed himself.

The motivations of these stories, however, are not purely individual. We should recall here the central role of the chigo in Tendai, at the heart of the symbolic device of royal enthronement. We have seen how repeated transgression—by the king and the youth Jidō—has become a driving force in the transmission of the rite. In the end, the chigo, all chigo, are said to be avatars of Kannon. Given this ideological and symbolical context, one should perhaps hesitate before considering that the sexual relations with a chigo are merely an ordinary form of homosexuality. We find here the same tendency as in "sexual theology" regarding hierogamy, that is, the fact of transforming sexual union into an expression of the religious principle, by sacralizing the partners and the act itself. Even if this is a typical case of "false consciousness," the latter is also part of reality, and one cannot reduce everything too quickly to hypocrisy. We must at least emphasize the specificity of the Buddhist homosexual tradition. Even if it is merely an attempt at euphemizing reality, it imprints its specific mark on Buddhism and Japanese culture. It is only during the Edo period that the tradition declines, giving way to "bourgeois" forms of homosexuality.

The case of the chigo exploitation raises a difficult question for the historian of religions, intent on preserving the religious value of the tradition. Like the "great cat massacre" studied by Robert Darnton, "one might want to 'understand' it, insofar as possible, but never with full empathy and always at a distance."[109] We should avoid, however, commodifying Buddhist homosexuality, as Tokugawa society (and some of its Western interpreters) did.

[109] Robert Darnton, *The Great Cat Massacre* (New York: Basic Books, 1984).

AFTERTHOUGHTS

T HE ABOVE DISCUSSION has tended to emphasize the monks' (and to a lesser extent the nuns') encroachments on Buddhist discipline rather than their observance of it. Undoubtedly transgression, the *nec plus ultra* of antinomianism, is easier to locate in the documents than obedience, the daily rice of monastic life. However, my intention in describing these transgressive feasts and fasts was not to indulge in titillating tales nor to endorse the kinds of anticlerical critiques we have examined, but rather to try to locate where the trouble lies, where the Buddhist sandal pinches. An idealized vision of Buddhism can only contribute to entertain the illusion—and at worst to create the condition of possibily of the very scandal—which it attempts to cover. A critical approach should try to explain these breaches to the rule, rather than blame or justify them.

How can we take into account the Buddhist will to transcendence—a will that drives practitioners to go beyond their immediate context—without underestimating the impact of the social and cultural context of the Buddhist institution? Clearly, we must abandon the image of an atemporal and unlocalized Buddhism, of a radically otherworldly teaching. We must question as well the widespread notion of an originally "pure" doctrine that, due to some monks' unfortunate concern for proselytizing and their compromise with the spirit of the time, happened to take one (or several) wrong turn(s). We will thus be led to reconsider the summary verdict passed against religious movements like Tantrism or "popular" Buddhism. Buddhism has been defined as a doctrine halfway between rigorism and transgression, between the two extremes of desire and nondesire. However, its much-vaunted "middle way" is itself double tracked and double edged: maintaining in principle a precarious balance between the two extremes, yet constantly torn in practice between these centrifugal tendencies. Once we reject the notion of a "pure," atemporal, and changeless doctrine, we are able to appreciate as a positive characteristic of Buddhism its flexibility, its singular capacity to adapt to the multiplicity of times and cultures.

The early Buddhist denial of sexuality responded to various motivations such as the refusal of desire, the fear of spiritual (and physical) impotence, and latent or patent misogyny. The point was also for clerics to distinguish themselves clearly as a group from lay practitioners, to draw conspicuous and hard-to-cross boundaries. Such was perhaps the main function of the Vinaya and its rites of passage, which are above all rites of demarcation. We noted the violent reaction of Vinaya legislators against these strange individuals, neither fish nor fowl, called *paṇḍaka*: beings who, by blurring genres and genders, seem to escape the "law of the genre" (*loi du genre*). Nevertheless, homosexuality was tolerated inasmuch as it clearly remained male and monastic, and did not call gender roles into doubt: like the ephebes of ancient Greece, the passive partners in Buddhist homosexuality were novices—children or adolescents—and not effeminate adults. Thus, the Buddhist saṅgha could preserve its integrity and its essential difference. Even in Japan, where homosexuality was culturally well accepted socially, it was for a long time perceived as an essentially monastic phenomenon. This remained true even after "male love" lost some of its "distinction" by diffusing into other social layers (first the aristocracy, then the warrior class, and finally the urban—and not so urbane—bourgeoisie).

Thus, either through observance of the rule or on the contrary through its transgression, monks have always claimed a distinct sexuality: the ideal chastity and ascesis of regular monks are as opposed to ordinary sexuality as to the sexual practices of Vajrayāna adepts. If clerical positions with regards to sexuality are hand-in-glove with the definition of the monastic group as such, it follows that the modification of one of these parameters (for instance, the adoption of new practices and conceptions, or the opening of Buddhism to new social categories) should have repercussions on Buddhism in its entirety.

My initial intention was to describe a complex and heterogeneous cultural phenomenon, the emergence of a Buddhist discourse on sexuality (and gender). Despite the fragmentary and multiple nature of this approach, or because of it, a sometimes uniform and simplistic scenario has tended to impose itself, which fails to do justice to the intricacy of the doctrines and of their sociohistorical contexts. This textual strategy has contributed to intensify the effects of the Buddhist ideology, an ideology that usually tried to reduce the multiplicity of possible attitudes toward sex and to circumscribe sexuality as a simple problem, liable to a single solution. We need to keep in mind that this reality was fundamentally different—singular, diverse, elusive, changing.

Having reached this point in the argument, some heuristic simplifications are no longer acceptable. I have tended, for instance, to identify the body and sexuality, at the risk of anachronistically projecting modern notions onto a traditional doctrine. As we know, sex and gender symbolism is extremely multivocal, and Buddhism is no exception in this respect. Feminine symbols, for instance, cannot be read simply as a reassertion of feminine values. In a teaching like Tantrism, where reversal and inversion are the name of the game, one should therefore not be surprised to see the allegedly inferior, that is, women, exalted as superior. This symbolic reversal characterizes only a liminal, paradoxical stage, and does not affect in practice the socially inferior status of women.

The same is true for the valorization—positive or negative—of the body. Buddhism has not explicitly identified the body and sexuality, nor has it constantly rejected the body as evil. Even when the Buddha is called the "great male," his masculine characteristics are not necessarily glorified. As Carolyne Bynum points out in the Christian context, the penis of Christ—in some medieval representations at least—meant above all suffering and purification.[1] Similarly, perhaps the famous "cryptorchidy" of the Buddha means less a denial of sexuality than an affirmation of his superhuman nature—which allows him to shift instantaneously from latency to actuality, from one mode of being to another. Thus, according to a commentary on the "horse-penis samādhi"—a form of esoteric concentration said to be that "of the secret organ, hidden as with the great male [the Buddha]": "Passions are manifested through error and eliminated through awakening, just as the horse's organ appears at the moment of the rut and hides right after."[2]

We noted at the beginning that, unlike Christianity, there has never been in Buddhism a full-fledged discourse on sexuality. Nevertheless, if Buddhism has never conceptualized sex and gender in the past, it may now have reached the point where it needs to do so. Indeed, the main aspects of Buddhist practice (interdictions, transgression, deliverance) are themselves today, in Western as in Asian cultures, affected by a modernity that leads to conceiving them more and more in terms of sexuality and gender difference. And if it is true that modernization requires the emergence of a lay Buddhism, it will be also necessary to address head-on problems that were kept until now among the "reserved" or insignificant questions (marriage and contraception). In the case of Japan, for instance, Buddhism has in the recent past found a growing number of female adherents through a reinterpretation and social reinscription of the cult of the Bodhisattva Jizō as means to solve the psychological sequels of the widespread practice of abortion. However, the Buddhist approach to contraception remains essentially negative and guilt-provoking, and responds only slowly to demographic and social changes.

As I argue in *Purity and Gender,* a consistent feminist critique could well shatter Buddhism in its foundations. It is indeed clear that not only the basic dogmas of Buddhism but the symbolic economy in which they are inscribed as well derive from a masculine ideology. The opening of

[1] See Bynum 1991: 92. For a different viewpoint, see Steinberg 1996.
[2] See *Hōbōgirin* 1: 16.

Buddhism to feminine values is therefore not without risks: it threatens to affect the very content of the Buddhist awakening, traditionally perceived as a rupture, a reversal, a social drama that is reenacted endlessly by hagiographical literature. Without essentializing feminine approaches, women practitioners tend to insist on the progressive, nondramatic, intimate character of their religious experience. One could assume that a greater emphasis on women's viewpoint would bring about some significant change regarding the classical schema of opposition or reversal between prohibition and transgression. We can suspect that this schema—reproduced in the present book—is one of the effects of the masculine ideology which has until now predominated in Buddhism.

The central role of interdiction and transgression in Buddhist soteriology, around which this study has tended (or vainly tried) to organize itself, needs therefore to be questioned in turn: not because these notions may be mere figments of the author's imagination, but on the contrary because they simply reproduce the male (hence partial in both senses: biased and incomplete) viewpoint of the Buddhist tradition—a tradition that nevertheless boasts of having transcended the extremes. As a paltry excuse, I may put forward that it is difficult to avoid, if not taking sides, at least taking note of the story as it has been told us—that is, from a viewpoint that implicitly excludes others (female and "neuter").

I acknowledge what my emplotment owes to Bataille's notions of taboo and transgression. Eroticism, like asceticism, is an attempt to go beyond the level of reproduction. Bataille defines eroticism as an approbation of life even into death. Transgression is the very movement of spirituality: to exceed all limits, to abide nowhere—as the *Vajracchedikā-sūtra* puts it. It is a constant violence to or violation of the homeostatic tendency of human nature, an ex-stasis, excess, hubris. Although there are obvious problems with such notions cross-culturally, I still believe that we can retain Bataille's insight that transgression is not a negation of the taboo; it goes beyond it and completes it.[3]

Finally, the fragments of a history of Buddhist sexuality that we have been able to examine, in particular in the Chinese case studied by van Gulik, strikingly recall, with their puritanic tone, the Victorian model analyzed by Foucault. As we know, Foucault called into question the "repressive model" of the Western history of sexuality, a model illustrated by Victorian society. Can we then apply this model to Asia, and more specifically to Buddhism? After all, if the Western discourse on sex is not, as one could have believed, a lifting of the interdiction, perhaps in the Chinese case too the model does not provide us with a key to understanding the story. Admittedly, the injunction to speak about sex in the

[3] Bataille 1957: 70.

mode of confession—voluntary or forced—is less central in the Asian societies studied here than in the West, but it is certainly not absent. To what extent the Buddhist ideology regarding sexuality corresponds to real practices remains to be seen. The few concrete exemples borrowed from the history of Chinese and Japanese Buddhism are too fragmentary, scattered, to be considered as probing. Documents are too terse or normative, and the reality of practices they refer to will continue—probably for a long time—to elude us. It is difficult to dig out the discourses of passive resistance, in particular those of women. Sometimes a story like that of "Loquacious Lotus" or of the Zen nun Eshun, whose chaste death may be read as a kind of protest against normative sexuality, show us how some of them could thumb their nose at Buddhism and the dominant culture it more or less willingly echoed. However, these voices are too isolated to represent anything more than the dotted line of a tradition of feminine sexuality and its resistance to male discourses on sex and gender.

According to the scenario adopted here, monastic norms and desires—which reflect the law of the male gender—are belied by social realities. If Buddhist ideology finds its limits in practice, however, it also succeeds in modifying these realities, and at the same time it also changes at their contact, thus filling the gap between ideal and practice by a lowering of this ideal and an opening onto the world. Because of this interpenetration, the tension between the two poles—ascetic religion and social world—tends to diminish, and Buddhism is in turn coopted by various social ideologies, some of which are anti-feminist, others not.

We must also insist on the obvious impossibility of treating a topic like "Buddhist" sexuality—even if it seems culturally external and sufficiently objectivized—without implicating oneself with one's desires and biases. The goal in the last analysis is to understand, through twists and turns, the shifting and sometimes interchangeable places of desire, interdictions, and transgression in one's own life. But why start from the primacy of desire, as I have done, rather than from that of the interdiction? We could as well have posited that desire is the outcome, not the presupposition, of the interdiction. We would then have obtained a scenario quite different from the one adopted here, probably equally valid—or invalid. Whatever hypothesis is used, however, the structural complicity of the interdiction and transgression remains.

Yet, as Bataille pointed out, by considering transgression from the outside, as an object to analyze, we still accept the premises of a discourse centered on the rule.[4] We may want at this point to bring into play what Foucault called the "speaker's benefit": the repressive model implies a

---

[4] See ibid., 43–44.

transgression in the very fact of speaking of Buddhist sexuality, of trying to create a more or less coherent discourse about it, where the tradition as a whole has shown a certain discretion.[5] There is transgression in the very fact of speaking of sex, of creating a (relatively) coherent discourse about it when the tradition itself has remained conspicuously prudish. Here we are confronted with the basic impudence, or even exhibitionism, of the scholar. Is he/she then simply trying to lift the repression, to retrieve silenced voices? Or does he/she participate, as Foucault thinks, in the very movement that he/she imagines himself/herself to be denouncing, a movement which always connects in new ways sex and desire to power? By trying to unmask a Buddhist economy of bodies and pleasures, what game are we playing? This is another question which, if it cannot be answered, needs at least to be raised at the end, if only to avoid too quick a conclusion.

Illustrating my favorite principle of "nothing is simple," the first model we have used—opposing in straightforward fashion norm and transgression—allowed us to see that transgression is not as transgressive as it appears, that it is itself more often than not essentially normative. The norm/transgression dichotomy still belongs to the structure. To show it, I have examined in the second part of the book the heterogeneous fields in the interstices of which the constellation of (or fragmented discourse on) Buddhist sexuality was able to emerge.

The Vinaya constitutes the most developed codification of the Buddhist discourse on sex. One can speak about sex—with details—only at the moment of the *poṣadha* (Pāli *uposatha*)—through the ritualization of a discourse otherwise prohibited. In Sino-Japanese Buddhism, however, sex seems to escape the obligation of being formulated, put into discourse, characteristic of Christian monachism (and to a lesser extent of early Buddhism: Indian legalism may also have the effect of limiting the offense to the deeds, and not pursuing it in thoughts).[6]

Buddhist discourse is transitive, and varies according to its audience. Thus, it can address itself to monks (monastic discourse), to rulers (state Buddhism and court Buddhism, two closely related yet sometimes quite different entities), and to the people (popular Buddhism). There is also a backlash discourse: once uttered, discourse can indeed be used by other people to other ends. Thus, the clergy talked about sexuality to control others (in particular clerics and women), but its discourse was co-opted

---

[5] See Foucault 1978: 6.

[6] "Cette matière ressemble à la poix qui, étant maniée de telle façon que ce puisse être, encore même que ce serait pour la jeter loin de soi, tache néanmoins et souille toujours." ("This matter is similar to pitch, for, however one might handle it, even to cast it far from oneself, it sticks nonetheless, and always soils.") See P. Segneri, *L'instruction du pénitent* (1695): 301, quoted in Foucault 1978: 19.

by others: whereas sexist commonplaces gave at times more power to women, the Vinaya may have suggested transgressive ideas to monks.

The principle of double ambivalence means that, although Buddhism is simultaneously liberating and repressive, its most sexist theses may not be as repressive as they look, nor its most equalitarian theses as liberating. Over against its orthodox discourse (which claims to be normative) emerges a backlash discourse: Buddhism is no longer agent or subject, but merely a narrative actor, an object acted upon. Thus, in the folkloric tradition, in imperial ideology, or in entertaining arts, we find Buddhist ideas that have gone wild—or wise.

The Buddhist discourse on sexuality intertwines many threads, among which the red thread of normative orthodoxy is only one, now visible, now covered by others. This dual—and doubly so—Buddhism echoes, counterbalances, makes a counterpoint to, or causes interference on the patriarchal ideology hawked by doctrines like Confucianism.

As it shifted from otherworldly asceticism to mundane asceticism, from a world-renouncing to a world-conquering ideology, Buddhism encountered sex in three major forms: as the principle of the world of individual and collective becoming; as one of the cardinal functions of local gods and religious specialists; and as the basis of sovereignty and kingship. Therefore, the Buddhist discourse on sexuality emerged in response to several different yet interrelated dynamics: as a partial explanation of the mechanism of individual karma; as a discourse on familial prosperity, which had been the preserve of Confucian ideology; as a way of taking into account the popular association of Buddhist deities and local gods, and the cosmological system derived from the yin-yang theories; and as a response to local strategies of power, most visible at court, but recurring at every level of society.

When we examine the anthropological structures of the Buddhist and Japanese *imaginaires*—in particular recurrent symbols like the dragon, the jewel (in the lotus), and the cave—it seems that the importance of female and sexual symbolism has considerably increased. However, the shift from male buddhas to female deities does not mean that Buddhism passed into female hands.

Another element to emphasize in the Japanese context is the importance of the vengeful spirits (*onryō* or *goryō*), and the fact that much in Japanese religious practice was based on fear. Far from being mere abstractions, hypostases (*suijaku*) of some divine or Buddhist principle, the goryō had a disturbing reality. They are the fault or the risk inherent in the system, the danger that makes sex necessary: in order to tame them (as in the case of Vināyaka), or to reestablish the harmonious alternation of yin and yang. Thus, the shift from goryō to *warei* (harmonious spirits), the euphemization, or the derisive laughter of Edo culture may indicate less a withdrawal of religiosity than a repression of fear through laughter, a repetition of Uzume's gesture. Buddhism was caught in this general movement of Japanese culture. Buddhist sexuality is a byproduct of this evolution.

The first chapter of this book was on the Law (rather than the norm). Foucault rejects the notion of Law, but the Law is ideologically the source, the starting point, of Buddhist thought. There is no way around it, but this necessary stage is what will allow us to question its primacy and relevance later on.

The recent (and future) evolution of Buddhism, which as been described (and invoked) by some as from a patriarchal to a non- (or post-)patriarchal society, is primarily a shift from a deployment of alliance to a deployment of sexuality.[7] What matters, in traditional Buddhist sexuality, is indeed the question of lineage, of alliance (and therefore also of patriarchy). Even sexual transgression—like its structural opposite, ascesis—was perceived essentially as a refusal of biological filiation and lineage. In this context, sexuality was primarily opposed to fertility.

In Buddhism as in the West, sexuality is intimately tied to power. However, I must also nuance my analysis of Buddhist power from a Foucaldian perspective. Power is not exerted from above but comes from below. We are rarely confronted with originary, global, and clear-cut cleavages that would determine local power relationships; rather, the multiple power relationships taking shape in families and other social groups produce larger effects of cleavage which, through local confrontations, run throughout the entire social body.[8] Instead of a two-tiered structure, we encounter mobile and transitory points of resistance, which produce unstable fault lines, fracturing groups and individuals. Buddhism is itself traversed by these power relationships. It reveals local tactics, not a global strategy. Thus, we cannot generalize and speak, for instance, of an unvaryingly sexist Buddhism: despite the conventional singular, Buddhism exists only in the plural. However, these Buddhisms reproduce and reinforce splits that already exist in a given society, power relationships that connect to each other in a network, following the apparent logic of a global strategy that retrospectively looks like a unitary and voluntary politics of sexuality.[9]

Discourses are not once and for all submitted to power, they can also become obstacle, resistance, starting point of an opposite strategy (for instance, the discourse on sodomy in Western culture). The same is true for the Buddhist discourse on the five feminine "obstacles": although it is

[7] Foucault 1978: 106.
[8] See ibid., 94–96.
[9] Ibid., 97–98.

fundamentally an alienating discourse, it can (and often did) become a factor of hope, a reason to claim gender equality. We can, in this case as in many others, observe the constitution of a "reverse discourse." Thus, if I had to rewrite this book (gods and buddhas forbid), I would try to use a tactical model rather than the model of the law and (dis)order. I would emulate Foucault's attempt to use a conception of power that substitutes the viewpoint of the objective for that of the law, the viewpoint of tactical efficacy for the privilege of the interdiction.[10]

A subtitle (or, as in Buddhist texts, a post-title) of this book could have been borrowed from Robertson Davies's novel, *What's Bred in the Bone.* Indeed, in the case of Buddhism, "what's bred in the bone returns in the flesh," in the sense that the Buddhist dream of purity led to the deviations and scandals we have seen; but one could also, inverting the saying, argue that what's bred in the flesh—the woman, or local cults—returns in the bone—that is, canonical Buddhism. In the nondualism of ultimate truth (the marrow of the Buddhist teaching), the distinction between the bones and the flesh is no longer valid, the essential "truth" of Buddhism is no different from its cultural "accidents." Thus, "pure" Buddhism develops hand in glove with its sexual "deviations."

Faced once again with an impossible attempt at closure, I have to (re)capitulate. In a typical relation of transference, the same movement that I detected in the sexual theology of medieval Japanese Buddhism— where the attempt at closure (through the elaboration of a Tantric ideology of the yin and yang) has liberated a "difference" that disseminates into a proliferation of "real" gods and goryō—has also been the failure of my narrative plot—which started as a simple binary (yin-yang-like) model of norm versus transgression (first part of the book), but which soon found transgression to be a problematic notion, which transgresses its limits and leads to complex overflows (second part). It is these overflows that I will try to channel or dike up in (by) *Erecting Obstacles.*

[10] Ibid., 102.

GLOSSARY

abhiṣeka (Skt.)	ritual of consecration by ablution (J. kanjō)
ajari (J.)	officiating priest
arhat (Skt.)	Buddhist saint who has attained enlightment
basara (J.)	extravagance, luxury; madness; unconventionality
bhikku (Pāli)	lit. "beggar"; a Buddhist monk
bodhi (Skt.)	awakening, enlightenment
bodhicitta (Skt.)	"thought of awakening"; semen
bodhisattva (Skt.)	one who has taken a vow to become a buddha
buppō (J.)	Buddhist Law
chigo (J.)	young boy, young novice
daijōsai (J.)	enthronement ceremony
devī (Skt.)	goddess
Dharma (Skt.)	lit., that which is real or true; Buddhist doctrine
dhyāna (Skt.)	meditation; trancelike meditative absorption
emaki (J.)	pictorial scroll
engi (J.)	genealogical tale
eta (J.)	outcast
geinō (J.)	arts of entertainment
gekokujō (J.)	"topsy-turvy world"
genpuku (J.)	coming-of-age ceremony
gojisō (J.)	attendant priest
hattō (J.)	ordinance
hinin (J.)	outcast
hongaku (J.)	innate enlightenment
honzon (J.)	object (of a ritual)
irui igyō (J.)	weird and strange; weird people
jisha (J.)	acolyte
jitō (J.)	military steward
kagema (J.)	male prostitute
kami (J.)	god or spirit
kasshiki (J.)	postulant
katabira (J.)	robe
kawaramono (J.)	outcast, "living on the river bank"
keikan (J.)	sodomy
mahāsukha (Skt.)	Great Bliss
matsuji (J.)	branch-temple
monogatari (J.)	literary stories
monogurui (J.)	madness
monzeki (J.)	abbot; Buddhist temples governed by an imperial prince
mudrā (Skt.)	seal; hand gesture; female partner
muen (J.)	without ties; unrelatedness, autonomy
nanshoku (J.)	male homosexuality

nenbutsu (J.)	invocation of the holy name of Amida Buddha
nyobon (J.)	lit. assaulting women; male intercourse with women
ōbō (J.)	royal law
ōchigo (J.)	older chigo
onryō (J.)	malevolent spirit
otogizōshi (J.)	narrative story
paṇḍaka (Skt.)	passive homosexual
pārājika (Skt.)	"defeat"; describes an offense calling for exclusion from the saṅgha
poṣadha (Skt.)	penance ritual
prajñā (Skt.)	wisdom
pāramitā (Skt.)	perfection of wisdom
prajnōpāya (Skt.)	union of wisdom and skillful means; perfect union of the Buddha with his śakti
sahaja (Skt.)	lit. "simultaneously arisen"; Tantric rite of preliminary bliss, preparatory for ultimate bliss
śakti	female companion of a deity, representing his energy
samādhi (Skt.)	meditative concentration; trance state attained through yoga
sambodhi (Skt.)	Illumination
saṃsāra (Skt.)	cycle of birth and death
saṅgha (Skt.)	the Buddhist community
saṅghādiṣeśa (Skt.)	offenses leading to temporary exclusion from the saṅgha
senryū (J.)	satirical verse
sennin (J.)	ascetic
setsuwa (J.)	Buddhist tales
shami (J.)	novice
shinwa (J.)	myth
shirabyōshi (J.)	dancing girl
shokunin (J.)	"artisan," outcast
shudō (J.)	"way of the youth"
siddha (Skt.)	saint famous for his powers (*siddhi*)
sokui kanjō (J.)	enthronement rites
sūtra (Skt.)	doctrinal discourse attributed to the Buddha
tengu (J.)	mountain spirit, goblin
terakoshō (J.)	temple page
ujidera (J.)	clan temple
upāya (Skt.)	skillful means
uposatha (Pāli)	penance ritual
vajra (Skt.)	diamond; thunderbolt; metaphor for the male organ in Tantrism
Vinaya (Skt.)	code of monastic discipline
wakamiya (J.)	young gods
wakashū (J.)	temple youth, young man

warawa (J.)	adolescent
yamabushi (J.)	mountain ascetic
zasu (J.)	head monk

BIBLIOGRAPHY

PRIMARY SOURCES

Abbreviations

DNBZ   *Dai Nihon bukkyō zensho.* Edited by Takakusu Junjirō et al. 150 vols. Tokyo: Dai Nihon bukkyō zensho kankōkai, 1913–1921. Reedited, 100 vols. Suzuki gakujutsu zaidan, ed. Tokyo: Kōdansha, 1970–1973.

NKBT   *Nihon koten bunkaku taikei.* Edited by Takagi Ichinosuke et al. 102 vols. Tokyo: Iwanami shoten, 1957–1968.

NKBZ   *Nihon koten bungaku zenshū.* Edited by Akiyama Ken et al. 51 vols. Tokyo: Shōgakkan, 1970–1976.

NSTK   *Nihon shisō taikei.* Edited by Ienaga Saburō et al. 67 vols. Tokyo: Iwanami shoten, 1970–1982.

PTS   Pāli Text Society.

SNKBT   *Shin Nihon koten bungaku taikei.* Edited by Satake Akihiro et al. 56 vols. Tokyo: Iwanami shoten, 1989–.

T.   *Taishō shinshū daizōkyō.* Edited by Takakusu Junjirō and Watanabe Kaigyoku. 100 vols. Tokyo: Taishō issaikyō kankōkai, 1924–1932.

Zuzō   *Taishō shinshū daizōkyō zuzōbu.* Edited by Takakusu Junjirō and Watanabe Kaigyoku. 12 vols. T. 86–97. Tokyo: Taishō issaikyō kankōkai, 1924–1935.

ZZ   *Dai Nihon zokuzōkyō.* Edited by Nakano Tatsue. 150 vols. Kyoto: Zōkyō shoin, 1905–1912. New edition, Taibei: Xinwenfeng, 1968–1970.

Collections

Chūsei hōsei shiryō shū. Edited by Satō Shin'ichi et al. Tokyo: Iwanami shoten, 1962.

Chūsei shintō ron. Edited by Ōsumi Kazuo. NSTK 19. Tokyo, 1977.

Dai Nihon shiryō. Series 4 and 5. Edited by Tōkyō daigaku shiryō hensanjo. 17 and 24 vols. to date. Tokyo, 1902–.

Guben xiaoshuo jicheng. 160 vols. Shanghai: Guji chubanshe, 1990.

Gunsho ruijū. Compiled by Hanawa Hokiichi (1779–1819). 24 vols. Tokyo: Naigai shoseki, 1928–1937.

Heian ibun. Edited by Takeuchi Rizō. 15 vols. Tokyo: Tōkyōdō shuppan, 1947–1980.

Jiu Tang shu (945). Attributed to Liu Xu (887–946). 16 vols. Beijing: Zhonghua shuju. 1975.

Jōdoshū zensho. 1911–1914. 20 vols. Reedited 1936. Tokyo: Sankibō busshorin, 1973.

Kamakura ibun. Edited by Takeuchi Rizō. 42 vols. to date. Tokyo: Tōkyōdō shuppan, 1971–.

Kōbō daishi zenshū. Kūkai (774–835). Tokyo-Kyoto, 1910. Reprint 8 vols. Kōyasan daigaku, Mikkyō bunka kenkyūjo, 1965.

Kojiruien. Edited by Kojiruien kankōkai. 60 vols. Reprint. Tokyo, 1931; reprint Tokyo: Yoshikawa kōbunkan, 1977.

Kokushi taikei. 1899. Revised edition by Kuroita Katsuichi. 66 vols. Tokyo: Yoshikawa kōbunkan, 1929–1964.

Ming Qing pinghua xiaoshuo xuan. Edited by Lu Gong. First Series. Shanghai, 1958.

Nihon koten bunkaku taikei. Edited by Takagi Ichinosuke et al. 102 vols. Tokyo: Iwanami shoten, 1957–1968.

Nihon koten bungaku zenshū. Edited by Akiyama Ken et al. 51 vols. Tokyo: Shōgakkan, 1970–1976.

Nihon shisō taikei. Edited by Ienaga Saburō et al. 67 vols. Tokyo: Iwanami shoten, 1970–1982.

Nihon zuihitsu taisei. Edited by Hayakawa Junzaburō et al. 81 vols. Tokyo: Yoshikawa kōbunkan, 1973–1979.

Sharebon taisei. Edited by Mizuno Minoru et al. 31 vols. Tokyo: Chūō kōronsha, 1978–1988.

Shin Nihon koten bungaku taikei. Edited by Satake Akihiro et al. 56 vols. Tokyo: Iwanami shoten, 1989–.

Shinshū shiryō shūsei. 36 vols. Kyoto: Dōbōsha, 1983.

Shinshū taisei. 36 vols. Tokyo: Shinshū tenseki kankōkai, 1916–1925. Reedited 30 vols. Tokyo: Kokusho kankōkai, 1974.

Shinshū zensho. 75 vols. Kyoto: Zōkyō shoin, 1913–1916. Reedited Tokyo: Kokusho kankōkai, 1971.

Sōtōshū zensho. 18 vols. Reedited by Sōtōshū zensho kankōkai. Tokyo: Sōtōshū shūmuchō, 1970–1973.

Tendaishū zensho. 25 vols. Tokyo: Daiichi shobō, 1973.

Xin Tang shu (1043–1060). Compiled by Ouyang Xiu (1007–1072), Song Qi (998–1061), et al. 20 vols. Beijing: Zhonghua shuju, 1975.

Zōho shiryō taisei. 4th ed. Kyoto: Rinsen shoten, 1985.

Zoku gunsho ruijū. Compiled by Hanawa Hokiichi. 1822. 34 vols. Tokyo: Zoku gunsho ruijū kanseikai, 1972.

Zoku zoku gunsho ruijū. Edited by Zoku gunsho ruijū kanseikai. 16 vols, 1906. Tokyo: Kokusho kankōkai, 1970.

Individual Works

Abhidharmakośa-śāstra. By Vasubandhu. T. 29, 1558. French translation by Louis de La Vallée Poussin. *L'Abhidharmakośa de Vasubandhu*. 6 vols. Paris: Geuthner, 1923–1931.

Aṅguttara-nikāya. Edited by R. Morris and E. Hardy. London: PTS, 1885–1900. Translated by F. L. Woodward and E. M. Hare. *The Book of Gradual Sayings*. 6 vols. PTS Translation Series 22, 24–27. London: Luzac, 1932–1936. Reprint 1960–1972.

Aki no yo no monogatari (ca. 1377). *Gunsho ruijū* 14, 311.

Asaba shō. By Shōchō (1205–1282). T., *Zuzō* 8–9.

Ashibiki-e. Edited by Komatsu Shigemi. Zoku Nihon no emaki, 25. Tokyo: Chūō kōron sha, 1978.

Avataṃsaka-sūtra (Huayan jing). T. 9, 278; T. 10, 279. Translated by Thomas Cleary. *The Flower Ornament Scripture.* Boston and London: Shambhala, 1984. Reprint 1993.

Azuma kagami. Anonymous. *Kokushi taikei* 32–33. Revised and expanded edition by Kuroita Katsumi. 60 vols. Tokyo: Yoshikawa kōbunkan, 1929–1967.

Besson zakki. By Shinkaku (1117–1180). T., Zuzō 3.

Bian er chai. Late Ming edition. Taibei: Palace Museum. Taibei: Tianyi chubanshe, 1990.

Bishamondō Kokinshū chū (14th c.). In Mikan kokubu kochūshaku taikei 4. 1935.

Biyan lu. By Xuetou Chongxian (980–1052). Commentary by Yuanwu Keqin (1063–1135). T. 48, 2003.

Bizei betsu. By Jien (d. 1225). In Tendai shūten hensanjo, ed. *Zoku Tendaishū zensho. Mikkyō* 3, *Kyōten chūshakurui* 2: 212–57. Tokyo: Shunjūsha, 1990. Also in Akamatsu Toshihide, *Kamakura bukkyō no kenkyū.* Kyoto: Heirakuji shoten, 1957: 317–35.

Bṛhadāraṇyaka Upaniṣad. Translated by Swāmī Mādhavānanda, Delhi: Advaita Ashrama, 1975.

Byakuhōshō. By Chōen (fl. 1278–1290). T., Zuzō 10.

Candamahāroṣana-tantra. Manuscript. Paris: Bibliothèque Nationale.

Chanyuan qinggui. By Changlu Zongze. ZZ 1, 2, 16, 5. Taibei ed., vol. 111.

Chanyuan zhuquanji duxu. By Guifeng Zongmi (d. 841). T. 48, 2015.

Chengshi lun (Satyasiddhiśāstra). T. 32, 1646.

Chigo kanjō shiki (beginning of Edo). Shinnyo Collection, Hieizan bunko.

Chigo kyōkun. By Sōgi. In *Gunsho ruijū* 14, 311.

Chōshūki. Vols. 16–17 in *Zōho shiryō taisei,* edited by Zōho shiryō taisei kankō-kai. Kyoto: Rinsen shoten, 1965.

Chūyūki. By Fujiwara no Munetada (1062–1141). 7 vols. *Shiryō taisei* 9–15. Revised and expanded edition. 99 vols. Kyoto: Rinsen shoten, 1965.

Dacheng wusheng fangbian men. T. 85, 2834.

Dai Birushana jōbutsu shinpen kaji kyō. T. 18, 848.

Dankai. By Tsumura Shōkyō. Tokyo: Kokusho kankōkai, 1970.

Dari jing yishi. By Yixing (683–727). ZZ 1, 36, 3–5. Taibei ed., vol. 36.

Da Song sengshi lue (977). By Zanning (919–1001). T. 54, 2126.

Da Tang xiyuji. By Xuanzang. T. 51, 2087. Japanese translation by Mizutani Shinjō. *Daitō Saiiki.* Chūgoku koten bungaku taikei 22. Tokyo: Heibonsha, 1971.

Dazhidulun. T. 25, 1509. French translation by Etienne Lamotte. *Le Traité de la Grande Vertu de Sagesse de Nāgārjuna.* 5 vols. Louvain: Institut Orientaliste, 1944–1980.

Denbu monogatari (ca. 1636–1643). Translated in Gary Leupp, *Male Colors: The Construction of Homosexuality in Tokugawa Japan.* Berkeley and Los Angeles: University of California Press, 1995.

Dharmaguptaka vinaya. T. 22, 1628.

Dhirghāgama (Chang ahan jing) . T. 1, 1.

Dīghanikāya. Translated by T. W. Rhys Davids and C.A.F. Rhys Davids. *Dialogues of the Buddha.* 3 vols. London: PTS, 1899, 1910, 1921. Reprint 1956, 1965, 1966.

Dunwu zhenzonglun (complete title: *Dacheng kaixin xianxing dunwu zhenzonglun*). T. 85, 2835.

Eihei shingi. By Dōgen. T. 82, 2584.

Fanwang jing. T. 24, 1484.

Fayuan zhulin (668). By Daoshi. T. 53, 2122.

Fozu tongji. By Zhipan. T. 49, 2035.

Fūryū Shidōken den. By Hiraga Gennai. *NKBT* 55: 153–224.

Genkō shakusho (1322). By Kokan Shiren (1278–1346). *DNBZ* 101 (ed. 1921); 1973 reprint 62, 470.

Genpei jōsuiki. In *Kōchū Nihon bungaku taikei* 15–16.

Gonshin shō (1414). By Enshun. *Zoku gunsho ruijū* 49: 636–53.

Guanfo sanmeihai jing. T. 15, 643.

Gujin xiaoshuo. By Feng Menglong. Beijing: Renmin wenxue chubanshe, 1958.

Gukanshō. By Jien. In Okami Masao and Akamatsu Toshihide, eds., *Gukanshō.* *NKBT* 86. Tokyo, 1967. See also *Kokushi taikei* 19. Translated by Delmer M. Brown and Ichirō Ishida. *The Future and the Past.* Berkeley and Los Angeles: University of California Press, 1979.

Gyokuyō. By Kujō Kanezane (1149–1207). 3 vols. Tokyo: Kokusho kankōkai, 1907.

Hachiman gudōkun. Text A: *Gunshō ruijū* 13; text B: *Zoku gunsho ruijū* 30. Both texts edited in Sakurai Tokutarō, Hagiwara Tatsuo, and Miyata Noboru, eds., *Jisha engi.* Nihon shisō taikei 20. Tokyo: Iwanami shoten, 1975.

Heike monogatari. Edited by Takagi Ichinosuke et al. *NKBT* 33. Tokyo, 1960. *Engyō-bon* recension edited by Yoshizawa Yoshinori, *Ōei shosha engyō-bon* Heike monogatari. Reprint Tokyo: Benseisha, 1977.

Hekizan nichiroku. By Unsen Taikyoku (1421–ca. 1472). Edited by Tsunoda Bun'ei and Gorai Shigeru. In Shintei zōho shiseki shūran kankōkai, ed., *Shintei zōho shiseki shūran* 26: 235–448. Kyoto: Rinsen shoten, 1927.

Hevajra-tantra. T. 18, 892. See David Snellgrove. *The Hevajra Tantra: A Critical Study.* London: Oxford University Press, 1959.

Hōjōki, Hosshinshū. Edited by Miki Sumito. Shinchō Nihon koten shūsei. Tokyo: Shinchōsha, 1976.

Hōkyō shō. By Yūkai (1345–1416). T. 77, 2456.

Honchō kōsōden (1702). By Shiban. *DNBZ* 63.

Honchō monzui. Kokushi taikei 29b. See also Osone Shōsuke, Kinpara Tadashi, and Goto Akio, eds., Shin Nihon koten bungaku taikei 27. Tokyo: Iwanami shoten, 1992.

Honchō shinsenden. By Ōe no Masafusa (1041–1111). Edited by Kawaguchi Hisao. Tokyo: Asahi Shinbunsha, 1967.

Hōnen shōnin gyōjō ezu. By Shunshō (1255–1335). In *Jōdoshū zensho* 16.

Hōnen shōnin zenshū. Edited by Kuroda Shindō and Mochizuki Shinkō. Kyoto: Shūsuisha, 1916.

Hōreki genrai shū, Zoku zuihitsu taisei, bekkan 6.

Hosshinshū. Compiled by Kamo no Chōmei. (1151–1213). In *Hōjōki, Hosshinshū*, edited by Miki Sumito. Shinchō Nihon koten shūsei. Tokyo: Shinchōsha, 1976.

Hyakurenshō. Anonymous (late 13th c.). *Shiryō taisei* 11.

Ihara Saikaku shū. Nihon koten bungaku zenshū. 3 vols. Tokyo: Shogakkan, 1971–1972.

Ikkyū banashi (1668). In Tsukamoto Tetsuzō, ed., *Zenrin hōwashū* 23. Tokyo: Yūhōdō, 1927.

Ikkyū shokoku monogatari. By Tsujimoto Motosada. 2 vols. 1844. In Kōda Rohan, ed., Nihon Bungei sōsho 18. Tokyo: Tōōdō, 1911.

Inryōken nichiroku. By Kikei Shinzui et al. *DNBZ* 75–78, 596 (vols. 133–137 in 1931 edition).

Ippen shōnin eden. Edited by Komatsu Shigemi. Tokyo: Chūō kōronsha, 1988.

Ishiyamadera engi emaki. In Komatsu Shigemi, ed., *Nihon emakimono*, vol. 7. Tokyo: Tōhō shoin, 1930.

Iwatsutsuji. In Asakura Haruhiko, ed., *Kanazōshi shūsei 5*. Tokyo: Tōkyōdō shuppan, 1984: 351–69.

Jakushōdō kokkyōshū. By Unshō (1614–1693). *DNBZ* 149.

Jiatai Pudeng lu. ZZ 2, 10, 1–2.

Jidian yulu. Edited by Lu Gong and Tan Tian. Guben pingjua xiaoshuo. Beijing: Renmin wenxue, 1984.

Jikkinshō. Edited by Nagatsumi Yasuaki. Iwanami bunko. Tokyo: Iwanami shoten, 1942.

Jingde chuandeng lu (1004). By Daoyuan (n. d.). T. 51, 2076.

Jingping mei cihua. By Xiaoxiaosheng (Ming). 4 vols. Hong Kong: Xinghai wenhua, 1987.

Jin Shu. By Fang Xuanling (578–648). 10 vols. Beijing: Zhonghua shuju, 1974.

Kakuzenshō. By Kakuzen (12th c.). T., Zuzō 4–5, 3022; *DNBZ* 53–56. (vols. 45–51 in 1921 edition).

Kashōki (1636). By Nyoraishi. Japanese translation by Watanabe Morikuni. *Kashōki*. Tokyo: Kyōikusha, 1979.

Kasshi yawa (ca. 1821). By Matsuura Seizan. Tokyo: Kokusho kankōkai, 1911.

Kathāvattu. Edited by A. C. Taylor. 2 vols. London: PTS, 1894–1897. Translated by C.A.F. Rhys Davids and S. Z. Aung. *Points of Controversy*. PTS Translation Series 5. London, 1915.

Keiran shūyōshū. By Kōshū (1276–1350). T. 76, 2410.

Kiyū shōran (1830). By Kitamura Nobuyo. 2 vols. Tokyo: Meicho kankōkai, 1970.

Kōbō Daishi ikkan no sho. In Mitsuo Sadatomo, ed., *Kinsei shomin bunka kenkyūkai* 13. Nanshoku bunken tokushū. Tokyo: Oranda shobō, 1952: 13–24.

Kōbō Daishi zenshū. By Kūkai (774–835). Edited by Mikkyō bunka kenkyūjo. 5 vols. Mt. Kōya: Mikkyō bunka kenkyūjo, 1970–1977.

Kogo shūi. By Inbe no Hironari (fl. 807). Edited by Nishimiya Kazunami. Tokyo: Iwanami bunko, 1991.

Kojidan (1212–1215). By Minamoto no Akikane. Edited by Kobayashi

Yasuharu. *Kojidan: Jō*. Koten bunko 60. Tokyo: Gendai Shichōsha, 1981. See also *Kokushi taikei* 18.

Kojiki. Edited by Kurano Kenji and Takeda Yūkichi. *NKBT* 1. Tokyo: Iwanami shoten, 1968. Translated by Donald L. Philippi. Tokyo: University of Tokyo Press, 1968; and Princeton: Princeton University Press, 1969.

Kokinshū chū. Edited in Mikan kokubun kochūshaku taikei, 4. 1935.

Kokon chōmonjū (1254). By Tachibana Narisue (fl. 1254). Edited by Nagazumi Yasuaki and Shimada Isao. *NKBT* 84.

Konjaku monogatari shū. Anonymous. Edited by Yamada Yoshio, Yamada Tadao, Yamada Hideo, and Yamada Toshio. 5 vols. *NKBT* 22–26.

Konku shō. In *Kinsei bukkyō shūsetsu* 1. Tokyo: Hirodani kokusho kankōkai, 1921.

Kōshoku gonin onna. By Ihara Saikaku. *NKBZ* 38: 305–423.

Kōshoku ichidai onna. By Ihara Saikaku. *NKBZ* 38: 425–583.

Kōshoku ichidai otoko. By Ihara Saikaku. *NKBZ* 38: 97–303.

Kuge shinsei. In *Zoku zoku gunsho ruijū* 7.

Kūya rui. By Minamoto Tamenori (d. 1011). *Zoku gunsho ruijū* 8.

Kyōunshū. By Ikkyū Sōjun (1394–1481). In Yanagida Seizan, ed., *Ikkyū, Ryōkan*. Tokyo: Chūō kōron, 1987.

Lidai fabaoji. T. 51, 2075.

Linji lu (full title: *Zhenzhou Linji Huizhao chanshi yulu*). T. 47, 1985.

Liushijia xiaoshuo. By Hong Pian. Edited by Tan Zhengbi (under the title *Qingpingshan tang huaben*). Shanghai, 1957.

Liuzu dashi fabao tanjing. T. 48, 2008.

Lun'yu. Harvard-Yenching Institute Sinological Series suppl. 16. *A Concordance to the Analects of Confucius*. Reprint Taipei: Chinese Materials and Research Aids Service Center, (1966) 1972.

Mādhyamikakārikā. By Nāgārjuna. T. 30, 1564.

Mahāparinirvāṇa-sūtra. Translated by Faxian. T. 1, 191.

Mahāparinirvāṇa-sūtra. T. 12, 365.

Mahāsāṅghika vinaya (Mohe sengqi lü). T. 22, 1425.

Mahāsāṅghika bhikṣuṇī vinaya. Translated by Hirakawa Akira, 1982.

Mahāvagga. In H. Oldenberg, *Vinaya-piṭaka* 1 (1879) Reprint London: PTS, 1964.

Mahāvairocana-sūtra. Translated by Śubhakarasiṃha and Yixing. T. 18, 848.

Mahāvastu. Translated by J. J. Jones. London: Luzac, 1949–1956.

Mahāyānasūtrālaṃkāra. By Asaṅga. Edited and translated by Sylvain Lévi. 2 vols. Paris: H. Champion, 1907–1911.

Majjhimanikāya. Edited by V. Trenckner. London: PTS, 1888.

Manzai Jugō nikki. *Zoku gunsho ruijū*, hoi (supplement) 1. Zuku gunsho ruijū kanseikai, 1932.

Mengqi bitan. By Shen Gua (1031–1095). Edited by Umehara Kaoru. *Mukei hitsudan*. 3 vols. Tokyo: Heibonsha, 1978–1981.

Mimibukuro. By Negishi Yasumori. Edited by Hasegawa Tsuyoshi. 3 vols. Tokyo: Iwanami shoten, 1991.

Mizu kagami. Maeda-ke bon (ca. 1191–1195). By Nakayama Tadachika. Kokushi taikei 21, 1. Tokyo: Kokushi taikei kankōkai, 1939.

Mohe zhiguan. By Zhiyi (538–597). T. 46, 1911.

Mon'yō ki. By Son'en Shinnō (1298–1356). T. *Zuzō* 11–12, 3216.

Mumyōzōshi. Edited by Kuwabara Hiroshi. Shinchō Nihon koten shūsei 7. Tokyo: Shinchōsha, 1976.

Nanhai jigui neifa zhuan. By Yijing. T. 54, 2125.

Nanshoku ōkagami. By Ihara Saikaku. *NKBZ* 39: 309–597. Translated by Paul Gordon Schalow. *The Great Mirror of Male Love.* Stanford: Stanford University Press, 1990.

Nara ibun. Edited by Takeuchi Rizō. 2 vols. Tokyo: Tōkyōdō, 1943–1944.

Nenashigusa kōhen. By Hiraga Gennai. Edited by Takagi Ichinosuke et al. *NKBT* 55: 95–151.

Nihon kiryaku. In *Kokushi taikei* 11.

Nihon ojō gokuraku ki (985–986). *DNBZ* 107; *Gunshō ruijū* 66.

Nihon ryōiki. By Kyōkai (fl. 823). Edited by Endō Yoshimoto and Kasuga Kazuo. *NKBT* 70. Translated by Kyoko Motomochi Nakamura, *Miraculous Stories from the Japanese Buddhist Tradition.* Cambridge: Harvard University Press, 1973.

Nihon shoki. (720). Edited by Sakamoto Tarō, Ienaga Saburō, Inoue Mitsusada, and Ōno Susumu. 2 vols. *NKBT* 67–68. Tokyo: Iwanami shoten, 1962–1967. See also *Kokushi taikei* 1.

Nomori no kagami. In *Gunsho ruijū* 21, 484.

Ōjō yōshū. By Genshin (942–1017). T. 84, 2682.

Qiantang huyin jidian chanshi yulu. Compiled by Wang Long (1569). In Lu Gong and Tan Tian, *Guben pinghua xianshuoji.* Beijing: Renmin wenxue, 1984.

Qingpingshan tang huaben. By Hong Bian (Ming). Shanghai: Shanghai guji, 1987.

Ratnakuṭa-sūtra. Translated by Bodhiruci et al. T. 11, 310.

Ritsuon sōbōden. In *DNBZ* 105.

Rokuharamitsuji engi. By Miyoshi Tameyasu (1049–1139).

Rou putuan. By Li Yu (end of Ming, beginning of Qing). Modern edition (no place, publisher, date).

Saddharmapuṇḍarīka-sūtra (Miaofa lianhua jing). T. 9. 262.

Saga monogatari. In Yokoyama Shigeru and Matsumoto Ryūshin, eds., *Muromachi jidai monogatari shūsei* 5. Tokyo: Kadogawa shoten, 1973–1988.

Saidaiji Eizon denki shūsei. Edited by Nara kokuritsu bunkazai kenkyūjo. Kyoto: Hōzōkan, 1977.

Samaññaphala-sutta. In *Dīghanikāya* 1. Edited by T. W. Rhys Davids and J. Estlin Carpenter. London: PTS, 1890.

Samantapāsādikā (Shanjian lü pipuosha). By Buddhagosa. T. 24, 1462. English translation by P. V. Bapat and Hirakawa Akira. *Shan-Chien-P'i-P'o-Sha.* Poona: Bhandarkar Oriental Research Institute, 1970.

Samguk yusa. By Ilyŏn. T. 49, 2039. Translated by Ha Tae-hung and Grafton K. Mintz. *Samguk Yusa: Legends and History of the Three Kingdoms of Ancient Korea.* Seoul: Yonsei University Press, 1972.

Sanbō ekotoba. In Yamada Yoshio. *Sanbōe ryakuchū.* Tokyo: Hōbunkan, 1951. English translation by Edward Kamens, *The Three Jewels: A Study and Translation of Minamoto Tamenori's* Sanbōe. Ann Arbor: Center for Japanese Studies, University of Michigan, 1988.

Sangō shiki. By Kūkai (775–835). *Kōbō daishi zenshū 3*.

Seisuishō (1623). By Anrakuan Sakuden. In Muto Sadao and Oka Masahiko, eds. *Seisuishō, Hanashibon taikei*. 20 vols. Tokyodō shuppan, 1975–1979. See also Suzuki Tōzō, ed. *Seisuishō*. 2 vols. Tokyo: Iwanami shoten, 1986.

Sengni niehai. Taibei: Tianyi chubanshe, 1990.

Senjūshō. Edited by Nishio Kōichi. Iwanami bunko. Tokyo: Iwanami shoten, 1970.

Shasekishū, by Mujū Ichien (1226–1312). Edited by Watanabe Tsunaya. *NKBT* 85. Tokyo: Iwanami shoten, (1966) 1975.

Shier lou. By Li Yu. In *Li Yu quanji*. Edited by Helmut Martin. 15 vols. Taibei, 1970.

Shingonshū kyōjigi. By Annen (841–?). T. 75, 2396.

Shin sarugaku ki. Edited by Kawaguchi Hisao. Tōyō bunko 424. Tokyo: Heibonsha.

Shintō shū. Modern Japanese translation by Kishi Shōzō. Tōyō bunko 94. Tokyo: Heibonsha, 1983.

Shin'yūki. NSTK 60: 7–25.

Shōbōgenzō. By Dōgen (1200–1253). T. 82, 2582.

Shoku Nihongi. SNKBT 12–15. Kokushi taikei, 2 vols. Tokyo: Yoshikawa kōbunkan, 1975.

Shouleng'yan jing. T. 19, 945.

Shōyūki. By Fujiwara no Sanesuke (957–1046). 3 vols. *Shiryō taisei*, bekkan 1–3.

Shūi kōtoku den (1301). By Kakunyo (1270–1351). Shinshū kana shōkyō 4.

Shutsujō kōgo. By Tominaga Nakamoto (1715–1746). Edited by Kyōdo Jikō. Tokyo: Ryūbunkan, 1982.

Sifen biqiuni chao. By Daoxuan (596–667). ZZ 1, 64, 1. Taibei ed., vol. 64.

Sifen lü (Dharmaguptaka vinaya). T. 22, 1428.

Sifen lü shanfan buque xingshi chao (630). By Daoxuan (596–667). T. 40, 1804.

Sifen lü shu. By Fali (569–633). ZZ 1, 65, 3–5. Taibei ed., vol. 65.

Soga monogatari. NKBT 88. Tokyo: Iwanami shoten, 1966.

Sokui hōmon. By Zonkai (1253–1332). Hieizan Bunko, Shinnyo zō (unpublished).

Song gaoseng zhuan. By Zanning (919–1001). T. 50, 2061.

Suetsumuhana. 1776–1801. 4 vols. Partial French translation in Jean Cholley, *Haiku érotiques*. Arles: Editions Philippe Picquier, 1996.

Sutta-nipāta. Sn 400, 609, 814, 835.

Taiheiki. I, II. Edited by Gotō Tanji and Kamata Kisaburō. *NKBT* 35, 36. Tokyo: Iwanami shoten, 1961.

Taiheiki. III. Edited by Yamashita Hiroaki. Shinchō Nihon koten shūsei. Tokyo: Shinchōsha, 1983.

Taiping guangji (978). By Li Fang (925–966) et al. Taibei: Guxin shuju, 1980.

Tang huiyao. Taibei: Shijie shuju, 1961.

Tōji Hyakugō komonjo. In *Kojiruien*, Shūkyōbu 2, 28.

Toribeyama monogatari. In *Gunsho ruijū* 14, 311.

Tsurezuregusa. By Urabe Kenkō (ca. 1280–1352). Edited by Kidō Saizō. Shinchō Nihon koten shūsei 10. Tokyo: Shinchōsha, 1977. English translation by William N. Porter. *The Miscellany of a Japanese Priest*. Rutland, Vt.: Charles E.

Tuttle, 1974; and by Donald Keene. *Essays in Idleness: The Tsurezuregusa of Kenkō.* New York: Columbia University Press, 1967.

Tsutsumi chūnagon monogatari. English translation by Robert L. Backus. *The Riverside Counselor's Stories: Vernacular Fiction of Late Heian Japan.* Stanford: Stanford University Press, 1985.

Ugetsu monogatari (1776). By Ueda Akinari. In Nakamura Yukihiko, ed., *Ueda Akinari shū. NKBT* 56. Tokyo, Iwanami shoten, 1959.

Uji shūi monogatari. Edited by Watanabe Tsuneya and Nishio Kōichi. *NKBT* 27. Tokyo: Iwanami shoten, 1960.

Ukiyo no arisama. Seikatsu shiryō shūsei 11.

Utsubo monogatari, vol. 1. Edited by Kōno Tama. *NKBT* 10. Tokyo: Iwanami Shoten, 1959.

Vimalakīrtinirdeśa (Weimojie jing). Translated by Zhi Qian (fl. 3rd c.). T. 14, 474. French translation by Etienne Lamotte. *L'enseignement de Vimalakīrti.* Louvain: Institut Orientaliste, (1962) 1987.

Vimuttimagga. T. 32, 1648. Translated by N.R.M. Ehara, Soma Thera, and Kheminda Thera. *The Path of Freedom.* Colombo: M. D. Gunasena, 1961.

Vinaya-piṭakam. Edited by H. Oldenberg. 5 vols. London: PTS, 1879–1883. Reprint 1964–1982.

Visuddhimagga. Edited by C.A.F. Rhys Davids. 2 vols. London: PTS, 1920–1921. Translated by Bhikkhu Nāñamoli. *The Path of Purification.* 2 vols. Colombo: Semage, 1956. Reprint Berkeley: Shambhala, 1976.

Wakan sansai zue. Compiled by Terashima Ryōan. 2 vols. Tokyo: Tōkyō bijutsu, 1970.

Xiyou ji. By Wu Cheng'en. 3 vols. Beijing: Renmin wenxue, 1984.

Xu gaoseng zhuan. By Daoxuan (596–667). T. 50, 2060.

Yamato monogatari. In Sakakura Atsuyoshi et al., eds., *Taketori monogatari, Ise monogatari, Yamato monogatari. NKBT* 9. Tokyo: Iwanami shoten, 1959.

Yanagidaru. Partial French translation in Jean Cholley, *Haiku érotiques.* Arles: Editions Philippe Picquier, 1996.

Yasaka jinja monjo. Compiled by Hirono Saburō. Yasaka jinja shamushō. 2 vols. Kyoto, 1939–1940.

Yijian ji. By Hong Mai. Edited by He Zhuo. 4 vols. Beijing: Zhonghua shuju, 1981.

Yōtenki. Zoku gunsho ruijū 48.

Youyang zazu. By Duan Chengshi. Edited by Imamura Yoshio. *Yuyō zasso.* 5 vols. Tokyo: Heibonsha, 1980–1981.

Zenkai shō. By Banjin Dōtan (1698–1775). T. 82, 2601.

Zenrin shōkisen. By Mujaku Dōchū (1653–1744). Kyoto: Baiyō shoin, 1909.

Zi buyu. By Yuan Mei (1716–1798). Shanghai: Shanghai guji chubanje, 1986.

Zōtanshū. Edited by Yamada Shōzen and Miki Sumito. Chūsei no bungaku. Tokyo: Sanmii shoten, 1973.

Zui puti (full title: *Jidian dashi zui puti quanzhuan*). In *Jidian dashi wanshi qiji, zui puti quanzhun,* edited by Baoren Tang, photo reproduction in vol. 73 of *Guben xiaoshuo jicheng.* See also *Gudai zhong pian xiaoshuo sanzhong,* edited by Guan Feimeng. Hangzhou: Zhejiang guji chubanshe, 1986.

Zuiweng tanlu (ca. 1150). By Jin Yingzhi. *Xinbian Zuiweng tanlu* edition. Shanghai: Gudian wenxue, 1958.

Zuting shiyuan (1108). By Muan Shanqing (fl. ca. 1100). ZZ 2, 18, 1. Taibei ed., vol. 113.

SECONDARY SOURCES

Abe Ryūichi. Forthcoming. *The Weaving of Mantra: Kūkai and the Construction of Esoteric Buddhist Textuality.*
Abe Shinji. 1981. *Hebigami denjōron josetsu.* Tokyo: Dentō to gendaisha.
Abe Yasurō. 1980. "'Iruka' no seiritsu." *Geinōshi kenkyū* 69: 16–38.
———. 1984. "Jidō setsuwa no keisei." *Kokugo kokubun* 600–601: 1–29, 30–56.
———. 1985. "Chūsei ōken to chūsei *Nihongi*: Sokuihō to sanjū shingisetsu o megurite." *Nihon bungaku* 34: 31–48.
———. 1988. "Seizoku no tawamure to shite no geinō: Yūjo, shirabyōshi, kusemai no monogatari o megurite." In Moriya Takeshi, *Geinō to chinkon: Kanraku to kyūzai no dainamizumu.* Tokyo: Shunjūsha.
———. 1989a. "Hōju to ōken: Chūsei ōken to mikkyō girei." In *Nihon shisō no shinsō.* Iwanami kōza tōyō shisō 16: *Nihon shisō* 2: 115–69. Tokyo: Iwanami shoten.
———. 1989b. "Nyonin kinzei to suisan." In Ōsumi Kazuo and Nishiguchi Junko, eds., *Josei to bukkyō.* Vol. 4: *Miko to joshin,* 153–240. Tokyo: Heibonsha.
———. 1990. "Jien to ōken: Chūsei ōken shinwa o umidashita mono." *Bessatsu Bungei,* special issue: *Tennōsei, rekishi, ōken, daijōsai,* 111–19. Tokyo: Kawade shobō shinsha.
———. 1992. "*Towazugatari* no ōken to buppō: Ariake no tsuki to Sutoku-in." In Akasaka Norio, ed., *Ōken no kisō e,* 2–66. Tokyo: Shin'yōsha.
———. 1993. "Jidō setsuwa to chigo." In Kamata Tōji, ed., *Ōdō shinkō.* Minshū shūkyōshi sōsho 27: 283–312. Tokyo: Yūzankaku shuppan.
———. 1995. "Irokonomi no kami: Dōsojin to aihōjin." In Yamaori Tetsuo, ed., *Nihon no kami.* Vol. 1: *Kami no shigen,* 121–72. Tokyo: Heibonsha.
Ackroyd, Joyce. 1959. "Women in Feudal Japan." In *Transactions of the Asiatic Society of Japan,* 31–68.
Addiss, Stephen. 1986. "The Zen Nun Ryonen Gensho (1646–1711)." In "Women in Buddhism" issue of *Spring Wind* 6 (1–3): 180–87.
Ahern, Emily M. 1975. "The Power and Pollution of Chinese Women." In Margery Wolf and Roxane Witke, eds., *Women in Chinese Society,* 193–214. Stanford: Stanford University Press.
Akamatsu Toshihide. 1957. *Kamakura bukkyō no kenkyū.* Kyoto: Heirakuji shoten.
Althusser, Louis. 1992. *L'avenir dure longtemps.* Paris: Stock/IMEC.
Amino Yoshihiko. 1978. *Muen. kugai. raku: Nihon chūsei no jiyū to heiwa.* Tokyo: Heibonsha.
———. 1993. *Igyō no ōken.* Tokyo: Heibonsha.
———. 1994. *Chūsei no hinin to yūjo.* Tokyo: Akashi shoten.
Andō Fumio. 1991. "Shinran ni okeru nyonin jōbutsu no mondai." In *Nihon bukkyō gakkai,* ed., *Bukkyō to josei,* 43–57. Kyoto: Heirakuji shoten.

Arai, Paula K. R. 1993. "Sōtō Zen Nuns in Modern Japan." In Mark R. Mullins, Shimazono Susumu, and Paul L. Swanson, eds., *Religion and Society in Modern Japan*, 203–18. Nanzan Institute for Religion and Culture. Berkeley: Asian Humanities Press.

Ariès, Philippe. 1982. "Réflexions sur l'histoire de l'homosexualité." In Philippe Ariès and André Béjin, eds., *Sexualités occidentales*, 81–96. Paris: Seuil.

Ariès, Philippe, and André Béjin, eds. 1982. *Sexualités occidentales*. Communications 35. Paris: Seuil.

Arntzen, Sonja. 1986. *Ikkyū and the Crazy Cloud Anthology: A Zen Poet of Medieval Japan*. Tokyo: University of Tokyo Press.

Astley, Ian. 1994. "Dairaku." In *Hōbōgirin* 7: 931–46. Paris: Adrien Maisonneuve.

Ayukai Funaoshin. 1932. *Zakkai*. Seoul: Chikazawa shuppan.

Backus, Robert L. 1985. *The Riverside Counselor's Stories: Vernacular Fiction of Late Heian Japan*. Stanford: Stanford University Press.

Bakhtin, Mikhail. 1984. *Rabelais and His World*. Translated by Hélène Iswolsky. Bloomington: Indiana University Press.

Balzac, Honoré de. (1846) 1993. *La cousine Bette*. Paris: Bookking International.

Bapat, P. V. 1957. "Change of Sex in Buddhist Literature." In *S. K. Belvalkar Felicitation Volume*, 209–15. Varanasi: Motilal Banarsidass.

Bapat, P. V., and Hirakawa Akira, trans. 1970. *Shan-Chien-P'i-P'o-Sha: A Chinese Version of Samantapāsādikā by Saṅghabhadra*. Poona: Bhandarkar Oriental Research Institute.

Barnes, Nancy Schuster. 1985. "Striking a Balance: Women and Images of Women in Early Chinese Buddhism." In Yvonne Yazbeck Haddad and Ellison Banks Findly, eds., *Women, Religion, and Social Change*, 87–111. Albany: State University of New York Press.

Baroni, Helen J. 1993. "Buddhism in Early Tokugawa Japan: The Case of Ōbaku Zen and the Monk Tetsugen Dōkō." Ph.D. dissertation, Columbia University.

Bataille, Georges. 1986. *Eroticism: Death and Sexuality*. Translated by Mary Dalwood. San Francisco: City Light Books.

———. 1991. *The Accursed Share: An Essay on General Economy*. Translated by Robert Hurley. 3 vols. New York: Zone Books.

Batchelor, Martine. 1990. "The Bodhisattva Precepts: The Formal Bi-weekly Purification Ceremony for Those Who Have Received the Bodhisattva Precepts; According to the Chinese Tradition as Recorded in the *Brahmajalasūtra*." Unpublished paper, Songgwang Sa Monastery, International Meditation Centre.

Bender, Ross. 1979. "The Hachiman Cult and the Dōkyō Incident." *Monumenta Nipponica* 34 (2): 125–52.

Beyer, Stephan. 1978. *The Cult of Tārā: Magic and Ritual in Tibet*. Berkeley and Los Angeles: University of California Press.

Bhattacharya, N. N. (1982) 1992. *History of the Tantric Religion: A Historical, Ritualistic and Philosophical Study*. New Delhi: Manohar.

Bialock, David T. 1997. "Peripheries of Power: Voice, History, and the Construction of Imperial and Sacred Space in the Tale of the Heike and other Medieval and Heian Historical Texts." Unpublished.

Blacker, Carmen. 1975. *The Catalpa Bow: A Study of Shamanistic Practices in Japan*. London: Allen and Unwin.

Bleys, Rudi C. 1996. *The Geography of Perversion: Male-to-Male Sexual Behaviour outside the West and the Ethnographic Imagination, 1570–1918*. London: Cassell.

Bloch, Maurice. 1992. *Prey into Hunter: The Politics of Religious Experience*. Cambridge: Cambridge University Press.

Bloch, Maurice, and Jonathan Parry, eds. 1982. *Death and the Regeneration of Life*. Cambridge: Cambridge University Press.

Blyth, Richard H. 1964. *Senryū: Japanese Satirical Verses*. Tokyo: Hokuseidō.

Bodiford, William M. 1993. *Sōtō Zen in Medieval Japan*. Honolulu: University of Hawaii Press.

Boswell, John. 1980. *Christianity, Social Tolerance, and Homosexuality: Gay People in Western Europe from the Beginning of the Christian Era to the Fourteenth Century*. Chicago: University of Chicago Press.

Bouchy, Anne-Marie [Anne]. 1983. *Tokuhon, ascète du nembutsu: Dans le cadre d'une étude sur les religieux errants de l'époque Edo*. Cahiers d'études et de documents sur les religions du Japon 5. Paris: E.P.H.E.

Bourdieu, Pierre. 1990. *Language and Symbolic Power*. Cambridge: Harvard University Press.

Bourke, John Gregory. 1891. *Scatologic Rites of All Nations*. Washington, D.C.: W. H. Lowdermilk.

Brantôme (Pierre de Bourdeille, Seigneur de). 1962. *Les dames galantes*. Paris: Librairie Générale Française.

Brazell, Karen, trans. 1973. *The Confessions of Lady Nijō*. London: Peter Owen.

———, ed. 1988. *Twelve Plays of the Noh and Kyōgen Theaters*. Ithaca: Cornell University, East Asia Program.

Brinker, Helmut. 1987. *Zen in the Art of Painting*. Translated by George Campbell. London: Arkana 1987.

Brock, Karen L. 1984. "Tales of Gishō and Gangyō: Editor, Artist, and Audience in Japanese Picture Scrolls." Ph. D. dissertation, Princeton University.

———. 1990. "Chinese Maiden, Silla Monk: Zenmyō and Her Thirteenth-Century Audience." In Marsha Weidner, ed., *Flowering in the Shadows: Women in the History of Chinese and Japanese Painting*, 185–218. Honolulu: University of Hawaii Press.

Broido, Michael M. 1988. "Killing, Lying, Stealing and Adultery: A Problem of Interpretation in the Tantras." In Donald S. Lopez, Jr., ed., *Buddhist Hermeneutics*, 71–118. Honolulu: University of Hawaii Press.

Brokaw, Cynthia J. 1991. *The Ledgers of Merit and Demerit: Social Change and Moral Order in Late Imperial China*. Princeton: Princeton University Press.

Brooks, Anne Page. 1981. "Mizuko kuyō and Japanese Buddhism." *Japanese Journal of Religious Studies* 8 (3–4): 119–47.

Brower, Robert Hopkins. 1952. "The *Konzyaku Monogatarisyū*: An Historical and Critical Introduction, with Annotated Translations of Seventy-Eight Tales." Ph. D. dissertation, University of Michigan.

Brown, Delmer M., and Ichirō Ishida. 1979. *The Future and the Past: A Transla-*

tion and Study of the Gukanshō, *an Interpretative History of Japan Written in 1219.* Berkeley and Los Angeles: University of California Press.

Brown, Judith C. 1986. *Immodest Acts: The Life of a Lesbian Nun in Renaissance Italy.* New York: Oxford University Press.

Brown, Peter. 1988. *The Body and Society: Men, Women, and Sexual Renunciation in Early Christianity.* New York: Columbia University Press.

Brundage, James A. 1987. *Law, Sex, and Christian Society in Medieval Europe.* Chicago: University of Chicago Press.

Buddhagosa. 1975. *The Path of Purification (Visuddhimagga).* Translated by Bhikku Nāñamoli. Kandy: Buddhist Publication Society.

Burlingame, E. W., trans. 1921. *Buddhist Legends.* Cambridge: Harvard University Press.

Buswell, Robert E., Jr. 1992. *The Zen Monastic Experience: Buddhist Practice in Contemporary Korea.* Princeton: Princeton University Press.

Butler, Katy. 1990. "Encountering the Shadow in Buddhist America." *Common Boundary* (May–June): 14–22.

Bynum, Caroline Walker. 1985. *Holy Feast and Holy Fast: The Religious Significance of Food to Medieval Women.* Berkeley and Los Angeles: University of California Press.

———. 1991. *Fragmentation and Redemption: Essays on Gender and the Human Body in Medieval Religion.* New York: Zone Books.

Cabezon, José Ignacio, ed. 1992. *Buddhism, Sexuality, and Gender.* Albany: State University of New York Press.

———. 1993. "Homosexuality and Buddhism." In Arlene Swidler, ed., *Homosexuality and World Religions,* 81–101. Valley Forge, PA: Trinity Press International.

Cahill, Suzanne E. 1985. "Sex and the Supernatural in Medieval China: Cantos on the Transcendent Who Presides over the River." *Journal of the American Oriental Society* 105 (2): 197–220.

Camporesi, Piero. 1995. *Juice of Life: The Symbolic and Magic Significance of Blood.* Translated by Robert R. Barr. New York: Continuum.

Cao Xueqin. 1973–1986. *The Story of the Stone.* Translated by David Hawkes. 5 vols. Middlesex: Penguin Books.

Chayet, Anne. 1993. *La femme au temps des Dalaï-lamas.* Paris: Stock-L. Pernoud.

Childs, Margaret Helen. 1980. "*Chigo Monogatari:* Love Stories or Buddhist Sermons?" *Monumenta Nipponica* 35 (2): 127–51.

———. 1985. "Kyōgen-kigo: Love Stories as Buddhist Sermons." *Japanese Journal of Religious Studies* 12 (1): 91–104.

———. 1991. *Rethinking Sorrow: Revelatory Tales of Late Medieval Japan.* Ann Arbor: University of Michigan, Center for Japanese Studies.

Choi Park-kwang. 1995. "Japanese Sexual Customs and Cultures Seen from the Perspective of the Korean Delegation to Japan." In *Sexuality and Edo Culture 1750–1850: Papers Presented,* 40–43. Bloomington: Indiana University Press.

Cholley, Jean. 1981. *Un haiku satirique: Le senryū.* Paris: Publications Orientalistes de France.

————, trans. 1996. *Haiku érotiques: Extraits de* La Fleur du bout *et du* Tonneau de Saule. Arles: Editions Philippe Picquier.

————, trans. 1997. *Manuel de l'oreiller pour posséder les femmes.* Arles: Editions Philippe Picquier.

Chou Yi-liang. 1944–1945. "Tantrism in China." *Harvard Journal of Asiatic Studies* 8: 241–332.

Clasquin, Michel. 1992. "Contemporary Theravāda and Zen Buddhist Attitudes to Human Sexuality: An Exercise in Comparative Ethics." *Religion* 22: 63–83.

Cleary, Thomas, trans. 1989b. *Entry into the Realm of Reality: The Text; A Translation of the Gaṇḍavyūha, the Final Book of the Avataṃsaka Sūtra.* Boston: Shambhala.

Cogan, J., trans. 1987. *The Tale of the Soga Brothers.* Tokyo: University of Tokyo Press.

Cole, Alan. 1996. "Mothers and Sons in Chinese Buddhism." Ph. D. dissertation, University of Michigan.

Collcutt, Martin. 1981. *Five Mountains: The Rinzai Zen Monastic Institution in Medieval Japan.* Cambridge: Harvard University Press.

Collectif. 1991. *Amour et sexualité en Occident.* Paris: Seuil.

Collins, Steven. 1982. *Selfless Persons: Imagery and Thought in Theravāda Buddhism.* New York: Cambridge University Press.

Covell, Jon Carter. 1980. *Unraveling Zen's Red Thread: Ikkyū's Controversial Way.* Elizabeth, NJ, and Seoul: Hollym International.

Cranston, Edwin A., trans. 1969. *The Izumi Shikibu Diary: A Romance of the Heian Court.* Cambridge: Harvard University Press.

Czaja, Michael. 1974. *Gods of Myth and Stone: Phallicism in Japanese Folk Religion.* New York and Tokyo: Weatherhill.

Dars, Jacques, trans. 1987. *Contes de la montagne sereine.* Paris: Gallimard.

Davies, Robertson. 1985. *What's Bred in the Bone.* New York: Viking.

Debergh, Minako. 1984. "Deux nouvelles études sur l'histoire du christianisme au Japon II: Les pratiques de purification et de pénitence au Japon vues par les missionnaires Jésuites au XVIe et XVIIe siècles." *Journal Asiatique* 272 (1–2): 167–216.

DeBernardi, Jean. 1987. "The God of War and the Vagabond Buddha." *Modern China* 13 (3): 310–32.

de Groot, J. M. 1893. *Le code du Mahāyāna en Chine: Son influence sur la vie monacale et sur le monde laïque.* Amsterdam, reprint Wiesbaden: Johannes Müller, 1976.

Deleuze, Gilles, and Félix Guattari. 1997. *Anti-Oedipus: Capitalism and Schizophrenia.* Translated by Robert Hurley et al. New York: Viking.

Delprat, Adriana. 1985. "Forms of Dissent in the *Gesaku* Literature of Hiraga Gennai (1728–1780)." Ph. D. dissertation, Princeton University.

Demiéville, Paul. 1932. "L'origine des sectes bouddhiques d'après Paramārtha." *Mélanges chinois et bouddhiques* 1: 15–64.

————. (1962) 1987. "Vimalakīrti en Chine." In Etienne Lamotte, *L'Enseignement de Vimalakīrti (Vimalakīrtinirdeśa).* Louvain: Institut Orientaliste, 1987: 438–55.

———. 1973. "Adieu maman." *Bulletin of the School of Oriental and African Studies* 36 (2): 271–86.

———. 1985. *Buddhism and Healing: Demiéville's Article "Byō" from Hōbōgirin.* Translated by Mark Tatz. Lanham, MD: University Press of America.

Dimock, Edward C., Jr. 1966. *The Place of the Hidden Moon: Erotic Mysticism in the Vaiṣṇava-Sahajiyā Cult of Bengal.* Chicago: University of Chicago Press.

Douglas, Mary. 1967. *Purity and Danger.* London: Routledge and Kegan Paul.

Dowman, Keith, trans. 1980. *The Divine Madman.* Clearlake, CA: Dawn Horse Press.

Duberman, Martin Bauml, Martha Vicinus, and George Chauncey, Jr., eds. 1989. *Hidden from History: Reclaiming the Gay and Lesbian Past.* New York: New American Library.

Dudbridge, Glen. 1978. *The Legend of Miao-shan.* Oxford Oriental Monographs, no. 1. London: Ithaca Press.

———. 1982. "Miao-shan on Stone: Two Early Inscriptions." *Harvard Journal of Asiatic Studies* 42: 589–614.

Dumézil, Georges. 1983. *La courtisane et les seigneurs colorés: Esquisses de mythologie.* Paris: Gallimard.

Durand-Dastès, Vincent. 1984. "Ji Gong et les personnages de bonzes dans le roman chinois en langue vulgaire." Unpublished.

Durt, Hubert. 1995. "L'apparition du Buddha à sa mère après son nirvāṇa: Le *Sūtra de Mahāmāya* (T. 383) et le *Sūtra de la mère du Buddha* (T. 2919)." Unpublished.

———. 1997. "Quelques aspects de la légende du roi Ajase (Ajātaśatru) dans la tradition canonique bouddhique." *Ebisu* 15: 13–27.

Dutt, Sukumar. 1960. *Early Buddhist Monachism.* Bombay: Asia Publishing House.

Dykstra, Yoshiko K., trans. 1976. "Tales of the Compassionate Kannon: The *Hasedera Kannon Genki.*" *Monumenta Nipponica* 31 (2): 113–43.

———, trans. 1983. *Miraculous Tales of the Lotus Sūtra from Ancient Japan: The Dainihon Hokekyōkenki of Priest Chingen.* Honolulu: University of Hawaii Press.

Eberhard, Wolfram. 1967. *Guilt and Sin in Traditional China.* Berkeley and Los Angeles: University of California Press.

Ebrey, Patricia Buckley. 1993. *The Inner Quarters: Marriage and the Lives of Chinese Women in the Sung Period.* Berkeley and Los Angeles: University of California Press.

Elster, Jon. 1983. *Sour Grapes: Studies in the Subversion of Rationality.* Cambridge: Cambridge University Press.

Elvin, Mark. 1984. "Female Virtue and the State in China." *Past and Present* 104: 111–52.

Endō Hajime. 1989. "Bōmori izen no koto: otto to tsuma, shinshūshi ni okeru josei no zokusei." In Ōsumi Kazuo and Nishiguchi Junko, eds. *Josei to bukkyō.* Vol. 3, *Shinjin to kuyō,* 41–80. Tokyo: Heibonsha.

———. 1992. "Chūsei bukkyō ni okeru 'sei': Kōfukuji sōjō 'jōhakai ishū' o tega-kari to shite." *Rekishi hyōron* 512: 19–34.

Enoki Katsurō, ed. 1979. *Ryōjin Hishō*. Tokyo: Shinchōsha.

Fabre-Vassas, Claudine. 1994. *La bête singulière: Les juifs, les chrétiens et le cochon*. Paris: Gallimard.

Fairweather, Ian. 1965. *The Drunken Buddha*. Brisbane: University of Queensland Press.

Falk, Nancy Auer. 1974. "An Image of Woman in Old Buddhist Literature: The Daughters of Māra." In Judith Plaskow and Joan Arnold, eds., *Women and Religion*, 105–12. Missoula, MT: Scholar's Press for the American Academy of Religion.

———. 1989. "The Case of the Vanishing Nun: The Fruits of Ambivalence in Ancient Indian Buddhism." In Nancy Auer Falk and Rita M. Gross, eds., *Unspoken Worlds: Women's Religious Lives*, 155–65. Belmont, CA: Wadsworth.

Falk, Nancy Auer, and Rita M. Gross, eds. 1980. *Unspoken Worlds: Women's Religious Lives in Non-Western Cultures*. San Francisco: Harper and Row.

Faure, Bernard. 1986. *Le Traité de Bodhidharma: Première anthologie du bouddhisme Chan*. Aix-en-Provence: Editions Le Mail.

———. 1987a. *La vision immédiate: Nature, éveil et tradition selon le* Shōbō-genzō. Aix-en-Provence: Editions Le Mail.

———. 1987b. "The Daruma-shū, Dōgen, and Sōtō Zen." *Monumenta Nipponica* 42 (1): 25–55.

———. 1991. *The Rhetoric of Immediacy: A Cultural Critique of the Chan/Zen Tradition*. Princeton: Princeton University Press.

———. 1994. *Sexualités bouddhiques: Entre désirs et réalités*. Aix-en-Provence: Le Mail.

———. 1996. *Visions of Power: Imagining Medieval Japanese Buddhism*. Princeton: Princeton University Press.

———. 1997a. "L'image de la mère dans le Zen Sōtō." In Jacqueline Pigeot and Hartmund O. Rottermund, eds., *Le vase de béryl: Etudes sur le Japon et la Chine en hommage à Bernard Frank*, 95–108. Arles: Editions Philippe Picquier.

———. 1997b. *The Will to Orthodoxy: A Genealogy of Early Chan*. Translated by Phyllis Brooks. Stanford: Stanford University Press.

Fields, Rick. *How the Swans Came to the Lake: A Narrative History of Buddhism in America*. Boston: Shambhala.

Filliozat, Jean. 1991a. "Continence and Sexuality in Buddhism and in the Disciplines of Yoga." In Jean Filliozat, *Religion, Philosophy, Yoga*, 327–39. Delhi: Motilal Banarsidass.

———. 1991b. "The Oedipus Complex in a Buddhist Tantra." In Jean Filliozat, *Religion, Philosophy, Yoga*, 429–38. Delhi: Motilal Banarsidass.

Fiser, Ivo. 1993. "Pāli Vinaya and Sanskrit Kāma-Śāstra." In N. K. Wagle and F. Watanabe, eds., *Studies on Buddhism in Honour of Professor A. K. Warder*, 57–65. South Asian Studies Paper 5. Toronto: University of Toronto, Centre for South Asian Studies.

Flandrin, Jean-Louis. 1981. *Le sexe et l'Occident: Evolution des attitudes et des comportements*. Paris: Seuil.

Forte, Antonino. 1976. *Political Propaganda and Ideology in China at the End of the Seventh Century: Inquiry into the Nature, Authors and Function of the Tun-huang Document S. 6502 Followed by an Annotated Translation.* Naples: Istituto Universario Orientale.

———. 1995. *The Hostage An Shigao and His Offspring.* Kyoto: Istituto Italiano di Cultura, Scuola di Studi sull'Asia Orientale.

Foucault, Michel. 1973. *The Order of Things: An Archeology of the Human Sciences.* New York: Vintage/Random House.

———. (1975) 1977. *Discipline and Punish: The Birth of the Prison.* New York: Vintage Books.

———. 1976. *Histoire de la sexualité. Vol. 1: La volonté de savoir.* Paris: Gallimard.

———. 1978. *The History of Sexuality.* Vol. 1: *An Introduction.* New York: Vintage-Random House.

———, ed. 1980. *Herculine Barbin: Being the Recently Discovered Memoirs of a Nineteenth-Century French Hermaprodite.* New York: Pantheon.

———. 1982. "Le combat de la chasteté." In P. Ariès and A. Béjin, eds., *Sexualités occidentales,* 26–40. Paris: Seuil.

———. 1985a. "Sexuality and Solitude." In Marshall Blonsky, ed., *On Signs,* 365–72. Baltimore: Johns Hopkins University Press.

———. 1985b. *The Use of Pleasure: The History of Sexuality.* vol. 2. Translated by Robert Hurley. New York: Vintage Books.

———. 1986. *The Care of the Self: The History of Sexuality.* Vol. 3. Translated by Robert Hurley. New York: Vintage Books.

———. 1995. *Dits et écrits.* (1954–1988). 4 vols. Paris: Gallimard.

Foucher, Alfred. 1949. *La vie du Buddha d'après les textes et les monuments de l'Inde.* Paris: Payot.

Frank, Bernard, trans. 1968. *Histoires qui sont maintenant du passé.* Paris: Gallimard.

———. 1989. "L'expérience d'un malheur absolu: son refus et son dépassement. L'histoire de la mère de Jōjin." *Comptes rendus de l'Académie des Inscriptions et Belles Lettres,* 472–88. Paris: Académie des Inscriptions et Belles-Lettres.

———. 1991. *Le panthéon bouddhique au Japon: Collections d'Emile Guimet.* Paris: Editions de la Réunion des Musées Nationaux.

———. 1995. "Amour, colère, couleur: Variations sur Aizen-myōō." In Gérard Fussman, ed. *Bouddhisme et cultures locales.* Paris: Ecole Française d'Extrême-Orient.

Freedberg, David. 1989. *The Power of Images: Studies in the History and Theory of Response.* Chicago: University of Chicago Press.

Freud, Sigmund. 1924. "The Psychogenesis of a Case of Homosexuality in a Woman." In Joan Riviere, ed., *Collected Papers* 2: 202–31. London: Hogarth Press.

———. (1930) 1994. *Civilization and Its Discontent.* New York: Dover Publications.

———. (1907) 1996. "Obsessive Actions and Religious Practices." In Ronald Grimes, ed., *Readings in Ritual Studies,* 212–17. Englewood Cliffs, NJ: Prentice Hall.

Fujii Masao. 1977. "Minzoku kankō ni mirareru aka to kuro no shōchōsei." In

Bukkyō minzoku gakkai, ed., *Bukkyō to girei: Katō Shōichi sensei koki kinen ronbunshū*, 203–37. Tokyo: Kokusho kankōkai.

Fuller Sasaki, Ruth. 1975. *The Recorded Sayings of Ch'an Master Lin-chi Hui-chao of Chen Prefecture*. Kyoto: Institute for Zen Studies.

Furth, Charlotte. 1986. "Blood, Body and Gender: Medical Images of the Female Condition in China, 1600–1850." *Chinese Science* 7: 43–66.

———. 1987. "Concepts of Pregnancy, Childbirth, and Infancy in Ch'ing Dynasty China." *Journal of Asian Studies* 46 (1): 7–35.

———. 1988. "Androgynous Males and Deficient Females: Biology and Gender Boundaries in Sixteenth- and Seventeenth-Century China." *Late Imperial China* 9 (2): 1–31.

———. 1994. "Rethinking van Gulik: Sexuality and Reproduction in Traditional Chinese Medicine." In Christina K. Gilmartin, Gail Herstatter, Lisa Rofel, and Tyrene White, eds. *Engendering China: Women, Culture, and the State*, 121–46. Cambridge: Harvard University Press.

Furukawa Makoto. 1994. "The Changing Nature of Sexuality: The Three Codes Framing Homosexuality in Modern Japan." Translated by Angus Lockyere. *U.S.-Japan Women's Journal, English Supplement* 7: 98–127.

Fussman, Gérard, ed. 1995. *Bouddhisme et cultures locales*. Paris: Ecole Française d'Extrême-Orient.

Gaignebet, Claude, and Marie-Claude Périer. 1990. "L'homme et l'excrétion: De l'excrété à l'exécré." In Jean Poirier, ed., *Histoire des moeurs. Vol. 1: Les coordonnées de l'homme et la culture matérielle*, 831–93. Encyclopédie de la Pléiade. Paris: Gallimard.

Girard, Frédéric. 1990a. *Un moine de la secte Kegon à l'époque de Kamakura, Myōe (1173–1232) et le "Journal de ses rêves."* Paris: Ecole Française d'Extrême-Orient.

———. 1990b. "Le Journal des rêves de Myōe, moine japonais de l'école Kegon." *Journal Asiatique* 278: 167–93.

Girardot, Norman J. 1983. *Myth and Meaning in Early Taoism: The Theme of Chaos (Hun-tun)*. Berkeley and Los Angeles: University of California Press.

Glassman, Hank. 1992. "Compassing *Mokuren no sōshi*: Textual and Thematic Approaches to a Tale from Late Medieval Japan." Unpublished.

Goodich, Michael. 1979. *The Unmentionable Vice: Homosexuality in the Later Medieval Period*. Santa Barbara: Rock-Erickson.

Goux, Jean-Joseph. 1990. *Symbolic Economies: After Marx and Freud*. Ithaca: Cornell University Press.

Grapard, Allan G. 1991. "Visions of Excess and Excesses of Vision: Women and Transgression in Japanese Myth." *Japanese Journal of Religious Studies* 18 (1): 3–22.

Greenblatt, Steven. 1986. "Loudun and London." *Critical Inquiry* 12 (2): 326–46.

Grimes, Ronald L., ed. 1995. *Readings in Ritual Studies*. Englewood Cliffs, NJ: Prentice Hall.

Groner, Paul. 1984. *Saichō: The Establishment of the Japanese Tendai School*. Berkeley: University of California, Buddhist Studies Series.

———. 1989. "The *Lotus Sūtra* and Saichō's Interpretation of the Realization of

Buddhahood with This Very Body." In George J. Tanabe, Jr., and Willa Jane Tanabe, eds., *The Lotus Sūtra in Japanese Culture*, 53–74. Honolulu: University of Hawaii Press.

———. 1990. "The *Fan-wang ching* and Monastic Discipline in Japanese Tendai." In Robert Buswell, Jr., ed., *Buddhist Apocrypha*, 251–90. Honolulu: University of Hawaii Press.

Gross, Rita M. 1986. "Buddhism and Feminism: Toward Their Mutual Transformation (1)." *Eastern Buddhist* (n.s.) 19 (1): 44–58.

Guth, Christine M. E. 1987. "The Divine Boy in Japanese Art." *Monumenta Nipponica* 42 (1): 1–24.

Ha Tae-hung and Grafton K. Mintz, trans. 1972. *Samguk Yusa: Legends and History of the Three Kingdoms of Ancient Korea*. Seoul: Yonsei University Press.

Hagiwara Tatsuo. 1983. *Miko to bukkyō shi: Kumano bikuni no shimei to tenkai*. Tokyo: Yoshikawa kōbunkan.

Halperin, David M. 1994. "Historicizing the Subject of Desire: Sexual Preferences and Erotic Identities in the Pseudo-Lucanian Erôtes." In Jan Goldstein, ed., *Foucault and the Writing of History*, 19–34. Oxford: Blackwell.

Halperin, David M., John J. Winkler, and Froma I. Zeitlin, eds. 1990. *Before Sexuality: The Construction of Erotic Experience in the Ancient Greek World*. Princeton: Princeton University Press.

Hamilton, Sue. 1995. "From the Buddha to Buddhagosa: Changing Attitudes toward the Human Body in Theravāda Buddhism." In Jane Marie Law, ed., *Religious Reflections on the Human Body*, 46–63. Bloomington: Indiana University Press.

Hanan, Patrick. 1981. *The Chinese Vernacular Story*. Cambridge: Harvard University Press.

Hardacre, Helen. 1983. "The Cave and the Womb World." *Japanese Journal of Religious Studies* 10 (2–3): 149–76.

Harper, Donald. 1987. "The Sexual Arts of Ancient China as Described in a Manuscript of the Second Century B.C." *Harvard Journal of Asiatic Studies* 47 (2): 539–93.

Harpham, Geoffrey Galt. 1987. *The Ascetic Imperative in Culture and Criticism*. Chicago: University of Chicago Press.

Hasegawa Kiyoko. 1980. *Onna no minzokushi*. Tokyo: Tokyo shoseki.

Hasegawa Masaharu. 1974. "Sei to sōbō: Chigo e no inori." *Kokubungaku kaishaku to kanshō* 18 (1): 57–62.

———. 1987. "Mōshigo, chigo, honjimono: Shōdō bungaku to shite no 'Shintōshū' o jiku ni." In Nihon bungaku gakkai, ed. *Nihon bungaku kōza* 4: *Monogatari, shōsetsu I*, 283–303. Tokyo: Taishukan shoten.

Hasekawa Kōzo and Tsukikawa Kazuo, eds. 1991. *Minakata Kumagusu nanshoku dangi: Iwata Jun'ichi ōfuku shokan*. Tokyo: Yasaka shobō.

Hazama Jikō. 1972. *Nihon bukkyō no kaiten to sono kichō: Nihon Tendai to Kamakura bukkyō*. 2 vols. Tokyo: Sanseidō.

Hecker, Hellmuth. 1982. *Buddhist Women at the Time of the Buddha*. Kandy: Buddhist Publication Society.

Hekma, Gert. 1994. "'A Female Soul in a Male Body': Sexual Inversion as Gender Inversion in Nineteenth-Century Sexology." In Gilbert Herdt, ed., *Third Sex, Third Gender: Beyond Sexual Dimorphism in Culture and History*, 213–39. New York: Zone Books.

Herdt, Gilbert, ed. 1994. *Third Sex, Third Gender: Beyond Sexual Dimorphism in Culture and History*. New York: Zone Books.

Herrmann-Pfandt, Adelheid. 1992–1993. "Ḍākinīs in Indo-Tibetan Tantric Buddhism: Some Results of Recent Research." *Studies in Central and East Asian Religions* 5–6: 45–63.

Hinsch, Bret. 1990. *Passions of the Cut Sleeve: The Male Homosexual Tradition in China*. Berkeley and Los Angeles: University of California Press.

Hirakawa Akira. 1960. *A Study of the Vinayapiṭaka*. Tokyo: Sankibō busshorin.

———. 1982. *Monastic Discipline for the Buddhist Nuns: An English Translation of the Chinese Text of the Mahāsāṃghika-Bhikṣuṇī-Vinaya*. Patna: Kashi Prasad Jayaswal Research Institute.

———. 1992. "The History of Buddhist Nuns in Japan." Translated by Karma Lekshe Tsomo and Junko Miura. *Buddhist-Christian Studies* 12: 147–58.

Hirano Umeyo, trans. N.d. *Buddhist Plays from Japanese Literature*. Tokyo: CIIB.

Hirazuka Yoshinobu. 1987. *Nihon ni okeru nanshoku no kenkyū*. Tokyo: Ningen no kagakusha.

Hōbōgirin: Dictionnaire encyclopédique du bouddhisme d'après les sources chinoises et japonaises. 1927–. Edited by Paul Demiéville et al. 8 vols. to date. Paris: Adrien Maisonneuve.

Holt, John C. 1983. *Discipline: The Canonical Buddhism of the Vinayapiṭaka*. Columbia, MO: South Asia Books.

Honda Yasuji. 1969. *Ennen*. Nihon minzoku geinō 3. Tokyo: Mokujisha.

Hori Ichirō. 1953. "Sō no saita to jiin no sezokuka." In Hori Ichirō, *Waga kuni minkan shinkō no kenkyū*. Vol. 2: *Shūkyōshi hen*, 367–79. Tokyo: Tōkyō sōgensha.

———. 1975. *Jōdai Nihon bukkyō bunkashi*. Vol. 2: *Jiin hen, sōni hen*. Tokyo: Rinsen shoten.

Horner, I. B. [Isabelle Blew]. (1930) 1975. *Women under Primitive Buddhism: Laywomen and Almswomen*. London: George Routledge and Sons. Reprint Delhi: Motilal Banarsidass.

———, trans. 1949–1966. *The Book of the Discipline (Vinaya-piṭaka)*. 6 vols. London: Luzac.

Hosokawa Ryōichi. 1987. *Chūsei no Ritsushū jiin to minshū*. Tokyo: Yoshikawa kōbunkan.

———. 1989. *Onna no chūsei: Ono no Komachi, Tomoe, sono hoka*. Nihon editā sukūru shuppanbu.

———. 1993. *Itsudatsu no Nihon chūsei: Kyōaku, ma no sekai*. Tokyo: JICC Shuppankyoku.

———. 1994. *Chūsei no mibunsei to hinin*. Tokyo: Nihon editā sukūru.

Hsiung Ping-ming. 1984. *Zhang Xu et la calligraphie cursive folle*. Paris: Collège de France.

Huang San and Jean Basse, trans. 1992. *Moines et nonnes dans l'océan des péchés*. Paris: Editions Philippe Picquier.

Hur, Nam-lin. 1992. "Popular Buddhist Culture in the Latter Tokugawa Period: A Study of Sensoji." Ph. D. dissertation, Princeton University.

Hurvitz, Leon, trans. 1956. "*Wei Shou,* Treatise on Buddhism and Taoism." In Mizuno S. and Nagahiro T., eds., *Yün-kang, The Buddhist Cave-Temples of the Fifth Century A.D. in North China.* Vol. 16, Supplement. Kyoto: Jinbun kagaku kenkyūjo.

Ichiko Teiji and Noma Kōshin, eds. 1976. *Otogizōshi, Kanazōshi.* Kanshō Nihon koten bungaku 26. Tokyo: Kadogawa shoten.

Ihara Saikaku. 1956. *Five Women Who Loved Love.* Translated by Wm. Theodore De Bary. Rutland, VT, and Tokyo: Charles E. Tuttle.

———. 1963. *The Life of an Amorous Woman (Kōshoku ichidai onna).* Translated by Ivan Morris. New York: New Directions.

———. 1969. *Five Women Who Chose Love. The Life of an Amorous Woman and Other Writings.* Translated by Ivan Morris. New York: New Directions.

———. 1990. *The Great Mirror of Male Love.* Translated by Paul Gordon Schalow. Stanford: Stanford University Press.

Iizuna Daiden. 1993. "*Kyōunshū* ni okeru 'nikushoku saitai' shi ni tsuite." *Indogaku bukkyōgaku kenkyū* 41 (2): 723–27.

Ilyŏn. 1972. *Samguk Yusa: Legends and History of the Three Kingdoms of Ancient Korea.* Translated by Ha Tae-Hung and Grafton K. Mintz. Seoul: Yonsei University Press.

Inagaki Taruho. 1969–1970. "Minakata Kumagusu chigo dangi." In Hagiwara Sachiko and Kawahito Hiroshi, eds., *Inagaki Taruho taizen* 6: 400–465. Tokyo: Genda shichōsha.

———. 1973a. "Nanshoku kō yodan." In *Minakata Kumagusu zenshū,* edited by Iwamura Shinobu. 9: 617–23. Tokyo: Heibonsha.

———. 1973b. *Shōnen'ai no bigaku.* Tokyo: Kadogawa shoten.

———. 1992. *Minakata Kumagusu chigo dangi.* Tokyo: Kawade shobō shinsha.

Inoue Mitsusada and Ōsone Shōsuke, eds. 1974. *Ōjōden, Hokke genki.* NSTK 7. Tokyo: Iwanami shoten.

Inoue Tamaki. 1993. "Symbolic Meanings of Shinran's Dream at Rokkakudō." Papers of the Sixth Biennial Conference of the International Association of Shin Buddhist Studies, Ōtani University, 1–16.

Ishida Jūshi, ed. 1972. *Kamakura bukkyō seiritsu no kenkyū: Shunjō risshi.* Kyoto: Hōzōkan.

Ishida Mitsuyuki. 1951. *Ganjin.* Kyoto: Hōzōkan.

Ishida Mizumaro. 1971. *Bonmōkyō.* Tokyo: Daizō shuppansha.

———. 1995. *Nyobon: Hijiri no sei.* Tokyo: Chikuma shobō.

Ishikawa Rikizan. 1986. "Chūsei Sōtōshū kirigami no bunrui shiron (8): Tsuizen, sōsō kuyō kankei o chūshin to shite (jō)." *Komazawa daigaku bukkyōgaku ronbunshū* 17: 179–213.

———. 1987. "Chūsei Sōtōshū kirigami no bunrui shiron (9): Tsuizen, sōsō kuyō kankei o chūshin to shite (chū)." *Komazawa daigaku bukkyōgakubu kenkyū kiyō* 45: 167–96.

Itō Kinkichi and Donald Richie, 1967. *Danjo-zō/The Erotic Gods: Phallicism in Japan.* Tokyo: Zufu shinsha, 1967.

Itō Masayoshi. 1972. "Chūsei Nihongi no rinkaku." *Bungaku* 40 (10): 29–48.
———. 1981. "Jidō setsuwa kō." *Kokugo kokubun* 49 (11): 1–32.
———, ed. 1983–1986. *Yōkyoku shū.* 2 vols. Shinchō Nihon koten shūsei 57, 73. Tokyo: Shinchōsha.
Iwamoto Yutaka. 1980. *Bukkyō to josei.* Tokyo: Daisan bunmeisha.
Iwata Jun'ichi. 1956. *Nanshoku bunken shoshi.* Tokyo: Koten Bunko. Reed. 1973, Toba: Iwata sadao.
———. 1974. *Honchō nanshoku kō.* Toba: Iwata Sadao.
Iyanaga Nobumi. Forthcoming. "Dākinī et l'empereur: Mystique bouddhique de la royauté dans le Japon médiéval."
Jaini, Padmanabh S. 1991. *Gender and Salvation.* Berkeley and Los Angeles: University of California Press.
Jang Hwee-ok. 1996. "Wŏnhyo and Rebirth Tales of Kwangdok and Omjang from Silla." *Acta Asiatica* 66: 57–68.
Joseishi sōgō kenkyūkai, ed. 1982. *Nihon josei shi.* 5 vols. Tokyo: Tokyo Daigaku shuppankai.
———, ed. 1983–1994. *Nihon joseishi kenkyū bunken mokuroku.* 3 vols. (1868–1981, 1982–1986, 1987–1991). Tokyo: Tōkyō Daigaku shuppankai.
———, ed. 1990. *Nihon josei seikatsu shi.* 5 vols. Tokyo: Tōkyō Daigaku shuppankai.
Jung-kwang. 1979. *The Mad Monk: Paintings of Unlimited Action.* Edited by Lewis Lancaster. Berkeley: Lancaster-Miller Publishers.
Kabilsingh, Chatsumarn. 1984. *A Comparative Study of Bhikkhuni Patimokkha.* Varanasi: Chaukhamba Orientalia.
Kaempfer, Engelbert. 1906. *The History of Japan, Together with a Description of the Kingdom of Siam, 1690–92.* Translated by J. G. Scheuchzer. 3 vols. Glasgow: James MacLehose and Sons.
Kageyama Haruki. 1975. "Matarajin shinkō to sono ihō." In Murayama Shuichi, ed., *Hieizan to Tendai bukkyō no kenkyū,* 317–40. Tokyo: Meicho shuppan.
Kamens, Edward. 1988. *The Three Jewels: A Study and Translation of Minamoto Tamenori's Sanbōe.* Ann Arbor: University of Michigan, Center for Japanese Studies.
———. 1990. *The Buddhist Poetry of the Great Kamo Priestess: Daisaiin Senshi and Hosshin Wakashū.* Michigan Monograph Series in Japanese Studies 5. Ann Arbor: University of Michigan, Center for Japanese Studies.
Kamikawa Michio. 1990. "Accession Rituals and Buddhism in Medieval Japan." *Japanese Journal of Religious Studies* 17 (2–3): 243–79.
Katō Genchi. 1924. "A Study of the Development of Religious Ideas among the Japanese People as Illustrated by Japanese Phallicism." *Transactions of the Asiatic Society of Japan,* 2nd series, 1, suppl: 5–22.
Katsuura Noriko. 1995. *Onna no shinjin: tsuma ga shukkeshita jidai.* Heibonsha sensho 156. Tokyo: Heibonsha.
Kavanagh, Frederick G. 1996. "An Errant Priest: *Sasayaki Take.*" *Monumenta Nipponica* 51 (2): 219–44.
Kawaguchi Hisao, ed. (1955) 1995. *Kohon setsuwa shū.* Tokyo: Iwanami shoten.
Kawai Hayao. 1992. *The Buddhist Priest Myōe: A Life of Dreams.* Translated by Mark Unno. Venice, CA: Lapis Press.

Keene, Donald, trans. 1961. *Major Plays of Chikamatsu*. New York: Columbia University Press.

———, trans. 1966. *Nō: The Classical Theatre of Japan*. Tokyo: Kōdansha.

———, trans. 1967. *Tsurezuregusa, Essays in Idleness*. New York: Columbia University Press.

———. 1977. "The Comic Tradition in Renga." In John Whitney Hall and Toyoda Takeshi, eds., *Japan in the Muromachi Age*, 241–77. Berkeley and Los Angeles: University of California Press.

Kelsey, W. Michael. 1981. "Salvation of the Snake, the Snake of Salvation: Buddhist-Shintō Conflict and Resolution." *Japanese Journal of Religious Studies* 8 (1–2): 83–113.

Ketelaar, James. 1990. *Of Heretics and Martyrs in Meiji Japan: Buddhism and Its Persecution*. Princeton: Princeton University Press.

Keyes, Charles F. 1986. "Ambiguous Gender: Male Initiation in a Northern Thai Buddhist Society." In C. W. Bynum, S. Harrell, and P. Richman, eds., *Gender and Religion*, 66–96. Boston: Beacon Press.

Kieschnick, John. 1997. *The Eminent Monk: Buddhist Ideals in Medieval Chinese Hagiography*. Kuroda Institute Series in East Asian Buddhism 10. Honolulu: University of Hawaii Press.

Kim [Kwon] Yung-hee, trans. 1994. *Songs to Make the Dust Dance: The Ryōjin Hishō of Twelfth-Century Japan*. Berkeley and Los Angeles: University of California Press.

Kitamura, Mariko, trans. 1980. "The Best Way Is to Keep Away from Them: Kamo no Chōmei's Views of Women in the *Hosshinshū*." *Journal of Asian Culture* 4: 1–20.

Kiyomoto Shūki. 1992. "Shinran ni okeru mukoku to kōsei." *Shinran to ningen*, 181–208.

Klein, Susan B. 1990. "When the Moon Strikes the Bell: Desire and Enlightenment in the Noh Play *Dōjōji*." *Journal of Japanese Studies* 17 (2): 291–322.

———. 1995. "Woman as Serpent: The Demonic Feminine in the Noh Play *Dōjōji*." In Jane Marie Law, ed., *Religious Reflections on the Human Body*, 100–36. Bloomington: Indiana University Press.

Ko, Dorothy. 1994. *Teachers of the Inner Chambers: Women and Culture in Seventeenth-Century China*. Stanford: Stanford University Press.

Kobayashi Taishirō. 1973. *Kobayashi Taishirō chosakushū*, vol. 1. Tokyo: Tankōsha.

Kobori Sōhaku and Norman Waddell, trans. 1970–1971. "*Sokushin-ki*, by Shidō Munan zenji," *Eastern Buddhist* (n.s.) 3 (2): 89–118; 4 (1): 116–23; 4 (2): 122.

Kodera, James Takashi. 1980. *Dōgen's Formative Years in China*. London: Routledge and Kegan Paul.

Kornfield, Jack. 1985. "Sex and Lives of the Gurus." *Yoga Journal*.

Ku Cheng-mei. 1984. "The Mahayanic View of Women: A Doctrinal Study." Ph. D. dissertation, University of Wisconsin-Madison.

Kuo Li-ying. 1994. *Confession et contrition dans le bouddhisme chinois du Ve au Xe siècle*. Paris: Ecole Française d'Extrême-Orient.

Kuratsuka Masaki. 1994. *Fujo no bunka*. Heibonsha Library 1200. Tokyo: Heibonsha.

Kurausu, F. 1988. *Meicho Edai: Sei Fūzoku no Nihon shi.* Tokyo: Kawade Shobō.

Kurihara Hiromi. 1991. "Shinran no joseikan." In Nihon bukkyō gakkai, ed., *Bukkyō to josei,* 59–78. Tokyo: Heirakuji shoten.

Kuroda Hideo. 1986a. *Sugata to shigusa no chūseishi: Ezu to emaki no fūkei kara.* Tokyo: Heibonsha.

———. 1986b. *Kyōkai no chūsei: Zōchō no chūsei.* Tokyo: Daigaku shuppankai.

Kuroda Toshio. 1975. *Nihon chūsei no kokka to shūkyō.* Tokyo: Iwanami shoten.

———. 1983. *Obō to buppō: Chūseishi no kōzu.* Kyoto: Hōzōkan.

Kvaerne, Per. 1975. "On the Concept of *Sahaja* in Indian Buddhist Tantric Literature." *Temenos* 11: 88–135.

Kwon, Yung-hee. 1986. "The Emperor's Songs: Go-Shirakawa and the *Ryōjin Hishō Kudenshū.*" *Monumenta Nipponica* 41 (3): 261–98.

La Vallée Poussin, Louis de. 1910. "The 'Five Points' of Mahādeva and the *Kathavattu.*" *Journal of the Royal Asiatic Society,* 412–23.

———, trans. 1923–1931. *L'Abhidharmakośa de Vasubandhu.* 6 vols. Paris: Geuthner. English translation by Leo Pruden. *Abhidharmakośabhāṣyam.* 3 vols. Berkeley: Asian Humanities Press, 1988–1989.

———. 1927. *La morale bouddhique.* Paris: Nouvelle Librairie Nationale.

———. 1937. "Musila et Narada: Le chemin du Nirvāṇa." *Mélanges chinois et bouddhiques* 5: 189–222.

LaCapra, Dominick. 1989. *Soundings in Critical Theory.* Ithaca: Cornell University Press.

Lachaud, François. 1997. "Le corps dissolu des femmes: Un autre regard sur l'impermanence." In Jacqueline Pigeot and Hartmund O. Rottermund, eds., *Le vase de béryl: Etudes sur le Japon et la Chine en hommage à Bernard Frank,* 47–62. Arles: Editions Philippe Picquier.

Lamotte, Etienne, trans. 1944–1980. *Le Traité de la grande vertu de sagesse de Nāgārjuna.* 6 vols. Louvain: Institut Orientaliste.

———. 1958. *Histoire du bouddhisme indien: Des origines à l'ère Saka.* Louvain: Institut Orientaliste.

———, trans. (1962) 1987. *L'enseignement de Vimalakīrti (Vimalakīrtinirdeśa).* Louvain: Institut Orientaliste. English translation by Sara Boin. *The Teaching of Vimalakīrti.* Sacred Books of the Buddhists 32. London: PTS, 1976.

———. 1974. "Passions and Impregnations of the Passions in Buddhism." In L. Cousins et al., eds. *Buddhist Studies in Honour of I. B. Horner,* 91–104. Dordrecht and Boston: D. Reidel Publishing Company.

Lang, Karen C. 1986. "Lord Death's Snare: Gender-Related Imagery in the Theragātha and the Therīgātha." *Journal of Feminist Studies in Religion* 2: 59–79.

———. 1995. "Shaven Heads and Loose Hair: Buddhist Attitudes towards Hair and Sexuality." In Howard Eilberg-Schwartz and Wendy Doniger, eds., *Off with Her Head: The Denial of Women's Identity in Myth, Religion, and Culture.* Berkeley: University of California Press.

Lanselle, Rainier, trans. 1987. *Le poisson de jade et l'épingle au phénix.* Paris: Gallimard.

Laqueur, Thomas. 1990. *Making Sex: Body and Gender from the Greeks to Freud.* Cambridge: Harvard University Press.

———. 1992. *La fabrique du sexe: Essai sur le corps et le genre en Occident.* Paris: Gallimard.

Law, Bimala Churn. (1927) 1981. *Women in Buddhist Literature.* Varanasi: Indological Book House.

Le Goff, Jacques. 1991. "Le refus du plaisir." In *Amour et sexualité en Occident,* 179–92. Paris: Seuil.

Lee, Peter H., trans. 1969. *Lives of Eminent Korean Monks: The* Haedong Kosŭng Chŏn. Harvard-Yenching Institute Studies 25. Cambridge: Harvard University Press.

Legendre, Pierre. 1974. *L'amour du censeur: Essai sur l'ordre dogmatique.* Paris: Seuil.

Legge, James, trans. 1965. *A Record of Buddhistic Kingdoms.* New York: Dover.

Lessing, Ferdinand D., and Alex Wayman. (1968) 1983. *Introduction to the Buddhist Tantric Systems.* Delhi: Motilal Banarsidass.

Leung, Angela K. 1983. "L'amour en Chine: Relations et pratiques sociales aux XIIIe et XIVe siècles (1)." *Archives de Sciences sociales des Religions* 56 (1): 59–76.

———. 1984. "Sexualité et sociabilité dans le *Jing Ping Mei,* roman érotique chinois de la fin du XVIème siècle." *Social Science Information* 23 (4–5): 677–700.

Leupp, Gary P. 1995. *Male Colors: The Construction of Homosexuality in Tokugawa Japan.* Berkeley and Los Angeles: University of California Press.

Lévi-Strauss, Claude. (1955) 1974a. *Tristes tropiques.* Translated by John Russell. New York: Atheneum.

———. 1974b. *Structural Anthropology,* vol. 2. Chicago: University of Chicago Press.

Lévy, André. 1978. *Inventaire analytique et critique du conte chinois en langue vulgaire.* 4 vols. Paris: Collège de France.

———. 1980. "Le moine et la courtisane." In Françoise Aubin, ed. *Etudes Song in memoriam Étienne Balazs,* ser. II, 2: 139–158. Paris: Ecole des Hautes Etudes en Sciences Sociales.

———, trans. 1985. *Fleur en fiole d'or (Jin Ping Mei cihua).* Bibliothèque de la Pléiade. 2 vols. Paris: Gallimard.

Levy, Howard S. 1965. *Two Chinese Sex Classics: The Dwelling of Playful Goddesses; Monks and Nuns in a Sea of Sins.* 2 vols. Asian Folklore and Social Life Monographs 75. Taipei: Chinese Association for Folklore.

———. 1971. *Sex, Love, and the Japanese.* Washington, D.C.: Warm-Soft Village Press.

———, trans. 1973. *Japanese Sex Jokes in Traditional Times: The Nun Who Rubbed and Thrusted, and Other Stories.* Washington, D.C.: Warm-Soft Village Press.

Lewis, I. M. (1971) 1989. *Ecstatic Religion: A Study of Shamanism and Spirit Possession.* London and New York: Routledge.

Li, Jung-hsi, trans. 1981. *Biographies of Buddhist Nuns: Pao-Chang's* Pi-ch'iu-ni chuan. Osaka: Tōhōkai.

Li Yu. 1990a. *The Carnal Prayer Mat (Rou Putuan)*. Translated by Patrick Hanan. New York: Ballantine Books.

———. 1990b. *Silent Operas (Wusheng xi)*. Edited by Patrick Hanan. Hong Kong: Chinese University of Hong Kong.

———. 1991. *De la chair à l'extase*. Translated by Christine Corniot. Arles: Editions Philippe Picquier.

Li Yuzhen. 1989. *Tangdai de biqiuni*. Taibei: Taiwan xuesheng shuju.

Liu Dalin, ed. 1993. *Zhongguo gudai xing wenhua*. 2 vols. Yinchuanshi: Ningxia renmin chubanshe.

Lopez, Donald S., Jr., ed. 1996. *Buddhism in Practice*. Princeton: Princeton University Press.

Luk, Charles. 1971. *Practical Buddhism*, Wheaton, IL: Theosophical Publishing House.

Lurie, Allison. 1984. *Foreign Affairs*. New York: Random House.

Maës, Hubert. 1970. *Hiraga Gennai et son temps*. Paris: Ecole Française d'Extrême-Orient.

———. 1979. *Histoire galante de Shidoken: Traduit de Fūrai Sanjin*. Paris: L'Asiathèque.

Mair, Victor A. 1986. "An Asian Story of the Oedipus Type," *Asian Folklore Studies* 45: 19–32.

Malalasekera, G. P., ed. 1961–. *Encyclopaedia of Buddhism*. Ceylon (Sri Lanka): Government Press.

Makita Tairyō, ed. 1970. *Rikuchō koitsu Kanzeon ōkenki no kenkyū*. Kyoto: Heirakuji shoten.

Malamoud, Charles. 1989. "Indian Speculations about the Sex of the Sacrifice." In Michel Feher, ed., *Fragments for a History of the Body, Part One*, 74–103. New York: Urzone.

Manaka Fujiko. 1979. "*Jichin oshō musōki* ni tsuite." *Bukkyō bungaku* 3: 32–39.

Marra, Michele. 1991. *The Aesthetics of Discontent: Politics and Reclusion in Medieval Japanese Literature*. Honolulu: University of Hawaii Press.

———. 1993a. "The Buddhist Mythmaking of Defilement: Sacred Courtesans of Medieval Japan." *Journal of Asian Studies* 52 (1): 49–65.

———. 1993b. *Representations of Power: The Literary Politics of Medieval Japan*. Honolulu: University of Hawaii Press.

Marx, Jacques, ed. 1990. *Religion et tabou sexuel*. Problèmes d'Histoire des Religions. Brussels: Editions de l'Université de Bruxelles.

Mather, Richard. 1981. "The Bonze's Begging Bowl: Eating Practices in Buddhist Monasteries of Medieval India and China," *Journal of the American Oriental Society* 101 (4): 417–24.

Matignon, Jean-Jacques. 1898. *Superstitions, crime et misère en Chine: Souvenirs de biologie sociale*. Lyon: A. Stork. Reedited as *La Chine hermétique*. Paris: Librairie orientaliste Paul Geuthner, 1936.

Matsuda Osamu. 1988. *Hanamojo no shisō: Nihon ni okeru shōnen'ai no seishinshi*. Tokyo: Peyotoru Kōbō.

Matsunaga Daigan and Alicia Matsunaga. 1972. *The Buddhist Concept of Hell*. New York: Philosophical Library.

Matsuo Kenji. 1988. *Kamakura shin bukkyō no seiritsu*. Tokyo: Yoshikawa kōbunkan.

Matsuoka Shinpei. 1993. "Chigo to tennōsei." In Kamata Tōji, ed., *Ōdō shinkō*. Tokyo: Yūzankaku shuppan.

McCullough, Helen Craig, trans. 1985. *Kokin wakashū: The First Imperial Anthology of Japanese Poetry*. Stanford: Stanford University Press.

————, trans. 1988. *The Tale of the Heike*. Stanford: Stanford University Press.

McCullough, William H. 1967. "Japanese Marriage Institutions in the Late Heian Period." *Harvard Journal of Asiatic Studies* 27: 103–67.

McMahon, Keith. 1995. *Misers, Shrews, and Polygamists: Sexuality and Male-Female Relations in Eighteenth-Century Chinese Fiction*. Durham and London: Duke University Press.

Michihata Ryōshū. 1979. *Chūgoku bukkyō shisōshi no kenkyū*. Kyoto: Heirakuji shoten.

Mikkyō jiten hensankai, ed. (1931) 1970. *Mikkyō daijiten*. 6 vols. Kyoto: Hōzōkan.

Mills, D. E., trans. 1970. *A Collection of Tales from Uji: A Study and Translation of* Uji Shūi Monogatari. Cambridge: Cambridge University Press.

Minakata Kumagusu. 1971–1975. *Minakata Kumagusu zenshū*. Edited by Iwamura Shinobu. Tokyo: Heibonsha.

————. 1973. "Notes and Queries, 1899–1933." In *Works in English by Kumagusu Minakata, 1893–1933*. Minakata Kumagusu, *Minakata Kumagusu zenshū* 10: 91–398. Edited by Iwamura Shinobu. Tokyo: Heibonsha.

————. 1991. "'Mara kō' ni tsuite." In Nakazawa Kenji, ed., *Jō no sekusorojii*, 195–234. Tokyo: Kawade bunko.

Minamoto Junko. 1981. *Kamakura jōdokyō to josei*. Kyoto: Nagata bunshodō.

————. 1993. "Buddhism and the Historical Construction of Sexuality in Japan." Translated by Hank Glassman. *U.S.-Japan Women's Journal, English Supplement* 4: 87–115.

Miyata, Noboru. 1979. *Kami no minzokushi*. Iwanami shinsho 97. Tokyo: Iwanami shoten.

————. 1983. *Onna no seiryoku to ie no kami*. Kyoto: Jinbun shoin.

————, ed. 1989. *Sei to mibun: Jakusha. haisha no shōsei to hiun*. Tokyo: Shunjusha.

————. 1993a. *Edo no hayarigami*. Chikuma gakugei bunko 980. Tokyo: Chikuma shobō.

————. 1993b. *Hime no minzokugaku*. Tokyo: Seidosha.

Miyatake Gaikotsu. 1923. *Senryū goi*. Tokyo: Seikōkan shuppan.

————. 1985–1992. *Miyatake Gaikotsu chosakushū*. Edited by Tanizawa Eiichi and Yoshino Takao. 8 vols. Tokyo: Kawade shobō.

Miyazaki Eishū. 1985. *Kishimojin shinkō*. Minshū shūkyōshi sōsho 9. Tokyo: Yūzankaku.

Mizuhara Gyōhei. 1931. *Jakyō Tachikawaryū no kenkyū*. Kyoto: Shibundō.

Moore, Jean Frances. 1982. "A Study of the Thirteenth-Century Buddhist Tale Collection *Senjūshō*." Ph.D. dissertation, Columbia University.

Moriyama Shōshin. 1965. *Tachikawa jakyō to sono shakaiteki haikei no kenkyū*. Tokyo: Shikanoen.

Morrell, Robert E. 1980. "Mirror for Women: Mujū Ichien's *Tsuma Kagami.*" *Monumenta Nipponica* 35 (1): 45–75.

———, trans. 1985. *Sand and Pebbles (*Shasekishū*): The Tales of Mujū Ichien, A Voice for Pluralism in Kamakura Japan.* Albany: State University of New York Press.

Morris, Ivan, ed. 1970. *Madly Singing in the Mountains: An Appreciation and Anthology of Arthur Waley.* New York: Walker.

Mujū Ichien. 1979. *Collection de sable et de pierres (Shasekishū).* Translated by Hartmut O. Rotermund. Paris: Gallimard.

Murakami, Yoshimi. 1974. "Affirmation of Desire in Taoism." *Acta Asiatica* 27: 57–74.

Muraoka Kū. 1975. *Ai no shinbutsu: Mikkyō to minkan shinkō.* Tokyo: Daizō shuppan.

Murcott, Susan, trans. 1991. *The First Buddhist Women: Translations and Commentary on the Therīgāthā.* Berkeley: Parallax Press.

Nagahara Keiji. 1979. "Medieval Origins of Eta-Hinin." *Journal of Japanese Studies* 5 (2): 385–403.

Nakamura Hajime, ed. 1981. *Bukkyōgo daijiten.* Tokyo: Tōkyō shoseki.

Nakamura Ikuo. 1992. "Tamayorihime to otome hinohime: Kodai ujizoku no soshin saiki to Yamato ōken." In Yamaori Tetsuo, ed., *Nihon ni okeru josei,* 5–73. Tokyo: Meicho kankōkai.

———. 1994. *Nihon no kami to ōken.* Kyoto: Hōzōkan.

Nakamura, Kyoko Motomochi, trans. 1973. *Miraculous Stories from the Japanese Buddhist Tradition: The* Nihon Ryōiki *of the Monk Kyōkai.* Cambridge: Harvard University Press.

———. 1983. "Women and Religion in Japan: Introductory Remarks." *Japanese Journal of Religious Studies* 10 (2–3): 115–21.

Nakazawa Shin'ichi, ed. 1991–1992. *Jō no sekusoroji.* Minakata Kumagusu korekushon. Kawade bunko. 4 vols. Tokyo: Kawade shobō shinsha.

Naomi Gentetsu. 1989. "Kōgo kara jotei he: Sokuten Bukō to henjo nanshi no ronri." In Ōsumi Kazuo and Nishiguchi Junko, eds., *Josei to bukkyō* 3: 167–206. Tokyo: Heibonsha.

Nara kokuritsu hakubutsukan, ed. 1975. *Jisha engi-e.* Tokyo: Kadogawa shoten.

Nattier, Jan. 1991. *Once upon a Future Time: Studies in a Buddhist Prophecy of Decline.* Berkeley: Asian Humanities Press.

Naylor, N. Christina. 1988. "Buddhas or Bitches: Nichiren's Attitude to Women." *Religious Traditions* 11: 63–76.

Ng, Vivienne W. 1987. "Ideology and Sexuality: Rape Laws in Qing China." *Journal of Asian Studies* 46 (1): 57–70.

———. 1989. "Homosexuality and the State in Late Imperial China." In Martin Bauml Duberman, Martha Vicinus, and George Chauncey, Jr., eds., *Hidden from History: Reclaiming the Gay and Lesbian Past,* 76–89. New York: New American Library Books.

Nihon bukkyō gakkai, ed. 1991. *Bukkyō to josei.* Kyoto: Heirakuji shoten.

Nishiguchi Junko. 1987. *Onna no chikara: Kodai no josei to bukkyō.* Heibonsha sensho 110. Tokyo: Heibonsha.

———. 1989a. "Ochō bukkyō ni okeru nyonin kyūzai no ronri: shussan no shuhō to goshō no kyōsetsu." In Miyata Noboru, ed., *Sei to mibun,* 129–67. Tokyo: Shunjūsha.

———. 1989b. " 'Josei to bukkyō' o meguru oboegaki: 'Ama to amadera' o megutte." In Ōsumi Kazuo and Nishiguchi Junko, eds., *Josei to bukkyō* 1: *Ama to amadera,* 279–89. Tokyo: Heibonsha.

———. 1989c. "Sei to chisuji." In Ōsumi Kazuo and Nishiguchi Junko, eds., *Josei to bukkyō* 4: *Miko to joshin,* 127–52. Tokyo: Heibonsha.

———. 1993. "Jōbutsu-setsu to josei: 'Nyobon-ge' made." *Nihonshi kenkyū* 366: 20–38.

Nishio Kōichi and Kishi Shōzō, eds. 1977. *Chūsei setsuwa shū: Kokon chōmonjū, Hosshinshū, Shintō shū.* Kanshō Nihon koten bungaku 23. Tokyo: Kadogawa shoten.

Niwa, Akiko. 1993. "The Formation of the Myth of Motherhood in Japan." Translated by Tomiko Yoda. *U.S.-Japan Women's Journal, English Supplement* 4: 70–82.

Nolot, Edith. 1991. *Règles de discipline des nonnes bouddhistes: Le Bhikṣuṇī-vinaya de l'école des Mahāsāṃghika-lokottaravādin.* Collège de France, Publications de l'Institut de Civilisation Indienne. Paris: Diffusion de Boccard.

Norman K. R., trans. 1971. *The Elders' Verses II: Therīgāthā.* PTS Translation Series 40. London: Luzac.

———, trans. 1989. *Poems of Early Buddhist Nuns.* Oxford: PTS.

Numa Gishō. 1989. "Kannon shinkō to bosei sūhai." In Miyata Noboru, ed., *Sei to mibun,* 169–206. Tokyo: Shunjusha.

Obeyesekere, Gananath. 1973. "The Goddess Patini and the Lord Buddha: Notes on the Myth of the Birth of the Deity." *Social Compass* 20: 217–29.

O'Flaherty, Wendy Doniger. 1973. *Asceticism and Eroticism in the Mythology of Śiva.* New York: Oxford University Press.

———. 1980. *Women, Androgynes, and Other Mythical Beasts.* Chicago: University of Chicago Press.

Ōgoshi Aiko, Minamoto Junko, and Yamashita Akiko. 1990. *Seisabetsu suru bukkyō: Feminizumu kara no kokuhatsu.* Kyoto: Hōzōkan.

Okada Hajime, ed. 1976–1984. *Haifū yanagidaru zenshū.* 13 vols. Tokyo: Sanseidō.

Okano Haruko. 1976. *Die Stellung der Frau im Shintō: Eine religionsphänomenologische und -soziologische Untersuchung.* Studies in Oriental Religions. Wiesbaden: Otto Harassowitz.

Ōkubo Ryōjun. 1981. "Genshi kimyōdan kanjō: mitsu ni shite mitsu ni arazu kanjō." *Tendai* 4: 37–46.

Oldenberg, Hermann, ed. 1879–1883. *The Vinaya Piṭakam.* 5 vols. London: PTS.

Ono Shihei. 1966. "Saiten setsuwa no seiritsu: Naikaku Bunko zō 'Sentō koin Saiten zenji goroku' ni tsuite." Reprinted in Ono Shihei, *Chūgoku kinsei ni okeru tanpen hakuwa shōsetsu no kenkyū,* 185–210. Tokyo: Hyōronsha, 1978.

Ōsumi Kazuo and Nishiguchi Junko, eds. 1989. *Josei to bukkyō.* 4 vols. Tokyo: Heibonsha.

Overmyer, Daniel L. 1985. "Values in Chinese Sectarian Literature: Ming and

Ch'ing Pao-chüan." In David Johnson, Andrew J. Nathan, and Evelyn S. Rawski, eds., *Popular Culture in Late Imperial China,* 219–54. Berkeley and Los Angeles: University of California Press.

Pachow, W. 1951–1955. "A Comparative Study of the *Prātimokṣa.*" In P. C. Bagchi, ed., *Sino-Indian Studies,* 4 (1–4): 18–196, and 5 (1): 1–45.

Paper, Jordan. 1990. "The Persistence of Female Deities in Patriarchal China." *Journal of Feminist Studies in Religion* 6: 25–40.

Parry, Jonathan. 1982. "Sacrificial Death and the Necrophagous Ascetic." In Maurice Bloch and Jonathan Parry, eds., *Death and the Regeneration of Life,* 74–110. Cambridge: Cambridge University Press.

Paul, Diana M. 1979. *Women in Buddhism: Images of the Feminine in Mahāyāna Tradition.* Berkeley: Asian Humanities Press.

———. 1980a. *The Buddhist Feminine Ideal: Queen Srmalā and the Tathāgatagarbha.* Missoula, MT: Scholars Press.

———. 1980b. "Empress Wu and the Historians: A Tyrant and Saint of Classical China." In Nancy Auer Falk and Rita M. Gross, eds., *Unspoken Worlds: Women's Religious Lives in Non-Western Cultures,* 191–206. San Francisco: Harper and Row.

Perera, L.P.N. 1995. *Sexuality in Ancient India: A Study Based on the Pāli Vinayapitaka.* Colombo: Karunaratna and Sons.

Péri, Noël. 1917. "Hāītī la Mère-de-Démons." *Bulletin de l'Ecole Française d'Extrême-Orient* 17: 1–102.

———. 1918. "Les femmes de Çākya-muni." *Bulletin de l'Ecole Française d'Extrême-Orient* 18: 1–37.

Pettazzoni, Raffaele. 1932. *La confession des Péchés,* vol. 2. Paris: Ernest Leroux.

Pflugfelder, Gregory M. 1990a. "Male-Male Sexual Behavior in Tokugawa Legal Discourse." Unpublished.

———. 1990b. "The Forbidden Chrysanthemum: Male-Male Behavior in Meiji Law." Unpublished.

———. 1992. "Strange Fates: Sex, Gender, and Sexuality in *Torikaeba Monogatari.*" *Monumenta Nipponica* 47 (3): 347–68.

———. 1996. "Cartographies of Desire: Male-Male Sexuality in Japanese Discourse, 1600–1950." Ph. D. dissertation, Stanford University.

Plutschow, Herbert E. 1983. "The Fear of Evil Spirits in Japanese Culture." *Transactions of the Asiatic Society of Japan* 3rd ser. 18: 133–51.

———. 1990. *Chaos and Cosmos: Ritual in Early and Medieval Japanese Literature.* Leiden and New York: E. J. Brill.

Poirier, Jean, ed. 1991. *Histoire des moeurs.* Encyclopédie de la Pléiade. 3 vols. Paris: Gallimard.

Prebisch, Charles S. 1974. "The *Prātimokṣa* Puzzle: Fact versus Fallacy." *Journal of the American Oriental Society* 94 (2): 168–76.

———. 1975. *Buddhist Monastic Discipline: The Sanskrit Prātimokṣa Sūtras of the Mahāsāṃghikas and Mūlasarvāstivādins.* University Park and London: Pennsylvania State University Press.

Quignard, Pascal. 1994. *Le sexe et l'effroi.* Paris: Gallimard.

Rabelais, François. 1955. *The Histories of Gargantua and Pantagruel.* Translated by J. M. Cohen. London: Penguin Books.

Rahula, Walpola. 1981. "Humour in Pāli Literature." *Journal of the Pali Text Society* 9: 156–73.

Ramanujan, A. K. 1982. "On Women Saints." In John Stratton Hawley and Donna Marie Wulff, eds., *The Divine Consort: Rādhā and the Goddesses of India*, 316–24. Berkeley: Berkeley Religious Studies Series.

Ratnapala, Nandasena. 1993. *Crime and Punishment in the Buddhist Tradition.* New Delhi: Mittal Publications.

Rhi Ki-yong. 1982. *Aux origines du "Tch'an-houei": Aspects bouddhiques de la pratique pénitentielle.* Seoul: Korean Institute for Buddhist Studies.

Rhys Davids, T. W., and Hermann Oldenberg, trans. 1885. *Vinaya Texts.* 3 vols. Sacred Books of the East. Oxford: PTS; reprint Delhi: Motilal Banarsidass, 1965.

Ridding, C. M., and Louis de La Vallée Poussin. 1920. "A Fragment of the Sanskrit Vinaya, Bhikṣuṇīkarmavacana." *Bulletin of the School of Oriental Studies* 1.

Robert, Yves, trans. 1989. *L'ivresse d'éveil: Faits et gestes de Ji Gong le moine fou.* Paris: Les Deux Océans.

Rotermund, Hartmund O. 1983. *Pélerinage aux neuf sommets.* Paris: Editions du CNRS.

Rousselle, Aline. 1988. *Porneia: On Desire and the Body in Antiquity.* Cambridge, MA: Basil Blackwell.

Roy, David Tod, trans. 1993. *The Plum in the Golden Vase or, Chin P'ing Mei.* Vol. 1: *The Gathering.* Princeton: Princeton University Press.

Ruan Fang-fu and Yung-mei Tsai. 1987. "Male Homosexuality in Traditional Chinese Literature." *Journal of Homosexuality* 14 (3–4): 21–33.

Ruch, Barbara. 1977. "Medieval Jongleurs and the Making of a National Literature." In John W. Hall and Toyoda Takeshi, eds., *Japan in the Muromachi Age.* Berkeley and Los Angeles: University of California Press.

———. 1990. "The Other Side of Culture in Medieval Japan." In Kozo Yamamura, ed., *The Cambridge History of Japan.* Vol. 3: *Medieval Japan*, 500–43. Cambridge: Cambridge University Press.

Rutt, Richard. 1961. "The Flower Boys of Silla: Notes on the Sources." *Transactions of the Korea Branch of the Royal Asiatic Society* 38: 1–66.

Saeki Junko. 1987. *Yūjo no bunkashi.* Chūōshinsho 853. Tokyo: Chūōkōronsha.

Saikaku. *See* Ihara Saikaku.

Sailley, Robert. 1980. *Le bouddhisme "tantrique" indo-tibétain ou "Véhicule de diamant."* Sisteron: Editions Présence.

Sakaida Shirō and Wada Katsushi, eds. 1943. *Nihon setsuwa bungaku sakuin.* Tokyo: Seibundō.

Sakurai Tokutarō, Hagiwara Tatsuo, and Miyata Noboru, eds. 1975. *Jisha engi.* Nihon shisō taikei 20. Tokyo: Iwanami shoten.

Sakurai Yoshirō. 1976. *Kamigami no henbō: Shaji engi no sekai kara.* Tokyo: Tōkyō daigaku shuppankai.

———. 1993. *Saigi to chūshaku: Chūsei ni okeru kodai shinwa.* Tokyo: Yoshikawa kōbunkan.

Sanford, James H. 1981. *Zen-Man Ikkyū.* Chico, CA: Scholars Press.

———. 1988. "The Nine Faces of Death: Su Tung-p'o's *Kuzō-shi.*" *The Eastern Buddhist* 21 (2): 54–77.

———. 1991a. "The Abominable Tachikawa Skull Ritual." *Monumenta Nipponica* 46 (1): 1–20.

———. 1991b. "Literary Aspects of the Dual Gaṇeṣa Cult." In Robert L. Brown, ed., *Ganesh*, 287–335. Albany: State University of New York Press.

Sasama Yoshihiko. 1989. *Kangiten (Shōten) shinkō to zokushin.* Tokyo: Yūzankaku.

———. 1991. *Benzaiten shinkō to zokushin.* Tokyo: Yūzankaku.

Saslow, James. 1989. "Homosexuality in the Renaissance: Behavior, Identity, and Artistic Expression." In Martin Bauml Duberman, Martha Vicinus, and George Chauncey, Jr., eds., *Hidden from History: Reclaiming the Gay and Lesbian Past,* 90–105. New York: New American Library.

Satō Kazuhiko. 1995. "Des gens étranges à l'allure insolite": Contestation et valeurs nouvelles dans le Japon médiéval." *Annales,* 50th year, 2: 307–40.

Sawada Mizuho. 1975. *Bukkyō to Chūgoku bungaku.* Tokyo: kokusho kankōkai.

Schalow, Paul Gordon. 1989. "Male Love in Early Modern Japan: A Literary Depiction of the 'Youth.'" In Martin Bauml Duberman, Martha Vicinus, and George Chauncey, Jr., eds., *Hidden from History: Reclaiming the Gay and Lesbian Past,* 118–28. New York: New American Library.

———. 1992a. "Kūkai and the Tradition of Male Love in Japanese Buddhism." In José I. Cabezon, ed., *Buddhism, Sexuality, and Gender,* 215–30. Albany: State University of New York Press.

———. 1992b. "Spiritual Dimensions of Male Beauty in Japanese Buddhism." In Michael L. Stemmeler and José Ignacio Cabezon, eds., *Religion, Homosexuality, and Literature,* 75–94. Las Colinas, TX: Monument Press.

———. 1993. "The Invention of a Literary Tradition of Male Love: Kitamura Kigin's *Iwatsutsuji.*" *Monumenta Nipponica* 48 (1): 1–31.

Schipper, Kristofer M. 1993. *The Taoist Body.* Translated by Karen Duval. Berkeley, Los Angeles, and London: University of California Press.

Schipper, Kristofer M. 1966. "The Divine Jester: Some Remarks on the Gods of the Chinese Marionette Theater." *Bulletin of the Institute of Ethnology: Academia Sinica* 21: 81–96.

Schopen, Gregory. 1988–1989. "On Monks, Nuns and 'Vulgar' Practices: The Introduction of the Image Cult into Indian Buddhism." *Artibus Asiae* 49 (1–2): 153–68.

———. 1995. "The Suppression of Nuns and the Ritual Murder of Their Special Dead in Two Buddhist Monastic Texts." Unpublished.

Schurhammer, Georg, S.J. 1982. *Francis Xavier: His Life, His Times.* Vol. 4: *Japan and China, 1549–1552.* Rome: Jesuit Historical Institute.

Schuster, Nancy. 1981. "Changing the Feminine Body: Wise Women and the Bodhisattva Career in Some *Mahāratnakasūtras.*" *Journal of the International Association of Buddhist Studies* 4 (1): 24–69.

Seaman, Gary. 1981. "The Sexual Politics of Karmic Retribution." In Emily Martin Ahern and Hill Gates, eds., *The Anthropology of Taiwanese Society,* 381–96. Stanford: Stanford University Press.

Segawa Kiyoko. 1963. "Menstrual Taboos Imposed upon Women." In Richard

Dorson, ed., *Studies in Japanese Folklore,* 239–50. Bloomington: Indiana University Press.

Sekiguchi Hiroko. 1982. "Kodai ni okeru Nihon to Chūgoku no shoyū. kazoku keitai no sōi ni tsuite: joshi shoyūken o chūshin to shite." In Joseishi sōgō kenkyūkai, ed., *Nihon josei shi.* Vol. 1: *Genshi, kodai,* 249–90. Tokyo: Tokyo Daigaku shuppankai.

Selby, Martha Ann. 1994. "Sanskrit Gynecologies: The Semiotics of Femininity in the *Caraka-* and *Śuśruta-saṃhitās.*" Unpublished.

Shahar, Meir. 1991. "Lucky Dog." *Free China Review* 41 (7): 64–69.

———. 1992. "Fiction and Religion in the Early History of the Chinese God Jigong." Ph. D. dissertation, Harvard University.

Shaw, Miranda. 1994. *Passionate Enlightenment: Women in Tantric Buddhism.* Princeton: Princeton University Press.

Shibayama Hajime. 1992. *Edo nanshoku kō: akusho hen.* Tokyo: Hihyōsha.

———. 1993. *Edo nanshoku kō: Wakashu hen.* Tokyo: Hihyōsha.

Shibuzawa Keizō, ed. 1965. *Emakimono ni yoru Nihon jōmin seikatsu ein.* 5 vols. Tokyo: Kadogawa shoten.

Sieffert, René, trans. 1986. *Supplément aux contes d'Uji.* Paris: Publications Orientalistes de France.

Siegel, Lee. 1987. *Laughing Matters: Comic Tradition of India.* Chicago: University of Chicago Press.

Sierksma, F. 1966. *Tibet's Terrifying Deities: Sex and Agression in Acculturation.* Rutland, VT, and Tokyo: Charles E. Tuttle.

Sinistrari d'Ameno, A. P. (1754) *De Sodomia: Tractatus in quo exponitur doctrina nova de Sodomia fœminarum a Tribadismo distincta.* Rome. Translated as *De la Sodomie (De Sodomia): Exposé d'une doctrine nouvelle sur la sodomie des femmes, distinguée du tribadisme.* Paris: Bibliothèque des curieux, n.d.

Sissa, Giulia. 1990. "Du désir insatiable au plaisir captive." In J. Marx, ed., *Religion et tabou sexuel,* 33–48. Brussels: Editions de l'Université de Bruxelles.

Skord, Virginia, trans. 1991. *Tales of Tears and Laughter: Short Fiction of Medieval Japan.* Honolulu: University of Hawaii Press.

Smith, Gary, ed. 1991. *On Walter Benjamin.* Cambridge: MIT Press.

Smyers, Karen A. 1983. "Women and Shinto: The Relation between Purity and Pollution." *Japanese Religions* 12 (4): 7–19.

Snellgrove. D. L. 1959a. *The Hevajra Tantra: A Critical Study.* London Oriental Series 6. London: Oxford University Press.

———. 1959b. "The Notion of Divine Kingship in Tantric Buddhism." In *The Sacral Kingship* (no editor). Leiden: E. J. Brill.

Soymié. Michel. 1956. *L'entrevue de Confucius et de Hiang To: Manuscrits tibétains et chinois.* Paris: Société Asiatique.

Spence, Jonathan. 1984. *The Memory Palace of Matteo Ricci.* New York: Penguin Books.

Spiro, Melford E. 1982. *Buddhism and Society: A Great Tradition and Its Burmese Vicissitudes.* 2nd ed. Berkeley and Los Angeles: University of California Press.

Sponberg, Alan. 1992. "Attitudes toward Women and the Feminine in Early Buddhism." In José I. Cabezon, ed., *Buddhism, Sexuality, and Gender*, 3–36. Albany: State University of New York Press.

Stallybrass, Peter, and Allon White. 1986. *The Politics and Poetics of Transgression*. Ithaca: Cornell University Press.

Stein, Rolf A. 1972. *Vie et chants de 'Brug-pa Kun-legs le yogin*. Paris: Maisonneuve et Larose.

———. 1974. "Etude du monde chinois: Institutions et concepts." In *Annuaire du Collège de France*, 499–517. Paris: Collège de France.

———. 1975. "Etude du monde chinois: institutions et concepts." In *Annuaire du Collège de France*, 481–95. Paris: Collège de France.

———. 1981. "Porte (gardien de la)." In Yves Bonnefoy, ed. *Dictionnaire des mythologies* 2: 280–94. Paris: Flammarion.

———. 1986. "Avalokiteśvara/Kouan-yin, un exemple de transformation d'un dieu en déesse." *Cahiers d'Extrême-Asie* 2: 17–80.

———. 1988. *Grottes-matrices et lieux saints de la déesse en Asie Orientale*. Paris: Ecole Française d'Extrême-Orient.

Steinberg, Leo. 1996. *The Sexuality of Christ in Renaissance Art and in Modern Oblivion*. 2nd ed. Chicago: University of Chicago Press.

Stevens, John. 1990. *Lust for Enlightenment: Buddhism and Sex*. Boston and London: Shambhala.

Strickmann, Michel. 1993. "The Seal of the Law: A Ritual Implement and the Origins of Printing." *Asia Major* 3rd series 6 (2): 1–83.

———. 1994. "Saintly Fools and Chinese Masters (Holy Fools)." *Asia Major* 3rd Series 7 (1): 35–53.

———. 1996. *Mantras et mandarins: Le bouddhisme tantrique en Chine*. Paris: Gallimard.

Strong, John S. 1979. "The Legend of the Lion-Roarer: A Study of the Buddhist Arhat Piṇḍola Bhāradvāja." *Numen* 26 (1): 50–88.

———. 1983. *The Legend of King Aśoka*. Princeton: Princeton University Press.

———. 1990. "Vinaya Violators." Paper read at the Conference "Compassion in Action: Towards an American Vinaya," Green Gulch Zen Center, CA, 3–8 June 1990.

———. 1995. *The Experience of Buddhism: Sources and Interpretations*. Belmont, CA: Wadsworth Publishing Company.

Strong, Sarah M. 1994. "The Making of a Femme Fatale: Ono no Komachi in the Early Medieval Commentaries." *Monumenta Nipponica* 49 (4): 391–412.

Suzuki Daisetsu. 1968. *Suzuki Daisetsu zenshū*. Vol. 3. Tokyo: Iwanami shoten.

Sweet, Michael J., and Leonard Zwilling. 1993. "The First Medicalization: The Taxonomy and Etiology of Queerness in Classical Indian Medicine." *Journal of the History of Sexuality* 3: 590–607.

Taga Munehaya. 1959. *Jien*. Tokyo: Yoshikawa kōbunkan.

———. 1980. *Jien no kenkyū*. Tokyo: Yoshikawa kōbunkan.

Taira Masayuki. 1992. *Nihon chūsei no shakai to bukkyō*. Tokyo: Hanawa shobō.

Takagi Tadashi. 1992. *Mikudarihan to enkiridera: Edo no rikon o yominaosu*. Tokyo: Kōdansha.

Takagi Yutaka. 1988. *Bukkyōshi no naka no nyonin*. Heibonsha sensho 126. Tokyo: Heibonsha.

Takahashi Tetsu. 1965. *Secret Heirloom Picture Scrolls*. Tokyo: Kōdansha shobō.

Takakusu Junjirō. 1896. "Pāli Elements in Chinese Buddhism: A Translation of Buddhagosa's *Samantapāsādīka*, a Commentary on the *Vinaya*, Found in the Chinese *Tripiṭaka*." *Journal of the Royal Asiatic Society*, n.s. 28: 415–39.

Takatori Ayumi. 1993. *Shintō no seiritsu*. Tokyo: Heibonsha.

Takemi Tomoko. 1983. "'Menstruation Sūtra' Belief in Japan." Translated by W. Michael Kelsey. *Japanese Journal of Religious Studies* 10 (2–3): 229–46.

Tanabe Miwako. "Chūsei no 'dōji' ni tsuite." *Nenpō chūseishi kenkyū* 9.

Tanaka Takako. 1989. "'Gyokujo' no seiritsu to genkai: 'Jishin oshō musōki' kara 'Shinran yume no ki' made." In Ōsumi Kazuo and Nishiguchi Junko, eds. *Josei to bukkyō*. Vol. 4: *Miko to joshin*, 91–126. Tokyo: Heibonsha.

———. 1992. *"Akujo" ron*. Tokyo: Kinokuniya shoten.

———. 1993. *Gehō to aihō no chūsei*. Tokyo: Sunakoya shobō.

———. 1995. "Torai suru kami to dochaku suru kami." In Yamaori Tetsuo, ed., *Nihon no kami*. Vol. 1: *Kami no shigen*, 173–208. Tokyo: Heibonsha.

———. 1996. *Sei naru onna: Chūjōhime*. Kyoto: Jinbun shoin.

Tara, Michael, trans. 1974. *Hathayogapradīpīka*. Paris: Fayard.

Tatz, Mark. 1986. *Asaṅga's Chapter on Ethics with the Commentary of Tsong-kha-pa, The Basic Path to Awakening: The Complete Bodhisattva*. New York: Edwin Mellen Press.

Tay, C. N. 1976. "Kuan-yin, the Cult of Half Asia." *History of Religions* 16 (2): 147–77.

Teele, Roy E., Nicholas J. Teele, and H. Rebecca Teele, trans. 1993. *Ono no Komachi: Poems, Stories, Nō Plays*. New York and London: Garland.

Teruoka Yasutaka. 1989. *Nihonjin no ai to sei*. Iwanami shinsho 92. Tokyo: Iwanami shoten.

Thurman, Robert A. F., trans. 1976. *The Holy Teaching of Vimalakīrti: A Mahāyāna Scripture*. University Park and London: Pennsylvania State University Press.

T'ien Ju-k'ang. 1988. *Male Anxiety and Female Chastity: A Comparative Study of Chinese Ethical Values in Ming-Ch'ing Times*. Leiden: E. J. Brill.

Tominaga Minamoto. 1982. *Shutsujō kōgo*. Gendai Bukkyō meicho zenshū. Tokyo: Ryūbunkan.

———. 1990. *Emerging from Meditation*. Translated by Michael Pye. Honolulu: University of Hawaii Press.

Topley, Marjorie. 1974. "Cosmic Antagonisms: A Mother-Child Syndrome." In Arthur P. Wolf, ed., *Religion and Ritual in Chinese Society*, 233–49. Stanford: Stanford University Press.

Tsai, Kathryn Ann. 1981. "The Monastic Order for Women: The First Two Centuries." In R. W. Guisso and S. Johannesen, eds., *Women in China: Current Reflections in Historical Scholarship. Historical Reflections* 8 (3): 1–20.

———. 1994. *Lives of the Nuns: Biographies of Chinese Buddhist Nuns from the Fourth to Sixth Centuries: A Translation of the* Pi-ch'iu-ni chuan, *compiled by Shih Pao-ch'ang*. Honolulu: University of Hawaii Press.

Tsuji Zennosuke. 1944–1955. *Nihon bukkyōshi*. 10 vols. Reedited Tokyo: Iwanami shoten, 1960–1961.

Tsunoda Bun'ei. 1985. *Taiken mon'in Tamako no shōgai: Shōtei hishō.* Asahi sensho 281. Tokyo: Asahi shinbunsha.

Tsunoda Ryusaku, Wm. Theodore de Bary, and Donald Keene, eds. 1964. *Sources of Japanese Tradition.* 2 vols. New York: Columbia University Press.

Ury, Marian, trans. 1979. *Tales of Times Now Past: Sixty-Two Stories from a Medieval Japanese Collection.* Berkeley and Los Angeles: University of California Press.

Van Gennep, Arnold. 1960. *The Rites of Passage.* Translated by Monika B. Vizedom and Gabrielle L. Caffee. Chicago: University of Chicago Press.

Van Gulik, Robert H. 1961. *Sexual Life in Ancient China: A Preliminary Survey of Chinese Sex and Society from ca. 1500 B.C. till 1644 A.D.* Leiden: E. J. Brill.

———. 1971. *La vie sexuelle dans la Chine ancienne.* Paris: Gallimard.

Verdier, Yvonne. 1979. *Façons de dire, façons de faire: La laveuse, la couturière, la cuisinière.* Paris: Gallimard.

Veyne, Paul. 1982. "L'homosexualité à Rome." In P. Ariès and A. Béjin, eds., *Sexualités occidentales,* 41–51. Paris: Seuil.

Vitiello, Giovanni. 1992a. "The Dragon's Whim: Ming and Qing Homoerotic Tales from *The Cut Sleeve.*" *T'oung Pao* 78: 341–72.

———. 1992b. "Taoist Themes in Chinese Homoerotic Themes." In Michael L. Stemmeler and José Ignacio Cabezon, eds., *Religion, Homosexuality, and Literature,* 95–103. Las Colinas, TX: Monument Press.

———. 1994. "Exemplary Sodomites: Male Homosexuality in Late Ming Fiction." Ph. D. dissertation, University of California-Berkeley.

Volpp, Sophie. 1994. "The Discourse on Male Marriage: Li Yu's 'A Male Mencius's Mother.'" *Positions* 2 (1): 113–32.

Wakatsuki Shōgo. 1971. "Edo jidai no sōryō no daraku ni tsuite: Sono shorei." *Komazawa daigaku bukkyōgakubu ronshū* 2: 5–19.

Wakita Haruko. 1984. "Marriage and Property in Premodern Japan from the Perspective of Women's History." Translated by Susanne Gay. *Journal of Japanese Studies* 10 (1): 77–99.

———, ed. 1985. *Bosei o tou: Rekishiteki hensen.* Vol. 1. Tokyo: Jinbun shoin.

———. 1992. *Nihon chūsei joseishi no kenkyū: Seibetsu yakuwari buntan to bosei. kasei. seiai.* Tokyo: Tokyo daigaku shuppankai.

———. 1993. "Women and the Creation of the *Ie* in Japan: An Overview from the Medieval Period to the Present." Translated by David P. Phillips. *U.S.-Japan Women's Journal, English Supplement* 4: 83–105.

Waley, Arthur, trans. (1921) 1976. *The No Plays of Japan.* Rutland, VT: Charles E. Tuttle.

———. 1932a. "New Light on Buddhism in Medieval India." *Mélanges chinois et bouddhiques* 1: 355–76.

———. 1932b. "An Eleventh-Century Correspondence." In *Etudes d'orientalisme publiées par le Musée Guimet à la mémoire de Raymonde Linossier.* Vol. 2: 530–45. Paris: Ernest Leroux.

Walters, Jonathan S. 1994. "A Voice from the Silence: The Buddha's Mother's Story." *History of Religions* 33 (4): 358–79.

Wang, Jing. 1992. *The Story of the Stone: Intertextuality, Ancient Chinese Stone*

Lore, and the Stone Symbolism of Dream of the Red Chamber, Water Margin, *and* The Journey to the West. Durham and London: Duke University Press.

Watanabe Tsuneo and Iwata Jun'ichi. 1989. *The Love of the Samurai: A Thousand Years of Japanese Homosexuality.* Translated by D. R. Roberts. London: GMP Publishers.

Watson, Burton. 1961. *Records of the Grand Historian.* New York: Columbia University Press.

Watson, James L. 1982. "Of Flesh and Bones: The Management of Death Pollution in Cantonese Society." In Maurice Bloch and Jonathan Parry, eds., *Death and the Regeneration of Life,* 155–86. Cambridge: Cambridge University Press.

———. 1985. "Standardizing the Gods: The Promotion of T'ien Hou ("Empress of Heaven") along the South China Coast." In David Johnson, Andrew J. Nathan, and Evelyn Rawski, eds., *Popular Culture in Late Imperial China,* 292–324. Berkeley and Los Angeles: University of California Press.

Watt, Paul. 1984. "Jiun Sonja (1718–1804): A Response to Confucianism within the Context of Buddhist Reform." In Peter Nosco, ed., *Confucianism and Tokugawa Culture,* 188–214. Princeton: Princeton University Press.

Wawrytko, Sandra A. 1993. "Homosexuality and Chinese and Japanese Religions." In Arlene Swidler, ed., *Homosexuality and World Religions,* 199–230. Valley Forge, PA: Trinity Press International.

Wayman, Alex. 1962. "Female Energy and Symbolism in the Buddhist Tantras." *History of Religions* 2: 73–111.

———. 1965. "The Five-fold Ritual Symbolism of Passion." In Kōyasan daigaku, ed., *Mikkyōgaku mikkyōshi ronbunshū,* 117–44. Kyoto: Naigai Press.

———. 1975. "Purification of Sin in Buddhism by Vision and Confession." In Sasaki Genjun, ed., *Bonnō no kenkyū,* 515–494 (sic). Tokyo: Shimizu Kōbundō.

———. 1977. *Yoga of the Guyasamājatantra: The Arcane Lore of Forty Verses. A Buddhist Tantra Commentary.* Delhi: Motilal Banarsidass.

———. 1983. "Male, Female, and Androgyne: Per Buddhist Tantra, Jacob Boehme, and the Greek and Taoist Mysteries." In Michel Strickmann, ed., *Tantric and Taoist Studies in Honour of R. A. Stein,* 2: 592–631. *Mélanges chinois et bouddhiques* 21. Brussels: Institut Belge des Hautes Etudes Chinoises.

Wayman, Alex, and Hideko Wayman, trans. 1974. *The Lion's Roar of Queen Śrīmālā: A Buddhist Scripture on the Tathāgatagarbha Theory.* New York: Columbia University Press.

Weidner, Marsha, et al. 1988. *Views from Jade Terrace: Chinese Women Artists 1300–1912.* Indianapolis: Indianapolis Museum of Art.

Welch, Holmes H. 1967. *The Practice of Chinese Buddhism, 1900–1950.* Cambridge: Harvard University Press.

White, David Gordon. Forthcoming. "Tantric Sects and Tantric Sex: The Flow of Secret Tantric Gnosis." In Elliot Wolfson, ed., *Rending the Veil.*

Wieger, Léon. 1910. *Bouddhisme chinois: Vinaya, Monachisme et Discipline; Hīnayāna, Véhicule inférieur.* Vol 1. Hien-Hien: Imprimerie de la mission catholique. Reprint Paris: Cathasia, 1951.

Wijayaratna, Mohan. 1990. *Buddhist Monastic Life According to the Texts of the Theravāda Tradition.* Translated by Claude Grangier and Steve Collins. Cambridge: Cambridge University Press.

———. 1991. *Les moniales bouddhistes: naissance et développement du monachisme féminin.* Paris: Editions du Cerf.

Wile, Douglas. 1992. *Art of the Bedchamber: The Chinese Sexual Yoga Classics, Including Women's Solo Meditation Texts.* Albany: State University of New York Press.

Willis, Janice Dean. 1985. "Nuns and Benefactresses: The Role of Women in the Development of Buddhism." In Yvonne Yazbeck Haddad and Ellison Banks Findly, eds., *Women, Religion and Social Change,* 59–85. Albany: State University of New York Press.

———. 1987. "Ḍākinī: Some Comments on Its Nature and Meaning." *The Tibet Journal* 12 (4): 19–37.

Wilson, Elisabeth. 1995. "The Female Body as a Source of Horror and Insight in Post-Ashokan Indian Buddhism." In Jane Marie Law, ed., *Religious Reflections on the Human Body,* 76–99. Bloomington: Indiana University Press.

———. 1996. *Charming Cadavers: Horrific Figurations of the Feminine in Indian Buddhist Hagiographic Literature.* Chicago: University of Chicago Press.

Winkler, John J. 1990. *The Constraints of Desire: The Anthropology of Sex and Gender in Ancient Greece.* New York and London: Routledge.

Wu Pei-yi. 1978. "Self-Examination and Confession of Sins in Traditional China. *Harvard Journal of Asiatic Studies* 39 (1): 5–38.

Yamaguchi Masao. 1977. "Kingship, Theatricality, and Marginal Reality in Japan." In Ravindra Jain, ed., *Text and Context: The Social Anthropology of Tradition.* Philadelphia: Institute for the Study of Human Issues.

Yamakami Izumo. 1994. *Miko no rekishi: Nihon shūkyō no botai.* Tokyo: Yūzankaku.

Yamamoto Hajime. 1995. "Jien to seiai: yurusarenai mono to yurusareta mono." *Nihon bunkagu* 44 (7): 23–30.

Yamamoto Hiroko. "Reikoku o meguru Jien no seishin shiteki ichi kōsatsu." In *Terakoya gogaku bunka kenkyūjo ronsō* 2.

Yamamoto Hiroko. 1987. "Yōshu to gyokujo." *Gekkan hyakka* 313: 7–16.

———. 1993. *Henjō fu: Chūsei shinbutsu shūgo no sekai.* Tokyo: Shunjūsha.

Yamaori Tetsuo. 1973. *Nihon bukkyō shisōron josetsu.* Tokyo: San-ichi shobō.

———. 1991. *Kami to okina no minzokugaku.* Kōdansha gakujutsu bunkō. Tokyo: Kōdansha.

———, ed. 1992. *Nihon ni okeru josei.* Tokyo: Meicho kankōkai.

———. 1995. "Nyoshin no tanjō." In Yamaori Tetsuo, ed., *Nihon no kami.* Vol. 2: *Kami no henyō,* 219–54. Tokyo: Heibonsha.

Yampolsky, Philip B., ed. 1990. *Selected Writings of Nichiren.* New York: Columbia University Press.

Yanagida Seizan, ed. 1970. *Daruma no goroku.* Tokyo: Chikuma shobō.

———, ed. 1974. *Zenrin shōkisen, Kattō gosen jikkan, Zenrin kushū benmyō.* 2 vols. Kyoto: Chūbun shuppansha.

———, ed. 1987. *Ikkyū, Ryōkan.* Daijō butten: Chūgoku, Nihon hen. Vol. 26. Tokyo: Chūō kōronsha.

Yanagida Seizan and Tokiwa Gishin, eds. 1976. *Zekkanron: Eibun yakuchū, gen-bun kōtei, kokuyaku.* Kyoto: Zenbunka kenkyūjo.

Yanagita Kunio. (1969) 1990. *Teihon Yanagita Kunio zenshū,* edited by Yanagita Tamemasa et al. 32 vols. Tokyo: Chikuma shobō.

———. 1990a. *Josei to minkan denjō.* In Yanagita Tamemasa et al., eds., *Yanagita Kunio zenshū* 10: 423–589. Chikuma bunko. Tokyo: Chikuma shobō.

———. 1990b. *Imōto no chikara.* In Yanagita Tamemasa et al., eds., *Yanagita Kunio zenshū* 11: 7–304. Chikuma bunko. Tokyo: Chikuma shobō.

———. 1990c. *Momotarō no tanjō.* In Yanagita Yamemasa et al., eds., *Yanagita Kunio zenshū* 10: 1–422. Chikuma bunko. Tokyo: Chikuma shobō.

Yokoi Yuho. 1976. *Zen Master Dōgen: An Introduction with Selected Texts.* New York: Weatherhill.

Yoshida Kazuhiko. "Ryūjo no jōbutsu." In Ōsumi Kazuo and Nishiguchi Junko, eds., *Josei to bukkyō.* Vol. 2: *Sukui to oshie,* 45–91. Tokyo: Heibonsha.

Yü Chün-fang. 1981. *The Renewal of Buddhism in China: Chu-hung and the Late Ming Synthesis.* New York: Columbia University Press.

———. 1990. "Feminine Images of Kuan-yin in Post-T'ang China." *Journal of Chinese Religions* 18: 61–89.

Zhang Dafu. 1957. *Zui puti,* ms. edition. Photographic reprint in *Guben xiqu congkan sanji,* Beijing.

Zito, Angela, and Tani E. Barlow, eds. 1994. *Body, Subject, and Power in China.* Chicago: University of Chicago Press.

Zürcher, Erik. 1959. *The Buddhist Conquest of China: The Spread and Adaptation of Buddhism in Early Medieval China.* 2 vols. Leiden: E. J. Brill.

———. 1991. *Bouddhisme, Christianisme et société chinoise.* Paris: Julliard.

Zwilling, Leonard. 1992. "Homosexuality as Seen in Buddhist Texts." In José I. Cabezon, ed., *Buddhism, Sexuality, and Gender,* 203–14. Albany: State University of New York Press.

Zwilling, Leonard, and Michael J. Sweet. 1994. "Like a City Aflame: The Third Sex, Bisexuality, and Sexual Object Choice in Jaina Commentarial Literature." Unpublished.

Zysk, Kenneth. 1991. *Asceticism and Healing in Ancient India: Medicine in the Buddhist Monastery.* New York: Oxford University Press.

INDEX